ACA Simplified

Smashing Strategic Business Management™ –
How to Pass the ACA Strategic Business Management Examination 2018

ICAEW
PARTNER IN
LEARNING

Recognised as an ICAEW Partner in Learning, working with ICAEW in the professional development of students

ICAEW takes no responsibility for the content of any supplemental training materials supplied by the Partner in Learning.

The ICAEW Partner in Learning Logo, ACA and ICAEW CFAB are all registered trademarks of ICAEW and are used under licence by ACA Simplified.

Disclaimer

The text in this book does not amount to professional advice on any particular technical matter and should not be taken as such. No reliance should be placed on the content as the basis for any investment or other decision or in connection with any advice given to third parties.

ACA Simplified expressly disclaims all liability for any losses or other claims, whether direct, indirect, incidental, consequential or otherwise arising in relation to the use of these materials.

We have made every effort to ensure that the materials are accurate and free from error. Please inform us immediately if you believe that you have discovered any problems with the text.

Whilst we strongly believe that our learning materials are an effective method of preparing for your examinations, ACA Simplified does not accept any liability whatsoever for your ultimate performance in the examination as a result of using this text.

Table of Contents

ACA Simplified SBM Mock Exams

We are pleased to present some further information on the original SBM mock examinations which we have written based on the 2018 SBM syllabus. Our mock examination packs include 2 full examination papers with model answers (a total of 4 SBM questions) per pack.

With the availability of 8 real SBM past papers and the ICAEW SBM Question Bank to practise, why would you want to purchase our mock exam pack?

1. Mock exams written specifically for SBM

As we explain in more detail in Appendix 5, many of the questions contained in the ICAEW SBM Question Bank are actually **amended versions of questions from the old TI Business Change paper** (whether from the Business Change Question Bank or Business Change past papers). Similarly, some of the official ICAEW Strategic Business Management mock exams provided to tuition providers are based on Business Change questions[1]. This means that **these questions have not been written from scratch specifically for SBM**: instead, the existing text has been reformatted into SBM-style Exhibits and the requirements have been amended. Given that SBM contains new topic areas (see chapters 18 and 19 for a listing) as well as a very different style of question format, we are uncertain that these "recycled" questions will be the optimum method of preparation.

In addition, the SBM examiners have explicitly stated that there is an intended balance between the different SBM disciplines (practical business advisory[2], financial reporting, audit and ethics) **across the 2 questions** within an SBM paper. **If you are practising single independent and self-contained questions from the Question Bank you will not be able to use this requirement for "balance" to help you practise your technique of predicting the mark allocation across a whole paper** (see chapters 3 and 5 for further discussion) so again these independent questions will not be an ideal way of preparing for SBM.

Our mock exam pack has instead been **written specifically for SBM**, avoiding these issues. We have written questions that include the new SBM syllabus content and which give you practice in predicting mark allocations across a whole paper (not possible when practising **individual** questions from the Question Bank). We have also reacted very carefully to examiner comments to understand how SBM will be examined in **future**, which may be a better form of preparation than using questions created for a different and **historic** syllabus (Business Change).

2. Realistic, "candidate-standard" model answers

One of the most common complaints amongst our students sitting SBM is that the model answers provided in the ICAEW Question Bank (and, to a lesser extent, in past papers and mock exams) are **impossible to achieve in the time available** – and we would agree and so would ICAEW: the model answer has intentionally been designed by ICAEW to cover a variety of possible angles that could be used to address the question. Whilst this is great as a learning aid (and ICAEW state that very full

---

[1] See Appendix 5 for full discussion and analysis.
[2] Please note that this is our own term to refer to what ICAEW term the "strategy" and "finance" elements of SBM: since these 2 elements will always be set in a combined way in the same question we prefer just to use a single term. We also use the term "practical" to emphasise that you need to make realistic and practical points.

4

answers are given so that students can learn as much as possible from their attempt) it does not help students to determine how much is realistically possible in the time available.

Therefore, our mock exam pack comes with what we call "**candidate-standard model answers**": in other words, an answer that we think is realistically possible in the time available, for a strong candidate with an average typing speed. **We have very carefully counted the number of words in our model answers to ensure that these are physically possible to construct in the time available** and we have also allowed for the fact that SBM requires more reading and planning time than other ACA papers (hence reducing the amount that can be written up in the time available).

We have carefully studied what the examiner wants to see (and does not want to see) in a good standard answer to create model answers which will **not intimidate you or damage your confidence** whilst at the same time showing you what you need to do to succeed in the time available.

In summary, the advantage of our mock pack over the other resources you have available is that our mocks will provide insight into what you should be doing to achieve a reasonable and realistic standard of answer: all other resources will provide you with lengthy "learning aids" rather than guidance as to what to do on the day.

3. Insights applied from the ICAEW Tutor Conferences

Our tutor team has attended all SBM Workshops at the ICAEW Tutor Conferences since 2014 and spent, listening to the feedback and viewpoints of the SBM examiner team on the first 8 real exam papers taken by candidates. We have carefully analysed these comments and have compared these to the recent real examinations to develop SBM mocks which respect the future progression and direction of the SBM examination.

4. Advice on mark allocation

The answer sections to our mock exams start with an explanation of how we allocated the marks for a question across the different Tasks. This will help you understand how the SBM examiners will themselves determine the mark allocation and will give you an opportunity to put into practice the various mark allocation estimation rules that we explain in this book: without the ability to understand the mark allocation, your time management will largely be guesswork. We believe that this is an improvement on the existing ICAEW resources which leave the crucial area of mark allocation unexplained.

5. Realistic question paper format

We provide our mock exams by email in PDF format. We have carefully formatted the question paper so that it reflects the narrow width page formatting of ICAEW computer-based assessment question papers, meaning that the question paper and computer-based assessment answer software can be loaded up side-by-side on a single screen in a similar manner to a real examination.

We have been very careful to make the exams look exactly like the real thing, even down to the font size and style, so that everything seems familiar on exam day.

6. Additional practice – vital in a practical paper such as SBM

Some students (and other tuition providers) are sceptical of the need for further mock examinations – there are now 8 real SBM papers available and the ICAEW Question Bank contains a large number of questions to attempt.

We would argue that it is important to recognise the **very open and unpredictable nature of the SBM examination**: this is not a closed subject like tax compliance or financial accounting where there are only a certain number of possible scenarios (i.e. rules) which can be tested – rather, it is a very practical, realistic test of business skills where the examiner can take the exam in many directions. In this sense, it is very similar to its predecessor paper (Business Change) – we have worked with many students who could pass all other ACA examinations easily but who became stuck at Business Change because it was too unpredictable and not something that could be drilled or rote-learned.

Therefore with SBM, **the more practice you can get the better** – there is unfortunately no set formula or narrow range of topics that you can guarantee to understand to pass the exam: **SBM is much more about practical skills, judgement and experience**. The more you can practice, the better.

7. Testing of topics without any other question practice available

We have been careful to include practice of certain key areas not yet tested in real past papers, mocks or the ICAEW Question Bank in order to avoid overlap with the SBM existing resources. As such, our mock examinations provide the only way to practise certain areas via an examination-style format since the relevant topics are not tested in any other available exam-standard questions.

Technique Improvement Service

Whilst we will provide you with a full "candidate-standard" model answer in our SBM mock pack, in an open and practical paper such as SBM, with its complicated holistic-marking methodology (see chapter 18) there are many plausible and acceptable ways of answering the same question. Therefore looking simply at our model answer may be insufficient to judge the quality of your own attempt, particularly if you have taken a different but reasonable interpretation of the question e.g. you have decided that the company should sell its loss-making division when our model answer shows more hope and suggests some ways to retain the division and improve its performance. We could both be right!

Our Technique Improvement Service provides a detailed tutor review of your attempts at our mock exams. We will not only provide you with an overall mark but will also work through and annotate your script on a line by line basis explaining what you are doing well and badly, aiming to boost your mark at all times. We will then also provide a separate report which analyses your script in more detail, emphasising any key points in our feedback and also correcting any technical issues. Overall, the service is not just about marking the script but also about providing detailed individual feedback on your script. Please see our website for further details.

Our fee for SBM TIS is £150 plus VAT per script assessed. We can assess attempts at our own mock examinations or at ICAEW SBM mocks or past papers.

In an unusual and technique-based examination like SBM, detailed tutor feedback can be vital, making the difference between a passing and failing script, even if you do know your technical content well: this is because SBM (just like the Case Study) is all about understanding what you need to be saying to **score marks** (not always the same thing as writing a **realistic, real-world report**).

Foreword to the 2018 Edition

Thank you for purchasing this 2018 edition of *Smashing SBM™ – How to Pass the ACA Strategic Business Management Examination*. We hope you will find it useful in your preparations for your examination.

We have reviewed and updated the 2017 edition of this book for the learning points raised by the 2017 SBM examinations and have also taken into account the points made by the SBM examiners at the SBM Workshop at the 2018 ICAEW Tutor Conference. We have also incorporated changes made in the 2018 Advanced Level syllabus (which, like in 2017, are minor in nature).

The 2017 examinations were largely in line with expectations and did not contain any surprises. Due Diligence was tested in both examinations so may perhaps be a bit less likely to be examined in 2018 and there was perhaps less emphasis on Big Data and cybersecurity than might have been expected from the syllabus updates on these areas in 2017 … but these areas remain "trendy" and (relatively speaking) "exciting" areas in accountancy so we would definitely recommend preparing yourself for possible Big Data and cybersecurity questions in 2018. These are definitely not the only learning points from the 2017 examinations so please read the rest of this book for full details.

We strongly recommend that you also consider purchasing our *Strategic Business Management Exam Room Notes 2018* as these will provide a useful complement to this book, which you can use both in the exam itself and also before the examination to quickly revise the most examinable SBM areas. Our *Strategic Business Management Exam Room Notes 2018* contain alphabetically-arranged summary reminders for all key SBM areas, based on our review of SBM past papers, ICAEW SBM mocks and SBM Question Bank questions.

We are also pleased to provide a fully updated 2018 edition of our SBM on-demand video course which contains over 40 hours of original content written and recorded by our team: look out for our detailed tutor Talkthroughs of the 2017 past papers plus some new content on (you guessed it!) Big Data and cybersecurity. Please see our website at **www.acasimplified.com** for more information on this course.

Do not forget to consider purchasing our SBM mock exams – we have carefully written some further practice exams for you, testing areas which are within the SBM syllabus but not tested so often in the existing materials. You can never do too much practice in an unpredictable examination like SBM so our mocks provide an ideal way to gain exposure to further scenarios. Please see page 4 of this book for further details.

Thank you again for purchasing this book and we hope you find it useful. Please do spend a bit of your preparation time focusing on the areas of **planning** and **mark estimation/time management** – if you can understand these 2 areas well, SBM is not the most technically demanding examination and you should have a good chance at scoring well.

Best of luck for your examination and thanks again for your purchase!

The ACA Simplified Team   **April 2018**

Foreword to the 2017 Edition

We have retained the Foreword to the 2017 edition (originally written in March 2017) of this book for your reference and to further explain what we are trying to achieve.

Thank you for purchasing this 2017 edition of *Smashing SBM™ – How to Pass the ACA Strategic Business Management Examination*. We hope you will find it useful in your preparations for this unusual examination.

We have reviewed and updated the 2016 edition for the learning points raised by the 2016 SBM examinations and also in relation to the points made by the SBM examiners at the SBM Workshop at the 2017 ICAEW Tutor Conference. We have also incorporated changes made in the 2017 SBM syllabus (which are minor in nature).

The 2016 examinations were largely in line with expectations and did not contain any surprises. As we had predicted, the Assurance area of Agreed Upon Procedures was finally tested. Other than the fact that the 2016 examinations tended to present the Task requirements "mixed into" the narrative (rather than as a single bullet point list at the end of the relevant question), the 2016 papers were standard in nature.

We strongly recommend that you also consider purchasing our *Strategic Business Management Exam Room Notes 2017* as these will provide a useful complement to this book, which you can use both in the exam itself and also to quickly revise the most examinable SBM areas. Our *Strategic Business Management Exam Room Notes 2017* contain alphabetically-arranged summary reminders for all key SBM areas, based on our review of SBM past papers, ICAEW SBM mocks and SBM Question Bank questions.

We were also pleased to launch our SBM on-demand video course for the November 2016 sitting. We have fully updated the course for the 2017 syllabus and have added further content. Please see our website at **www.acasimplified.com** for more information on this course.

Don't forget to consider our SBM mock exams – we have carefully written some further practice exams for you, testing areas which are within the SBM syllabus but not tested so often in the existing materials. You can never do too much practice in an unpredictable examination like SBM so our mocks provide an ideal way to gain exposure to further scenarios. Please see page 4 of this book for further details.

You can also sign up to our Twitter feed @acasimplified to be automatically notified as soon any new materials or courses are launched.

Thank you again for purchasing this book and we hope you find it useful. Please do spend a bit of your preparation time focusing on the areas of **planning** and **mark estimation** – if you can understand these 2 areas well, SBM is not the most technically difficult examination and you should have a good chance at succeeding.

Best of luck for your examination!

The ACA Simplified Team   **May 2017**

Foreword to the 2016 Edition

We have retained the Foreword to the 2016 edition (originally written in March 2016) of this book for your reference and to further explain what we are trying to achieve.

Thank you for purchasing this 2016 edition of *Smashing SBM™ – How to Pass the ACA Strategic Business Management Examination.*

We are very pleased to be launching this second edition of *Smashing SBM™*, following an excellent and enthusiastic student response to the first edition published in 2015. Having written the book solely in response to student requests connected to our reputation for providing effective tips to strategic business examinations such as the ACA Case Study (see our book *Cracking Case™*), it was perhaps not too surprising to see our best case forecasts for the book fulfilled!

We have thoroughly updated all the text to take into account the learning points from the 2015 real SBM examinations and 2015 official ICAEW SBM mock examinations, as well as the updates made to the ICAEW Study Manual for the 2016 syllabus.

We hope you will find this book useful in your preparations for SBM. The SBM examination is unusual in nature, having only 2 questions and a lot of Exhibit information to read. Additionally, the question paper does not split the number of marks down into the separate Tasks required. Using this book, however, should provide you with some **effective planning strategies** and an ability to **correctly estimate the number of marks available for each Task**, thereby allowing you to manage your time well.

The book also includes detailed revision notes and tips on the key areas of practical business advisory (otherwise known as the combination of Business Strategy and Financial Management), assurance and ethics.

The first part of the book explains how to plan and estimate the mark allocation. We also review some useful points from the examiners' feedback in this part. The second part of the book then includes revision of technical content on key areas before ending with some further tips from the examiners and from us.

From the feedback received from students who purchased this book and also from students on our SBM tuition courses, we know that the book does pair up well with our *Strategic Business Management Exam Room Notes*. Our *Exam Room Notes* provide an alphabetical set of summarised notes covering all key areas that are likely to be tested in the SBM examination (based on reviewing the SBM syllabus, SBM past papers, SBM mock exams and similar resources for the previous Business Change examination on which SBM extensively draws). The *Exam Room Notes* cover both numerical and narrative aspects.

We are aware that due to extremely high demand for our *Strategic Business Management Exam Room Notes* at the 2015 sittings, Amazon experienced several stockouts and students had to wait to receive their copy of the book. Whilst all students did receive their copy before the examination, please note that we have now been informed by Amazon that they have placed the 2016 version of this book into a special supply arrangements to avoid a recurrence of this issue. Even so, we would advise you to obtain your copy of the *Exam Room Notes* well before the examination: this is not only to avoid any potential supply chain issues but also because it is it vital for you to use the *Exam Room Notes* in all your practice attempts so that you become familiar with where the content can be found and what reminders are included. It is always slightly alarming to see the number of copies of our books sold just 1 or 2 weeks before the examination as we do try to publish these several months in advance on the basis that you can obtain best value by purchasing the books as early as possible. Therefore please do pick up your copy of the sister publication to this book as soon as possible.

We received a large amount of positive feedback on the 2015 edition of this book. We have therefore broadly retained the same structure and format as last year but as always we do welcome your constructive feedback on any improvements or areas you think we should add to the book.

As we go to press, we are in the process of preparing further SBM resources which we hope to be able to launch before the July 2016 sitting but which should certainly be in place for the November 2016 sitting. Please keep an eye on our website at **www.acasimplified.com** and also consider subscribing to our newsletter: see the subscription box on our website to sign up to the newsletter.

You can also sign up to our Twitter feed @acasimplified to be automatically notified as soon any new materials or courses are launched.

Thank you again for purchasing this book and we hope you find it useful. Please do spend a bit of your preparation time focusing on the areas of **planning** and **mark estimation** – if you can understand these 2 areas well, SBM is not the most technically difficult examination and you should have a good chance at succeeding.

Best of luck for your examination!

The ACA Simplified Team   **March 2016**

PS. If you found the book useful, why not include a review at Amazon.co.uk? In this competitive market, honest reviews from students are one of the best ways to help future students understand the benefits of our publications and this in turn allows us to put more resources into developing new and innovative approaches to help you in your studies.

Foreword to the 2015 Edition

We have retained the Foreword to the 2015 edition (originally written in April 2015) of this book for your reference and to further explain what we are trying to achieve.

Thank you for purchasing this 2015 edition of *Smashing SBM™ – How to Pass the ACA Strategic Business Management Examination*.

It is with great pleasure that we are launching this, the first edition of *Smashing SBM™*. Following the success of our similar *Cracking Case™* publication and after repeated requests to provide a similar student-focused textbook on what you **really** need to do to pass the ACA examinations, we are now pleased to launch *Smashing SBM™*.

After 2 sessions of tutoring SBM and, perhaps more importantly, having now had the opportunity to review and analyse 2 real SBM examination papers (July 2014 and November 2014) and to attend the related ICAEW Tutor Conference workshops in 2014 and 2015, we feel it is an appropriate time to set down in paper some of our thoughts on this unusual examination. Hence this book.

Smashing SBM™ is intended to provide an **original, practical and coherent planning framework** to tackle this relatively unusual examination. It is also designed to provide you with a **focus for your revision time**: we have even included some specific revision questions for you to attempt to help promote this. Finally, *Smashing SBM™* aims to explain **how your script will be assessed** so that you can write in the correct style and with the correct emphasis.

ICAEW have stated that SBM is intended to be a "bridge" to the Case Study examination. Hence our "money bridge" on the front cover. Beyond marketing imagery, however, we have fully integrated this bridge concept into our approach to writing this book: like the Case Study, SBM is fundamentally about providing practical business advice to a client after very quickly absorbing a large amount of information, organising this into a coherent and appropriate plan and then producing your answers in an organised and balanced report format.

How will *Smashing SBM™* help you to prepare for the exam?

- By helping you to manage your time by **allocating the right amount of effort to each individual Task** (using our **MAP planning technique**)

- By helping you to **work on your report-writing skills and writing style** to ensure that you only cover the relevant areas and that you write concisely

- By helping you to **revise key technical areas**, through explaining to you which areas to focus on, providing you with revision notes within this book and providing you with selected practice questions from our Financial Management and Business Strategy and Technology Professional Level Q&A publications

- By giving you insight into what the examiners are **trying to do with this examination** and by **explaining how the marking works**

As we have already established a highly successful Case Study programme, including our *Cracking Case™* student-focused textbook, and as SBM is assessed using the same skills framework as Case

Study (see chapter 4), we believe that we should be well-placed as a tuition company to provide a similar original and market-leading approach to SBM.

We therefore very much hope that you will find this book useful. We have worked hard to ensure that all material is useful and relevant so we do recommend that you read the book in full a few times: chapter 2 provides an overview of what each chapter is designed to do in order to give you an advance understanding of what we are trying to achieve in the book as a whole.

We can only improve our materials and continue to anticipate the requirements of ACA students with your feedback and suggestions so please do contact us at **getqualified@acasimplified.com** if you have any feedback, whether positive or negative.

We hope that *Smashing SBM™* proves useful and we wish you all the best with your examination. Please do let us know how you got on and how this book may have helped you along the way.

Best wishes and good luck!

The ACA Simplified Team   **April 2015**

PS. If you found the book useful, why not include a review at Amazon.co.uk and/or on Twitter (using our Twitter handle **@acasimplified**)? In this competitive market, honest reviews from students are one of the best ways to help future students understand the benefits of our publications.

Smashing SBM™: Our Terminology

As we have created our own original planning technique and perspective for the SBM examination, it is necessary to introduce our own terminology to refer to our planning approach and related aspects of the examination. Please note that the following terms are not official ICAEW terminology and have been **developed specifically for *Smashing SBM*™** – as such, you should not use them in your SBM report answer: the terms are merely used for tutorial and illustrative purposes.

MAP

Acronym for **Mark Allocated Plan**, our unique form of planning sheet. Rather than terming our planning sheets simply a "Plan", we have added the words "Mark Allocated" to emphasise that a crucial element of planning for an examination such as SBM (where the precise mark allocation is not indicated to candidates) must involve **estimating the mark allocation**: only once you have determined this should you turn to the traditional planning phase of deciding exactly what to write. In other words, the **mark allocation** estimate must come first before any **planning** takes place – hence MA **before** P.

The term MAP is also designed to emphasise that your plan must give **direction** to your answer – without an effective MAP you could end up wandering off the mark-scoring path or head off in a completely incorrect direction. Therefore the term MAP emphasises that a good plan should give you **guidance** and **direction**.

Task

This is our own terminology for each of the specific requirements mentioned in the SBM question paper. **Generally**, the Tasks will be contained in a single Exhibit at the very end of the question in a **numbered list**: however, in some SBM examinations there was a further "hidden" Task contained in an earlier Exhibit (without an obvious number marker: see discussion in chapter 7). Therefore always review the Exhibits fully before determining what your answer should contain.

Our MAP planning sheets provide space for you to write a quick summary of the main Task. Our MAPs also provide reminders of how to estimate the mark allocation for each Task. Use these aspects of our MAPs to ensure that you do not forget to do important parts of the question and to ensure that you allocate your time sensibly.

Sub-Task

A sub-Task is an element within one of the numbered (or "hidden") Tasks. Often a Task will have 2-3 sentences and in this case there would be 2-3 sub-Tasks. However, in some instances there may be different sub-Tasks within a single sentence. See the examples below, taken from the November 2014 SBM examination:

"Question 1

The FFT Board would like DH to prepare a report which:

(1) Explains the decline in FFT's profit over the years ended 31 December 2012, 31 December 2013 and 31 December 2014. Recommend action which may improve profitability in future."

Here sub-Task (a) would be to **explain the decline in profit**; sub-Task (b) would be to **provide recommendations** to improve profitability.

"Question 2

The WS Board would like XYZ to prepare a report which addresses the following:

(2) Using Exhibit 3A and 3B, so far as the information permits, explain with supporting calculations why the actual profit differs from the budgeted profit for each of the two divisions, and for the company as a whole, for the year ended 30 September 2014."

Here sub-Task (a) would be to explain why **performance for the 2 divisions differs** from budgeted profit; sub-Task (b) would then apply a similar analysis to the **company as a whole**. Notice how there are 2 different sub-Tasks within a **single** sentence in this second example: therefore do not assume that the number of **sentences** or number of **individual bullets** is necessarily a good indicator of the number of sub-Tasks.

Our MAP planning sheets provide space for you to write a quick summary of each sub-Task. We believe that this is a very important part of your planning because filling out the sub-Task column will ensure that you have not missed anything crucial within your answer. It will also ensure that you give a good enough emphasis to all sub-Tasks: this is crucial to impress the examiner and failure to complete all sub-Tasks well (or omission of some sub-Tasks completely) will severely limit your grade.

Part 1 – How to Plan

Chapter 1   Introduction: This Book and Why We Wrote It

Learning Points

After reading this chapter, you must be able to:

1. understand the reasons why this book has been written
2. understand the basic structure of the book (chapter 2 will provide more details)
3. understand how SBM requires a different approach to your other ACA examinations

---

1.1   How and Why We Have Written This Book

We were delighted to launch *Smashing SBM™ – How to Pass the ACA Strategic Business Management Examination* with the 2015 edition of the book.

We now have 8 full real SBM exams to analyse so after teaching SBM since the examination was first introduced in July 2014 and after attending various SBM workshops at the ICAEW Tutor Conference, we think that it is now possible to offer some evidentially-based tuition tips and planning advice in a book format. Hence *Smashing SBM™*.

We also know that, following the release of our highly successful book *Cracking Case™ – How to Pass the ACA Case Study*[3], a publication which provides a unique planning technique successfully used by 2 ICAEW prize winners in 2014, there is a need to provide students with a **more practical and innovative approach to planning** than is often otherwise available: in developing our techniques, we believe very strongly in trying to listen to examiner feedback at the ICAEW SBM Workshops and in looking at how our own students are performing – if this means rejecting a "normal" method of planning or even what the textbook says the examination is about, then so be it! **We are only interested in methods that actually work.**

1.2   What Does the Book Aim to Do?

Smashing SBM™ contains a large number of chapters and topic areas but, fundamentally, we are aiming to do 4 things with the book:

1. help you to understand **how to estimate the marks available for the different question Tasks**, thus guiding you towards an appropriate allocation of your time

2. help you to understand **what skills the examiners are looking to see** and therefore **how the examination is marked**

---

[3] At certain points in 2014, 2015, 2016 and 2017, *Cracking Case™* was placed within the top 1,000 bestselling books on Amazon.co.uk – not bad for an accountancy textbook! The strong student feedback recorded on Amazon.co.uk further reflects how this book has been received within the student community and indicates the difference that an effective planning approach can make.

3. help you to focus your **revision onto areas that are more likely to come up in the real exam** (in some cases, such as chapters 10 to 17, *Smashing SBM™* will even provide you with **original revision resources of our own**)

4. provide you with an **overarching planning framework which takes into account the above 3 factors** – we call this planning approach **MAP**, firstly because the technique is intended to give you focus and direction (just like a real-world "map") and also because MAP stands for "Mark Allocated Plan": this reflects our view that it is pointless to plan your report in SBM without first estimating **how the marks will be allocated**. But without studying the techniques contained in *Smashing SBM™*, estimating this mark allocation will be difficult.

1.3   Basic Structure of the Book

The first part of the book (chapters 1 to 8 inclusive) contains detailed reviews of the style, format and marking approach used in SBM – you might regard these chapters as **explaining the nature and requirements of the examination paper**. Part 1 ends with a review of examiner comments regarding the 8 real examinations sat since July 2014 when SBM was first examined – a very useful source of information but one which, in our experience, is underutilised by students.

The second part of the book (chapters 9 to 20 inclusive) then tries to help you make a start on your revision and explains what you should be doing in practice to pass the examination. Hence we include chapter 18 (examiner comments from the SBM Workshops at recent ICAEW Tutor Conferences) and chapter 19 (an examiner article from VITAL magazine) to reinforce how the technical content revised in chapters 9 to 17 should be applied in practice.

In addition to these 2 main parts of the book, we then also provide our Appendices which provide our MAP templates (tailored to Q1 and Q2) plus examples of how to complete your MAPs for a real SBM exam paper (using the example of the November 2014 exam).

For a more detailed review of the structure of the book, on a chapter by chapter basis, please see chapter 2.

1.4   How to Use the Book

We strongly recommend that you read the book in full before attempting any SBM papers. Although we do make reference to the SBM real exams, SBM ICAEW mocks and SBM Electronic Question Bank questions, we have been careful not to reveal the correct answers at any point – therefore although you will gain **some** idea of the content of some of these papers if you read the book before attempting your papers, we do not believe that you will have had so much pre-warning as to what to do as to make sitting the papers pointless: on the contrary, if you sit all the papers first and only then come to read the book and understand our planning technique then you will have no more papers available to practise (unless you purchase our mocks of course! See page 4 for details).

Therefore, **please read the book in full and experiment with designing your own MAPs before attempting any SBM papers**. We then recommend that you return to the book after you have had

18

some practice of sitting SBM exams: this practice will reveal your own personal weak areas to work on so you will know which parts of the book to prioritise.

Once you have read the book a few times, the chapters in Part 1 will hopefully become less important for you to revisit: **you should by then be familiar with our planning approach, the format of the exam and examiner comments**. If so, you can then move on to focus on the chapters in Part 2 which contain revision of **technical content**: it is unlikely that you will have mastered all of this content fully from a few readings so you need to concentrate on studying these areas right through to the exam day.

Hopefully, after understanding both planning (Part 1) and the technical content (Part 2) you should be well placed to "**smash SBM**"!

Chapter 2   Overview of *Smashing SBM*™: Chapter by Chapter

Learning Points

After reading this chapter, you must be able to:

1. understand what each chapter of *Smashing SBM*™ is designed to do
2. recognise that all chapters have been carefully written to provide different information
3. identify the chapters that are of most value to you personally
4. understand which chapters must be read again just before the examination

---

2.1   Chapter by Chapter Overview of *Smashing SBM*™

Having explained our thinking behind the creation of this book in the previous chapter, we will now preview the remaining chapters of the book, aiming to explain what each chapter is designed to achieve.

We recommend that you review this overview carefully **before** reading the rest of the book: this will give you an understanding of what each chapter will contribute to your approach to the SBM examination. You can then revisit this overview when you re-read the book to ensure that you have covered those chapters which are of most benefit to you personally.

2.2   Overview of Chapter Content and Aims

Chapter 1: Introduction: This Book and Why We Wrote It

This chapter explains why we have written this book and what the book is designed to achieve.

Chapter 2: Overview of *Smashing SBM*™: Chapter by Chapter

Chapter 2 is the chapter that you are currently reading. It provides an overview of the book so that you know what will be covered. Certain chapters will be of more importance to you personally so please try to make a note of the matters that may be particularly important for you to cover.

Chapter 3: The Nature of the Examination and the Examination Paper

This chapter analyses the 8 real SBM papers which were available at the time of writing as well as the SBM Sample Paper produced by ICAEW ahead of the first sitting of SBM in July 2014. It aims to use this analysis to help you understand what the **typical format of the examination will be**, including the expected Exhibit length and number of Tasks for both Q1 and Q2. This will in turn **help you to understand how to allocate your time**.

20

Chapter 4: SBM, Case Study and the 4 Case Skills "Lenses" Translated

SBM has been specifically designed by ICAEW as a **skills "bridge"** to help students develop the practical analysis and report-writing skills needed to succeed in the final Case Study examination. In line with this aim, the SBM examiners have confirmed that the **4 general Case Study skills areas will be used when designing the SBM paper – these 4 areas** (which we call "lenses" to indicate that you should "view" the information in a particular way to achieve the marks) **must also be addressed in your answer**. Therefore in this chapter we explain what the 4 broad Case Study skills areas are and how to "translate" these slightly technical terms into report answers.

Chapter 5: Need Direction? Use a MAP!

This chapter introduces our unique planning methodology, which we call **MAPs** or **Mark Allocated Plans**. MAPs provide a way of planning your answer which takes into account the fact that you will only be given a general 60 or 40 global question mark allocation rather than a specific mark allocation for different Tasks and sub-Tasks: therefore a vital first step in an effective SBM exam strategy must be to estimate how many marks are likely to be available for the different elements and therefore how much time to devote to each aspect of your answer. To some extent, most of the other chapters in the book feed into this fundamental question of **likely mark allocation**: therefore we introduce the concept of the MAP quite early on in the book.

Chapter 6: The Correct SBM Writing Style

This chapter explains how to write as succinctly as possible, whilst still picking up the marks, when answering SBM questions. We will look at some of the examiner's advice on the **most efficient methods of writing**, ensuring that you get the relevant technical points and definitions into your answers without wasting too many words or falling into the trap of writing out accounting standards without any application.

Chapter 7: Analysis of the SBM Past Papers

Real SBM examination papers are the best source of evidence on the format and focus of the examination. Together with the related examiner commentary (analysed in chapter 8: see below), a careful review of past papers can provide some important tips and hints as to what will be expected in the examination. **In this chapter we therefore carefully review the SBM past papers in detail. We review the format of the examination, the type of Tasks requested, the Exhibit length and the allocation of marks across the different SBM subject areas** (i.e. practical business advisory, financial reporting, audit and ethics).

Chapter 8: Useful Points from the Examiners' Comments on the Past Papers

In this chapter, we carefully review the comments made by the examiners in the model answers and markschemes for all SBM past papers available at the time of writing. Although these comments are available to students via the model answers downloadable from the ICAEW website, **we are aware that most students do not read these comments or at least do not look at them in detail**: hence **we collate and compare the comments to identify the patterns in these papers**. This allows us to identify some **common weaknesses** and, conversely, the **common strengths** of the best performing scripts. Armed with this knowledge, you can adapt your answering style so that you **provide the kinds of answer that the examiners like to see**.

Chapter 8 completes Part 1 of the book on the nature and requirements of typical SBM papers so we then move into Part 2 of the book where we look at technical aspects of SBM.

Chapter 9: The Mini-Case Study: What To Do and What Not To Do

The SBM examiners have confirmed that Q1 will always account for a higher proportion of the marks than Q2: **Q1 will be allocated between 55 and 65 of the 100 marks available**. It has also been stated that Q1 will be a **mini-Case Study** that integrates several aspects of a business problem. Given the mark allocation, **it will be hard to pass the examination without a strong performance in Q1** and therefore we provide a full chapter explaining the best way to attack this style of question.

Chapters 10 to 14: Revision of Specialist Audit & Assurance Topics

As SBM will tend to test specialist assurance areas rather than statutory audit (the separate Corporate Reporting paper provides ample testing of the process of statutory audit) then there is a risk that you could be **throwing away valuable marks by not knowing how to address specialist assurance areas such as corporate governance, internal audit, Agreed Upon Procedures or Due Diligence** (amongst other topics). Chapters 10 to 14 therefore provide revision and self-test questions to study these specialist areas, which are usually understood poorly by students.

Chapter 15: Practical Business Advisory: Revision of Key Topics

This chapter performs a similar role to the chapters on Specialist Audit & Assurance areas, but with an **emphasis on Practical Business Advisory (PBA) points** (i.e. strategy, financial management and practical advice). Here we draw upon the types of scenario seen in the 8 real SBM papers set to date and also on the SBM Sample Paper.

Chapter 16: Revision of Key Business Strategy and Financial Management Topics

As you may be aware, we produce books containing **hundreds of short-form self-test questions (Q&As) for all Professional Level papers**. We have carefully selected the most useful questions from our **Business Strategy and Technology** and **Financial Management Q&As** and we reproduce these for your revision in this chapter. As discussed in more detail in chapter 18, the examiner has emphasised that Business Strategy and Financial Management topics remain very important in SBM so we wanted to provide you with a very quick revision method.

22

As also indicated in chapter 18, the SBM examiners have urged candidates to thoroughly revise the Financial Accounting and Reporting syllabus. **Unfortunately, given the breadth of FAR, it is not possible to provide a set of short form questions in this book as there is just too much to cover: for a very quick method of revising, we recommend that you instead separately obtain our *Advanced Level Financial Reporting Exam Room Notes 2018*.**

We do believe that a full and thorough revision of the Professional Level will put you in a very good place to attempt SBM so please do consider purchasing the **full versions** of our Business Strategy and Technology, Financial Management and Financial Accounting & Reporting Q&As – **the very short question format will be an ideal way of revising knowledge that you should already have** and will be better than getting out your Professional Level Study Manual or (even worse) full past paper questions!

Chapter 17: Ethics: Revision and Application to SBM

We know that every SBM paper will have between **5 and 10 marks for ethics**. Although this is not a huge total, **at the margin those marks could be crucial**. We also know from the ICAEW SBM Workshops that the examiners are looking for **something different in ethics answers at the Advanced Level (compared to the Professional Level)**. This chapter therefore reviews the examiner comments and expectations and also provides some different **ethical frameworks** that you can use to generate an interesting and well-structured answer.

Chapter 18: Comments from the ICAEW Tutor Conferences

Our tutor team attended the **SBM Workshops at recent ICAEW Tutor Conferences, obtaining insights into what the examiners are trying to do with the SBM**. In this chapter we provide some useful notes on the most important points discussed. Please do read this chapter very carefully: **without understanding what SBM is designed to test, there is no way to anticipate the future direction of the examination or tailor your answering style to what the examiners want to see**.

Chapter 19: Summary of VITAL Magazine Article on SBM

In April 2014, shortly before the first sitting of the new SBM examination, ICAEW provided a one page summary of the **new format of the examination, together with some tips on what to revise**. As we are aware that many students do not regularly read VITAL, and as you probably do not collect copies of VITAL to refer to, we have summarised the article in this chapter.

Chapter 20: Advice for Exam Day

As an Advanced Level examination, SBM is an "**open book**" examination. In this chapter we provide some advice on how to **manage your exam room resources** so that these are neither too short (lacking information) nor too extensive (resulting in information overload and an inability to find information under time pressure). We also provide **some further practical tips and explain why purchasing our *SBM Exam Room Notes* book would create a perfect partner publication for the technique set out in this book, giving you all the resources you really need to pass SBM**.

Appendix 1 – MAP for SBM Q1

Appendix 1 contains our **first Mark Allocated Plan or MAP**, specifically created for Q1. Our Q1 MAP contains space to write in a brief summary of each Task and sub-Task, make a note of what technical content to include and create an estimate of the number of marks available, based on the principles set out in this book. Our Q1 MAP also contains Q1-specific reminders of likely mark allocations and reminders of what skills to demonstrate to the marker.

Rather than just uncritically applying our Q1 MAP, we would strongly recommend that you take Appendix 1 as a guide to the creation of your **own personalised MAP**: this will allow you to find a format that works for you personally – perhaps you may wish to incorporate more personal reminders as you complete SBM past papers and mock exams and identify your weaknesses. We would recommend that you retain the basic general format and approach of our MAPs but a **personally-designed and individual version is always likely to be the best approach**.

Appendix 2 – MAP for SBM Q2

Appendix 2 contains our **second Mark Allocated Plan or MAP**, specifically created for Q2. We follow the same approach as in Appendix 1 but adjusting for the different nature of Q2.

Again, we would recommend that you use our suggested MAP as the basis of your **own personalised version**.

Appendix 3 – Example Completed MAPs: November 2014 Examination Paper

Our third Appendix contains an **example of a set of completed MAPs, based on how we would have used the MAP approach if we had needed to sit the November 2014 SBM paper**.

Please note that we completed these MAPs as part of the process of writing a textbook rather than under time and other examination pressures. As such, we have been able to take our time and even use the suggested answer to provide a "**perfect**" example of how a MAP should be completed. You will have to work under more time pressure and therefore **please try not to be intimidated or worried about the example MAPs** – these are really an "ideal" example and **you will be able to pass the examination well with a much more basic or "rough" version than what we have here** since many other students will not be aware of the need to plan so carefully and will not even have the MAP technique available to them.

Appendix 4 – Sample Pages from ACA Simplified *SBM Exam Room Notes*

Our ***SBM Exam Room Notes*** provide a "sister" publication to *Smashing SBM™* by providing notes that can be used in the examination. *Smashing SBM™* should be studied and used well before the examination but, as a book of general examination advice, *Smashing SBM™* is not specifically designed for quick reference on examination day (although you may wish to tag and highlight certain sections) – our *SBM Exam Room Notes* are, however, designed for very quick alphabetical reference in the examination. To provide you with an example of how the Exam Room Notes are designed to work, Appendix 4 includes some sample pages.

Appendix 5 – SBM ICAEW Revision Resources: Some Important Points to Note

In the final element of the book, we review the ICAEW SBM mock exams, ICAEW Question Bank, Sample Paper and Electronic Question Bank to provide **some warnings on which preparation questions are likely to be most representative of SBM questions**: as we show in Appendix 5, some Question Bank and even mock exam questions are **based on Business Change questions from the old Technical Integration syllabus**. It seems unlikely that these will be as helpful for practice as questions which have been written **from scratch for SBM** (like our own mock exams) and hence Appendix 5 contains a list of priority questions – very useful if you do not have time to practise all available preparation questions.

Chapter 3   The Nature of the Examination and the Examination Paper

---

Learning Points

After reading this chapter, you must be able to:

1. understand some basic principles behind the design of SBM as an assessment method
2. understand the typical format and length of the various elements of an SBM paper
3. understand the number and types of Task and sub-Task generally found in Q1 and Q2
4. appreciate that some Tasks require a high investment of reading time relative to the marks available

---

3.1   SBM: The Nature of the Examination

Before we get into the details of how to tackle SBM (including our **unique MAP planning methodology**), in this chapter we will highlight some important and unique characteristics of SBM as an examination, compared to other ACA examinations. We include this information at the start of the book because we believe that you need to keep this information in mind **throughout your preparation for SBM**.

In the second half of the chapter we analyse the available SBM papers to develop an "anatomy" of a typical SBM paper, looking at the **length of Exhibits generally given, the content of those Exhibits and the number of Tasks required to be completed**. We again provide this information near the start of the book as it is important to bear this data in mind **throughout your preparation**: analysis of what a paper will typically look like will also hopefully do something to reduce your worries about the **very long and open nature of the SBM examination paper**.

Here is a reminder of the expected marks breakdown by discipline, according to the examiners:

Topic	Standard weighting
Strategy	35-45%
Finance, valuations & investment appraisal	30-40%
Financial reporting[4]	15-20%
Assurance	10%
Ethics	5-10%

Given the importance of the first 2 categories and the fact that these disciplines are always tested in the same Tasks (whereas financial reporting, assurance and ethics are often tested on their own in separate, single discipline Tasks), for the purposes of this book we merge the categories of "Strategy" and "Finance, valuations & investment appraisal" into a single category which we call "practical

---

[4] The SBM examiners generally use the term "corporate reporting" to refer to this topic but because we think this may lead to confusion with the separate Corporate Reporting ACA paper, we have adopted the term "financial reporting" to refer to this part of the syllabus. By "financial reporting" we do **not** just mean the lessons that you learned in the Financial Accounting and Reporting paper but also the **new** rules that you learn from the Advanced Level study materials.

business advisory" or PBA: we study and analyse these 2 disciplines together because they are always tested in **combined Tasks** and so you need to understand the integration. Please see chapter 15 for detailed notes on PBA but, for the moment, note that this topic area is the **single most important element within the SBM syllabus**.

3.2 The "Accountant in Business" – Not the "Strategist in Business"

At both the 2014 and 2015 ICAEW Tutor Conferences, the examiners made a pointed remark which we feel is very important – it was stated that SBM "**has not been designed to be an exam that could be passed by an MBA student but rather as an exam that can only be passed by a Chartered Accountant**". What does this difference mean?

According to the examiners, an MBA-style examination has a **purely strategic focus** and does not test the candidate's understanding of the **financial reporting implications** of a strategic project or proposal. On the other hand, a paper which can only be passed by a Chartered Accountant (such as SBM) is one where the strategic impact on the **financial statements** will form part of the assessment.

As such, you should always bear in mind the phrase the **"Accountant in Business"** when writing your answer[5]: the examiners are interested in the **interplay between strategic decisions and financial reporting/audit issues** so it follows that you should keep both your **Strategist and Accountant hats on** when answering the questions.

Note that unless an SBM Task explicitly relates to financial reporting, you are unlikely to be given any reminders by the question wording that the "**Accountant in Business**" perspective is the one that the examiners are expecting you to show. Therefore do try to include relevant points regarding the impact on the financial statements **even where not specifically requested to do so**: you will be rewarded for this work.

3.3 Understanding the Examination Paper Material and Requirements

As SBM has been designed as a "bridge" to the final Case Study examination in which your challenge on exam day will be to review and analyse a further 10-12 pages of unseen material, one of the primary skills which you will need to develop in preparing for and sitting SBM is to develop an ability to **quickly and efficiently read and organise large volumes of information**. The amount of information you will be given for each question will be **significantly higher in SBM compared to any prior ACA paper** as there are only 2 questions to attempt in SBM: the ICAEW examiners have deliberately reduced the number of questions from the previous 3 questions in old Technical Integration paper in Business Change so that you can be given **more stimulus material to work with**, helping to "bridge" the skills gap to the Case Study.

The amount of exam paper material in SBM can appear overwhelming and this is only made worse by the fact that you will not be given any guidance as to how to allocate your time within each question

---

[5] As you will see, the second or "reminder" page of our MAP planning sheets contain plenty of reminders to adopt this perspective in your answers: we make no apology for any repetition as it is simply too important to your performance that you understand that this is what the examiners want to see.

because you will only be told the **total** mark allocation. **We therefore strongly believe that the key to succeeding in SBM is to develop an appropriate planning strategy**: hence the first part of this book will focus exclusively on explaining how to use our unique MAP planning sheets.

The most important element of your planning in SBM will involve predicting the number of marks available for each element of Q1 and Q2. Without a sensible estimate you could end up writing too much on insignificant areas. Our planning technique is constructed around this very point. **We have therefore carefully developed 11 specific mark estimation Rules to help you estimate a mark, and therefore time, allocation.**

In addition, it will not be possible to correctly estimate the number of marks available for each Task and sub-Task if you have not carefully taken the time to understand **exactly what the question is asking you to do**. Sometimes you will be given several numbered or bulleted points, helpfully splitting the question out for you already but on other occasions you will just be given a dense, multi-sentence block of text and will therefore have to carefully pick through the text to work out the number of different elements that you need to complete. In certain cases (such as the November 2014 real examination) there will even be **further Tasks mentioned outside of the list given at the end of the question paper** and hence mixed in or "hidden" within the text[6] i.e. mixed into the introductory material at the start of the question and before the first numbered "Exhibit". **It is therefore unfortunately necessary to read all the scenario information first before you can start your planning**, further increasing the challenge of the examination.

Overall, then, reading and planning skills are absolutely vital to the examination. Our MAP planning sheets contain reminders of the principles contained in this book but in order to use the MAPs effectively please do read all of our advice regarding **planning** and **interpretation of the questions** very carefully indeed.

Whilst it will take some time to explain our MAP technique, if you can correctly learn how to apply our **11 Rules** you will be in a significantly better position than other students who are being taught that the mark allocation between Tasks is likely to be "about equal" – just about the worst advice regarding SBM that we have ever heard![7]

3.4   A Bridge to the Case Study – Therefore Apply Case Study Skills

The ICAEW examiners have explicitly designed SBM to be a "bridge" to the Case Study examination after feedback from employers and tuition providers that the unusual nature and format of the Case Study was too much of a change for students to cope with in the absence of any preparatory steps: SBM will therefore "bridge" the skills gap.

This means that you should be thinking along the lines of the Case Study and using the same perspectives. However, if you are taking SBM before Case Study (as is the most common scenario)

---

[6] At the SBM Workshop at the 2014 ICAEW Tutor Conference, the examiners noted that many students missed an important "hidden" ethics Task in the November 2014 paper. Whilst not indicating that all papers will use this approach, there were certain strongly expressed requests for tutors to ask students to look through **all** the stimulus materials for a question before deciding what the requirements of the question actually are. This tactic has been used again in subsequent SBM papers so consider yourself warned!

[7] As such, it was disappointing to hear another large tuition provider make this very statement at the SBM Workshop at the 2015 ICAEW Tutor Conference.

then you obviously will not know what this will mean in practice. We will explain the necessary skills throughout the remainder of the book and we also include reminders on our MAP planning sheets. To anticipate the discussion of chapter 4, we would summarise the SBM-relevant Case Study perspectives as:

Keep your points practical – try to ensure a balance between using technical accounting concepts and giving very simple, practical advice which does not have to be rocket science: in chapter 8 we review some of the typical practical advice often given in the Case Study and you will see that the points are relatively basic and more about common sense than the intricacies of hedge accounting!

Apply scepticism – question the information given (politely!) and also look at what information has not been given but which is necessary to make an informed decision: as in the Case Study, the examination paper will not **remind** you to adopt a sceptical approach as by this stage in your studies and development as a potential Chartered Accountant you are expected to deploy this perspective **by default**.

Apply judgement as to what you discuss and adopt the client's perspective: cover the big picture in a helpful and succinct manner – you cannot discuss everything of interest in the time available so just as in Case Study you need to use judgement to select the points that are really key for the client to know. Carefully reviewing past papers is one of the best ways to identify what points are likely to score so we will provide such an analysis in this book.

3.5 "No Taxation in SBM"? Don't Get the Champagne Out Just Yet!

We are aware that some other tuition providers have been informing students that SBM will not involve any taxation issues. The most common statement we heard from students who used to ask whether to do the old style Business Change (Technical Integration) paper or move across to SBM was therefore that "there is no tax in the Advanced Level", probably followed by a sigh of relief (unless they happen to be a tax geek)!

It is thankfully **almost correct** that there are no tax issues to worry about in SBM, if by "tax" we mean the complicated UK tax rules which used to be tested under the old Technical Integration papers and which have now been moved down to the Professional Level paper in Business Planning: Taxation.

However, you should be aware that at **the 2014, 2015 and 2016 ICAEW Tutor Conferences the examiners did reserve the right to introduce "simple, fictional" tax questions**: in this kind of hypothetical question, all necessary tax rules will be given to the student in the question, rather than being based on prior knowledge of a real world tax system (the UK). **No complex rules will be used as the examiners said they were not looking to catch students out** by doing anything too complicated.

In theory, this should mean that you ought to be able to put together all the pieces of the tax puzzle live in the examination room but, of course, in practice this could be easier said than done: hence this statement that tax can still be tested is not the best of news.

In order to try to anticipate some of the "generic" rules that may be tested, we would advise you to revise the following basic **principles** of taxation (independent of precise UK tax rules):

1. **Trading losses** (including common restrictions and planning opportunities such as groups)

2. **Capital Allowances** (perhaps for integration into an NPV or cash flow model)

3. **Taxation of an individual** (perhaps as part of the analysis of a remuneration strategy)

4. **Liquidation and transfers of trade and assets** (key business change possibilities)

Again, in preparing for this possibility you should not be revising the details of UK tax rules, but rather the general **principles**, as it is likely that the fictional tax rules will be simpler versions of the UK approach (in order that candidates have some familiarity with the principles available).

Unless the examiner has asked students to consider the taxation position of a fictional country (per the above), we would expect all other questions to say something along the lines of "not to worry about tax for now". **Given that this will always be said, we would not expect any marks to be available for points such as "consider the tax implications" or (an even worse use of time) the calculation of capital allowances or tax losses etc**.

Put another way, only consider tax issues if there is a **very big hint in the question** i.e. a set of fictional country rules. **Otherwise do not try to score points with generic ideas**.

3.6 Not MC² But Rather MS²

We will review the examiner comments on the recent real exam papers in chapter 8. One of the most important remarks that we will see (and repeatedly so) is that the **examiners like to see points that are specific to the scenario**, rather than points that can always be made for any business.

As an example, if the examiners provide company-specific data and performance indicators (such as revenue per passenger and occupancy rates for an airline, for example) then **these must be used**: students should not just rely on indicators such as gross profit margins or total revenue as you will be throwing away marks by being so **generic** in approach.

Related to this point, we will see in chapters 7 and 8 that the examiners will often introduce a "twist" so that the scenario is unusual in some way. For example, perhaps the goodwill calculation shows a negative result or a "bargain purchase" rather than the expected positive figure. Or maybe one of the apparent ethical issues is not actually a serious matter after all. This is another way in which the examiner can check that you are responding to the **specific question set**, rather than "answering on auto-pilot" by not really responding to the specific and carefully designed scenario data.

To help with this process, we suggest that you remember the mnemonic **MS²** – **M**ake **S**cenario-**S**pecific remarks.

If you can just remember and apply **MS²** then you will automatically have dealt with the most common problem in a failing SBM script (see chapter 18).

3.7 SBM Exam Papers: The Typical Format

Having reviewed the above points, in the remainder of this chapter we will spend some time analysing the recent SBM examination papers and also the official ICAEW Sample Paper with a **particular focus on the likely format and structure of the examination paper itself**. We do this to help you prepare yourself for the **likely format** and also to warn you regarding some potential time traps in the way the examination paper information is presented and formatted.

Since SBM involves provision of extensive amounts of information and scope to vary the marks breakdown between perhaps 55:45 up to 65:35 in favour of Q1 versus Q2, the examiners definitely do have scope to change the format of SBM significantly from paper to paper.

Even so, **we would expect the format to remain largely in line with the 8 real exams and single Sample Paper available at the time of writing**. Therefore, whilst always being careful to respond to your own specific exam, we do think it is helpful to prepare yourself mentally for the standard format of an SBM paper and hence we provide an "anatomy" of the currently available papers in the remainder of this chapter.

The tables below aim to summarise the basic characteristics of each element of the exams. We must first, however, explain some of the **terminology** that we will be using in the tables.

The reference to numbered "**Exhibits**" is hopefully self-explanatory.

By "**Introduction**" we mean the text found before any of the Exhibits – typically this will provide some guidance as to the position that the client company finds itself in and will thus "set the scene". However, **do not regard this information as pure background**: you may well have to introduce some of the data into your answer and in **the November 2014 and both 2015 real examinations, the "Introduction" in fact contained an additional Task which might have been missed if you only read the numbered list of Tasks presented at the end of the question text**[8]. The 2016 examinations (other than July 2016 Q2) and July 2017 Q1 and November 2017 Q2 had each Task separately stated at the end of the applicable Exhibit (rather than using a consolidated list of all Tasks at the end of the question) so this problem should have been less likely to occur. (July 2016 Q2, July 2017 Q2 and November 2017 Q1 had a single listing of all Tasks, either near the start or right at the end of the question.)

We therefore recommend that you read the "introduction" text very carefully indeed: **with respect to the subsequent "Exhibits", the examiners are reasonably kind** as each Exhibit is relatively self-contained and will relate to only 1 or 2 Tasks (sometimes emphasised by brackets in the question wording) **but in the "Introduction" text there may be points which relate to any or all Tasks**. Therefore we would strongly advise you to adopt some kind of **quick annotation technique to make sense of the introductory text**: annotation of each subsequent Exhibit is perhaps less important as you can just look at particular Exhibits for particular Tasks (whilst still looking out for connections and the overall "big picture" of the scenario).

---

[8] See chapter 18 for further discussion of the implications of missing this "hidden" requirement – in the November 2014 examination, the examiners indicated that there was a clear correlation between candidates who missed this aspect of the exam and those candidates who **failed the examination overall**. Therefore, be warned – **the introductory material is very important**.

By "**Task list**" we mean the list of numbered requirements normally found in a consolidated list at the end of the question (or occasionally at the start of the question) (except in the 2016 examinations (other than July 2016 Q2) and in July 2017 Q1 and November 2017 Q2, where each Task was individually set out after the applicable Exhibit rather than in a consolidated list covering all Tasks), and which sets out the main requirements for your answer. The official ICAEW terminology is "requirement" but we use the term "Task" in this book – it is just a bit easier to write.

In producing the tables below, we are not just interested in showing how long each Exhibit tends to be and what it contains – we are also trying to show some of the typical Tasks or topic areas that have been tested so far to date (see the "Content" column for this important detail). Overall, the information in the tables should hopefully help you focus your revision onto the right areas.

As we believe that **Q1 and Q2 are fundamentally different styles of question**, we have chosen to analyse Q1s and Q2s in separate tables: **this will make the different patterns easier to spot**.

3.8   Anatomy of the SBM Past Papers: Question 1

Question 1   Exhibits and Exhibit length

July 2014			November 2014		
Element	**Content**	**Length (Pages)**	**Element**	**Content**	**Length (Pages)**
Introduction	Background	2.00	Introduction	Background	1.25
Exhibit 1	Industry	0.75	Exhibit 1	Industry	0.65
Exhibit 2	The client	0.75	Exhibit 2	The client	0.50
Exhibit 3	Financial information	1.00	Exhibit 3	Financial information	1.00
Exhibit 4	FX risks	0.50	Exhibit 4	Financial reconstruction	1.00
Exhibit 5	Acquisition	0.50	Exhibit 5	Leasing	0.25
Exhibit 6	Tasks	0.70	Exhibit 6	Journalist e-mail	0.75
			Exhibit 7	Tasks	0.50
Total		**6.20**	**Total**		**5.90**

July 2015		
Element	**Content**	**Length (Pages)**
Introduction	Background	2.00
Exhibit 1	The client	1.00
Exhibit 2	Expansion strategies	1.00
Exhibit 3	Financing	0.50
Exhibit 4	Financial information	1.25
Exhibit 5	Collaboration offer	1.00
Exhibit 6	Tasks	0.50
Total		**7.25**

November 2015		
Element	**Content**	**Length (Pages)**
Introduction	Background	1.25
Exhibit 1	Industry	1.00
Exhibit 2	The client	0.75
Exhibit 3	Financial information	1.00
Exhibit 4	Acquisition	2.00
Exhibit 5	Financing	0.50
Exhibit 6	Tasks	0.50
Exhibit 7	Telephone conversation	0.25
Total		**7.25**

July 2016		
Element	**Content**	**Length (Pages)**
Introduction	Background	1.50
Exhibit 1	The client	1.50
Exhibit 2	Expansion strategy	1.00
Exhibit 3	Exchange rate risks	1.00
Exhibit 4	Warehouse proposal	1.00
Exhibit 5	Brand development	1.50
Exhibit 6	Ethical matter	0.50
Total		**8.00**

November 2016		
Element	**Content**	**Length (Pages)**
Introduction	Background	1.00
Exhibit 1	The client	2.00
Exhibit 2	Project proposals	2.50
Exhibit 3	Redundancies	1.00
Total		**6.50**

July 2017		
Element	Content	Length (Pages)
Introduction	Background	1.50
Exhibit 1	Industry and client	1.00
Exhibit 2	Financial information	1.00
Exhibit 3	Contract negotiations	1.00
Exhibit 4	Hedging	1.25
Exhibit 5	Long-term strategy	1.00
Exhibit 6	Ethical matter	0.50
Total		7.25

November 2017		
Element	Content	Length (Pages)
Introduction	Background	1.50
Exhibit 1	The client	1.00
Exhibit 2	Proposed MBO	1.00
Exhibit 3	Business plan	2.00
Exhibit 4	Financial forecasts	1.25
Exhibit 5	Ethical matter	0.25
Total		7.00

Question 1   Number of sub-Tasks to complete

July 2014			
Task	Sub-Tasks	Total marks	Marks per page[9]
1	1	19	8
2	3	16	32
3	3	14	18
4	2	11	22

November 2014			
Task*	Sub-Tasks	Total marks	Marks per page
1	1	13	6
2	2	25	25
3	2	10	40
4	1	6	8
Hidden*	1	6	8

* Note that an additional Task was set in the Introduction element of Q1 so we have included this here as a "hidden" Task. See further discussion above.

July 2015			
Task	Sub-Tasks	Total marks	Marks per page
1	3	23	11
2	3	10	20
3	2	10	20
4	2	9	9
Hidden*	3	8	8

November 2015			
Task	Sub-Tasks	Total marks	Marks per page
1	4	35	11
2	2	9	18
3	2	9	5
Hidden*	1	7	28

* Note that an additional Task was set in the Introduction element of Q1 so we have included this here as a "hidden" Task. See further discussion above.

_____

[9] In all these tables, "page" means "page of Exhibit material". All figures have been rounded to the nearest whole page. Note that the marks **per page** figure in our tables may exceed the **total** marks for that Task – for example, if the Task has a total of 12 marks based on only one third of a page of material to read, then on a pro-rata full page equivalent basis the marks per page would be 36 (12 marks for just 1/3 of a page so 3 x 12 on a pro-rata full page basis). Please use the "Total Marks" column to see the total marks available for each Task.

July 2016			
Task	Sub-Tasks	Total marks	Marks per page
1	2	11	6
2	2	13	13
3	3	15	15
4	3	14	10
5	1	7	14

November 2016			
Task	Sub-Tasks	Total marks	Marks per page
1	2	16	8
2	2	9	4.5
3	1	12	6
4	2	6	3
5	2	12	12
6	1	7	7

July 2017			
Task	Sub-Tasks	Total marks	Marks per page
1	3	23	9.2
2	3	18	14.4
3	3	13	13
4	1	8	16

November 2017			
Task	Sub-Tasks	Total marks	Marks per page
1	2	22	8.8
2	3	12	12
3	3	7	3
4	1	8	4
5	1	9	36

Question 1   Anatomy Summary

We can see that there will normally be either 6 or 7 Exhibits and then generally 4 specifically-stated Tasks (plus a potentially "hidden" Task as in the November 2014 and 2015 papers). The November 2015 Q1 had a very long first Task which was worth 35 marks and contained 4 separate sub-Tasks so this is probably why there were only 3 specific Tasks in total, plus an additional "hidden" Task on ethics. The November 2016 Q1 is another "outlier" as it only contained 3 Exhibits and was relatively short at only 6.5 pages in total.

After the scene-setting "Introduction" text, Exhibit 1 will tend to focus on the client and its industry and Exhibit 2 will describe the client in more detail or look at project proposals. Exhibit 3 will often provide financial information (IS and/or SFP). The remaining Exhibits will then vary depending on the specific scenario. The final Exhibit will set out the Tasks but in the 2016 papers and July 2017 Q1 the Tasks were presented separately at the end of each Exhibit so look out for this in future (in November 2017 Q2 there was a single consolidated list of all Tasks, provided near the start of the question). November 2015 Q1 is again and exception here as there was one final short Exhibit **after** the Tasks list in this exam.

With respect to Exhibit length, the "standard" first 3 Exhibits will tend to account for approximately 2 to 2.5 pages of information. The remaining Exhibits other than the final Exhibit setting out the Tasks will generally be quite short and account for only 1-2 pages of information each. Therefore, it appears that **most of the information will relate to the more predictable parts in terms of Exhibit content**: the industry background, the client and the financial analysis which are needed for **Task 1**.

Since Task 1 (generally, financial analysis) will require you to read as far as Exhibit 3 this means that in effect around **half to two-thirds of the information given** (ignoring the Introduction) **will relate to the first Task only**. Put another way, the other 3 Tasks will have to be based on the remaining and normally shorter Exhibits (plus perhaps a few points from the Introduction information).

35

This means that there is potentially a very serious time-trap built into Task 1 – you will have to read and use around 50% of the information for only 25% of the Tasks. Although the marks are weighted towards Task 1 and therefore more time should be allocated to Task 1, you will have to be careful not to become bogged down in the details, compromising the rest of your answer.

Put another way, there will be a **very favourable ratio of marks per page of material that you need to read for Tasks 2 to 4** so you must ensure that you get around to these elements in good time. Some of these later tasks will be self-contained and will require only half a page to be read but you will get perhaps as many as 10 marks for such a Task … **half as much as the long Task 1 which could require you to read 6 times as much information!** We can see from the tables that more marks per page of Exhibits are available for Tasks 2 to 4[10]. Based on the tables above (and as further demonstrated below), it is thus important not to become bogged down in the first Task[11].

In terms of the number of sub-Tasks to complete, it seems likely that Task 1 will often focus on only a single sub-Task (review of financial performance). Then the other Tasks will vary in terms of the number of sub-Tasks but will tend to have more than 1 element to attack. Therefore, you should, as a general rule, be **looking at doing more than one thing in your answers to Tasks 2-5 in a standard Q1**. As such, using **headings** will be a very good idea. We have allowed for this general requirement to complete multiple sub-Tasks in our MAPs.

As a final matter, we would note that the Exhibit length of **Q1 appears to have increased in length, based on the 2015, July 2016 and 2017 examinations** – the amount of Exhibit material was **at least 7 pages** in all of these papers, an increase of around 1 page compared to 2014. In this context, it is going to be even more important to manage your time carefully and avoid the time-trap which is Task 1! Having said this, the November 2016 Q1 was a little shorter at around 6.5 pages.

---

[10] Please note that our estimate of the Exhibit pages per mark excludes the Introduction material as it is hard to allocate this to any specific Task or sub-Task (it could be relevant to any Task) whereas generally specific Exhibits map to specific Tasks.
[11] The time trap set by the examiners here is precisely the same as that set by Requirement 1 of the Case Study examination. See our book *Cracking Case™ – How to Pass the ACA Case Study* for further details.

36

3.9 Anatomy of the SBM Past Papers: Question 2

Question 2 Exhibits and Exhibit length

July 2014		
Element	Content	Length (Pages)
Introduction	Background	1.50
Exhibit 1	The client	0.50
Exhibit 2	Procurement	1.25
Exhibit 3	Demand forecast	0.75
Exhibit 4	Factory financing	0.25
Exhibit 5	Tasks	0.75
Total		5.00

November 2014		
Element	Content	Length (Pages)
Introduction	Background	1.33
Exhibit 1	The client	0.67
Exhibit 2	Tender	0.67
Exhibit 3	Budget data	1.25
Exhibit 4	Acquisition	0.5
Exhibit 5	Tasks	0.5
Total		4.92

July 2015		
Element	Content	Length (Pages)
Introduction	Background & Tasks	2.00
Exhibit 1	Industry	0.50
Exhibit 2	The client	0.50
Exhibit 3	Strategy A	0.50
Exhibit 4	Strategy B	0.50
Exhibit 5	Financial Information	0.25
Exhibit 6	Financial statements	1.00
Total		5.25

November 2015		
Element	Content	Length (Pages)
Introduction	Background	1.00
Exhibit 1	The client	1.00
Exhibit 2	Sale of division	0.50
Exhibit 3	Cash	0.50
Exhibit 4	Use of cash	0.50
Exhibit 5	Tasks	0.50
Total		4.00

July 2016		
Element	**Content**	**Length (Pages)**
Introduction	Background	1.00
Exhibit 1	The client	1.00
Exhibit 2	Governance	0.50
Exhibit 3	Financial Information	1.00
Exhibit 4	Data management	0.50
Exhibit 5	Sustainability	0.25
Exhibit 6	Tasks	0.50
Total		**4.75**

November 2016		
Element	**Content**	**Length (Pages)**
Introduction	Background	1.00
Exhibit 1	Industry	0.75
Exhibit 2	Project proposal	2.00
Exhibit 3	Financial Information	1.00
Exhibit 4	Fuel cost data	1.00
Total		**5.75**

July 2017		
Element	**Content**	**Length (Pages)**
Introduction	Background	1.25
Exhibit 1	Industry and client	1.00
Exhibit 2	Financial information	1.50
Exhibit 3	Corporate recovery plan	0.33
Exhibit 4	Financial reconstruction	1.00
Exhibit 5	Due Diligence	0.50
Total		**5.58**

November 2017		
Element	**Content**	**Length (Pages)**
Introduction	Background	1.00
Exhibit 1	Industry and client	0.75
Exhibit 2	Financial information	2.00
Exhibit 3	Expansion plan	1.50
Total		**5.25**

Question 2   Number of sub-Tasks to complete

July 2014			
Task	Sub-Tasks	Marks	Marks per page
1	2	16	8
2	2	11	44
3	2	7	14
4	1	6	12

November 2014			
Task	Sub-Tasks	Marks	Marks per page
1	1	10	8
2	1	13	10
3	2	8	6
4	2	9	18

38

July 2015			
Task	Sub-Tasks	Marks	Marks per page
1	2	8	8
2	2	14	28
3	2	14	28
4	1	4	4

November 2015			
Task	Sub-Tasks	Marks	Marks per page
1	2	21	14
2	2	10	20
3	2	9	18

July 2016			
Task	Sub-Tasks	Marks	Marks per page
1	2	14	7
2	2	9	5
3	2	5	10
4	1	5	10
5	2	7	14

November 2016			
Task	Sub-Tasks	Marks	Marks per page
1	3	9	5
2	1	8	4
3	2	7	7

July 2017			
Task	Sub-Tasks	Marks	Marks per page
1	3	12	3
2	1	5	2
3	2	7	21
4	2	14	14

November 2017			
Task	Sub-Tasks	Marks	Marks per page
1	2	16	9
2	2	7	7
3	1	7	3
4	2	6	3
5	1	6	3

Question 2   Anatomy Summary

We can see that there will tend to be 4 or 5 Exhibits in Q2.

Exhibit 1 will tend to focus on describing the client in more detail. There will not always be a specific industry background Exhibit, unlike in Q1 – industry background information may of course be included in the Introduction section. There will then tend to be 3 Exhibits specific to the scenario. One of these 3 Exhibits will be relatively lengthy at 1 page or more. The final Exhibit will then set out the Tasks to be completed (with the exception of November 2016 Q2 and November 2017 Q2 where each Task was set out separately within the relevant Exhibit).

Unlike in Q1, **there does not seem to be the same risk of falling into a time-trap with Task 1 in Q2** because in Q2 the first Exhibit is clearly separate from the other Exhibits (compared to the "group" of the first 3 Exhibits in Q1 which often **all** need to be integrated into the first Task describing financial performance, hence leading to the risk of a time trap). In Q2, the information on the client is relatively short at between half to two thirds of a page and this information will be separate from the other Tasks and Exhibits. This is in line with the examiners' statements (see chapter 18) that Q1 will be a single integrated "mini-Case Study" whilst Q2 will contain Tasks that are more separate and not as integrated.

Looking at the number of sub-Tasks, there is no real pattern and a roughly equal likelihood of just 1 or, alternatively, 2 sub-Tasks per Task, with 2 sub-Tasks per Task becoming more common in the

2015 and 2016 papers. **To date, Q2 has rarely had a Task with 3 sub-Tasks (see November 2016 and July 2017 for examples), which is different to Q1 where Tasks with 3 sub-Tasks are relatively common**[12].

Overall, then, the structure of Q2 is **less certain** than Q1.

3.10   Summary of Findings on the SBM Past Papers

Based on the above, we suggest that a typical SBM paper will look as follows:

Question 1

Approximately **7** pages of Exhibits to read, tested via approximately **9** total Tasks and sub-Tasks

Question 2

Approximately **5** pages of Exhibits to read, tested via approximately **8** total Tasks and sub-Tasks

Looking at things from the point of view of "absorption time" (the amount of time taken to read the Exhibits), **the marks available for Q1 appear attractive**: generally, this question will carry 50% more marks than Q2 (60 marks versus 40 marks[13]) but will have only 2 more pages or 40% more to read (7 pages versus 5 pages). Similarly, in Q1 you will generally have 1 more Task/sub-Task than Q2 but this is only 12.5% more Tasks for 50% more marks (9 total Tasks and sub-Tasks versus 8 total Tasks and sub-Tasks). This confirms our view that you should definitely attempt Q1 first (see also our arguments in chapter 9 and the examiners' statement in chapter 18 that Q2 will be used to a provide a marks balance across SBM areas, based on what Q1 has already tested, suggesting again that you should do Q1 first) **provided that you develop the discipline to avoid the possible "time trap" connected with Task 1 in Q1**.

3.11   Anatomy of the SBM Sample Paper: Question 1

We will now undertake a very similar analysis of the single available official ICAEW Sample Paper, which was issued before the July 2014 examination.

Unlike some of the other ICAEW practice materials for SBM (see Appendix 5), the Sample Paper was drafted from scratch specifically for SBM by the ICAEW examiner team: the Sample Paper was also extensively discussed at the July 2014 SBM Workshop at the ICAEW Tutor Conference. We therefore believe that this paper is a very accurate representation of how a real examination might look.

---

[12] Notice the difference with Q2 in the Sample Paper, as discussed below.
[13] Please note that this is just an approximation: the examiner has stated that Q1 could account for as many as 65 marks – whilst this would probably involve adding Tasks and sub-Tasks to Q1 and removing the same from Q2, this would imply that Q1 was worth 86% more marks than Q2 (65 marks versus 35 marks, or 86% more).

Nevertheless, as it is not technically a real past paper, we have separated the analysis from the 8 real papers reviewed above.

Question 1   Exhibits and Exhibit length

Sample Paper		
Element	**Content**	**Length (Pages)**
Introduction	Background and Tasks	2.0
Exhibit 1	The client	0.75
Exhibit 2	The target	0.25
Exhibit 3	Acquisition assumptions	1.0
Exhibit 4	Target financials	2.0
Exhibit 5	Brand valuation	0.5
Exhibit 6	Pension	0.5
Exhibit 7	Surveyor report	0.25
Total		**7.25**

Question 1   Number of sub-Tasks to complete

Sample Paper			
Task	Sub-Tasks	Marks	Marks per page
1	2	12	6
2	2	17	14
3	2	10	10
4	2	10	20
5	1	6	12

Based on the above data, comparing the Sample Paper Q1 with the "real" Q1s seen in the past papers available at the time of writing, we would note the following:

The Sample Paper Exhibits appear longer than the 2014 papers at 7.25 pages versus around 6 pages in the 2014 papers but the Sample Paper is in line with Q1 in the more recent 2015, 2016 and 2017 papers

The Sample Paper Tasks were included as a consolidated list in the Background section on page 2 of the Exhibits rather than in a final Exhibit – this has happened in some past papers but other past papers (particularly in recent years) have sometimes separately stated each Task within the relevant Exhibit, rather than using a consolidated list (whether at the start or end of the question)

The order of the Exhibits is different in the Sample Paper with the financials (for a target in an acquisition) being introduced **slightly later than in the real papers** (at Exhibit 4 rather than at Exhibit 3 as in the real papers)

The number of sub-Tasks is very evenly spread with 2 sub-Tasks per Task in the Sample Paper compared with a more uneven spread in the real papers

Despite these differences, the focus of Sample Paper Q1 is on a very typical scenario of a valuation and therefore this paper provides some very useful revision of relevant technical areas.

Question 2   Exhibits and Exhibit length

Sample Paper		
Element	Content	Length (Pages)
Introduction	Background	1.5
Exhibit 1	Bank letter	1.0
Exhibit 2	Corporate Governance	0.5
Exhibit 3	Refinancing packages	1.0
Exhibit 4	Client financials	1.0
Exhibit 5	Tasks	0.5
Total		5.5

Question 2   Number of sub-Tasks to complete

July 2014			
Task	Sub-Tasks	Marks	Marks per page
1	1	10	5
2	3	21	11
3	2	7	4
4	3	7	7

Comparing the Q2 in the Sample Paper with the Q2s in the real exams, the Exhibit length and provision of the Tasks in the final Exhibit is more consistent with the real exams than Sample Paper Q1. However, again the financial information is introduced later than normal in the Sample Paper.

Overall, the Sample Paper appears to be a good representation of a real examination but you should definitely bear in mind that **Sample Paper Q1 contains a lot more Exhibit material than the 2014 real examinations but is in line with the more recent real examinations** so whilst the Sample Paper will be a time pressured paper to attempt, it should be a good source of practice. The ordering of the Exhibits is also slightly different in the Sample Paper: again, it is **Q1 where the difference is more pronounced**.

3.12 Anatomy of a Typical SBM Paper: Conclusions

It may seem a bit strange to count the number of pages, Tasks and sub-Tasks in the manner undertaken here but hopefully you will see that there are **patterns** and therefore that you can prepare yourself for the likely format of the exam paper.

You have also been made aware that, particularly in Q1, the ratio of marks per page of Exhibits is relatively poor in certain Tasks (such as Task 1) and, accordingly, much more favourable in the other Tasks for those questions. This will hopefully help you to use your time effectively: if you can get through Task 1 in Q1 without wasting too much time then you should be rapidly able to accumulate marks.

We have also been able to show that it is **relatively rare for a Q1 Task to have no sub-Tasks** and therefore if you feel you are focusing on just one area (a lack of headings for different elements of your answer would be another clue) then you **may well have missed something**: therefore, go back to the question wording to find out what you are not doing.

Regarding Q2, we have shown that **there will not generally be more than 2 sub-Tasks** for any particular question and the ratio of marks per page of Exhibits is more evenly distributed across different Tasks than in Q1. There is hence not such a risk of falling into a timetrap in Q2. Tasks with 2 sub-Tasks are extremely common in Q2 so **ensure that you spend enough time reading the question wording and filling out the sub-Task column in our MAPs to ensure you cover all requested elements**: otherwise you will generally be limiting your marks by around 50% each time in any given Q2 Task.

Finally, we have shown that, in overall terms and assuming you do not fall into a timetrap, **Q1 has a very favourable number of marks available relative to the amount of information to absorb: therefore we strongly recommend that you start with Q1**.

Chapter 4   SBM, Case Study and the 4 Case Skills "Lenses" Translated

---

Learning Points

After reading this chapter, you must be able to:

1. understand the "skills bridge" from SBM to the Case Study
2. adopt the standard Case Study "lenses" to provide value-added remarks in SBM
3. understand how our MAP planning sheets incorporate reminders of the Case Study "lenses"

4.1   Bridging the Skills Gap to Case Study

As noted elsewhere in this book[14], and as reflected in the cover design for the 2015 edition of this book, SBM has been explicitly designed as a "**bridge**" between the Professional Level and the final unusual Case Study examination. Our understanding is that, according to employer feedback to ICAEW, many students have been finding the step up to the Case Study examination to be too much of a change from the previous examinations: the amount of information to be analysed in Case is high and the questions are also relatively "open" or unguided, relying on your judgement (and prior knowledge of what will be rewarded with marks) to decide what to write.

Therefore SBM has been introduced to give students an opportunity to learn how to **deal with a high volume of information** (although less than Case Study) and also to **develop judgement** in how to respond to very "open" questions, with up to 65 marks available (for Q1).

We do strongly agree that SBM helps students to develop the skills needed to do well in Case Study but **we would note that SBM and Case are marked in very different ways**: the Case Study markscheme is unique and highly unusual whereas SBM uses a more traditional approach (albeit not on the half mark or full mark per point approach at the Professional Level: see chapters 8 and 18). Therefore whilst the **skills are definitely shared**, and whilst we will analyse these skills in detail in this chapter, please do bear in mind that nothing is really shared with Case in terms of **marking approach**[15].

With this caveat in mind (a caveat which is more for your general understanding than because it affects the rest of this chapter), we will explain and analyse the Case Study skills areas (which we term the Case Study "lenses" – i.e. ways in which you should **look** at information). The examiners have confirmed (see chapter 18) that the **4 Case Study skills areas are used to develop the SBM examination paper and the approved markscheme** so the more you can adopt this way of looking at or using the data, then the better the likely outcome for your SBM mark.

---

[14] See, in particular, chapter 19 on the description of SBM by ICAEW in the ACA student magazine VITAL.
[15] See our popular book *Cracking Case™ – How to Pass the ACA Case Study* for a detailed analysis of the unique Case marking approach, together with our suggested approach to "cracking" the secrets of the markscheme.

4.2   The 4 Case Study Skills "Lenses" Translated

In terms of ICAEW language, the 4 skills areas assessed in a Case Study markscheme are defined as:

1.   **Assimilating & Using Information**

2.   **Structuring Problems & Solutions**

3.   **Applying Judgement**

4.   **Conclusions & Recommendations**

Why do we talk about "**translating**" the lenses? As you may agree, some of the above terms are somewhat technical in nature and **do not necessarily explain what you need to do in terms of writing an answer**: the term "Conclusions & Recommendations" is obviously pretty clear but what does "**Applying Judgement**" or "**Assimilating & Using Information**" actually mean in practice (and in terms of what you should write on the page)? This is why we need to "**translate**" the terms into more useful suggested output for you.

Based on our experience of teaching Case Study, the 4 lenses can be translated into SBM outputs as follows:

1. Assimilating & Using Information

- Identifying the **key information** to be used

2. Structuring Problems & Solutions

- Using the key information to produce **results** (such as percentage changes or a valuation estimate)

- **Basic descriptive** comments on the results (up/down, marginal change, substantial change)

3. Applying Judgement

- **Deeper descriptive** comments (patterns, changes, concerns, opportunities)

- Adopting the perspective of the "**Accountant in Business**" – how do **cash flows** and **business impacts** interact with **accounting rules**?

- Exercising **professional scepticism** – what is missing or wrong with the data?

4. Conclusions & Recommendations

- Briefly **summarising** your main points (Conclusions)

- Offering **practical advice and suggestions on the way forward** (Recommendations)

4.3   Implications of the "Lenses" for your SBM Answers

The SBM examination paper will **not** remind you that the above skills areas are expected in your script: you are just supposed to know (or hopefully have been taught!) that this is how the SBM examination paper is assessed.

Therefore, our first implication of the "lenses" for your SBM answers is to say that **you must find a way of reminding yourself that all these skills must be demonstrated in your answer**. Our MAP planning sheets will help by providing you with reminders on the second page of the MAP but it is still up to you to instinctively apply the "lenses" when deciding what to comment on. You can work on this through your mock exam attempts.

From our tuition courses, **we find that the first 2 skills lenses** (Assimilating & Using Information and Structuring Problems & Solutions) **tend to be covered quite well by students**: by identifying the key scenario information and turning this into calculations or tabular presentation (or the equivalent process for purely narrative content), most students will be answering these areas without consciously trying to do so. In our opinion, it is the **Applying Judgement** and **Conclusions & Recommendations** skills lenses that require more conscious effort. Therefore in the next 2 sections, we explain how to use these "lenses" in practice.

4.4   Professional scepticism (Applying Judgement lens)

One easy way to demonstrate the **Applying Judgement** skill is to exercise **professional scepticism over the information which you have been given**: at the SBM Workshop at both the 2014 and 2015 ICAEW Tutor Conferences, the examiners **criticised the lack of scepticism** in student answers and this is also routinely mentioned as a skills weakness in the Case Study.

Learn from this in SBM by ensuring that you politely raise queries as to the validity of data – **try not just to say that something has "not been substantiated" or "has not been proven"**: try to make the point more interesting by **giving a reason as to why the information appears to be incorrect** (e.g. it is double the profit margin of last year) or **perhaps explain the implications of the figure being incorrect** (e.g. if the discount rate applied is too low, then the NPV will be significantly overstated).

Based on a review of **Case Study** papers, some **scepticism** points to consider include:

- Information based on **forecasts** is **inherently unreliable** and may change

- Important model variables are **missing** (with examples)

- **Seasonality** considerations have not been built into the model

- Assumptions regarding **immediate sales** are unrealistic

- Margins or key figures are **out of line with the historic evidence**

- **Sensitivity** calculations should be performed

- **Methodology** (accounting profits, NPV, payback period) has weaknesses (with examples)

- **Forecast** period is **too long or too short**

- Lack of **detailed quantitative data**

- Information is based on **press reports** only

- Information is based on **initial discussions** only – things could change

- **Query the position of the provider of the information** – do they have a reason to distort the figures?

We can see that scepticism is both a case of querying **the information** and also often a case of querying **the methodology** used and even querying **the source** of the information.

Based on a review of **SBM** exams, scepticism points made to date include:

- **Stripping out particular activities or events enables underlying activities to be analysed** but judgement is required and errors could be made (July 2014 real paper Q1)

- **Allocation of overheads** in the management accounting system has a significant impact on results (July 2014 real paper Q1)

- There is a **lack of information** to determine whether price discounting or a change in product mix has affected results (July 2014 real paper Q1)

- **Ability and knowledge of staff at client is unknown** and may not be specialised enough (July 2014 real paper Q1)

- **Four years may be too short a planning horizon** to evaluate the outlay on a factory (July 2014 real paper Q2)

- **Assumed** exchange rates **could vary** over the long term (July 2014 real paper Q2)

- The **outcomes** of future contract **renegotiations are not known** (July 2014 real paper Q2)

- The difference between an 8% and 5% interest rate is **material** but the reasons for the difference need to be confirmed (November 2014 real paper Q1)

- A reconstruction scheme requires shareholders to inject funds and it is **not known** if this will occur (November 2014 real paper Q1)

- **Assurance over the project profit figure should be obtained** because this will make a crucial difference to whether the scheme will work (November 2014 real paper Q1)

- There is **no supporting evidence for the figures provided** and management have a strong incentive for optimism to persuade shareholders to invest (November 2014 real paper Q1)[16]

- Management accounting allocation of overheads is **arbitrary** and leads to a distortion of profit (November 2014 real paper Q2)

- **Weaknesses in the management accounting allocation** might lead to the wrong decision on whether to drop a supplier (November 2014 real paper Q2)

- The client company should consider a **range of currency fluctuations** and not just the fluctuation between sterling and a single foreign currency (July 2015 real paper Q1)

- Not **all** costs will be incurred in sterling (July 2015 real paper Q1)[17]

- Various points raised regarding the data provided as part of a set of **forecasts**, to be reviewed as an assurance exercise under ISAE 3400 (July 2015 real paper Q1)

- Uncertainty of the ability to **repay a loan** and therefore the going concern basis of the client company (July 2015 real paper Q1)

- The client company has no **existing presence** in the sector and so lacks **knowledge, experience** and **core competences** (July 2015 real paper Q2)

- Any PE valuation must be treated with caution due to the difficulty of finding **comparator companies** (July 2015 real paper Q2)

- It is uncertain whether the current levels of **profitability** (used in the valuation model) can be maintained in **future** (July 2015 real paper Q2)

- **Missing information on fixed and variables costs** makes it impossible to estimate the full impact of the loss of a contract (July 2015 real paper Q2)

- Loss of a contract could have further **reputational impacts** which have not been modelled in the financial information (July 2015 real paper Q2)

- Scepticism of the **Financial Director's valuation** is needed as the valuation produced is not **in line with the results of other techniques** (July 2015 real paper Q2)[18]

- Use of a dividend valuation model based only on **proposed** dividends rather than dividends actually paid is problematic, particularly if there is **no information on cash available** (July 2015 real paper Q2)

- There may be unexpected **costs of integration** and **synergy gains** are not confirmed or **guaranteed** (November 2015 real paper Q1)

---

[16] In relation to this point, the term "professional scepticism" is even used in the model answer – this is definitely not something to do in Case Study as the term itself should not be written into your answer (instead you should just apply professional scepticism as a skill).
[17] Again, in relation to this point, the term "professional scepticism" is even used in the model answer.
[18] Again, in relation to this point, the term "professional scepticism" is even used in the model answer.

- Due Diligence is very useful but **may not identify all issues** (November 2015 real paper Q1)

- It is **not known** how certain stakeholders with **high shareholding percentages** will react (November 2015 real paper Q1)

- Incorrect estimates of fair value would be particularly significant in respect of a "**landbank**" if the relevant company is a **property developer** – this is likely to be one of its main assets (November 2015 real paper Q1)

- Further **market research** on the target market is needed before reaching a final decision (July 2016 real paper Q1)

- All NPV figures are dependent on the accuracy of **assumptions** (July 2016 real paper Q1)

- Debt and equity are not the **only** alternative financing methods – others should be considered (July 2016 real paper Q1)

- The implication of a **perpetuity** (constant renewal of a contract) cannot be assumed in reality (July 2016 real paper Q1)

- A **casual conversation** may not be a **reliable** source of information and information obtained from such a source would need to be **verified** independently (July 2016 real paper Q1)

- Data on some key operating costs is **missing**, **preventing an analysis** of operating margins (July 2016 real paper Q2)

- Profit data has not been provided on several **key product lines** so the analysis is necessarily limited in nature (July 2016 real paper Q2)

- There is no information on the **rate of returns** and product **quality** (July 2016 real paper Q2)

- The data currently being gathered by the Board is **too aggregated** to be of use (July 2016 real paper Q2)

- The final part of Q2 asked candidates to indicate which **additional data** would be required for a better analysis – this was effectively an opportunity to exercise **scepticism of the data already provided** (July 2016 real paper Q2)

- The results of the different alternative financial models are **very close** so **additional** financial and non-financial information needs to be considered (November 2016 real paper Q1)

- Certain key factors are **not adjusted for** in the models and some form of **averaging** over different years is probably also advisable (November 2016 real paper Q1)

- It is **unreasonable** to compare 2 NPV calculations if the projects cover **different time periods** (November 2016 real paper Q1)

- The **useful life assumption** makes a huge **difference** to the results of the calculation and so should be checked carefully (November 2016 real paper Q1)

- An evaluation of **management performance** over a particular time period must factor in the impact of variables **outside** the control of management as these may have **interfered** with the efforts of management (November 2016 real paper Q1)

- The **first step** in an **ethical** evaluation is to **establish the facts accurately** (November 2016 real paper Q1)

- The decision to invest must **not** be taken **purely on the results of the NPV calculation** – there may be **other** factors to consider (November 2016 real paper Q2)

- Further information should be obtained on **how the discount rate has been calculated** and **how sensitive** the NPV is to the discount rate (November 2016 real paper Q2)

- The **price reduction** is **certain** if the agreement is made whereas **volume** increases are only an **estimate** which could have been made by the customer in a **self-interested** way to persuade the client to accept new contract conditions (July 2017 real paper Q1)

- Forecasts **exclude** important elements such as tax, interest and investment in PPE – a more comprehensive cash flow forecast is advised (July 2017 real paper Q1)

- **Opportunity cost** may not have been considered correctly in the model (July 2017 real paper Q1)

- Extent of **counterparty risk** is **not known** (July 2017 real paper Q1)

- An ethical concern relates **only to one member of the Board** and there is **no evidence** that the Board in general has done anything wrong (July 2017 real paper Q1)

- The **limited period of time** available is unlikely to be sufficient to establish evidence to support the projections – market research would be needed as to the likelihood of the projected sales being achieved (July 2017 real paper Q2)

- The valuation depends on the **forecasting being reliable** and the **discount rate being appropriate and stable over time** (November 2017 real paper Q1)

- The revenue growth rate is a **fundamental assumption** that **drives** much of the increase in the value of the equity from the MBO – therefore, this growth rate needs to be **substantiated** (November 2017 real paper Q1)

- The valuation model **assumes that surplus cash can be distributed to shareholders** and does not need to be **retained for investment** to generate future cash flows (November 2017 real paper Q1)

- There may be **unrecognised** asset values in **intangibles** (November 2017 real paper Q1)

- The forecast's working assumptions made by the management team may not be **realistic** – the assumption that cash flows are **indefinite** needs to be evaluated carefully, given the relatively **short-term strategy** proposed (November 2017 real paper Q1)

- The management team is subject to various **conflicts of interest** and may **lack commitment to the MBO** – other members of the team appear to **lack suitable finance expertise** (November 2017 real paper Q1)

- Financial, commercial and operational Due Diligence is strongly advised to **substantiate** key facts (November 2017 real paper Q1)

- Although the joint arrangement offers modest and temporary benefits, there may **only be a five-year horizon** to the activities (November 2017 real paper Q2)

- Assurance over the proposed joint arrangement is strongly advised to **substantiate** key facts (November 2017 real paper Q2)

- **Manipulation of accounting policies and estimates should not be reflected in valuation models** as this will overstate growth (Sample Paper Q1)

- There may be **unrecognised** assets, liabilities and provisions which should be included in a valuation (Sample Paper Q1)

- Financial Due Diligence procedures can only provide **limited assurance** (Sample Paper Q1)

- **Statutory accounts should not be used directly for valuations** – they are not prepared for this purpose (Sample Paper Q1)

- An **effective tax rate of 25%** used in all working assumptions is a "**crude assumption**" as it does not separate current tax from deferred tax (Sample Paper Q1)

- The **perpetuity** assumption appears **unrealistic** (Sample Paper Q1)

- Not realistic to assume constant prices and costs assumed into **perpetuity** (Sample Paper Q1)

- **Not clear how the cost of equity has been arrived at** and whether this is a real or money rate (Sample Paper Q1)

- The **proposal** to integrate companies of such different sizes and with such different strategies is **questionable** (Sample Paper Q1)

- The **cash flow model should be amended** to include the reduction in interest payments which will result when an overdraft is repaid (Sample Paper Q2)

- The client should assume that new funds will be provided by the bank – **no offer has been made** but rather the bank has merely indicated "the minimum conditions for consideration" of a new loan application (Sample Paper Q2)

- There does not seem to be **any reason** for the assumption that the new loan will be at the same rate as the existing loan (Sample Paper Q2)

- There is **uncertainty over the fair value of options** as they are not traded – a model such as Black-Scholes or Monte Carlo simulation could be used (Sample Paper Q2)

Scepticism is not the **only** way to use the Applying Judgement lens (see the other bullet points under Applying Judgement noted above on page 45) but it does seem to be rewarded in most SBM examinations so it is worth developing this skill, particularly as there is a strong overlap (see above) with the similar professional scepticism points that will be rewarded in your final Case Study examination.

4.5   Practical recommendations (Conclusions & Recommendations lens)

As will be seen in chapter 8, the examiners do tend to note that many students **did not draw an appropriate conclusion or offer any recommendations** on what to do. This is perhaps because the question wording will often not specifically remind you to provide a conclusion or any recommendations.

Therefore ensure that you **proactively** build the Conclusions & Recommendations lens into your answers. **Recommendations need to be as practical as possible** and should not normally relate to "pure accountancy" points such as reviewing journal entries or performing stock takes – rather the points should be **business-friendly and practical**. Please see our chapter on practical business advisory or PBA points (chapter 15) for further suggestions but based on our review of Case Study papers[19], points which are rewarded with marks tend to fall into 8 main category areas:

- Reconsider **pricing** (including discounts)

- Look at ways to **reduce costs**

- Look at the **timing** of the project – is it too soon or too late? Is delay possible?

- Impact on **staff** – managing business change

- Does the company have the **capacity** to do this kind of activity or to pay for the acquisition?

- **Further information** should be gathered (with examples)

- **Discuss and negotiate** – involve and consider the positions of all stakeholders

- Consider **alternative** options and strategies

The Case Study also always rewards a recommendation of which strategic option to pick or pursue and **therefore whether to proceed with a project**.

These Recommendations provide quite a broad range of possible points: **therefore always ensure that your points demonstrate the MS^2 quality**: the above points are just suggestions rather than points that will always apply in every case.

Based on a review of the **SBM** real exams and the SBM Sample Paper, Recommendations points have included:

---

[19] See our book *Cracking Case™ – How to Pass the ACA Case Study* for a detailed discussion of relevant practical points in the Case Study.

- Examine **capacity** in more detail – temporarily reduce output and activities until demand recovers (July 2014 real paper Q1)

- Reduce **price** provided that demand is elastic (July 2014 real paper Q1)

- Increase advertising and marketing **expenditure** (July 2014 real paper Q1)

- Consider **rebranding** (July 2014 real paper Q1)

- Set up a **contingency plan** to deal with similar issues if they reoccur in future (July 2014 real paper Q1)

- Undertake a **public relations** exercise (July 2014 real paper Q1)

- Improve **quality** (July 2014 real paper Q1)

- Continue to use existing supplier as this supplier is reliable but undertake **negotiations** on price and service, perhaps raising the possibility of moving to a different supplier to encourage a better deal (July 2014 real paper Q2)

- **Negotiate** an approach under which the commitment to the existing supplier is made conditional on service levels being achieved (July 2014 real paper Q2)

- **Improve operating efficiency** and review operating management procedures and productivity (November 2014 real paper Q1)

- Raise production **capacity** by investing in new assets (November 2014 real paper Q1)

- Increase **prices** until excess demand is removed (November 2014 real paper Q1)

- **Renegotiate** the existing contract with the customer (November 2014 real paper Q1)

- Strategy 1 should be preferred because it is superior in terms of **satisfying customer needs**, even though it has a higher **cost** than Strategy 2 – it also has **higher revenue** and allows for **local** supply methods (July 2015 real paper Q1)

- The company should take a **selective** approach, rather than expanding **too rapidly** in an unfocused manner (July 2015 real paper Q2)

- A market segment with **high levels of competition** and **low barriers to entry** is unlikely to be very **profitable** (July 2015 real paper Q1)

- **Threats** should be adequately **reviewed** and **assessed** (July 2015 real paper Q1)

- A **share for share** exchange could be a **lower risk option** as it does not increase **gearing** – this also preserves **liquidity** and **debt capacity** (November 2015 real paper Q1)

- Finance Method A is preferred **despite its higher cost** because it has **better currency matching with Australian operations, a longer loan period which helps liquidity and**

avoids a mismatch in loan periods as would happen under Finance Method B (July 2015 real paper Q1)

- Sell **directly from the UK** when **initially** entering the market but then **revise** this if sales take off significantly (July 2016 real paper Q1)

- Perform **market research** before deciding on a **final strategy** (July 2016 real paper Q1)

- A **positive NPV appears good** but bear in mind the **40% probability of the result being negative** if a different outcome happens (July 2016 real paper Q1)

- **Invest** in the warehouse but any **commitment should be delayed as long as possible** to gain the maximum amount of **information** from market entry (July 2016 real paper Q1)

- In addition to confirming the **valuation** in a proposed brand sale, consider **strategic factors** such as the **loss of the ability to benefit from the brand in future** and the **impact** of the actions of **other companies** if the brand is any way shared with other entities (July 2016 real paper Q1)

- Consider **risk**, including renegotiation risk, as well as the **NPV result** (November 2016 real paper Q1)

- Consider **flexibility** of the options – purchasing one aircraft and leasing a second aircraft may provide a good blend of **affordability** and **flexibility**, compared to purchasing or leasing **both** aircraft (November 2016 real paper Q2)

- The **amount of hedging** used will depend on the **risk appetite** of the Board (November 2016 real paper Q2)

- An advantage of **not hedging all** fuel purchases is that this is more **flexible** if demand is not as high as expected (November 2016 real paper Q2)

- Something needs to be done regarding the relevant customer, given their **importance** to the business (July 2017 real paper Q1)

- The client should develop alternative strategies to **reduce dependency** on a particular customer in future (July 2017 real paper Q1)

- Alternative strategies to deal with problems facing the business could involve seeking **new products** and **new markets** – **speciality** breads with **high margins** may be an opportunity to **expand** or the company could look at **non-bread baked items** – the company could also look at **new geographical markets** (July 2017 real paper Q1)

- Any doubts over the **short-term viability** of the company resulting from the change in credit terms should be considered (July 2017 real paper Q1)

- A **detailed cash flow forecast** is needed (July 2017 real paper Q2)

- The client should consider acquiring the **equity** of its target as well as the target's **debt** (July 2017 real paper Q2)

54

- **All assumptions should be re-evaluated** in order to reduce the key risk of overpayment for the target (November 2017 real paper Q1)

- It may be advisable for the **client** (investor) **to appoint at least 1 member of the Board** of the target to represent its **interests** and to gain **access to information** (November 2017 real paper Q1)

- The proposed joint arrangement appears to offer modest and temporary benefits but also involves **major risks** such as a short five-year horizon – therefore the preferred recommendation is to set up a **subsidiary** rather than become involved in a **joint arrangement** (November 2017 real paper Q2)

- Even **after** Due Diligence has been undertaken, there should be **ongoing monitoring** of any joint arrangement (November 2017 real paper Q2)

- **Recommendation to proceed** with a particular financing option, based on cost and other factors (Sample Paper Q2)

- **Recommendation of an alternative financing option** if the preferred option is not ultimately possible (Sample Paper Q2)

Again, hopefully if you take a few moments to compare the bold "trigger words" in the Case Study Recommendations list as compared to the SBM Recommendations list, you will see a clear overlap with the general areas identified regarding the Case Study: areas such as **pricing**, **capacity**, **negotiations** and **whether to proceed** definitely seem to be shared. This should provide you with assurance of the types of point which are likely to be rewarded in SBM and also, again, means that preparing for SBM really does help you cross the later "bridge" into the Case Study.

4.6   Conclusions, Recommendations and the Formatting of Your Report

We have indicated above that the Conclusions & Recommendations "lens" is often not adopted by students. You may therefore find it helpful **to add a reminder to your planning sheets** to include these section headings (our MAPs already include reminders because of the importance of this point).

However, as the table below shows, the Conclusions & Recommendations skill/lens is not something that is necessarily reflected in **section headings**, at least based on the model answers for recent SBM papers:

Paper	Q1		Q2	
	Conclusions heading?	Recommendations heading?	Conclusions heading?	Recommendations heading?
Nov 2017				Yes (in middle of answer)
July 2017	Yes (in middle of answer)		Yes (in middle of answer)	
Nov 2016	Yes**** (in middle of answer)	Yes (in middle of answer)		Yes (at end of answer)
July 2016		Yes (in middle of answer)		
Nov 2015		Yes*** (at end of answer)		
July 2015		Yes (in middle of answer)		Yes (at end of answer)
Nov 2014		Yes (in middle of answer)	Yes (in middle of answer)	
July 2014		Yes* (at end of answer)		Yes** (in middle of answer)
Sample Paper			Yes (in middle of answer)	Yes (at end of answer)

* Headed up as "Actions that could be taken"
** Headed up as "Advice"
*** Headed up as "Response"
**** Headed up as "Summary"

As we can see, the model answers apparently do not always require Conclusions or Recommendations headings (a Conclusions heading is definitely less common than a Recommendations heading): the model answers will instead very often offer Conclusions and Recommendations "mixed in" with the main narrative or "as you go along" but on other occasions will use a dedicated report section heading.

For this reason, our MAPs do not stipulate that you must use Conclusions or Recommendations as a heading and we instead include a reminder on page 2 of the MAP to adopt this perspective generally.

From an examination technique perspective and given the apparent propensity of students not to remember to offer Conclusions and Recommendations, you may still want to build these headings into your answer. **Here you should note that when the headings have been included in the above SBM papers they have not necessarily been right at the end of all the Tasks**: sometimes if there is a particularly long Task (hence worth a lot of marks) then there will be a Recommendations or Advice section just for that Task, before the rest of the answer is then completed. As such, we would definitely aim to view Conclusions & Recommendations as a **skill or perspective** rather than just **a heading in a set position** – a **skill or perspective** is something that, like the **professional scepticism** used to fulfil the Applying Judgement criterion, can be used **throughout an answer** and not just at the end.

Chapter 5   Need Direction? Use a MAP!

Learning Points

After reading this chapter, you must be able to:

1. understand the concept of a Mark Allocated Plan or MAP
2. understand how use of a MAP will give valuable direction to your answer
3. understand how to apply our "Rules of Thumb" to estimate the mark allocation of any SBM question

---

5.1   The Most Important Skill for SBM Planning – Predicting the Mark Allocation

Unlike all Professional Level papers (except the Business Planning papers), the Advanced Level papers provide no clear breakdown of the mark allocation within a question: you will simply be told that a group of Tasks, which have been bundled into a single question, has a total allocation of, say, 60 or 55 marks – it will then be up to you to decide how much each Task is worth[20].

Whilst this lack of clarification can be tremendously frustrating for students, the argument of the examiners is that the Advanced Level examinations are designed to test your **practical advisory skills**: one of these skills involves identifying **what is important and what is not**, so that your client advice can be relevant and to the point. To use 2 phrases often used by the SBM examiners, your client needs to know the "**big picture**" and you need to "**make the numbers talk**": the client is not interested in some obscure IFRS paragraph number relating to the treatment of transaction costs on an exotic put option – they want to know what the financial instrument will cost, how this will be funded and whether the instrument is right for the business.

Whether you agree that not indicating the mark allocation is an appropriate test of these professional skills or not, at least you now know the reasoning behind leaving you to estimate the marks available for each element. We just have to live with it!

As a result of the uncertainties created by this approach, we strongly believe that the **single most important skill to develop for SBM is to effectively predict the number of marks for each Task within a question**. Whilst you are unlikely to get the allocation perfectly correct, making an attempt to identify the correct allocation will place you at a significant advantage over students who are naively assuming that the mark allocation is equally spread over the different Tasks.

---

[20] As explained on page 14, we use the term "Task" to refer to a sub-component of each question. This will normally be indicated by a number such as (1), (2), (3) and so on. However, one important point noted by the SBM examiners at the 2015 Tutor Conference was that in the November 2014 real examination many candidates missed a further Task that was written into the narrative Exhibits (rather than being separately identified by a numbered element at the end of the Exhibits): the examiners reused this technique in the 2015 examinations and also in July 2017 Q1 where a partner request to consider ethical issues was not mentioned again when the Tasks to complete were stated in various lists throughout the question text. Our term "Task" also includes these "hidden" elements. Within each Task, there may be further sub-elements which we term "sub-Tasks": these will sometimes be indicated by a separate bullet marker for each sub-Task but, as with the main Tasks, this may not **always** be the case so do not rely simply on bullets as an indicator: in some cases, a single bullet could have 2-3 sentences attached, requiring different elements to be completed and we would term each of these as a "sub-Task" if they involved different activities. For further examples, see chapter 7 which reviews the recent SBM past papers.

In section 5.5 below we set out 11 Rules that you can use to estimate the mark allocation: whilst we strongly urge you to learn these methods well, please note that, due to the importance of this aspect of SBM, our planning sheets (MAPs) incorporate some useful reminders. We then apply these 11 Rules in chapter 7 where we review the SBM past papers in detail. We will show you that the MAP mark estimation techniques will effectively predict the unequal mark breakdown between different Tasks within both Q1 and Q2. **Using this technique will therefore give you an initial indication of how to allocate time within your answer.**

5.2   Our Planning Technique: MAPs

MAP stands for "Mark Allocated Plan". We do not call our planning sheets simply "planning sheets": rather, for SBM, we think that **estimating the mark allocation has to be built into your planning approach and as such we have named our planning sheets as "Mark-Allocated Plans"**.

Hopefully this will serve as an important reminder of what we are trying to do in planning – we are trying to give the correct **direction** to your answer, navigating your writing towards points that matter and also spending enough time on sections that are likely to be **heavily rewarded**. Just as in the real world, without a MAP, you will be relying on luck to get to the right destination.

Example pro forma MAPs for SBM Q1 and Q2 are presented in Appendix 1 and 2[21]. We also provide an example of a completed MAP for the November 2014 examination in Appendix 3. We have produced slightly different MAPs for each question as we believe that the emphasis is likely to be different.

Please now take a moment to look at the Q1 and Q2 MAPs provided in Appendix 1 and 2.

The components of a MAP are as follows:

1. Rows – we provide various rows for you to complete with the Tasks and sub-Tasks required. We recommend that you complete the first 2 columns of each row with a brief description of what is required in note form (perhaps 5-10 words maximum). This will prevent you forgetting to do things and will also force you to think about the likely mark allocation.

2. Columns – we provide several columns which should be completed only **after you have populated all the row headings in the first column** i.e. after you have effectively and carefully split out the Tasks into sub-Tasks and therefore have a full but **quick reference statement of what the question is asking you to do**.

The third column should then be completed with the key technical content that you need to mention (e.g. specific IFRSs or IASs or perhaps key models or equations).

---

[21] For production reasons, we have had to produce our MAPs in portrait format – you may wish to create your own MAPs in landscape format to provide more space for notes. Alternatively, you may wish to use more than one planning sheet per question (particularly for Q1), again to provide more space for notes. The MAPs contained in our Appendices are purely for **guidance** purposes and like all elements of this book are copyright of ACA Simplified and therefore not to be photocopied.

After thinking about which technical content is relevant, you should complete the fourth column with your estimate of the **number of marks** available (based on the techniques and 11 Rules explained below).

Next complete the fifth column with an estimated amount of **time** to allocate to each element, based on the number of estimated marks. Rather than specifying a fixed factor such as "1.8 minutes per mark" we suggest that you find a personalised figure, taking into account how long you personally take to read and plan – **we do not want to force you into any particular value and of course the key is obviously to work as quickly as possible!** (For the purposes of the completed MAP in Appendix 3, we have assumed 1.75 minutes of writing time per mark.)

We would **not** advise you to allocate 2.1 minutes per mark (3h30 / 100 marks) for writing time as is sometimes suggested by other tuition providers as this ignores the fact that you need to spend some time reading and planning all your answers: therefore the time available for **writing up** your answers will always be less than the full amount available.

The final column should be completed once you know the time allocation for each element: this will tell you when to stop writing on that issue and move on.

You will now have a completed MAP which gives clear direction to your answer and also gives you a more scientific way of deciding how much time to spend on your various destinations along the way.

3. The 11 Rules – the rules at the bottom of the MAP provide a reminder of the rules that we suggest that you apply to estimate the number of marks. We strongly recommend that you commit these rules to memory so that you can apply them instinctively but we include them at the bottom of the MAP just in case you cannot remember under examination pressure. The 11 Rules are discussed in more detail below.

5.3   The MAP Timing Column – Get a Silent Stopwatch

We are aware that the planning sheets of some other providers suggest that you set timings such as "9.30am – 9.45am: plan answer; 9.45am to 10.15am: financial reporting element" and so on.

We believe that it is much simpler and effective to start your timings at zero and then build upwards as you work down the fourth column of your MAP. You are much less likely to get the timing wrong when working in this way and you will also not have to spend any thinking time at all working out that, for example, at 9.37am you have 38 minutes until 10.15am. This is wasted effort in an examination scenario, particularly when you only have 2 questions to answer, and it can easily lead to a big error in timing if you miscalculate the difference as, say, 28 minutes.

We therefore recommend that you obtain a silent stopwatch and simply start this once your MAP is complete and you are ready to start writing up your answer (including making a start on your calculations). Then simply count upwards from 00:00 based on the timings developed within the MAP where each Task will be given a certain amount of time. This is easier than getting confused or even making costly mistakes while thinking about what the time is out there in the real world.

5.4 Complete the MAPs quickly

We very much hope that the MAP sheets will provide a more effective method of planning out your answer but **be careful not to overanalyse or overplan** – the examination is very time-pressured and you have a lot of material to read and write about. The most important parts of the MAP are in fact the **first things** that you should be adding: namely, a split of the Task into sub-tasks with brief row headings and then your estimated number of marks and related timings. Beyond this, be careful as to how much detail you add in[22].

5.5 Predicting the Mark Allocation: The 11 Rules

When estimating the number of marks available for a particular Task and its related sub-Task, we recommend that you apply the following rules (in approximate order of importance, from most frequently used to least frequently used):

Rule 1 – Exhibit length & number of Exhibits mentioned in the Task wording – as shown in the following chapters, there is a very strong relationship between the length of the Exhibits that you need to consider and the amount of marks for that question: **the longer the length of the Exhibits, the more marks available**. Additionally, if the question wording specifically asks you to **consider several Exhibits** then the marks for the Task will be relatively higher.

Rule 2 – Dedicated Exhibits mean more marks – generally, if the Task has references to an Exhibit or set of Exhibits which are **only to be used for that specific Task** it will be worth more than a question which has no such specific references.

Rule 3 – Financial information means more marks – as you may expect in an accountancy examination, if the Exhibits for a Task contain financial or numerical information then the Task will have a relatively higher number of marks available. However, always apply rule 5 below when subsequently creating your split between narrative and numerical marks.

Rule 4 – Task wording and formatting – generally, the longer the Task wording, the more marks available. If there are **several sentences in the Task wording**, the Task will be relatively **highly rewarded**. If there are **bullet points** included then again the Task will be **highly rewarded**.

Rule 5 – Is the Task a numerical one? Apply the 33:66 rule – clearly there will be some reward for calculations (although not as much reward as you may expect for an accountancy examination: see discussion in chapter 18) but the marks for the narrative analysis of those figures will be disproportionately rewarded with generally a 33:66 split **in favour of narrative**. Therefore, please do **discuss** the figures sufficiently by allowing for a decent number of narrative marks in your MAP estimate.

Rule 6 – Consider which question you are attempting and the topic area – if you are attempting Q1 and are looking at PBA (practical business advisory) then this tends to be rewarded

---

[22] In suggesting a rapid but focused approach to planning, our advice is in line with our advice for Case Study where we strongly disagree with the very detailed plans advocated by some other providers: planning does not in itself gain you any marks unless the points are also written up.

disproportionately highly[23]; on the other hand, an Assurance Task in Q1 is very unlikely to be worth more than 10 marks.

Rule 7 – Is the Task a multi-discipline Task? – if the Task appears to involve **more than one discipline** (strategy/PBA, financial reporting, assurance and ethics) then it will be a highly rewarded Task. On the other hand, if the Task just involves one discipline other than PBA then it is likely to be worth less than 10 marks

Rule 8 – When completing your second question, consider your estimates for your first question – the examiner has stated that Q2 will be used to provide the necessary "balance" across the topic areas of strategy (which we call PBA or Practical Business Advisory), financial reporting, assurance and ethics (see chapter 3 and chapter 19). Therefore if Q1 had particularly few marks for financial reporting then if you see financial reporting in Q2 it is likely to be disproportionately rewarded. Similarly, if there was no ethics element in Q1, then ethics will attract quite a lot of marks in Q2.

Rule 9 – Ethics will generally be 6-8 marks per Task – this Rule is hopefully pretty self-explanatory.

Rule 10 – Comparison of financing methods is normally 8 marks or so – again, this Rule is hopefully self-explanatory – by "comparison of financing methods" we mean a comparison between 2 different loans or, alternatively, between using a loan and equity, or a loan versus a lease, and so on. We would suggest 8 marks as a good initial estimate in such cases.

Rule 11 – Narrative risks/strategy discussion is normally 8 marks or so – we would generally suggest that there will be 8 marks for a narrative-only discussion of risks or strategy issue if there are no figures or calculations involved.

To remind you of these rules, we have provide simplified summaries/reminders at the bottom of our MAPs as follows – hopefully now that we have explained the rules above then the summaries below will be a bit more "catchy" and will help you remember the points easily:

---

[23] The case of Q1 practical business advisory creates a conflict between our different Rules: the **question wording** will be **short** but the **Exhibit length** will be **long** (probably involving multiple Exhibits). **The Exhibit length overrides the short nature of the question and a large number of marks will be available**. This is because part of the skill being assessed in this style of question is whether you will direct your attention to the key numerical story, rather than analysing all possible numerical aspects: leaving the question wording short and open allows the examiner to test your judgement regarding what matters to the client in the numbers.

Rule 1 – Exhibit length & number of Exhibits to consider

Rule 2 – Dedicated Exhibit or not?

Rule 3 – Financial information?

Rule 4 – Task wording length and bullets (overridden by Rule 1)

Rule 5 – 33:66 rule (if a numerical question)

Rule 6 – Which question and which discipline?

Rule 7 – Multi-discipline?

Rule 8 – Balancing rule

Rule 9 – Ethics 6-8 marks

Rule 10 – Financing comparison 8 marks

Rule 11 – Narrative risks/strategy 8 marks

We put these 11 Rules to the test in chapter 7 which analyses the recent SBM past papers. We will show you that the 11 Rules really do work as a way to estimate the marks available.

Although our MAPs will provide reminders, please do commit the above 11 Rules to memory so that you can use them "instinctively" and hence save time.

Chapter 6   The Correct SBM Writing Style

Learning Points

After reading this chapter, you must be able to:

1. understand the importance of writing concisely in "almost bullet-like" style
2. understand how to remove irrelevant, time-wasting material from your own writing
3. understand the significant time savings which are possible with the correct style

---

6.1   The Easiest Way to Fail SBM – Poor Time Management

The easiest way to fail SBM is to **run out of time to complete your second question to a good enough standard**. Typically, this will happen because you have fallen into the **"time trap" purposefully set by the examiner in Q1** (see chapter 3 for further discussion of the Q1 time trap). Alternatively, it could happen because your writing style is **too wordy** or perhaps because you have taken the requirement to **write a "report" a little bit too literally**, thereby including sentences to introduce different sections, link elements together and generally write in the way that you would write in a real world report (rather than something that you have to rush out in 3.5 hours!).

Whilst all ACA examinations are highly time-pressured, we believe that **time mismanagement is particularly likely to happen in SBM because you only have 2 questions to attempt** (the lowest number of questions of any ACA examination) and therefore it can seem easy to relax, starting Q1 with the thought that you have over 2 hours in which to complete this question and therefore that you have plenty of time. **In reality, you need to be working at a very high speed right from the first minute of the examination.** Whilst our MAPs will help you to **focus onto the right areas** and so get you working effectively right from the moment that you turn the examination paper over, you also need to ensure that your write up of your MAPs is **as time-efficient as possible so that your plan can be turned into as many marks as you can manage in the time available**.

In this chapter, we will try to explain some of the weaknesses in SBM writing style that we frequently see in our taught course students (at the **start** of their studies with us, naturally!). Our suggestions are obviously relevant to SBM but **also to Corporate Reporting and Case Study**: time mismanagement is even more of a problem in Case Study so another aspect of the skills "bridge" to that final unusual examination will be covered through your work to implement the recommendations of this chapter.

6.2   The Correct SBM Writing Style: Some Recommendations

Succinct writing on a range of areas

The examiners consistently comment that they **do not want to have hugely detailed answers to any individual Task** – they instead want to see that you can achieve to an acceptable standard across a **range of areas**, rather than being a narrow specialist in one particular area. Given the number of Tasks set in any SBM question, **the only way to fulfil this range within the time available is to ensure you are writing very succinctly**.

A good rule of thumb is to try to write in **"almost bullet-like" sentences**. In other words, all your sentences should be capable of being turned into bullets with the removal of just a few words. Therefore you must get as close as possible to bullet points but without literally writing bullets (which you must not do as your answers must be in full sentences). As an exercise, **have a look at some of the sentences in this chapter or in the rest of this book** and try to rewrite them in as short a format as you can – we definitely break the "almost bullet-like" rule on many occasions but then we did not write the book in 3.5 hours so we can afford a little bit of slack and of course we wanted you to have an exercise to do ...

As you write your mock attempts, try to critically assess whether you are being as succinct as you really could be. You can definitely work on this element by going back and literally writing out your mock answer text again (using a computer so that you can "tinker" with the wording to find the most succinct phrasing). Working through each page on a line by line basis will help you to identify what you personally need to avoid doing. You may be surprised by the results of this exercise: many students report being able to trim their text down by 1/3 or more.

Another tip is that as we know what some of the sections of the report are likely to look like[24] then you should be able to work out some **standard and efficient phrases** that you will always use in these elements. Spending some time before the examination to make these sentences as clean and clinical as possible really could be worth it.

Use section headings to save words and focus your attempt onto the right areas

At the 2014, 2015, 2016 and 2017 SBM Workshops at the ICAEW Tutor Conferences, the examiners stated that a **key differentiator** between a good script and a failing script was often that the good script was better organised through **the use of section headings**. The examiners therefore advised all tutors to tell students to start each Task and sub-Task on a **separate page and always starting within a heading** so that each part of the report looks at a different area.

Using section headings will also ensure that you answer each part of the question to a good standard: if you have all your points in one long unheaded section then it is easy to kid yourself that you have done a good job of covering a range of points whereas if you have instead first set up your **skeleton structure** with clear headings for each Task and sub-Task then it will be **very easy to see when you have not done enough on a particular area**: your relevant section will be too short and this is something that will be glaringly obvious.

Another reason to use headings is that **headings can save you words and therefore time**: you will no longer have to signal to the examiner that you are switching to a different element of your answer through introductory language such as "Turning now to consider the impact of recent changes on staffing arrangements": you can just use a heading called "Staff arrangements" and the

---

[24] For example, financial performance analysis will be needed in Q1, somewhere you will need to discuss ethics using a standard framework to generate ideas (see chapter 17) and financial reporting points will require reference to IFRSs followed by application to the scenario (see below).

examiner/reader will be given the same amount of guidance but using 2 words rather than 12 (time saving: 83%!).

Inline definition of IFRS

In the financial reporting aspects of SBM, we know that you will need to demonstrate your knowledge of key IFRS rules and will have to then apply these rules to the scenario set.

At the 2015 SBM Workshop at the ICAEW Tutor Conference, the examiners confirmed that simply writing out the relevant standard will attract "little or no credit": in some cases, the markscheme might award minimal marks for correctly identifying the applicable standard (provided that this is not blatantly obvious[25]) but **in most cases there would be no marks awarded at all just for writing out the rules**. As such, you are potentially going to completely waste your time in any copying out of accounting rules.

What the examiners are interested in is whether you can correctly **apply** the relevant rules to the scenario. You show this by **applying** the rules rather than simply **writing** the rules out. This means that a more efficient approach is to use what we call an "**inline definition**" approach.

What is "inline definition"? This is best illustrated by 2 examples. In the first example, we apply what we call a "copying out approach", an approach that we see very often with taught course students at the start of our courses. In the second example, we instead apply an "inline definition" approach where we show the same amount of knowledge of IFRS but in a **fraction of the words required** and, secondly, **in which, because of the sentence structure and focus, all points will automatically connect with the scenario**.

For the purposes of illustration, we have created a fictional company called Example plc, which we have assumed has some matters to consider under IAS 38 regarding its development costs.

Method 1 – Copying out approach

"IAS 38 defines intangible assets as non-monetary assets which are without physical substance and which are identifiable, meaning that the asset is separable (capable of being separated and sold) or arises from contractual or other legal rights. An intangible asset can be recognised when it is probable that the future economic benefits that are attributable to the asset will flow to the entity and the cost of the asset can be measured reliably.

Under IAS 38, all research costs must be expensed but development costs can be capitalised if the technical and commercial feasibility of the asset for sale or use have been established. This requires the following:

- Intention to complete the asset

---

[25] For example, if the scenario relates to financial instruments then merely identifying that IAS 39 is relevant would not be something that attracts credit but if the question concerns an operating lease then there might be some credit for going into the relevant section of IAS 17 as it would have required some technical skill to identify that **operating lease** rules in IAS 17 were the relevant rules. However, just stating that IAS 17 applies would not, in itself, attract credit.

65

- Availability of economic resources to complete the asset
- Ability either to use or sell the asset
- Ability to demonstrate how the asset will generate future economic benefits

Looking at the position of Example plc, the project to improve efficiency in the production of widgets should not be capitalised as development expenditure as the Board Minutes indicate that a decision has not yet been made on whether to complete the asset and there is uncertainty as to the resources required. However, it is clear from the independent valuation report that there is a market for improved widgets as over £10m of sales have been achieved by Competitor plc in the last month."

224 words

Method 2 – Inline definition: IFRS criteria mentioned in the same line as scenario data

"IAS 38 is the relevant standard for the project to improve efficiency in production of widgets as we need to determine whether the costs are research (expensed) or development (capitalised).

The Board Minutes indicate a lack of certainty over "intention to complete the asset" (key IAS 38 requirement for capitalisation) and there is no certainty of the "availability of economic resources to complete the asset" (IAS 38) because the Finance Director has indicated that loans and staff may be reallocated to different projects.

However, there is evidence of a "potential inflow of economic benefits to the entity" (IAS 38) and "an ability to use or sell the asset" because the independent valuation report shows high sales of improved widgets. No information at all has been provided on "reliable measurement of cost" (IAS 38) (although it appears that the project has been tracked independently within the management accounts) so this is another indicator that capitalisation is not yet possible."

158 words or 71% of the length of the example under Method 1 above

Hopefully from the above exercise you can see that it is possible to make **more relevant points in fewer words** – the second example in fact applies IAS 38 rules more carefully, giving scenario-specific or MS^2 points at all times but using only **71% of the time required to write the first example**. If you therefore adopt the correct **inline** writing style, passing will be much easier – sometimes "less is more"!

Using the word "because": potential impact on marginal scripts

Linked to our above points on the benefits of inline definition, during the SBM Workshop at the 2015 ICAEW Tutor Conference, the examiners commented that if they had one tip for "marginal students" (i.e. students who were very close to passing SBM) it would be to use the word "because" a bit more. Why? Because (!):

1. Using the word "because" ensures that you are explaining **why** something should be done or **why** a particular IFRS applies: you are therefore showing your **reasoning** to the examiner and therefore the examiner can award marks (perhaps only partial marks, but still marks) for that thinking, even if your conclusion is ultimately wrong. Therefore, for example, immediately treating a lease as an operating lease without properly explaining why this is the right approach will mean giving up a lot of marks even if your approach is actually correct (and if your approach is wrong you will not be getting anything since there is no reasoning for the marker to assess when determining whether any partial credit should be given).

2. The examiners in some cases need to **see the reasoning and not just the conclusion or recommendation**: if you have been asked to provide recommendations on how to boost staff morale during a period of change, saying simply that a "profit sharing arrangement should be implemented" will not attract any marks at all as this does not show **why** this is the right decision **in this case** – the examiners are **obsessed** with ensuring that **only scenario-specific points are rewarded**, rather than rote-learned lists of generic or "boilerplate" answers taken from a student's "open book" resources so using the word "because" ensures that you **connect the point to the data**.

    A profit sharing arrangement is probably **always** going to be a reasonable suggestion but precisely because it can **always** be used it is **not an interesting or insightful point unless you use the word "because" to turn it into something relevant to the specific scenario**: that will require some skill so it will be rewarded whereas just copying something out will not.

3. Using the word "because" will ensure that you **turn towards justification and reasoning fairly soon in your answer** and hence you will avoid any risks in merely copying out, which is simply not rewarded.

The examiners specifically stated that "most" marginal candidates would have passed the examination if they had simply used the word "because" a bit more. **We would take notice of this warning.**

6.3   Writing Efficiently in SBM: Some Phrases to Avoid

Based on the above advice and our reviews of student scripts from our taught courses, here are some suggested phrases and points that are best avoided for the purposes of the SBM exam:

Introductory sentences

It is completely **unnecessary to introduce each Task or sub-Task: just get on with the analysis**. Therefore sentences such as "In this part of the report, we will analyse the financial performance of Example plc over the past 12 months" are completely unnecessary as there will be no marks on the markscheme for this kind of language. Just use a heading of "Financial performance" and get on with your analysis!

Link sentences

There is no need to write beautiful linkages between paragraphs as this again will not be rewarded. Therefore phrases such as "Following on from the above analysis of profit per year ..." or "In contrast to the improvement in gross margin ..." are a waste of time. The marker cannot award any marks for these **linkages** between points: **marks can only be awarded for the points themselves**.

Enumerative sentences

There is no need to say "Another factor which may be affecting the market for widgets is ..." – **just state the factor itself!**

Section sentences

There is no need to say "In conclusion ..." or "As a recommendation we would advise": if you are using section headings (as advised above) such as "Conclusions" or "Recommendations" then the marker will know which section you are addressing: once again, **just get on with the analysis rather than introducing it**.

Although some of the unnecessary phrases identified above may not appear to use up many words, if you are making these mistakes repeatedly throughout the exam then the cumulative effect can be surprisingly large: even if you only waste 200 words in total across the whole paper (for reference, **even the few examples given in quotation marks in this section 6.3 amount to 57 words already ...**) then that is **several minutes** of writing up time – if you could pay someone to have a further few minutes of time in an ACA examination then perhaps we should not ask too closely what you would do but our advice is a free (and much more ethical!) way of gaining the same amount of time so go for our option!

Whilst we realise that you are probably keen to start reading the rest of this book to learn more about the examination, marking approach, technical points and so on, we would close this chapter by emphasising once again that **perhaps the single most important improvement that most students can make is to their SBM writing style** – this is why we have included our points early in this chapter 6 so please do not forget about our points just because it is within the "introductory" part of the book.

Chapter 7   Analysis of the SBM Past Papers

Learning Points

After reading this chapter, you must be able to:

1. understand the tendencies in the mark allocation of SBM past papers
2. appreciate how our MAP "11 Rules" fit well with the SBM past paper mark allocations
3. understand the balance between narrative and numerical marks in the SBM past papers
4. appreciate some of the typical practical business areas which were considered

---

7.1   The Best Evidence on Content and Marks Allocation – Real ICAEW Papers

At the time of writing (March 2018), 8 real examination papers had been set by ICAEW after the introduction of this new paper under the evolved ACA syllabus (which entered into effect for the Advanced Level from July 2014). This provides us with 8 full examination standard papers to analyse in order to understand the likely format and requirements of the examination.

This chapter will go into considerable analytical detail. This level of analysis is necessary as we believe that real papers are the best examples of what the examination will be like in future[26] but with relatively few real example papers available we need to extract as many learning points as possible.

7.2   The July 2014 Paper: A Brief Overview

The first real SBM paper contained 2 questions:

1. **Funnel Cruises plc**, worth 60 marks

2. **Landex plc**, worth 40 marks

We will analyse both questions under 2 specific headings:

- **Mark allocation by SBM topic area** (practical business advisory, financial reporting, Specialist Audit & Assurance, ethics)

- **Mark allocation applying the 11 Rules** (see chapter 5)

---

[26] See Appendix 5 for our explanation of why the ICAEW Question Bank and mock examinations may not be as useful guidance as real past papers.

7.2.1 Funnel Cruises (60 marks)

This question concerned a large client, Funnel Cruises, which provided international cruise services. The candidate assumes a role in advising the client shortly after the retirement of the Finance Director. Despite a considerable downturn in performance, FC was considering the acquisition of a company called Coastal Hotels.

1. Mark allocation by SBM topic area

Funnel Cruises contained the following elements:

1. Analysis of FC financials with explanations of the reasons for a decline in performance (19 marks)

2. Evaluation and discussion of different methods of hedging, including derivatives (16 marks)

3. Valuation of a possible acquisition and the financial reporting implications and assurance procedures required (14 marks)

4. Quantification of the impact of a food poisoning incident and making related recommendations (11 marks)

Based on the above, we would suggest that the composition of the marks in Q1 was as follows:

Practical business advisory	50
Financial reporting	7
Audit & Assurance	3
Ethics	0
Total	**60**

We would expect the heavy emphasis on practical business advisory areas such as analysing management accounts and "non-pro-forma" calculations (i.e. reacting to a specific strategic scenario) to continue in Q1 as this was typical in Q1 of the old Business Change paper (which was also informally termed the "mini-case" question by the examiners).

2. Mark allocation applying the 11 Rules

As always, only the total number of marks was indicated for students: we have derived our own Task-specific breakdown of the marks by looking at the markscheme (obviously not something available when sitting the exam!).

Using the rules outlined in chapter 5, we would suggest that the following techniques could have been used to correctly estimate the split of the total of 60 marks into the different Tasks[27]:

Task 1 – Extensive Exhibits and so 19 marks (Rules 1 & 2)

Task 1 on analysis of the FC financials was the single most important Task in terms of the mark allocation, which is consistent with our rule to look at the amount of financial information made available: Exhibit 3 was composed entirely of management accounts figures together with **additional operational results measures**. This combination should have alerted candidates to the high number of marks available as there was plenty of opportunity to make MS^2 points regarding the scenario-specific operational measures (in addition to traditional figures used for financial reporting such as revenue, gross profit and so on). In addition, Exhibit 1 and Exhibit 2 contained further details on the background to FC's operations which should have led students to see that the examiner wanted a connection to be made between Exhibits 1, 2 and 3 within this answer (Rules 1 & 2): as such, there was an extensive amount of Exhibit material to this Task.

Task 2 – Dedicated Exhibit with numbers and narrative so 16 marks (Rules 1, 2 & 5)

Task 2 on hedging was the second most important Task in the mark allocation. This Task had an entire Exhibit (Exhibit 4) dedicated only to foreign currency risks, including numbers and narrative information (Rule 2). The amount of information was significantly longer than Exhibit 5 (used in the next Task) which related exclusively to the potential acquisition of Coastal Hotels. As such, using our suggestion of looking at the length of the Exhibit as initial guidance, Task 2 on hedging would be predicted to be awarded more marks than Task 3 and this was the case (Rule 1). Rule 5 (the 33:66 Rule) should then be used to split into the appropriate amount of numerical and narrative work.

Task 3 – Short Exhibit but several sub-Tasks so 14 marks (Rules 1, 3, 4, 5 & 7)

Task 3 contained a relatively short Exhibit (Exhibit 5), providing outline data for Coastal Hotels, the proposed target of an acquisition. The Exhibit was short at only half a page but the Task was split into 3 separate elements, including practical business advisory work (a valuation), financial reporting work and discussion of assurance issues (Due Diligence) (Rules 1, 3, 4 & 7). Hopefully our rule to look at the number of disciplines covered would have alerted students to the fact that there were more marks available than could be suggested just from looking at the short Exhibit length. Rule 5 (the 33:66 Rule) should then be used to split into the appropriate amount of numerical and narrative work.

Task 4 – No separate Exhibit but extensive narrative and detailed requirements so 11 marks (Rules 1, 2 and 4)

Task 4 did not have its own separate Exhibit as the information on the food poisoning issue was all described in the first part of the exam paper before the Exhibits. Lacking a dedicated Exhibit should indicate a relatively low share of marks.

However, just under a quarter of the text in the first part of the exam paper (in our terminology, the "Introduction" section: see page 31) related to the food poisoning incident and the text clearly included

---

[27] We recommend that you keep a finger in page 60 providing our summary of the 11 Rules so that you can quickly flick back and check your understanding as we work through the July 2014 paper.

a percentage figure, suggesting that a calculation was possible: therefore, the number of marks should be estimated to be a bit higher than otherwise indicated by the lack of a dedicated Exhibit. The Task requirements were also quite detailed and asked the candidate to "calculate and explain" the impact and also to "recommend any operational actions". As such, there were 3 elements to address so at a minimum of, say, 3-4 marks per Task then hopefully students would have known that the allocation could not be below 10 marks.

Overall, this Task required use of several different rules to correctly estimate the mark allocation.

The 11 Rules and July 2014 Q1 Mark Allocation: Summary

Overall, the July 2014 paper fits well with our suggestion to look at **Exhibit length**, the **number of sub-Tasks**, the **existence of a dedicated Exhibit** and the **nature of the question wording** as your 4 criteria in deciding the spread of marks. The spread was unequal, with a range between 11 and 19 marks. However, there were no indications that any Task was minor in nature so this should have maintained the minimum estimate at around 10 marks and then use of the Rules based on Exhibit length and sub-Tasks could have operated to indicate the greater importance of Tasks 1, 2 and 3 (in decreasing order of importance).

7.2.2   Landex (40 marks)

This question concerned a large manufacturer of high quality watches. Landex was based in the UK but exported worldwide. The Landex Board was faced with a strategic choice: continue to work with an existing supplier that was struggling to keep up with expansion, rely on multiple suppliers or set up its own factory in a developing nation.

1. Mark allocation by SBM topic area

Landex plc contained the following elements:

1. Evaluation and comparison of 3 procurement proposals, explaining operational and strategic implications (16 marks)

2. Provision of reasoned advice on 2 bonds, including the financial reporting treatment (11 marks)

3. Discussion of 2 ethical issues concerning a supplier and its related parties (7 marks)

4. Outlining of the corporate governance and financial reporting issues involved in working with a new supplier (6 marks)

Based on the above, we would suggest that the composition of the marks in Q2 was as follows:

Practical business advisory	16
Financial reporting	14
Audit & Assurance	3
Ethics	7
Total	**40**

Hopefully you can see that our Rule that ethics will account for 6-8 marks was proven correct in this paper. The significance of financial reporting tasks is noteworthy: however, this would not be surprising applying the balance rule: there was relatively little financial reporting in Q1 so to achieve the target balance of 15-20 financial reporting marks across the paper as a whole (see chapter 3 and chapter 19) then a mark of around 12-15 marks would be needed in Q2 – and this was what was awarded.

2. Mark allocation applying the 11 Rules

The range of marks for different Tasks in this question was from a minimum of 3 for corporate governance issues to 16 for calculations regarding the 3 proposals. Was this something that our 11 Rules would have helped students to determine? [28]

Task 1 – Extensive question wording and 2 Exhibits to be integrated so 16 marks (Rules 1, 2 & 4)

Looking more closely at the Tasks set out in Exhibit 5, the **length of the question wording** (Rule 4) would be a pretty good guide to the correct number of marks in Q2: Task 1 has the most words/requests and clearly emphasises that 3 different proposals are being discussed: the request also clearly identifies 2 Exhibits to be used (unlike the other 3 Tasks which mention either a single Exhibit or none at all). With 3 different issues to look at then assuming at least 5 marks for each proposal (given the requirement for calculations) would result in a good approximation to the correct number of marks at 16 marks.

Alternatively, our suggestion to look at the length of the Exhibits included would also have worked as a predictor: Task 1 specifically asked candidates to use 2 different Exhibits (Exhibit 2 and 3). Taken together, these Exhibits account for 2 of the 5 pages which make up Q2. Is it a coincidence that 2/5 x 40 marks = 16 marks, the exact number of marks available for Task 1?

Task 2 – 2 bullets so a significant Task but less so than Task 1 (Rules 1, 2 & 8)

Task 2 contains 2 bullets so is clearly a significant part of the question but with only 2 issues compared to Task 1's 3 issues we would expect 2/3 of the marks … and this is almost exactly what happened: Task 2 was worth 11/16 or 69% of the marks available for Task 1.

Alternatively, looking at the matter based on the length of the Exhibits, Task 2 was the only other Task to reference a specific Exhibit so on our 11 Rules it would have to account for more marks than

---

[28] We recommend that you keep a finger in page 60 providing our summary of the 11 Rules so that you can quickly flick back and check your understanding as we work through the July 2014 paper.

either Task 3 and 4 – this was the case and in fact Task 2 accounted for approximately the same number of marks as Tasks 3 and 4 **combined** (11 marks for Task 2 versus a total of 13 marks for Task 3 plus Task 4). Once again, this emphasises that if there is a reference to a dedicated Exhibit in the question wording then the relevant Task will be more important.

Hopefully candidates would have applied the balancing rule (Rule 8) to Q2 with respect to the financial reporting of the bond: there was almost no financial reporting in Q1 so this would then suggest that any opportunity to test financial reporting in Q2 would have been very important in the markscheme[29].

Task 3 – Ethical focus (Rule 9)

Task 3 related to ethics only. Our ethics Rule suggests that around 6-8 marks will be available for an ethics question and this is exactly what happened.

Task 4 – A very brief request (Rules 2 & 4)

Task 4 contained a very brief request simply to "set out" the corporate governance and financial reporting issues: at just one sentence, this is the briefest statement of all questions and, as such, Task 4 was the lowest weighted element at 6 marks.

7.3   Some Reflections on the July 2014 Markscheme and Model Answer

As we have shown above, our 11 Rules would have worked well as a method of predicting the mark allocation in both questions. In some cases, a single Rule would have been enough – in others, there would have been a need to apply more than one Rule or to think in **overall paper** terms by using the balancing rule: for example, this would have indicated a relatively high reward for financial reporting issues in Q2 since there were few financial reporting issues in Q1.

The July 2014 markscheme definitely supports our argument to look firstly at the **Exhibit length and number of Exhibits to consider** when assessing the likely number of marks available. Task 1 contained the shortest instructions on what to do with just one sentence compared to 3 or 4 sentences for all other Tasks yet **Task 1 contained the highest number of marks of any Task** in the paper as it required usage of **3 Exhibits**. From looking purely at the amount of instruction given, one might conclude that Task 1 would be the least important since there were no bullets or sub-Tasks allocated. Therefore, the Exhibit length Rule does seem to overrule the Task wording length Rule. This is what we mean by the need for **judgement** in some cases.

Another hint would be to remember which question you are looking at – Q1 is always likely to involve a lot of marks for **practical business advisory** (which was precisely the focus of Q1 Task 1 in July 2014). The final hint was to read the question wording very carefully: Task 1 asked students to use

---

[29] Here we have assumed that you have completed Q1 first: the balancing rule would also work the other way around of course – if you had completed Q2 first and noticed that Task 2 was very heavy on financial reporting then accordingly you could have used Rule 8 to realise that there would not be many financial reporting marks available in Q1.

Exhibit 3 "and the other information provided" whereas all other Tasks either referred to a single Exhibit or no Exhibit at all[30].

We hope that the above review shows you how to apply the 11 Rules in practice and also gives you confidence that the Rules do work. We will now go through the same process but looking at the November 2014 examination paper.

7.4   The November 2014 Paper: A Brief Overview

The second real SBM paper contained 2 questions:

1. **Firebrand Forklift Trucks Ltd**, worth 60 marks

2. **Washing Solutions Ltd**, worth 40 marks

We will analyse both questions under the same 2 standard headings as in the previous chapter:

- **Mark allocation by SBM topic area** (practical business advisory, financial reporting, audit, ethics)

- **Mark allocation applying the 11 Rules** (see chapter 5)

7.4.1   Firebrand Forklift Trucks Ltd (60 marks)

This question concerned a large client, Firebrand Forklift Trucks, which manufactured forklift trucks from a factory in Wales. The trucks were exported globally. The candidate assumes a role advising the client in the context of a shortage of funds and an inability to repay a loan and overdraft. The Board was therefore considering putting the company into administration.

1. Mark allocation by SBM topic area

Firebrand Forklift Trucks contained the following elements:

1. Analysis of the reasons for a decline in FFT's profit over several years together with a suggestion for actions which could improve profitability (13 marks)

2. Evaluation of a proposed financial reconstruction scheme (including calculations), containing analysis of the benefits and risks for various stakeholders followed by discussion of the financial reporting of a loan (17 marks + 8 marks)

---

[30] We might also note that Task 1 was the only Task where the question wording refers to an Exhibit in the Task wording itself (rather than being placed in round brackets, as is the case with all the other references to Exhibits). This was presumably a further attempt by the examiners to reinforce to students that they needed to "use Exhibit 3 and the other information provided" – these were the very first words in the Task!

3. Evaluation (including calculations) of the benefits and risks of leasing, compared with selling, forklift trucks, as well as the financial reporting implications of leasing the trucks (5 + 5 marks)

4. Advice to the FFT Board on a response to an email received from a journalist regarding an ethical issue (6 marks)

In addition to the above points listed in the final Exhibit (Exhibit 7), there was an additional "hidden" Task:

5. Advice to the engagement partner of the candidate's own accounting firm (rather than the client) as to the ethical implications of giving advice to FFT regarding FFT's response to an email from the journalist (6 marks)

Many candidates missed this additional Task and therefore immediately lost 6 marks or 10% of the marks available for Q1.

Based on the above, we would suggest that the composition of the marks in Q1 was as follows (equivalent marks from the July 2014 paper (see previous chapter) are included in brackets for comparison purposes):

Practical business advisory	35	(50)
Financial reporting	13	(7)
Audit & Assurance	0	(3)
Ethics	12	(0)
Total	**60**	**60**

We can see that practical business advisory was again very important in Q1 but in the November examination financial reporting and particularly ethics were given a lot more importance.

2. Mark allocation applying the 11 Rules

As always, only the total number of marks for the question as a whole was indicated for students. We have therefore derived a Task-specific breakdown of the marks from the markscheme. Here we are interested in whether the principles outlined in chapter 5 would be an effective way of estimating how to split the marks and therefore your time[31].

Task 1 – Reasonably detailed Exhibits with financials so 13 marks (Rules 1, 2, 3 and 5)

At first sight, and considering that this Task involved analysis of the financial information, it seems puzzling that there were only 13 marks available for this task compared to the 19 marks available in July 2014. This would appear to be even stranger when we consider that:

---

[31] We recommend that you keep a finger in page 60 providing our summary of the 11 Rules so that you can quickly flick back and check your understanding as we work through the November 2014 paper.

1. there were 3 years of information to analyse in the November 2014 paper (compared to 2 years of information in July 2014)

2. the November 2014 paper provided both an income statement and SFP (compared to only an income statement in July 2014)

3. in both papers, there was approximately the same amount of information in Exhibit 2 (half a page of company details) and Exhibit 3 (a full page of management accounting information)

However, with a more careful appraisal of the information (and of course with a considerable benefit of hindsight and the availability of the markscheme!) perhaps some important rules can be developed.

We would firstly note that in the November 2014 paper, the company background contained no numbers whereas in the July 2014 there were several scenario-specific numbers which could have been integrated into the financial analysis: for example, the number of ships and the passenger capacity of the company ships. Therefore, perhaps the examiners thought that the numerical analysis in July 2014 could have been more specific to the scenario and therefore more marks were available.

We would then note that in the November 2014 paper, the Income Statement was presented at a summary level and **did not contain a breakdown within key captions** such as revenue, cost of sales or distribution and administration costs. On the other hand, in the July 2014 paper, candidates were rewarded for analysis of different revenue streams and changes in different key costs: this was possible because a detailed split out of these amounts was provided to candidates. Again, perhaps the examiners thought that the numerical analysis in July 2014 could be more detailed and therefore more marks were available.

Although the November 2014 paper contained an SFP (unlike in July 2014) the SFP provided was extremely basic with just 3 asset categories and 3 liability categories, 2 of which were bank loans and a bank overdraft and hence tested in other elements of the question. Hence candidates could not analyse the SFP in much detail.

Finally, we would note that in the November 2014 examination paper, candidates were provided with just 3 types of operating data compared to the 8 types of operating data provided in July 2014. Once again then, the July 2014 paper permitted a much more detailed numerical analysis and hence there were another 6 marks in Task 1 of the earlier paper.

This analysis provides us with a valuable lesson: **do not assume that Task 1 in Q1 will always be the most important task and make a judgement once you have seen how much information is available**. Try to look at how much information is provided **compared to the 2 real papers we have analysed here**, as well as compared to any other practice exams which you have done.

Task 2 – Exhibits containing many numbers and 2 bullet-points on several different topic areas so 25 marks (Rules 1, 2, 3, 4, 5 and 7)

Task 2 on the proposed financial reconstruction was, in terms of marks, the most important Task in Q1. Exhibit 4 clearly provided a large number of figures to work with (approximately 15 different figures) and the examiners made it clear that they wanted a separate financial reporting analysis of the reconstruction through use of a second bullet point in the list of Tasks in the final Exhibit for the question.

Although there were 25 marks for this Task as a whole (a number well above any number of marks for a Task in the July 2014 paper), there were really **2 quite separate tasks** to do here: the numerical analysis involving practical business advisory skills was worth 17 marks which is in fact very close to the 16 marks for a similar task in the July 2014. **It is only really the incorporation of financial reporting into the November 2014 Task 2 which boosts the marks up.** At 8 marks for financial reporting, a relatively standard or expected amount of emphasis was given to FR issues.

Task 3 – Short Exhibit but 2 clear sub-Tasks so 10 marks (Rules 2 and 4)

This Task had an approximately equal number of marks as the same task in the July 2014 paper. The November 2014 Task 3 involved practical business advisory to calculate the benefits and risks of leasing trucks followed by an explanation of the financial reporting consequences.

The equivalent Task in the July 2014 paper was worth a further 4 marks (14 marks compared to 10 marks in November 2014) but comparing the 2 papers shows us that there were more numbers to work with in Exhibit 5 in July 2014 than in November 2014. Arguably, the financial reporting issues in July 2014 (Groups) were also more difficult from a technical point of view compared to November 2014 (Leases) so this would be another reason why the marks were slightly higher in the earlier paper.

Despite this variance, Task 3 was the third most important Task in both papers and this is consistent with our emphasis on Exhibit length since both papers had an exhibit of between one-third and half a page only. As such, the relevant Exhibit was one of the shortest on each paper and hence this Task was not given a high number of marks in relative terms.

Task 4 – No separate bullets and ethical in nature so 6 marks (Rule 9)

In the November 2014 examination, this Task was the only Task not to have 2 bullet-point requests (other than the financial analysis Task 1 which we know will always have quite a few marks despite only a short request). This would hopefully have alerted candidates to the relatively low number of marks available, given a dedicated and relatively lengthy (half page) Exhibit. The question wording was not as demanding as in July 2014 as there was no request to "calculate and explain" since there were no numbers to work with.

At the same time, however, an accurate estimate of the number of marks for this Task would probably only have been possible in practice if a candidate had correctly identified that there was an additional ethical Task (a somewhat "hidden" Task: see Task 5 below) – the hidden Task contributed another 6 ethical marks regarding the same scenario. As such, if we look at the **2 different ethical issues** together, the length of Exhibit 6 is a good indication of the total number of marks: at two-thirds of a page and 12 marks, this fits with our rule on Exhibit length. Again, however, this would have required the candidate to recognise that there were **2 Tasks in relation to ethics** based on the same relatively lengthy Exhibit.

Task 5 – Hidden and hence no separate Exhibit so 6 marks (Rule 9)

As noted above, this Task was not clearly stated for candidates in the terms of reference at the end of Q1: **candidates had to spot the request from the partner of the candidate's accounting firm on page 3 of the examination paper which asked for an analysis which was "in addition" to the other Tasks requested.**

For this very reason, there was no statement in the question to use a specific Exhibit and the issue related in the end to the same ethical issue as in Exhibit 6. Hopefully candidates would therefore have treated Task 4 and Task 5 as part of the same broad ethical topic and based on our Rule that ethics will account for 6-8 marks per issue such a candidate would have concluded that there were approximately **12 marks for Task 4 and Task 5 combined**.

The 11 Rules and November 2014 Q1 Mark Allocation: Summary

Overall, based on the above, we believe that the November 2014 Q1 fits well with our standard 11 Rules as outlined in chapter 5 and as already explored in detail in the previous chapter. In other words, **looking at the Exhibit length, the number of sub-Tasks, the nature of the question wording and the number of different topic areas included** would have helped you correctly decide the spread of marks. In the November 2014 paper, the range of marks in the different Tasks was technically between 6 and 25 marks. However, based on the analysis above we would regard the range as really being between 12 and 17 if judged on a sub-Tasks basis[32]. This is very much in line with the previous July 2014 paper so our advice that a Q1 Task should always carry at least 10 marks in Q1 remains valid.

In conclusion, we believe that our 11 Rules work well for both Q1s examined so far. However, given the length of the discussion above, and the fact that you will have to work through this thought process in an amount of time significantly less than that taken to read our analysis (i.e. you will need to reach your judgement within a few minutes at a maximum) it is important that you reread and work through the points made above so that you can reach your judgement in a more **instinctive** way and hence work **much more quickly**.

We have included reminders on our MAPs to assist with this process but we cannot emphasise enough how important it is to strike a balance between correctly allocating your marks/time to the different sub-Tasks and leaving enough time to actually attempt those tasks to a good standard. You need to keep practising and therefore developing the skills needed to reach the correct judgement very quickly, based on our 11 Rules and the various considerations therein.

To help build this skill, you may wish to look at several SBM past papers rather than using the ICAEW Question Bank: the past papers provide 2 full and "paired up" questions which are designed to be taken together and which therefore reflect the expected allocation of SBM syllabus marks across the paper (set of 2 questions) as a whole – on the other hand, each question in the Question Bank is designed to be taken on an individual basis rather than as part of a set of 2 questions so taking Question Bank questions will not build your ability to understand the mark allocation across an SBM

---

[32] These numbers are arrived at by grouping the 2 ethics sub-Tasks (since these concerned the same general ethics area) and splitting the 25 marks in Task 2 into 17 marks for practical business advisory and 8 marks for financial reporting.

paper as a whole (for example, you cannot use the balancing rule when taking Question Bank questions because these are standalone questions rather than part of a 2 question paper).

7.4.2   Washing Solutions Ltd (40 marks)

This question is, in our opinion, the most difficult SBM question set to date. This is because it tested areas that arguably[33] would not have been studied by students since the Management Information Certificate Level paper (i.e. technical issues that may not have been studied by candidates for several years) such as **allocation of overheads and management accounting methods**. Without an understanding of this area, it would have been difficult to gain the 50% of the Q2 marks allocated to calculations. Additionally, one of the sub-Tasks relating to Due Diligence was harder than it could have been (see discussion below).

In this question it would be even more important to estimate the marks available for **other areas** and ensure that you are attacking all the easier sub-Tasks by carefully adding these to your MAP and following our reminders on what to talk about.

The question concerned a client with 2 divisions, each manufacturing a different type of washing machine. The company had recently experienced very poor financial results after an apparent mistake in their costing methodology (based on a cost-plus approach). Candidates were required to explain why actual profits departed from budgeted profit and a possible opportunity to sell one division to a rival company.

1. Mark allocation by SBM topic area

Washing Solutions contained the following elements:

1. Analysis and explanation for a decline in the tendering success rate of one division, compared to the prior year (10 marks)

2. Explanation, with calculations, of the reasons why actual profits differ from budgeted profit for each of the 2 divisions and for the company as a whole in the most recent reporting period (13 marks)

3. Analysis and explanation of the effect of overhead cost allocations on pricing (8 marks)

4. Explanation of the strategic, operating and financial factors that the client should consider before deciding whether to sell a division, together with risks and Due Diligence procedures in respect of receiving shares in the purchaser as consideration for the sale (9 marks)

Unlike Q1, there does not appear to have been any "hidden" sub-Task in Q2 – all Tasks were set out in the final Exhibit (Exhibit 5).

---

[33] The examiners would probably respond that (1) all brought forward knowledge is potentially examinable and/or (2) the SBM Study Manual does contain additional technical content regarding costing methods such as ABC and absorption costing.

Based on the above, we would suggest that the composition of the marks in Q2 was as follows (equivalent marks from the July 2014 paper (see previous chapter) are included in brackets for comparison purposes):

Practical business advisory	31	(16)
Financial reporting	4	(14)
Audit & Assurance	5	(3)
Ethics	0	(7)
Total	**40**	**40**

We can see that this question was very heavily based on PBA concepts: without recognising the impact of the cost-plus approach and the overhead allocation method, it would have been difficult to make any of the necessary PBA points. As far as we can see, there were only very minimal financial reporting issues (on inventory and impairment) to consider in this question – this fits with the "balancing rule" as Q1 reviewed above contained 13 financial reporting marks.

In many ways, this Q2 reminds us of the type of Q3 that would sometimes crop up in the previous Business Change paper: a type of practical financial analysis with no real financial reporting or assurance aspects and therefore a potentially dangerous question if you do not enjoy thinking on your feet in an examination setting.

1. Mark allocation applying the 11 Rules

As always, only the total number of marks for the question as a whole was indicated for students. We have therefore derived a Task-specific breakdown of the marks from the markscheme. Here we are interested in whether the principles outlined in chapter 5 would be an effective way of estimating how to split the marks and therefore your time[34].

Task 1 – relatively short Exhibit length so only 10 marks (Rules 1, 2, 4 and 5)

At first sight, many candidates may have assumed that Task 1 would be the Task which accounted for the most marks: on its face, the Task asks for a comparison across 2 different years with respect to a full Exhibit of information. Many candidates may therefore have assumed that this Task would be the equivalent of the standard financial analysis Task (Task 1) in Q1. However, in practice, this task was worth less than Task 2 and had almost the same marks value as the purely numerical Task 4. What is going on here?

Looking more carefully, the question refers to only one Exhibit (compared to the 2 Exhibits mentioned in Task 2: see below) and the financial information provided is quite limited: although it refers to 2 different years, it is information of a "Key Performance Indicator"-type rather than a full Income Statement. As such, it is similar to the operational data that candidates can often find at the bottom of all the information given in the financial analysis Task in Q1 i.e. the additional "icing on the cake"

---

[34] We recommend that you keep a finger in page 60 providing our summary of the 11 Rules so that you can quickly flick back and check your understanding as we work through the November 2014 paper.

type of data rather than the bulk of the main data itself. This may explain why there were not so many marks available because it was not possible to do a huge amount of different things with the data: looking at the model answer, the calculations are largely common sense percentage changes or average figures rather than anything that requires a financial accounting background.

There was also no need to cross apply information from different Exhibits as candidates were told just to use Exhibit 2. For example, information on the company background was not needed for this answer.

Looking at Exhibit length, it is clear that Exhibit 2 is significantly shorter than the 2 Exhibits used in the next Task (Task 2). The numbers are also much less complicated. The total Exhibit length of the 2 Exhibits used in Task 2 is approximately 40% longer than the single Exhibit used for Task 1 (after allowing for spacing and tables etc) and in line with this the number of marks available for Task 2 is 30% higher than for Task 1 (13 versus 10).

Taking all these factors into account, it makes more sense that Task 1 did not have as many marks available as Task 2. However, **given that Task 2 was much harder, we suspect that many candidates would have tried to compensate by writing far too much for Task 1**. The analysis here shows that unfortunately it is not possible to compensate for a difficult PBA question by writing a lot of material on simpler financial analysis-style questions: always use the 11 Rules to estimate the number of marks and if after using these rules it appears that **unfortunately the harder Tasks are going to be awarded substantially more marks, then this is just the way it is** and you will not be helping yourself in any way by trying to compensate with a longer answer for a simpler Task.

Task 2 – Complex number work from 2 Exhibits so 13 marks (Rules 1, 3, 4 and 5)

We have already partly explained the mark allocation for this Task in our discussion of the previous Task. To repeat, there were clearly 2 detailed Exhibits which had to be used in full to arrive at a good answer. Secondly, the information was sufficient to prepare a mini "Income Statement" (or at least a contribution analysis) and candidates were also asked to explain the differences in the figures (therefore requiring some narrative work). As such, this was effectively a financial analysis type question (similar to a standard Task 1 in Q1) but with the added difficulty of having to prepare the figures first.

Overall, the 11 Rules should have made it very clear that this was the focal point of the whole question and hence it is not surprising that there were a large number of marks available. As well as allowing a year on year comparison, the numbers also required comparison between 2 different divisions: therefore, you in fact needed a 4 column approach rather than the normal 2 column approach to analysing changes over time. This is again an indication of the complexity of the figures and thus the marks available. In fact, part of the next Task could really be understood as an extension of the same overall points on costing: on this basis there would be approximately 18 marks for this concept. Again, this reflects our 11 Rules on Exhibit length and numerical complexity.

Task 3 – no new Exhibit and some basic financial reporting elements so 8 marks (Rules 2, 3 and 5)

As noted above, this Task extended a similar line of thinking on overhead costs allocations as was used in the previous Task. Candidates were not asked to read any further Exhibits for this Task and there was in fact only 1 further Exhibit for Q2 which was used for Task 4.

Candidates were given 2 sub-Tasks in this Task: further analysis of overheads and pricing and the impact of these methods on financial reporting of inventories. This should have alerted candidates to the fact that the calculations element (the first element) could not have been given a huge number of marks because there was a requirement for some financial reporting discussion. In fact, there were only 4 marks for the calculations, the same as for the financial reporting element.

Based on our 11 Rules, candidates should have considered how complex the financial reporting issues could be. The issue was the valuation of inventories, which is one of the first topics studied in your ACA qualification: the topic did not relate to group accounting, financial instruments or some other complicated accounting concept. Therefore, hopefully candidates would have realised that only around 4-5 marks would be available.

Task 4 – narrative only with 2 elements so 9 marks (Rules 1, 3 and 4)

The final Task was purely narrative in nature. Given the difficulty of the calculations, we are not surprised that the examiner's report indicates that many candidates attempted this Task first: this was probably sensible because it is a Task which is independent of the calculations and so could have been a safe option if candidates were worried about their upcoming numerical answers.

Although the Task wording did not specifically refer to an Exhibit by number, there was one remaining Exhibit (Exhibit 4) which had not been used to this point: in referring to the offer from Hexam to acquire one of the divisions, it should really have been clear that the examiner was expecting you to use Exhibit 4. This Exhibit is relatively short at half a page with only some simple numbers (on the percentage shareholding of different groups). On this basis, we would probably estimate around 4-5 marks for work involving the Exhibit. There was then clearly a separate assurance task involving Due Diligence procedures but with no numbers so an assumed allocation of around 4-5 marks would have worked well.

The 11 Rules and November 2014 Q2 Mark Allocation: Summary

Overall, based on the above, we believe that the November 2014 Q2 fits well with our 11 Rules as outlined in chapter 5 and as already explored in detail in the previous chapter. In other words, looking at the Exhibit length, the number of sub-Tasks, the nature of the question wording and the number of different topic areas included would have helped you correctly decide the spread of marks.

Although we strongly disagree with the advice that you should assume a roughly equal number of marks for each Task (advice which we know some other tuition providers are giving to students), the mark spread in this question (judged on a Task basis) was between a minimum of 8 marks (Task 3) and a maximum of 13 marks (Task 2). As such, it is the closest we have come to an equal weighting in any SBM question set in 2014 but even so you should be spending another 10 minutes on a question worth 13 marks compared to a question worth 8 marks so it is still useful to use the MAPs to allocate time.

This shows that our slightly more scientific approach of estimating the marks can cope well both with the normal situation where there is a very unequal spread of marks (all questions other than November 2014 Q2) and the exception to the rule where to spread is more equal. Our technique is still better than just assuming an equal spread as most of the time this will be far from correct.

The November 2014 Paper: One Last Important Reminder

This chapter is quite dense so we recommend that you re-read it several times so that you can see how to apply the 11 Rules in practice. Therefore you should automatically pick up this issue but as an important reminder we would like to emphasise again that in Q1 in the November 2014 paper the financial performance analysis Task (Task 1) was not the most important Task in terms of mark allocation. We have already identified that Task 1 in Q1 is a potential time trap (see chapter 3) because the amount of Exhibit material to absorb per mark available is relatively low (and also because this will be a standard and "familiar" kind of question) so our finding here that Task 2 in Q1 was actually more important in the November 2014 paper[35] is a **further warning not to try to pass Q1 just from a brilliant Task 1**.

7.5   The July 2015 Paper: A Brief Overview

The third real SBM paper contained 2 questions:

1. **Commex Cables plc**, worth 60 marks

2. **Paige plc**, worth 40 marks

We will analyse both questions under 2 specific headings:

- **Mark allocation by SBM topic area** (practical business advisory, financial reporting, Specialist Audit & Assurance, ethics)

- **Mark allocation applying the 11 Rules** (see chapter 5)

7.5.1   Commex Cables (60 marks)

This question concerned a large client, Commex Cables, which manufactured cables for the mining industry. The candidate assumes a role in advising the client on its plans to enter overseas markets, either via a subsidiary or distribution centre in Australia.

---

[35] To repeat, Task 2 carried a lot of marks because it contained lengthy Exhibit information, 2 separate bullet points for the sub-Tasks and covered multiple SBM disciplines (PBA and financial reporting).

1. Mark allocation by SBM topic area

Commex Cables contained the following elements:

1. NPV calculations for 2 strategies and evaluation of related supply chain issues (23 marks)

2. Comparison of 2 financing strategies (10 marks)

3. Provision of assurance to lenders under ISAE 3400 (10 marks)

4. Identification of key financial reporting issues from the strategies (9 marks)

5. Ethical issues arising from transactions at unusual rates and with potential benefits for company directors (8 marks)

Based on the above, we would suggest that the composition of the marks in Q1 was as follows:

Practical business advisory	33
Financial reporting	9
Audit & Assurance	10
Ethics	8
Total	**60**

The inclusion of both financial reporting and assurance Tasks in this question reduced the number of marks available for practical business advisory compared to some papers but practical business advisory was clearly still the main focus.

2. Mark allocation applying the 11 Rules

As always, only the total number of marks was indicated for students: we have derived our own Task-specific breakdown of the marks by looking at the markscheme.

Using the rules outlined in chapter 5, we would suggest that the following techniques could have been used to correctly estimate the split of the total of 60 marks into the different Tasks[36]:

Task 1 – Extensive Exhibits, financial information, multi-discipline and question bullets so 23 marks (Rules 1, 3, 4 & 7)

This first Task asked for evaluation of 2 different strategies via an NPV approach so immediately it would be clear that a lot of marks were available. In addition, this Task was the only Task to use bullet points in the list of Tasks: this should have been another indicator that the mark allocation would be

---

[36] We recommend that you keep a finger in page 60 providing our summary of the 11 Rules so that you can quickly flick back and check your understanding as we work through the July 2015 paper.

high. The Task required both Financial Management and Business Strategy skills so could be considered multi-discipline in nature (mark estimation rule 7).

Task 2 – Short Exhibit but long Task wording so 10 marks (Rules 1, 4 & 10)

Given the short nature of the Exhibit relevant to this Task, the number of marks is definitely towards the top end of what one might expect. It might have been possible to work this out by first working out the other Tasks. As there were 2 different financing methods to evaluate in a numerical way, it was perhaps a reasonable first step to think that there would be at least 4 marks per financing method. The wording which sets up the Task is also relatively long and asks candidates for a third element (an explanation of why the interest rate differs between the 2 financing methods) so this would be another indicator of a reasonable number of marks for this Task. Overall, however, this was the hardest Task to estimate correctly based on our rules.

Task 3 – Assurance with no Assurance in Q2 so balancing rule and 10 marks (Rule 8)

We know that Assurance should generally be worth 10 marks across the paper as a whole and given that there was no Assurance tested in Q2, we could be confident that there would be around 10 marks for this skill and therefore this Task.

Task 4 – Direction towards an Exhibit but not a dedicated Exhibit and short Task wording so 9 marks (Rules 2 & 4)

In this Task, the number of marks for financial reporting is towards the middle of the spectrum for this skills area. It may have been possible to identify this from looking at Rule 2 – the Exhibit to which candidates were directed to answer this question was shared with Task 1 so there was no dedicated Exhibit and accordingly the marks were relatively lower.

Additionally, the Task wording was very brief (the shortest of all Tasks listed) so Rule 4 would suggest that not too many marks were available.

Task 5 – Ethics so apply ethics 6-8 rule (Rule 9)

Along with the Assurance Task (Task 3), this Task would have been easy to work out. The question wording was very clear that this whole Task was ethical in nature. As there were 2 different ethical issues to look at, the estimate would have to be at the top end of the range and so an estimate of 8 marks would have been correct.

The 11 Rules and July 2015 Q1 Mark Allocation: Summary

Overall, the July 2015 paper fits well with our suggestion to look at **Exhibit length**, the **number of sub-Tasks**, the **existence of a dedicated Exhibit**, whether the Task is **multidiscipline**, the **balancing rule** and the **nature of the question wording** as your criteria in deciding the spread of marks. The spread was unequal, ranging from 8 marks to 23 marks. However, there were no indications that any Task was minor in nature so this should have maintained the minimum estimate at around 10 marks and then use of the Rules based on Exhibit length and sub-Tasks could have operated to indicate the greater importance of Tasks 1, 2 and 3 (in decreasing order of importance).

7.5.2 Paige plc (40 marks)

This question concerned a producer of processed, packaged foods. The performance of a subsidiary had declined since acquisition so the candidate was asked to analyse 2 potential strategies to improve performance. As part of this exercise, it was necessary to analyse the nature of the market environment facing the group.

1. Mark allocation by SBM topic area

Paige contained the following elements:

1. An assessment of the market environment and related risks (8 marks)

2. An evaluation of Strategy A (14 marks)

3. An evaluation of Strategy B, including valuation elements (14 marks)

4. A reasoned recommendation on which strategy to adopt (4 marks)

As noted elsewhere in this book, it is relatively unusual for a separate Task to be specifically allocated to recommendations – normally, these marks are mixed in with the marks for the underlying analysis. We will therefore not analyse this as a separate Task with respect to our rules.

Based on the above, we would suggest that the composition of the marks in Q2 was as follows:

Practical business advisory	40
Financial reporting	0
Audit & Assurance	0
Ethics	0
Total	**40**

In other words, the whole of this question related to practical business advisory – this is highly unusual but could perhaps be anticipated from use of Rule 8 (Balancing rule) as Q1 contained both Assurance and financial reporting issues so had already used up a lot of the mark allocation for those elements.

2. Mark allocation applying the 11 Rules[37]

Task 1 – Short Exhibit length, no Dedicated Exhibits, no financial information and short Task wording so 8 marks (Rules 1, 2, 3 & 4)

Unlike many SBM papers, the first Task in this instance was not a long financial performance review or similar. It was in fact a purely **narrative** analysis of the market background. The Exhibits on the market and the background of the relevant subsidiary were very short at only half a page or less each: many other questions have had longer Exhibits in relation to the market and company. This should have indicated that there were not huge number of marks available here. The Task wording was the shortest of any Task so this was again a hint that this Task would have attracted the fewest marks.

Task 2 – Dedicated Exhibit and long Task wording length so 14 marks (Rules 2 & 4)

This Task was the Task with the joint highest number of marks in this question. The Task wording made it clear that Exhibit 3 needed to be used and this Exhibit is specific only to the strategy analysed in this Task. Additionally, the Task wording is relatively lengthy and asks for a view on no less than 4 different proposals.

These facts should have alerted candidates to a high number of marks for this Task.

Task 3 – Dedicated Exhibit, financial information and long Task wording length so 14 marks (Rules 2, 3 & 4)

In a similar way to the previous Task, the fact that there was a different dedicated Exhibit for this Task together with the lengthy Task wording that included 2 sub-numbered elements (not strictly speaking bullet markers but the same principle) should have indicated that the Task would be worth quite a few marks.

In addition to the above, this Task was really the only numerical element of Question 2 so there would clearly have been some marks for this.

We would note that the marks allocated to Task 2 and Task 3 were identical, even though there were no numbers to use in Task 2. The reason for this appears to be that in the purely narrative Task 2, candidates had to evaluate 4 different potential sub-strategies whereas in the numerical Task 3, candidates only really had to look at 1 valuation area. In addition, as we have emphasised in many places in this book, there is more emphasis than you might expect for an accountancy exam in SBM on narrative elements so this should always be borne in mind. On this basis, it is not hugely surprising to see the same number of marks for Task 2 and 3.

7.6   The November 2015 Paper: A Brief Overview

The fourth real SBM paper contained 2 questions:

---

[37] We recommend that you keep a finger in page 60 providing our summary of the 11 Rules so that you can quickly flick back and check your understanding as we work through the July 2015 paper.

1. **Riller**, worth 60 marks

2. **Kinn plc**, worth 40 marks

We will analyse both questions under 2 specific headings:

- **Mark allocation by SBM topic area** (practical business advisory, financial reporting, Specialist Audit & Assurance, ethics)

- **Mark allocation applying the 11 Rules** (see chapter 5)

7.6.1   Riller (60 marks)

This question concerned a large client in the housebuilding industry. The company was recovering from a long recession in the industry but had managed to build up a large "landbank" which was its main asset. To expand its operations, the company was considering the acquisition of another company in a different part of the UK.

1. Mark allocation by SBM topic area

Riller contained the following elements:

1. Performance review, consideration of a potential acquisition price and financial reporting issues (35 marks but with 6 marks for financial reporting)

2. Comparison of 2 financing strategies (9 marks)

3. Considerations regarding Due Diligence procedures (9 marks)

4. Ethical issues in connection with potential inducements or bribery (9 marks)

Based on the above, we would suggest that the composition of the marks in Q1 was as follows:

Practical business advisory	38[38]
Financial reporting	6
Audit & Assurance	9
Ethics	7
Total	**60**

Task 1 contained more sub-Tasks than we have seen in any other SBM paper with 4 sub-Tasks being required. The final one of these on financial reporting would normally be split into a separate Task. To make it easier to match up our discussion with the question paper, we have not split this financial

---

[38] Calculated as 35 marks in Task 1 less 6 financial reporting marks in Task 1 plus 9 marks in Task 2.

reporting Task out into a separate Task and will instead discuss it within Task 1 below. However, this explains why there were quite so many marks for Task 1 on this paper

2. Mark allocation applying the 11 Rules

As always, only the total number of marks was indicated for students: we have derived our own Task-specific breakdown of the marks by looking at the markscheme.

Using the rules outlined in chapter 5, we would suggest that the following techniques could have been used to correctly estimate the split of the total of 60 marks into the different Tasks[39]:

Task 1 – Extensive Exhibits, financial information, multi-discipline and question bullets so 38 marks (Rules 1, 3, 4 & 7)

The above Rules should have indicated that this was definitely a major task as there was a lot of information and a lot to do, including various numerical elements. The question ranged over performance review, valuations and financial reporting so was clearly multidiscipline in nature. The question had 4 different bullet point markers allocated (the most we have seen in any single SBM Task) so this was again an indicator of a lot of marks being available.

Within the total of 35 marks, only 6 marks were allocated to the financial reporting issues on consolidation. Although the Task wording directs students specifically to Exhibit 4 in relation to the financial reporting issues (something which could have indicated a possible dedicated Exhibit on financial reporting), the amount of material in relation to financial reporting in Exhibit 4 is very minimal, being around 5% of all the text in that Exhibit. This should therefore have been an indication that the relevant issues would not have attracted many marks.

In fact, Question 2 contained quite a few more marks for financial reporting (9 marks) through a more detailed question so use of the balancing rule and knowledge that there are only a maximum of around 15 marks in total for financial reporting across the paper as a whole could also have helped allocate a small number of marks here.

Task 2 – Short Exhibit but long Task wording so 9 marks (Rule 4)

We have seen above that the discussion of 2 different financing methods in Question 1 in the July 2015 paper attracted 10 marks. This Task was very similar to the July 2015 Task and this time it attracted 9 marks. In other words, a very similar number of marks for the same style of Task.

In this case, there were specific bullet point markers in the Task wording (something which would normally indicate quite a few marks to be allocated) but one of these reminded students to offer a recommendation rather than setting a separate sub-Task (considering that you should always be recommending in SBM anyway). Additionally, the Exhibit text relevant to the 2 financing options was very short.

---

[39] We recommend that you keep a finger in page 60 providing our summary of the 11 Rules so that you can quickly flick back and check your understanding as we work through the November 2015 paper.

Task 3 – Assurance and no Assurance in Q2 so balancing rule and 9 marks (Rule 8)

We know that Assurance should generally be worth 10 marks across the paper as a whole and given that there was no Assurance tested in Q2, we could be confident that there would be around 10 marks for this skill and therefore this Task. In this case, there were 9 marks so not a material difference from our prediction.

Task 4 – Ethics so apply ethics 6-8 rule (Rule 9)

Along with the Assurance Task (Task 3), this Task would have been easy to work out. The question wording was very clear that this whole Task was ethical in nature. The marks allocated fell right in the middle of our suggested range of 6 to 8 marks.

Overall, Question 1 was a good fit with the predictions from our Rules.

7.6.2 Kinn plc (40 marks)

This question concerned a listed engineering company with various different divisions. The company had performed poorly in recent years and was considering a restructuring. The Board required advice from the candidate about the impact of the disposal of a division, use of the cash generated and interest rate risks.

1. Mark allocation by SBM topic area

Kinn plc contained the following elements:

1. A review of forecast financial performance together with discussion of the financial reporting implications of the sale of the division (IFRS 5) (21 marks with 9 marks for financial reporting)

2. Analysis of interest rate hedging techniques (10 marks)

3. Discussion of alternative use of funds from the sale of a division together with financing considerations (9 marks)

Based on the above, we would suggest that the composition of the marks in Q2 was as follows:

Practical business advisory	31
Financial reporting	9
Audit & Assurance	0
Ethics	0
Total	**40**

As with Question 1 from this paper (see above), the financial reporting Task was mixed in with the first Task in this question, rather than being split out as normal. We know from the model answer that there were 9 marks for this element alone as the markscheme does split out the financial reporting component into a separate Task. However, to make it easier to compare our points back to the question paper we have left this financial reporting element as part of Task 1 here.

2. Mark allocation applying the 11 Rules[40]

Task 1 – Financial information, long Task wording length with bullets and multi-discipline so 21 marks (Rules 3, 4 & 7)

This first Task clearly asked for numerical analysis and there are some lettered sub-Tasks to complete (not literally bullets but the same principle). The Task wording is longer than any other Task in this question. The Task also involves different disciplines as there are some practical business advisory and financial reporting implications to consider.

In respect of the financial reporting issues, which in some papers would have been presented as a separate Task, we would note that the number of marks at 9 marks is significantly higher than the financial reporting issues in Question 1 of this paper (see above). The reason for this appears to be that the examiners wanted a variety of points to be made in connection with IFRS 5 in this question whereas in Question 1 there were only 6 marks for various consolidation and IFRS 13 issues. It is not completely clear why there were so many more marks available for IFRS 5 issues in Question 2 but we would bear this in mind for future reference.

Task 2 – Financial information and Dedicated Exhibit so 10 marks (Rules 2 & 3)

This Task required use of brought forward knowledge from the Financial Management paper in relation to interest rate derivatives. It was clearly a numerical question, giving the Task a few more marks than would otherwise be expected (Rule 3) and there was a dedicated Exhibit 3 which was not used in any other Task. This should have indicated that there were a reasonable number of marks available but there were no bullet point markers so the number of marks did not go too high and remained at 10 marks.

Task 3 – Dedicated Exhibit, financial information and Task wording length (Rules 2, 3, 4 & 10)

This final Task allocated 9 marks for the analysis of 2 alternative issues in relation to financing. There was a dedicated Exhibit 4, indicating that there would be a reasonable number of marks. The Task wording for Task 3 was almost identical in length to Task 2 and the number of marks between these 2 Tasks was also identical, thus indicating the benefit of looking at the amount of Task wording when deciding on the mark allocation.

We have seen in 2 other instances in relation to the 2015 papers (see above) that if there are 2 issues to consider in relation to **financing** then there will tend to be around 8 to 10 marks available and this was the case again here. This has led us to create our Rule 10.

---

[40] We recommend that you keep a finger in page 60 providing our summary of the 11 Rules so that you can quickly flick back and check your understanding as we work through the November 2015 paper.

7.7 The July 2016 Paper: A Brief Overview

The fifth real SBM paper contained 2 questions:

1. **Kiera Healy Company**, worth 60 marks

2. **Quinter**, worth 40 marks

We will analyse both questions under 2 specific headings:

- **Mark allocation by SBM topic area** (practical business advisory, financial reporting, Specialist Audit & Assurance, ethics)

- **Mark allocation applying the 11 Rules** (see chapter 5)

7.7.1 Kiera Healy Company (60 marks)

This question involved a manufacturer of luxury toiletries. The company was considering international expansion into the US, subject to a review of the relevant risks. The company was also considering selling one of its brands to another company.

1. Mark allocation by SBM topic area

Kiera Healy Company contained the following elements:

1. Review of strategic and operating issues relating to an international expansion (11 marks)

2. Analysis of foreign currency risk (13 marks)

3. Financial reporting implications of investments in a warehouse (15 marks)

4. Branding and assurance procedures (14 marks)

5. Ethical issues in relation to governance (7 marks)

Based on the above, we would suggest that the composition of the marks in Q1 was as follows:

Practical business advisory	24
Financial reporting	15
Audit & Assurance	14
Ethics	7
Total	**60**

2. Mark allocation applying the 11 Rules

As always, only the total number of marks was indicated for students: we have derived our own Task-specific breakdown of the marks by looking at the markscheme.

Using the rules outlined in chapter 5, we would suggest that the following techniques could have been used to correctly estimate the split of the total of 60 marks into the different Tasks[41]:

Task 1 – Extensive Exhibits and financial information and multi-discipline (Rules 1, 3 and 7)

This first Task clearly involved a lot of Exhibit information to analyse, including a large amount of financial information. It would also have been clear that the Task was multidiscipline in nature and would therefore fall under the "practical business advisory" element of SBM which we know from discussion elsewhere in this book will always account for a lot of marks.

Task 2 – Dedicated Exhibit and financial information (Rules 2 and 3)

This Task had a dedicated Exhibit as the information was clearly only usable for a derivatives calculation. This would indicate that a good number of marks would be available. Additionally, derivatives calculations obviously involve financial information by definition so this would again boost the score up slightly.

Task 3 – Dedicated Exhibit and multi-discipline (Rules 2 and 3)

This Task clearly involved both financial reporting and an NPV calculation and therefore was multidiscipline in nature, indicating a high mark. There was also a Exhibit which only had to be used for this Task so the dedicated Exhibit rule applied.

Task 4 – Assurance (Rule 6)

We know that Assurance should always be between 10 and 15 marks in an SBM examination. Therefore, asking which discipline is involved would have helped estimate the mark correctly here.

Task 5 – Ethics so apply ethics 6-8 rule (Rule 9)

This Task would have been easy to work out. The question wording was very clear that this whole Task was ethical in nature. The marks allocated fell right in the middle of our suggested range of 6 to 8 marks.

7.7.2   Quinter (40 marks)

This question involved an importer of electrical goods which was planning to list on the AIM market before 2020.

---

[41] We recommend that you keep a finger in page 60 providing our summary of the 11 Rules so that you can quickly flick back and check your understanding as we work through the July 2016 paper.

1. Mark allocation by SBM topic area

Quinter contained the following elements:

1. Performance analysis of financial and operating data (14 marks)

2. Identification of additional data that the Board should have to help in its decision-making (9 marks)

3. Financial reporting relating to inventories (5 marks)

4. Discussion of corporate governance and performance improvement (5 marks)

5. Evaluation of sustainability policy (7 marks)

Based on the above, we would suggest that the composition of the marks in Q2 was as follows:

Practical business advisory	28
Financial reporting	5
Audit & Assurance	7
Ethics	0
Total	**40**

2. Mark allocation applying the 11 Rules

As always, only the total number of marks was indicated for students: we have derived our own Task-specific breakdown of the marks by looking at the markscheme.

Using the rules outlined in chapter 5, we would suggest that the following techniques could have been used to correctly estimate the split of the total of 40 marks into the different Tasks[42]:

Task 1 – Extensive Exhibits, dedicated Exhibit, financial information and multi-discipline (Rules 1, 2, 3 and 7)

This Task clearly involved more Exhibit data than any of the other Tasks so was always going to be worth a lot of marks. Additionally, students should have known that performance reviews are given quite a lot of weighting in the marks available. The Task also had a dedicated Exhibit which contained financial information only so therefore the dedicated Exhibit and financial information rules would both apply.

---

[42] We recommend that you keep a finger in page 60 providing our summary of the 11 Rules so that you can quickly flick back and check your understanding as we work through the July 2016 paper.

Task 2 – Dedicated Exhibit and bullet points (Rules 2 and 4)

This Task had a dedicated Exhibit on decision-making and data management by the Board. Additionally, the Task wording contained bullet point markers (unlike most of the other sets of question wording) so should accordingly have been given a few more marks in your estimate.

Task 3 – Exhibit length and balancing rule (Rules 1 and 8)

This Task did not have a dedicated Exhibit and only had a few lines relating to inventories in one of the other Exhibits. In addition, a lot of financial reporting marks had already been allocated in Q1 so applying the balancing rule would mean that there were just a few marks remaining here.

Task 4 – Tricky!

The mark allocation here was difficult to estimate in advance – most of the Assurance marks would have appeared to have been used up by Q1 but there were a further 5 marks available for the area of corporate governance, which is usually classed within the Assurance marks. This Task was therefore a rare exception to the normal rules as arguably there were too many Assurance marks in this paper as a whole.

Task 5 – Dedicated Exhibit and discipline (Rules 2 and 6)

Again, the dedicated Exhibit rule would have helped for this Task. Together with Task 2, this Task was the only Task to have bullet point markers in the question wording, suggesting to add a couple more marks to your estimate.

As already noted, there was a lot of Assurance in this paper and arguably the 7 marks relating to environmental issues here could be classed as Assurance marks within the Environmental and Social Audits and Assurance element of the syllabus. At the same time, the question was relatively practical and did not require detailed knowledge of Assurance rules so perhaps the examiners are treating environmental advisory points as part of Practical Business Advisory.

In this case, there is definitely a learning point to take away from this paper as it could mean there will be additional marks for environmental issues over and above those allocated to Assurance in the paper as a whole.

7.8   The November 2016 Paper: A Brief Overview

The sixth real SBM paper contained 2 questions:

1. **Wooster**, worth 62 marks

2. **Phantom West Airlines**, worth 38 marks

We will analyse both questions under 2 specific headings:

- **Mark allocation by SBM topic area** (practical business advisory, financial reporting, Specialist Audit & Assurance, ethics)

- **Mark allocation applying the 11 Rules** (see chapter 5)

7.8.1 Wooster (62 marks)

This question related to a luxury sports car manufacturer which had suffered from underinvestment and lost competitiveness against rivals. The company was considering 2 methods of improving performance.

1. Mark allocation by SBM topic area

Wooster contained the following elements:

1. A financial appraisal of a project (16 marks)

2. Identification of KPIs in relation to sustainability (9 marks)

3. A financial appraisal of a second project (12 marks)

4. Financial reporting considerations in relation to a factory closure (6 marks)

5. Analysis of financial and operating data (12 marks)

6. Ethical issues in relation to redundancies and share options (7 marks)

Based on the above, we would suggest that the composition of the marks in Q1 was as follows:

Practical business advisory	40
Financial reporting	6
Audit & Assurance	9
Ethics	7
Total	**62**

2. Mark allocation applying the 11 Rules

As always, only the total number of marks was indicated for students: we have derived our own Task-specific breakdown of the marks by looking at the markscheme.

Using the rules outlined in chapter 5, we would suggest that the following techniques could have been used to correctly estimate the split of the total of 62 marks into the different Tasks[43]:

Task 1 – Extensive Exhibits, financial information and long Task working (Rules 1, 3 and 4)

This Task contained a lot of Exhibit material to read, much of which was financial in nature. The Task wording was also long (and longer than any other Task). Therefore it was worth the most marks.

Task 2 – No dedicated Exhibit and Assurance, with no Assurance in Q2 (Rules 2, 6 and 8)

We know that Assurance will be worth 10-15 marks across the paper as a whole. There were no Assurance marks at all in Q2 so we assume that the reason the mark here was towards the bottom end of the 10-15 marks bracket was due to the fact that the Assurance request was found within a longer Exhibit – there were only 4 very short paragraphs on Assurance to consider.

Task 3 – Extension of Task 1

This Task was based on the same Exhibits as Task 1 so the mark was similar. The mark was slightly lower as candidates were asked to focus on a financial analysis of project 2 whereas the analysis of project 1 (Task 1) also had to look at supply chain issues.

Task 4 – Balancing rule with plenty of Financial Reporting marks in Q2 (Rule 8)

Here the balancing rule would have worked very well indeed because there were a lot of Financial Reporting marks in Q2.

Of course, the challenge here is that if you are attempting Q1 first then you may not have known what was coming in Q2. We leave it your discretion as to whether you think it is going to be useful to quickly look at the requirements for Q2 when determining the mark allocation for Q1 in relation to areas such as Assurance or financial reporting.

Task 5 – Detailed Exhibit and financial information (Rules 1 and 3)

This Task required review of a detailed set of financial and operating data contained in Exhibit 1. The data provided not only the standard metrics such as revenue and profit but also some company specific operating data in relation to the number of cards sold and the number of employees at the company. This would have provided plenty of data to analyse.

Based on our review of other past papers above, an allocation of around 12-14 marks for a performance review in Q1 does seem relatively common.

Task 6 – Ethics so apply ethics 6-8 rule (Rule 9)

This Task would have been easy to work out. The question wording was very clear that this whole Task was ethical in nature. The marks allocated fell right in the middle of our suggested range of 6 to 8 marks.

---

[43] We recommend that you keep a finger in page 60 providing our summary of the 11 Rules so that you can quickly flick back and check your understanding as we work through the November 2016 paper.

7.8.2 Phantom West Airlines (38 marks)

In this question, candidates had to advise a UK-based scheduled airline which specialised in long haul flights. The company had the opportunity to operate a new route to India and as a second matter wanted some advice on whether to hedge its fuel costs.

1. Mark allocation by SBM topic area

Phantom West Airlines contained the following elements:

1. Calculation of project revenue (9 marks)

2. A comparison of financing methods for a new aircraft (8 marks)

3. Financial reporting issues relating to the 2 finance methods (6 marks)

4. Financial reporting impact of a cash flow hedge (7 marks)

5. Analysis of hedging strategies relating to fuel prices (8 marks)

Based on the above, we would suggest that the composition of the marks in Q2 was as follows:

Practical business advisory	25
Financial reporting	13
Audit & Assurance	0
Ethics	0
Total	**38**

2. Mark allocation applying the 11 Rules

As always, only the total number of marks was indicated for students: we have derived our own Task-specific breakdown of the marks by looking at the markscheme[44].

We would note that the mark allocation of this question was extremely even between the different Tasks, with most Tasks being 7 or 8 marks and then with one Task having 9 marks and another just 6 marks. This is in line with the relative Exhibit length as the Exhibits for Tasks 4 and 5 are almost identical in length, at one page each. The amount of Exhibit material for Task 3 on financing methods is relatively short and hence this Task had the lowest number of marks.

---

[44] We recommend that you keep a finger in page 60 providing our summary of the 11 Rules so that you can quickly flick back and check your understanding as we work through the November 2016 paper.

The balancing rule (Rule 8) would also have been helpful as there had been 6 financial reporting marks in Q1 already (see above) so as financial reporting is not supposed to account for more than 20 marks in total, that would leave 14 or so for Q2 – in fact, there were 13 marks for financial reporting, which is not a material difference from the estimate of 14.

On this basis, we have not worked through each separate Task as we believe that the above analysis of the Rules should explain the position fully.

7.9   The July 2017 Paper: A Brief Overview

The seventh real SBM paper contained 2 questions:

1. **Best Baked Bread**, worth 62 marks

2. **Moonbeam Marine Yachts**, worth 38 marks

We will analyse both questions under 2 specific headings:

- **Mark allocation by SBM topic area** (practical business advisory, financial reporting, Specialist Audit & Assurance, ethics)

- **Mark allocation applying the 11 Rules** (see chapter 5)

7.9.1   Best Baked Bread (62 marks)

This question related to a listed bakery company which had come under pressure from its largest customer (SaveLow), putting pressure on financial performance. The company also had to deal with price volatility in one of its main raw materials (wheat).

1. Mark allocation by SBM topic area

Best Baked Bread contained the following elements:

1. Analysis of a proposed contract renewal with SaveLow, including the impact on liquidity, cash flows and strategy (23 marks)

2. Analysis of hedging for changes in the price of wheat, including discussion of financial reporting implications (18 marks)

3. Preparation of a forecast of operating profit and discussion of financial reporting implications (13 marks)

4. Ethical issues arising from the use of low quality wheat (8 marks)

Based on the above, we would suggest that the composition of the marks in Q1 was as follows:

Practical business advisory	42
Financial reporting	12
Audit & Assurance	0
Ethics	8
Total	**62**

2. Mark allocation applying the 11 Rules

As always, only the total number of marks was indicated for students: we have derived our own Task-specific breakdown of the marks by looking at the markscheme.

Using the rules outlined in chapter 5, we would suggest that the following techniques could have been used to correctly estimate the split of the total of 62 marks into the different Tasks[45]:

Task 1 – Extensive Exhibits, financial information, multi-discipline and long Task wording (Rules 1, 3, 4 and 7)

This Task required 3 lengthy Exhibits to be read, with a lot of financial information to work through. The Task was also multi-discipline in nature. The Task wording was the longest of any of the Tasks. Therefore, a substantial number of marks were available for this Task.

Task 2 – Long, dedicated Exhibit, financial information and multi-discipline (Rules 1, 2, 3 and 7)

This Task had a dedicated Exhibit which was only relevant to this part of the question. The Exhibit was also quite long at over a page. Candidates had to look at the operational impact of using wheat derivatives but also had to discuss the financial reporting consequences, making the Task multi-discipline in nature. For these reasons, this Task attracted the second highest number of marks.

Task 3 – Short Exhibit (Rule 1)

Although this Task involved financial forecasting of performance and might therefore have been assumed to attract a lot of credit, the Exhibit material was very short at just half a page (plus the text setting the question requirements). Therefore, although there was a dedicated Exhibit with financial information and some fairly lengthy text setting out the question requirements, the short nature of the Exhibit appears to have "overruled" these other mark estimation rules. This is an important learning point to take away, given that this is a relatively recent past paper.

---

[45] We recommend that you keep a finger in page 60 providing our summary of the 11 Rules so that you can quickly flick back and check your understanding as we work through the July 2017 paper.

Task 4 – Ethics (Rule 9)

This Task was easy to estimate as it was a fairly standard SBM ethics type of question and therefore fell within our estimated range of 6-8 marks.

Overall, the mark allocation in this question appears to fit well with our mark allocation rules but we would definitely draw your attention to the unusually low number of marks given for Task 3, despite this involving a financial forecast which might ordinarily have led students to suspect that a lot of marks were available. As noted above, the Exhibit length for this Task was very short. Relatedly, we would note that a lot of marks were available for the derivatives Task (Task 2), given that there were a couple of different hedges to consider and that candidates also had to look at financial reporting issues. Please bear these points in mind for the next time you have a forecast within a question that also looks at hedging issues.

7.9.2   Moonbeam Marine Yachts (38 marks)

In this question, candidates had to advise a private equity firm (RFI) which specialised in the purchase of distressed investments and was considering investing in a yacht manufacturing company (MMY). Candidates had to advise on appropriate Due Diligence procedures and had to review some proposals for the financial reconstruction of the proposed target.

1. Mark allocation by SBM topic area

Moonbeam Marine Yachts contained the following elements:

1. Due Diligence procedures and financial reporting (12 marks)

2. Explanation of current financial position and viability as a going concern (5 marks)

3. Evaluation of the potential return from a proposed corporate recovery plan (7 marks)

4. Appraisal of 2 alternative proposals for the financial reconstruction of the target (14 marks)

Based on the above, we would suggest that the composition of the marks in Q2 was as follows:

Practical business advisory	25
Financial reporting	4
Audit & Assurance	9
Ethics	0
Total	**38**

2. Mark allocation applying the 11 Rules

As always, only the total number of marks was indicated for students: we have derived our own Task-specific breakdown of the marks by looking at the markscheme[46].

Task 1 – Balancing rule (Rule 8)

As there were no marks for Assurance in Q1, the balancing rule could be used to estimate that there would be around 10 marks for Assurance in Q2 in order to provide the correct balance of marks across SBM syllabus areas in the examination as a whole (Assurance must always account for around 10 marks per paper, according to the examiners).

The Task also required some financial reporting points so there would be a few marks for these – the balancing rule could also be applied here since we have seen that there were 12 marks for financial reporting in Q1, meaning that there would not be a huge number of marks for the same discipline in Q2. The balancing rule would therefore have been very handy for this Task. Please note that the Exhibit relevant to this part of the question was very short at only half a page so the balancing rule and requirement for Assurance to constitute 10 marks per paper appears to overrule Rule 1 on Exhibit length (and also Rule 2 on a dedicated Exhibit since the relevant Exhibit was only applicable to this first Task).

Task 2 – Very lower number of marks … but short Task text (Rule 4)

The number of marks available for this Task was surprisingly low at only 5 marks as there was quite a lot of Exhibit material (including financial information) to take into account to explain the financial position of the company. However, it is noticeable that Task 2 had the shortest instructions to the candidate of any Task in Q2 (only a single sentence of 1.5 lines of text) so this was perhaps a clue that there would not be many marks available. We would also note that the question only asked about "financial position" and not about "financial performance" so there was no need to look at the Income Statement.

Looking at the model answer, no calculations were required and the points were rather straightforward: the target had breached 2 debt covenants, its assets had low net realisable values and losses before tax were being made but EBITDA was positive so operational cash flows might be reasonable (further information would be required).

We think it is very likely that many candidates would have done too much for this Task as it could potentially have been interpreted as a performance review question. This is another reason why it is important to apply judgement by looking at the mark allocation for all Tasks rather than making any assumptions about individual Tasks. If a candidate had interpreted this Task as a performance review and engaged in a lot of ratio analysis then this would simply have wasted a lot of time as only 5 marks were available. Therefore, always consider the likely mark allocation of all other Tasks before deciding on the allocation for a particular Task.

---

[46] We recommend that you keep a finger in page 60 providing our summary of the 11 Rules so that you can quickly flick back and check your understanding as we work through the July 2017 paper.

Tasks 3 & 4 – Exhibit length (Rule 1)

It is helpful to deal with these 2 Tasks under the same heading because we can use our rule on Exhibit length to allocate the marks here. Exhibit 3 was relevant to Task 3 and consisted of approximately half a page of text – Exhibit 4 was relevant to Task 4 and consisted of a full page of text. Based on the ratio of Exhibit lengths, Task 4 could therefore have been expected to account for twice as many marks as Task 3 and that is exactly what happened in practice because Task 4 was worth 14 marks whereas Task 3 was worth 7 marks.

Both Tasks required calculations and had roughly the same amount of text to set up the requirements of the Task. Additionally, both Tasks had their own dedicated Exhibit. It was therefore the Exhibit length that made the difference to the marks available because otherwise the mark allocation would have been equal based on our dedicated Exhibit (Rule 2), financial information (Rule 3) and Task wording length (Rule 4) rules.

7.10   The November 2017 Paper: A Brief Overview

The eighth real SBM paper contained 2 questions:

1. **Gemstone Jewellery**, worth 58 marks

2. **Hayfield**, worth 42 marks

We will analyse both questions under 2 specific headings:

- **Mark allocation by SBM topic area** (practical business advisory, financial reporting, Specialist Audit & Assurance, ethics)

- **Mark allocation applying the 11 Rules** (see chapter 5)

7.10.1 Gemstone Jewellery (58 marks)

In this question, the candidate worked for a venture capital firm (ICF) which specialised in providing equity and debt capital for management buyouts (MBOs). ICF was considering an investment into Gemstone Jewellery which owned and operated a chain of retail jewellery shops. The candidate was required to forecast the value of Gemstone's equity, consider Due Diligence procedures, discuss financial reporting issues and consider ethical issues arising from the proposed MBO.

1. Mark allocation by SBM topic area

Gemstone Jewellery contained the following elements:

1. Preparation of a forecast of the value of Gemstone's equity at 2 different dates, with supporting explanations (22 marks)

2. Discussion of the potential benefits and risks of the MBO for ICF, the MBO team and Gemstone's bank (12 marks)

3. Discussion of appropriate Due Diligence procedures in relation to key financial, commercial and operational risks (7 marks)

4. Explanation of the financial reporting implications of Gemstone's strategies to sell a workshop, undertake refurbishment and use a sale and leaseback arrangement (8 marks)

5. Ethical issues arising from potentially untransparent action by a member of the Gemstone Board (9 marks)

Based on the above, we would suggest that the composition of the marks in Q1 was as follows:

Practical business advisory	34
Financial reporting	8
Audit & Assurance	7
Ethics	9
Total	**58**

2. Mark allocation applying the 11 Rules

As always, only the total number of marks was indicated for students: we have derived our own Task-specific breakdown of the marks by looking at the markscheme.

Using the rules outlined in chapter 5, we would suggest that the following techniques could have been used to correctly estimate the split of the total of 58 marks into the different Tasks[47]:

Task 1 – Extensive Exhibits and financial information (Rules 1 and 3)

At 22 marks, Task 1 was towards the top end of what we would normally see for an SBM valuations question. However, candidates had to read several pages of information and integrate a range of issues in order to be able to perform the calculation. The question wording specifically asked for a free cash flow (FCF) model to be used, meaning that very detailed NPV-style calculations were required – FCF requires more calculations than other valuation models so this would obviously boost the mark.

---

[47] We recommend that you keep a finger in page 60 providing our summary of the 11 Rules so that you can quickly flick back and check your understanding as we work through the November 2017 paper.

Task 2 – Extensive Exhibits, detailed Task wording and bullets and adapted Rule 11 (Rules 1, 4 and 11)

Rule 11 states that there will normally be 8 marks for a discussion of risks/strategy but Task 2 in this question had 12 marks available. This obviously exceeds 8 marks but note that the question wording specifically asked candidates to consider 3 different stakeholders, which is fairly high. Candidates would also have had to absorb quite a lot of information (essentially the same amount of information as was required for Task 1 which, as indicated above, was quite extensive) in order to be able to deal with this Task.

Finally, we would note that the task wording for Task 2 was quite detailed and used specific bullet points (unlike any of the other Tasks in Q1) so this should have served as a further indicator that a lot of marks would have been on offer.

For these reasons, it was perhaps not too surprising to see the risks discussion exceed our 8 mark general prediction because there were some further indicators to consider. This reminds us to always apply judgement when using our mark estimate rules.

Task 3 – Balancing rule (Rule 8)

It would have been quite hard to correctly estimate the number of marks available for Due Diligence in Task 3. There was no specific Exhibit (or section within an Exhibit) which related specifically to this Task so the Exhibit length rule could not be used. In fact, candidates would have had to read most of the Exhibits for the question as a whole in order to be able to address this Task specifically.

Therefore, ordinarily one would have expected quite a few marks to be available. However, Assurance was also tested in Q2 in this examination and the number of marks available for Assurance in each question was approximately equal. There may therefore be something to be said for quickly looking at the Tasks for both questions before determining your Q1- or Q2-specific marks estimate. Obviously, this would use up valuable time but perhaps if you look at the Tasks simply to determine the basic focus (PBA, financial reporting, Assurance or ethics) then you may be able to get the information required without going into the details, thereby losing too much time and perhaps creating confusion by having too many Tasks in your head at the same time.

Task 4 – Dedicated Exhibit, short Task wording length and Balancing rule (Rules 2, 4 and 8)

At only 8 marks, there were not all that many marks available for this Task despite the fact that there was a dedicated Exhibit and several different financial reporting issues to deal with. However, it is noticeable that the Task wording was the shortest of any of the Tasks so this should have been an indication not to allocate too many marks.

Additionally, there were quite a few marks available for financial reporting in Q2 so it would not have been possible to allocate too many marks for financial reporting to Q1 since the examination paper as a whole would then have breached the total number of marks permitted for this syllabus area. We would therefore make some of the same points in relation to the Balancing rule as were made regarding Task 3 above: subject to time constraints, it can sometimes be beneficial to see what is set in the other question in the examination paper when determining how many marks to allocate to certain Tasks. Again, you will have to find a way of doing this quickly under time pressure by

106

identifying the focus of the Tasks in the other question without looking at that other question in too much detail.

Task 5 – Ethics (Rule 9)

This Task was easy to estimate as it was a fairly standard SBM ethics type of question. Strictly speaking, the marks available slightly exceeded our 6-8 marks estimate but only by 1 mark so this would not really have caused too many problems.

7.10.2 Hayfield (42 marks)

In this question, candidates had to advise a company that manufactured high quality heavy equipment for the construction industry. Candidates had to review performance against budget (including analysis of variances), discuss the company's hedging strategies and consider strategies for overseas expansion.

1. Mark allocation by SBM topic area

Hayfield contained the following elements:

1. Analysis of performance against budget (16 marks)

2. Explanation of why a loss was being made on currency hedging and explanation of the financial reporting implications of the loss (7 marks)

3. Evaluation of potential strategies for overseas expansion (7 marks)

4. Consideration of the financial reporting implications of overseas expansion (subsidiary or joint arrangement) (6 marks)

5. Discussion of how Assurance procedures (including Due Diligence) could be used to reduce the level of risk involved in working with a partner organisation (6 marks)

Based on the above, we would suggest that the composition of the marks in Q2 was as follows:

Practical business advisory	30
Financial reporting	6
Audit & Assurance	6
Ethics	0
Total	**42**

2. Mark allocation applying the 11 Rules

As always, only the total number of marks was indicated for students: we have derived our own Task-specific breakdown of the marks by looking at the markscheme[48].

Task 1 – Exhibit length, financial information and Task wording length and bullets (Rules 1, 3 and 4)

This Task contained very long Task wording with 2 overall bullet points to consider: within the first bullet point there was then a separate split into 6 further bullet points that needed to be considered as reconciling factors. This was the most extensive use of different bullets in any Task wording that we have seen in SBM so it should have been an indication that a lot of marks would have been available.

Additionally, as the Task involved a reconciliation between actual operating profit and budgeted operating profit, the Task was clearly financial in nature so again the mark allocation would have been quite high.

Task 2 – Short Exhibit length and no dedicated Exhibit (Rules 1 and 2)

Although this Task related to hedging and derivatives (an area which normally attracts quite a few marks in SBM), there was very little Exhibit text to read at only one-third of a page: this is much less than is frequently seen in SBM hedging and derivatives questions. Additionally, and again like many other examples of SBM hedging and derivatives questions, there was no dedicated Exhibit for this Task as the information was instead included as part of a longer Exhibit which was relevant to various different Tasks. Accordingly, the mark allocation for this Task was relatively modest at just 7 marks.

Task 3 – Narrative risks/strategy 8 marks (Rule 11)

It should have been easy to estimate the mark allocation for this Task as it involved a narrative-only discussion of overseas expansion strategies. Additionally, there were 2 different strategies to consider and this "two-fold" element is also very common in narrative risks/strategy questions in SBM. Therefore, the mark allocation was very much in line with our 8 mark rule for this type of question.

Task 4 – No dedicated Exhibit and Balancing rule (Rules 2 and 8)

There were 2 main financial reporting issues to consider: a joint arrangement versus a new subsidiary. As these are relatively complicated financial reporting areas, perhaps an assumption of 4 marks per issue would have been reasonable, given that SBM is not designed as a financial reporting exam so the marks per issue would be less than in CR. Assuming 4 marks per issue for both issues would suggest an estimate of 8 marks which was not too far off the 6 marks that could have been awarded in practice for this Task.

---

[48] We recommend that you keep a finger in page 60 providing our summary of the 11 Rules so that you can quickly flick back and check your understanding as we work through the November 2017 paper.

The information necessary to deal with this question was not contained in a dedicated Exhibit and was instead mixed into an Exhibit which also needed to be used for Task 3. This should therefore have indicated that there would not be a huge number of marks available.

Finally, we noted that there were a few marks for financial reporting issues in Q1 so awarding more than 7 or 8 marks for financial reporting in Q2 would not have been possible without potentially breaching the maximum number of marks that can be awarded in the examination as a whole for this topic area, according to the examiners.

Task 5 – No dedicated Exhibit and Balancing rule (Rules 2 and 8)

Our analysis here is essentially the same as for Task 4 above but now applied to Assurance. There was no Exhibit specific to this Task and quite a few marks had already been awarded for Assurance in Q1. Therefore, it would definitely not have been possible to award the 10 full marks for Assurance here in Q2 and the allocation was therefore somewhat lower at 6 marks.

Even so, we would note that with 7 marks for Assurance in Q1, the total of 13 marks for Assurance in this past paper as a whole was relatively high and, indeed, slightly above the 10 marks which the examiners have suggested will normally be available. Once again, it is important to use your judgement rather than regarding either our own mark estimate Rules or the statements of the examiners as imposing strict quantitative limits in all cases. Both our own mark estimate Rules and the statements of the examiners should be treated as approximate indicators only.

Chapter 8   Useful Points from the Examiners' Comments on the Past Papers

---

Learning Points

After reading this chapter, you must be able to:

1. spot the patterns in examiner comments regarding "weak" and "strong" scripts
2. implement an approach that avoids the failings of "weak" scripts

---

8.1   Useful Points in the Examiners' Comments

As under the old Technical Integration syllabus papers and other "evolved ACA" papers, SBM examination paper markschemes contain a grey-shaded box area after each question which contains comments from the examiners. As tutors, we believe that these comments are really gold dust[49] and definitely something to study carefully because they explain key student mistakes[50]. **However, we know that students rarely look at this useful information (or do not look at it in detail).** Therefore, we present here a summary of key learning points in this chapter, based on reviewing the comments on the SBM past papers available at the time of writing.

8.2   July 2014 Examiners' Comments

Question 1   Funnel Cruises plc

Task 1   Performance analysis (review of management accounting information)

This Task was the first analysis of financial information under the new evolved syllabus "mini-Case" style questions so we strongly advise you to read the examiner comments carefully to understand what is required.

Weak answers

- Made **insufficient use** of the data

- Made **only occasional references** to the data

- Calculated gross profit and operating profit margin but did not go beyond this to calculate **scenario-specific** indicators (such as revenue generated per customer)

---

[49] This is another way in which SBM serves as a "bridge" or precursor to the Case Study examination – candidates would have to be insane to attempt the Case Study without taking the time to read the sample scripts and related examiner comments (available from the ICAEW website). Get into training for this by reading the SBM examiner comments well.
[50] Issues which a large number of students got wrong are areas which are more likely to be re-examined in subsequent examination sessions … including yours, so take note of anything done really badly.

- Did not react well to the fact that the data was **quarterly** in nature (rather than including a single, obvious prior year comparator)

- Merely noted that figures or ratios had gone up or down without explaining **why**

- Wasted time by explaining **trivial cost changes** rather than concentrating on the **key issues**

Strong answers

- Used a **table of data at the start** of their answer

- Used the **operating data to provide analysis based on passenger numbers**, occupancy, ships, fuel and asset values. In other words, they calculated **scenario-specific or MS^2** results.

- Interpreted the quantitative analysis to demonstrate **cause and effect relationships** to build an explanation of underlying events

- Recognised the **interconnectedness** between different markets/demand for different services and **allowed for this when stripping out the data**

Task 1 Summary

We can see a range of strengths and weaknesses above. How can this be summarised? Perhaps we can say that points which are more **scenario-specific** are the ones made by strong candidates whereas weaker candidates provide analysis which is too **generic**. As such, you will need to work hard at developing your reading skills in order to absorb the material very quickly and use the reading time to draw out **scenario-specific** points. Given the time pressures, we know that it is easier said than done to advise you to "take your time" before starting your answer but it really does appear that just a bit more time reading the **specifics** and avoiding the temptation to dive in with **generic** calculations will be worth it.

Secondly, the inability to prioritise through a focus on trivial issues reflects a lack of use of the Structuring Problems & Solutions lens (see chapter 4).

Task 2   Foreign exchange issues (use of hedging methods)

Here the examiners introduced a twist – the company was paid in advance, **before** providing its services, so the usual generic points on the risks caused by incurring costs and only receiving revenue later when the exchange position may have worsened (or, more optimistically, improved) **did not apply**. Once again, paying careful attention to the **specifics** of the scenario would have been very beneficial.

Weak answers

- Provided **long lists** of all the different derivatives possible

- Discussed non-operating cash flows when this was **not requested** by the question

- **Reproduced a general section from the learning materials** on foreign currency risk management

- The multilateral netting off calculation was weak because many candidates were **unable to correctly convert into £s as the base currency of the company**

Strong answers

- Provided a bespoke solution which was specific to the client and scenario

Task 2 Summary

Other than the issue of correct calculations, the main difference here again seems to be whether the discussion is **specific** enough to the question set or more generic in nature. With respect to the remark on reproduction of the learning materials, perhaps this indicates a potential disadvantage of having all your notes to hand – please observe this warning, whether you are using the ICAEW Study Manuals, your own notes or our *SBM Exam Room Notes*: **use the materials as scenario-specific reminders and not something to just copy out**.

Task 3   Acquisition of Coastal Hotels (financial reporting and Due Diligence)

Again, the examiners provided a "twist" or difference to many valuation questions – the company was loss-making and therefore valuation techniques such as a cash flow model or EBITDA would not be appropriate. This twist was designed to get students thinking about alternatives (and perhaps adjustments to make) in the valuation.

Weak answers

- Stated that net assets could be a good starting point for negotiations but **did not expand on this point** (i.e. did not look at limitations with this measure)

- Discussed use of a cash flow or EBITDA model to estimate the valuation of the company, despite the fact that the company was **loss-making** and therefore these methods would not be appropriate[51]

- Ignored the fact that **losses were being made in the period until the date of acquisition**

- The financial reporting treatment of **negative goodwill was done very poorly**

Strong answers

- Used **headings** for all the **different Due Diligence processes** that could be undertaken

- Provided a reasoned response on **who** should carry out the Due Diligence

- Identified that the key issue was one of **independence**

Task 3 Summary

Once again, the fact that the company was loss-making was a **scenario-specific** point which the examiner wanted you to spot. Therefore we would make the same point once again – make **scenario-specific points**. MS[2] is the way to go! The lack of querying of the net assets method reflects a lack of use of the **Applying Judgement** (professional scepticism) lens (see chapter 4).

We are surprised to see that the financial reporting treatment of negative goodwill was done poorly – this should have been familiar from the Professional Level and presumably students should have had good notes to refer to. However, this reminds us of the **examiners' unhappiness with understanding of Group topics**[52] so revise this area well.

More positively, the Due Diligence element appears to have been done well with candidates making use of their notes to develop appropriate **headings**. **The examiners commented favourably on use of headings** and we think that it is sensible to provide headings, not only to attract the marker's attention and obtain the marks but also to structure your answer and ensure that you are making enough points across a range of areas, rather than concentrating too much on one idea: if you are using headings you will quickly notice this because different sections will obviously be too short.

---

[51] The background information provided a reminder to students by stating (page 4) that "A particular issue is that Coastal is making losses, so I am not sure whether the normal methods of valuation using earnings or cash flow would be appropriate."
[52] The 2015 edition of the Corporate Reporting Study Manual added many pages of additional Groups practice. At the SBM Workshop at the 2014 ICAEW Tutor Conference, the examiners were very disappointed indeed with performance on a Groups question in the November 2013 sitting of the Business Change paper: at the next examination sitting and the first example of the evolved ACA papers, a Groups financial reporting question (with an "unusual" position i.e. negative goodwill) was tested in the July 2014 paper (as discussed here in this section). This reflects our warning that if something is done badly at a prior sitting it will be tested again in the near future.

113

Task 4   **Food poisoning incident** (calculation of impact)

Candidates needed to estimate the impact on profit of a food poisoning issue. The "twist" here was that some costs were fixed whilst others were variable – therefore the 10% change mentioned should only have been applied to certain costs.

Weak answers

- **Assumed that all costs were variable** and hence applied a broad 10% decrease

- Did not discuss the impact in **detail**

Strong answers

- Noticed that a 10% fall in revenue resulted in a **much greater decrease** in profits

- Provided a **reasonable discussion on the actions that should be taken** by the company to reduce the impact on profit

Task 4 Summary

Aside from the need to read the question carefully to identify the impact of the 10% cost reduction (and specifically which costs would be affected), the fact that stronger candidates noted the connection between revenue and profit again shows the need to consider **interdependencies** in the figures. Of course, these interdependencies cannot be known or predicted in advance so this again forces students to consider **scenario-specific** points.

Question 2   **Landex plc**

Task 1   **Operating and strategic evaluation** (evaluation of 3 procurement proposals)

This Task required candidates to evaluate 3 proposals relating to procurement, providing an NPV calculation for each type. Candidates also had to look at the strategic and operational implications of the different options.

Weak answers

- Included revenue in their calculations for all the proposals, despite the fact that the **revenue streams were common to all the procurement options** and would not affect the decision of which supplier to select

- Made errors regarding the **foreign currency rate** and **discount rate** used

Strong answers

- Set out the calculations in a **structured year by year format**

- Recognised the **key risks** and the **differences for each proposal** (an extended supply chain for one proposal and high fixed costs plus exchange rate risk for another proposal)

- Provided a **conclusion** which matched with their discussion

Task 2   **Financing decision** (bond calculation, including the effective interest rate)

Candidates had to calculate the effective interest rate on 2 different bonds, one in a foreign currency and one in the domestic currency (sterling).

Weak answers

- Failed to allow for the fact that the **bond was in a foreign currency** and therefore the effective interest rate should take into account the expected maturity value in pounds sterling before applying the fourth root formula (as the bond was a 4 year bond)

- Failed to adjust for **issue costs** (by using a Debit entry on the loan) and therefore started with the wrong value for the effective interest rate[53]

- Failed to carry out **a reasonableness test which would have suggested that the interest rate should be close to 5%** – the issue costs are relatively immaterial at 2% so even after allowing for these then the effective interest rate should have been close to the 5% coupon rate (the actual answer was 5.57%)

Strong answers

As the examiners noted that the bond calculation question was very poorly answered, no particular points on strong answers were indicated.

It is worth noting the comment that "even where calculations were incorrect, appropriate advice based on candidates' own figures was awarded full credit". This emphasises that the important thing is to have a good attempt at the figures but not to worry about absolute perfection if this gets in the way of writing about those figures. As indicated in chapter 5, there is an approximately **33:66 split between numerical and narrative marks**.

---

[53] Many students apparently ended up with a 5% effective interest rate on a 5% coupon bond, making their calculations unnecessary. If there are no issue costs and no discount/premium on redemption then the effective rate is indeed equal to the coupon rate and no calculations are needed … which strongly suggests that in the examination things will not be so simple and therefore the effective interest rate will **differ** from the coupon rate.

Task 3   **Ethical issues** (supply contract and related parties)

Candidates were required to assess whether there were any ethical reasons why a supply contract with a particular provider needed to be maintained and secondly a potential conflict of interest in awarding a contract to a company run by the brother of the Finance Director.

Weak answers

- "Sat on the fence" and **did not provide clear advice**

- **Drifted into the financial reporting obligations** of related parties rather than looking at **ethical** issues (the financial reporting issues were tested under the next, separate Task)

Strong answers

- Reasonably **concluded** that there were **no ethical grounds** requiring a particular supply contract to be in place

- Explored **ethical principles first and then looked at how these applied** to the decision process on procurement[54]

- Look both at issues which were **actual** problems and issues which **could be** problems from a certain point of view (perceptions of the matter)

With respect to the stronger answers, we can see here an example of **nuance** in SBM – in one of the ethical issues there was in fact no ethical problem so the examiners were trying to test if candidates could resist the "knee-jerk" reaction and automatically find a serious ethical issue on every occasion.

Task 4   **Corporate governance issues** (regarding ethical issues)

Weak answers

- Asserted that the brother was a related party **without justifying this conclusion**

- Provided **extreme suggestions** on the role of the Finance Director

Strong answers

- Provided **good coverage** of the required disclosures

---

[54] See chapter 17 for a detailed review of frameworks/principles.

Again, we see the interest of the examiners in avoiding "extreme" positions in ethics scenarios. At both the 2014 and 2015 ICAEW Tutor Conferences, the examiners remarked that the Advanced Level will not test ethics in the same way as at the Professional Level and so it is expected that candidates will have a greater appreciation of potential **nuances**, rather than **extreme positions** or the knee-jerk reaction to "immediately resign from the engagement or call the Ethics Helpline".

July 2014 Examiner Comments – The Importance of MS^2

There are clearly many instances above where the requirement to make **scenario-specific** points distinguished strong from weak candidates and (relatedly) ensured that stronger answers provided added-value advice that extended beyond generic or obvious points that were effectively simply copied from the study materials. We cannot stress how important it is to follow MS^2 in your answers.

8.3   November 2014 Examiners' Comments

Before we analyse the examiner comments in more detail, it is important to note that the comments were significantly shorter in November 2014 than in July 2014: generally the examiner provided less than half the amount of discussion in November 2014 compared to the first SBM Paper in July 2014. This is a particular problem with respect to November 2014 Q2 where there is very little discussion at all.

Even so, we will still analyse whatever information we do have available because any "gold dust" (see above) has some value.

Question 1   Forklift Trucks Ltd

Task 1   Performance analysis (review of accounts for 3 recent reporting periods)

This Task was only the second analysis of financial information under the new involved syllabus "mini-Case" style questions. The indications are that this will be a significant part of any Q1 (although the emphasis was lower in this second example of financial performance analysis: see chapter 7) so we recommend that you look at the examiner comments carefully: **there are always going to be many marks available for this skills area**.

As this was the second attempt at this style of question, fortunately the examiner comments are significantly shorter. Overall, the examiner appeared to be happier with this example of a Q1 Task 1 than in July 2014, perhaps suggesting candidates are improving and responding to feedback. This is very similar to what has happened in one of the easier parts of the Case Study paper at the next level up and therefore we would issue the same warning as we have done in our book *Cracking Case™ – How to Pass the ACA Case Study*: **if you do not do as good a job of the basics as everyone else is doing, you are automatically at a significant disadvantage**, especially when the marks are moderated depending on general performance.

Weak answers

- Provided only **random calculations mixed in** with their narrative

117

Strong answers

- Used a **table of data at the start** of the answer

- Calculated relevant **additional metrics** to further the discussion and particularly to help **make recommendations**

Task 1 Summary

The points here regarding whether to use a table of numbers at the start of the question or whether to mix in your calculations as you go in your narrative are consistent with the July 2014 paper. In other words, the **examiners definitely favour an approach based on provision of an initial table of figures**, followed by usage of those figures.

Again, better candidates calculated **relevant metrics** which were specific to the business rather than relying on standard or **generic** "accountant's" figures.

There is thus a consistent pattern here in what the examiner wants to see in Q1 Task 1: learn from this.

Task 2   Financial reconstruction (impact of business change and financial reporting)

Here the examiner was more disappointed with performance: there was a clear distinction between strong and weak candidates based on the following factors:

Weak answers

- Failed to provide **specific points or sections for different stakeholder groups** and instead included all their discussion and points **merged together** into one common narrative on all stakeholders

- Did not **provide calculations** to support their points

- Accepted the income projections at face value and **did not apply professional scepticism**

- Provided financial reporting remarks which were **mainly descriptive rather than applied to the question set**

Strong answers

- Identified the **correct figures for the funds generated on liquidation, the amount the bank would recover and also the amount the liquidator could pay to creditors** who held a floating charge

- Had a **separate section for each of the major stakeholders**, a list of factors which were very specific for that group and supporting calculations

- Created a **separation** between (1) the financial reconstruction and (2) the liquidation

- Exercised **professional scepticism** by suggesting that the income projections could be optimistic or overstated

- Noted the impact of the **potential reluctance of shareholders** to reinvest

- Discussed the **accounting standards which relate to going concern** and avoided an answer which was largely descriptive of the standards: in other words, the standards were applied to the specific question set

Task 2 Summary

Perhaps we should perform a word count of the number of times that the examiners' comments use the term "specific" in a positive manner, contrasting with the negative "generic" word! Time and again, this is what the examiner says is a distinguishing factor between strong and weak candidates.

We would also note that this is another occasion where the examiner expresses a strong preference for **different sections (i.e. headings) within a particular Task**: for example, it was considered a characteristic of better candidates to separate the financial reconstruction and liquidation elements and also to provide separate sections for different stakeholders, rather than merging all points into one section.

We would strongly agree with the impact of using different section headings and we always advise our taught course students to use this approach in all ACA papers[55]. Section headings are useful in many ways: (1) they can ensure that you give a good spread of different points (2) they can ensure that you answer all elements of the question and provide enough detail within each element (in order to justify having a section heading for that part, you will need to find enough points to say) and (3) they make it very easy for the marker to see the number and range of points on each area: given the "holistic" and therefore slightly subjective aspect to the SBM marking, anything that impresses the marker or makes their life easy is worth doing.

Here the examiner explicitly criticised the lack of use of the **Applying Judgement** lens, through a lack of **professional scepticism**. The very term "professional scepticism" is used in the criticism so there is really no excuse for not using this skill in your own examination.

---

[55] At an extreme, in our opinion, the correct section headings in the Case Study are actually known in advance **and only by sticking to these headings are you likely to succeed in the exam**. See our book *Cracking Case™ – How to Pass the ACA Case Study* for more information on how to structure your Case Study approach.

Task 3   Leasing proposal (financial reporting)

After the tricky financial reconstruction question, this Task concerned a relatively straightforward leases question, concentrating on a common ACA financial reporting topic of operating leases versus finance leases.

Weak answers

- Used an **annual interest rate** rather than the correct quarterly interest rate: lease payments were to be made on a quarterly basis but the interest rate given in the question was clearly an annual rate

- **Treated the lease as a finance lease** even though the residual/disposal value at the end of the lease was very low (indicating that FFT retained the risks of ownership) and the lease term was significantly less than the useful life of the asset

Strong answers

- Provided a **good discussion of the financing package**, looking at some **practical business impacts** such as **cash, liquidity, capacity**: in other words, there was an awareness of the general background of the company

Task 3 Summary

Looking at the points made regarding weaker answers, the issue of the quarterly versus annual interest rate was perhaps a slightly sneaky trick by the examiners and hopefully something specific to this question: it appears to have caught out a large number of candidates anyway. If we assume therefore that it is a relatively unusual point, there is not really much to be learned from this issue as it hopefully will not recur.

This leaves the other weakness as a failure to apply the correct financial reporting treatment. Again, unfortunately, this is not hugely illuminating as obviously it is a good idea to get your treatment correct. Overall, then, there is not a huge amount of useful information here.

Regarding the stronger answers, the point is, once again, that stronger candidates are good at making points which are **specific to the scenario**. Once again, then, follow our advice (as indicated on our MAPs) to apply the **MS²** approach.

Task 4   Ethical issue (email from journalist)

This issue concerned an email received from a journalist which stated that information on the health consequences of the products provided by FFT was about to be published into the public domain.

120

Weak answers

- Did not appreciate the **limits of corporate responsibility** i.e. that the way in which FFT's products were ultimately used was the responsibility of customers and not FFT

Strong answers

- Suggested that FFT could **remind customers about the correct usage of its products** and consider a cessation of sales to customers who could not prove that the products were being used in the correct way

Task 4 Summary

This was a relatively short and simple task and so there are not many examiner comments to appreciate. However, notice that (yet again!) a good response requires the use of **MS²** through the specific and intelligent suggestion that although FFT is not responsible for the actions of its customers, a nuanced response would be to **communicate with them** and ensure that they fully understand the impact of using the products in the wrong way.

Task 5   **"Hidden" ethical issue** (ethics of advising FFT on the journalist's email)

As indicated in chapters 7 and 18, **the hardest aspect of this Task was in fact to spot that it was required in the first place!** We have noted that many students did not identify that this Task was required because it was not included in the separate Exhibit at the end of the question. This point was raised by the examiners at the 2015 Tutor Conference: tutors were strongly advised to warn candidates **not to assume that all Tasks would be given "on a plate"** at the end of the question. **We believe that this was definitely a strong hint as to how the Tasks may be set out in future.**

Weak answers

- **Failed to spot that the Task was even required at all** (see above)

- Provided **generic description** focusing on advocacy and self-interest threats but failing to discuss the main issues of **transparency and honesty**

- **Merged this answer in with the previous Task rather than keeping the issues completely separate** (as suggested by the nature of this Task, which involved advising the Partner of our own advisory firm, rather than the client – the previous Task provided advice to the client)

Strong answers

- The examiner was very unhappy with performance here and did not indicate how any strong answers had been written.

Further Useful Comments on Q1

In addition to the above Task-specific points, the examiner provided the following advice to candidates:

- **Ensure that your answer to each Task is separately and clearly identified**

- **Start each Task on a new page with a clear heading for each Task**

- **Answer the Tasks in the order in which they appear on the question paper: this is not a requirement but it will often be advantageous because the earlier Tasks will generate data or discussion which may be relevant to later Tasks within the same question**

All these points seem sensible and, again, were made directly by the examiner so we advise that you take them on Board.

Question 2   Washing Solutions Ltd

As noted above, the comments regarding Q2 are particularly short. Even so, there are some useful points to see and we will still analyse the information fully.

Task 1   Explanation for decline in tendering performance (Industrial Division tender analysis)

This Task required candidates to explain why one division was struggling to win tenders, compared to good performance in prior years.

Weak answers

There were very few weak answers as candidates "performed very well" on this Task. Accordingly, there are no real issues of weakness to note. This is perhaps because of the **relatively small amount of numerical information and the fact that only one Exhibit needed to be considered. In other words, it was obvious what you needed to do** and there was no possibility of looking at an issue which the examiners did not consider important.

Strong answers

Although general performance was very strong, the best candidates of all were able to understand the **underlying causes of poor performance and to provide reasoned recommendations**

122

Here we would note, in particular, that the question wording did not specifically ask for any **recommendations**. This shows the importance of bearing in mind the "Case Study"-style "lenses" which we explained in detail in chapter 4. **You should bear these perspectives in mind in all answers as it is clear from the above remark that the examiners consider answers that go beyond the wording of the question will be rewarded if the points are reasoned and within the standard 4 perspectives.**

Task 2 **Actual v budgeted profit** (understanding of the impact of overhead calculations)

This was a very tricky Task, requiring use of concepts potentially not studied for some years by many candidates (see above). Perhaps unsurprisingly, the examiner stated that, overall, responses were "disappointing".

Weak answers

- Used **poor presentation** which was hard to follow

- **Incorrectly calculated** actual and budget statements

- **Incorrectly calculated** total overhead figures

- **Failed to explain or demonstrate** in numerical terms the differences between actual profits and budgeted profit

- Provided **general discussions** rather than reasoned arguments[56]

Strong answers

Unfortunately, no aspects of stronger answers were noted – **the examiners were generally disappointed with performance**.

---

[56] Page 16 of the markscheme provides a criticism that "the narrative frequently substituted reasoned arguments with general discussion of" but does not complete the sentence: therefore we cannot be sure exactly what the criticism is here. This is in line with the rather short nature of the comments regarding Q2. The examiner comments on the July 2014 paper are definitely a better source of information.

Task 3 **Overhead allocation and inventories** (pricing decisions and financial reporting)

Weak answers

- Failed to identify the incremental costs as one labour hour plus the variable overhead elements on labour hours: this could also be described as a **lack of professional scepticism** over the client's approach, even though there was a big hint in the initial information at the start of the question that there was a problem or error somewhere in the costing technique

Strong answers

- Correctly recognised IAS 2 as the **relevant reporting standard to discuss** and **applied this to the specific scenario set**

- **Queried the client's approach** and instead suggested that the additional costs of quality were simply one further labour hour (£8) plus the connected variable overhead element of that labour hour (£16) rather than the figure given by the client

Task 4 **Sale of division and Due Diligence** (risks and assurance)

As noted, many candidates answered this element first, probably because the numerical aspects looked difficult. The examiner does not say whether answering this element first was a good or bad thing: as there is no criticism of this, we will assume that the examiner was happy with this approach (at the end of Q1 the examiner does say that the Tasks (or "requirements" in examiner language) may be attempted in any order) and it certainly does not seem to have impacted on performance or this would have been noted.

Weak answers

- Provided **general Due Diligence procedures** rather than focusing on the specific question of the issue of **using shares as consideration**

Strong answers

- Split the discussion under the **headings** provided in the question: namely, **strategic factors, operating factors and financial factors**. The examiner emphasised that this was a "good approach".

Once again, where does the weakness come from? **Use of generic lists and answers rather than the application of MS^2.**

8.4 July 2015 Examiners' Comments

Question 1 Commex Cables plc

Task 1 NPV analysis (overseas investment)

This task was a fairly straightforward foreign currency NPV calculation which used a perpetuity approach and only a few rows of calculations – it was nowhere near as complicated as a typical Financial Management NPV calculation at the Professional Level. The Task also required some sensitivity analysis and narrative discussion of the supply chain. It was therefore a long task with a variety of things to do.

We are aware that many candidates were thrown by the fact that there was no performance review in this first Task of Question 1. This was certainly unusual but there is nothing in the syllabus or examiner comments to say that Task 1 of Question 1 will always be a performance review so please be prepared for different possibilities.

Weak answers

- Made errors in respect of the cash flow **timings**

- Discounted the **perpetuity** incorrectly

- Unnecessarily **recalculated** the cash flows even though these were clearly given in the question

- Ignored the question wording regarding **when** an exchange rate change would occur

- Could not solve for the **sensitivity rate**

- Failed to calculate the **exchange rate which would result in a zero NPV**, as required by the question – instead, candidates **picked different exchange rates** and discussed these or calculated the IRR of each project

- Used the framework of translation risk, transaction risk and economic risk but **without applying** this in any way to the scenario

- Were not clear whether a **depreciation** or **appreciation** of the foreign currency was necessary to result in a zero NPV

- Gave a **generic response** on the supply chain with **little or no application to the scenario**

- Failed to **split** the answer to consider goods and services aspects **separately** – similarly, few candidates split maintenance services and emergency responses into different markets with different supply chain issues

Strong answers

- Used the **framework** of translation risk, transaction risk and economic risk **with application to the scenario**

- Commented on **both** strategies within the supply chain element of the question

- Treated the **different** types of product and service that the company provided **separately**, with discussion of **different** impacts on each stream under each strategy

Task 1 Summary

Here we can see the examiners' typical concern with the lack of **scenario-specific** points. It also seems that students were relatively unconfident with calculating the **breakeven exchange rate** so we would advise you to work through this question a few times – it is one of those occasions where the answer seems very obvious and even easy when you have the luxury of time to think about it but you need to prepare a standard approach for quick use in the exam.

Secondly, we would note that the examiners wanted students to **split** the company's business into goods and services, and then to split the services element into different types as well, in order to give an answer which has **points specific to each stream**. This is really another way of making **scenario-specific** points. It is highly likely that you will have to analyse a business with different revenue streams in your own examination so do bear this point in mind.

Task 2   Debt finance (comparing 2 loan options)

This Task covered one of the examiners' favourite areas of financing methods. We have stressed at various places in this book how important it is that you understand the different ways this can be tested. This Task involved the comparison of 2 different financing approaches – this is also a very common SBM scenario.

Weak answers

- Failed to **compare** the **different** features of the 2 loans by analysing the loans completely separately

- Failed to answer the question regarding the **differences in interest rates** or gave only very brief answers to this element

- Did not provide an **explanation** for their **recommendation** over which loan to take – or **failed to provide** any recommendation at all

Strong answers

- Discussed the currency issues relating to **each** method and the **detailed terms** of each loan such as the guarantee, security being offered and length of each loan

Task 2 Summary

Here we can see that the examiners wish you to make a **comparison** between different loans rather than look at them separately. The examiners also want you to give a **properly explained** recommendation – this is a reminder of the Case Study "lens" of Conclusions & Recommendations: as we have stressed in various places in this book, you should always be looking for opportunities to recommend but make sure you use the examiners favourite word "**because**" (see chapter 18) when doing so.

Task 3   Assurance (Due Diligence)

This Task involved a very common assurance area in SBM so students should have been well prepared. However, the examiners noted that the question received a "mixed response".

Weak answers

- Ignored the question wording which specifically asked students **not** to give a **list** of assurance procedures

- Failed to **split** their answer to look at **each loan separately**

- Failed to comment on the need to provide **evidence of security** for the loans or the type of charge that could be taken out over the assets – the impact of this evidence on the assurance work needed to be spotted by candidates

Strong answers

- Correctly identified that the prospective information was **questionable**

- Identified the **key issues** for lenders and how an assurance report would help the lenders

Task 3 Summary

Here the main problem seems to be that candidates did not read the question properly and therefore **listed out** Due Diligence procedures on "autopilot". Other than this, there do not seem to have been any major problems and this is in line with the fact that assurance questions are normally relatively easy, provided that you respond to the specific question set.

We would make a note of the importance to lenders of providing **evidence** of security and considering the types of charges used – given that **loans** are a **very common focus** of SBM questions, it follows that you may well have to look at **assurance** in relation to loans so these points would then be relevant again.

Task 4   Financial reporting (subsidiary, division and other matters)

This Task required candidates to identify that a subsidiary needed to be consolidated but a division would **not** require consolidation. There were also some financial reporting issues in relation to foreign currency, construction costs, related parties, contingent liabilities and operating segments.

Weak answers

- Did not pitch the answer **widely enough** to consider a **range** of financial reporting issues and so missed issues such as construction contracts, related parties and contingent liabilities

Strong answers

- Recognised that **IFRS 8** was relevant to the scenario

- Recognised that a subsidiary **is** consolidated but a division **is not**

Task 4 Summary

Provided that candidates spot the financial reporting issues, they seem to be able to pick up the marks in SBM. Notice the reference to the fact that many students did not have a wide enough **range** of financial reporting points – they did spot the most obvious issues in relation to consolidation but there were other matters to consider as well.

Task 5   Ethics (collaboration and Director interests)

This Task asked students to analyse 2 issues, both involving potential conflicts of interest or deals on terms other than arm's length.

Weak answers

- Suggested **few** or **no actions**

- Suggested actions which were **extreme**, **inappropriate** or **generic** such as "speak to the ICAEW"

Strong answers

- Looked **separately** at the 2 issues and suggested **different** sensible actions to take

- Recognised that a subsidiary **is** consolidated but a division **is not**

Task 5 Summary

Here we can see how important it is to offer some advice on **actions** to take – if you follow the advice set out elsewhere in this book, then you should automatically be doing this under the "**Mitigation**" component of our suggested **IIR** ethics analysis framework.

Please also note that the examiners are not looking for **extreme** actions in response to ethical issues – please see chapter 18 for more on this. Regarding the July 2015 examination, the examiners commented that

> "Even though it is reassuring to see candidates taking ethics seriously, some candidates fail to see that this is a very sensitive area and often appear to believe that they are "playing safe" when they suggest the most extreme actions, when they may not be a necessary or appropriate response."

Question 2   Paige plc

Task 1   Risk analysis (review of the market environment)

This Task required candidates to provide a **primarily narrative** analysis of the market environment, with a particular emphasis on **risks**. Although the question wording did not require it, many candidates used a standard **model** such as PESTEL or Porter's Five Forces.

Weak answers

- Focused too much on the **company** and did not make enough specific reference to the **market environment**

- Did not separately address the 2 elements of the Task on the "**market environment**" and "**key risks**", respectively – instead, there was just a general discussion of the issues more generally

Strong answers

- Used **various models** to answer the question, giving a good **structure** to the answer and ensuring that candidates addressed key issues

- Used the **financial information given in the question scenario** to make sensible comments about the market environment and related risks

Task 1 Summary

Here we can see that the examiners do like to have a **structure** to the answer – the use of **models** would have given candidates various **headings** to structure their answer and it was also noted that it was considered a "weak" approach to mix the market environment and key risks in a **single** discussion rather than splitting these out: again headings could have helped here.

Task 2   Strategy A (narrative analysis of first strategy option)

In this Task, candidates had to consider a number of proposals to change the company's service provision. The evaluation was primarily narrative in nature.

Weak answers

- Gave **bullet point lists** without developing the points raised – for example, they simply commented that a strategy option would "cost a lot" with no **further discussion or explanation**

- Provided **only brief conclusions** or did not provide **conclusions at all**

- Provided **conclusions** that often **only summarised** what had **previously been stated**

Strong answers

- Provided **detailed discussions** of the benefits and risks specific to each strategy based on what had been identified in the first Task

- Discussed **each possible option** within Strategy A individually with **separate** discussion of advantages and disadvantages of each option within the strategy

Task 2 Summary

The problem here seems to have been that answers were too **brief**, both in relation to the main strategy analysis and also the related conclusions. Note that it appears that the examiners want the conclusion section to add a bit **more value** than **simply repeating what you have already stated**: this can perhaps be automatically achieved by ensuring that you have some **recommendations** within this section.

Please also note that the examiners **praised students** who used points developed in an **earlier Task** when answering this Task. Although Question 1 is designed to be the integrated "mini-case study" in which several parts of the question will be interrelated, it appears that you should look out for opportunities to create **connections** between Tasks even in Question 2.

Task 3   **Strategy B** (narrative analysis of second strategy option)

This Task was similar to the previous Task but it had more of a numerical element since it involved different valuation methods and comments on the validity of those methods. The examiners reported that this section received a "mixed response" and that the valuation elements received "very varied answers".

Weak answers

- Simply **stated** it would be good to have a cash injection into the business – there was no attempt to analyse how this **might be used** or the **possible returns** from that injection so the answer was **too brief**

- Were unable to apply a **range** of different valuation methods and comment on their validity

- Struggled to cope with the **calculations** needed for valuations

- Struggled to **work backwards** from a given WACC to arrive at the implied cost of equity

- Picked up the **wrong values** for debt and equity from the question

Strong answers

- Made **good** general comments on the potential benefits **and** risks of the strategy

- Made use of **ROCE** – note that it was stated that only the "**strongest candidates**" specifically mentioned this concept

- Made good comments on a **range** of different valuation techniques that could be used and summarised these appropriately – note that it was stated that only the "**very strongest candidates**" could do this

- Answered the **asset-based valuation model element** very well

Task 3 Summary

Considering the importance of valuations to the SBM syllabus, and the fact that valuations are already covered in the earlier Financial Management paper, we continue to be **surprised** by statements such as the fact that **only** the "**very strongest candidates**" were able to use valuations models and criticise these effectively. It seems to us that the area of valuations is relatively straightforward and predictable so **we are not sure why students are struggling** – on the other hand, perhaps it is a good thing that candidates seem to struggle with this area as it means it will **continue to be tested in future** and therefore if you can prepare this area well there is a good chance you will have an opportunity to collect a good number of marks and distinguish yourself from many other candidates.

It is also clear that many students struggled to apply a **familiar calculation in an unfamiliar way**: in this case, students struggled to work the familiar WACC calculation backwards in the unfamiliar scenario where they were given the WACC rather than having to calculate this. We have spotted that this has been tested now in a couple of SBM papers so please make sure you are able to manipulate the algebra correctly. Please see chapter 15 for a review of the way that "backwards" workings have been used in SBM to date.

Task 4   Recommendations

Rather unusually, this final element of the question specifically asked students to give some recommendations and allocated a Task to this. As we have indicated elsewhere in this book, normally you will not be given a prompt to offer recommendations (or conclusions) so you should be looking to offer these wherever relevant anyway but in this particular Task, the examiners gave you a very clear hint what to do.

Weak answers

- Gave **one sentence**, **unsubstantiated** recommendations

- Failed to make **any** recommendations at all

Strong answers

- Presented quite **detailed, reasoned recommendations**

Task 4 Summary

Relatively little feedback was given by the examiners on this unusual component of the question. It is particularly **surprising** that some students failed to make any recommendations **at all** when a specific Task was (unusually) allocated to this in the question. This would seem to suggest, once again, that candidates need to be aware of just how important it is to offer recommendations in SBM, whether prompted or unprompted.

We would also note that the examiners consider that a 1 sentence recommendation is unlikely to be sufficient as it needs to be **substantiated**. Again, your friend here is the word "**because**" (see chapter 18 for more on this word from the examiners).

8.5   November 2015 Examiners' Comments

Question 1   Riller

Task 1   Performance review and acquisition price (data review and valuation models)

This Task was very long, ranging over performance analysis, evaluation and even financial reporting issues. The Task was worth 35 marks in total and accordingly there are quite a few positive and negative examiner comments to consider here.

Weak answers

- **Randomly** generated their ratios rather than considering the ratios **relevant to the question**

- Failed to produce a **data table** of ratios at the start and instead had data points "**woven**" into the narrative

- Failed to consider the more **question specific ratios** such as price per household, cost per household or average time to sell – instead, candidates focused on straightforward ratios such as gross profit margin, net profit margin and gearing

- Ignored **financial position** or treated it in a trivial manner in the narrative discussion

- Failed to provide **reasons** for **movements** in the ratios based on causal factors in the data and information

- Failed to **use the data** when evaluating "strategic, operational and financial" considerations

- Did not recognise **quality** differences in the houses being produced – instead, comments focused on geography and **generic** acquisition factors such as culture and management styles

- Made no comment on the **debts** that would be **brought into the SFP on acquisition**

- Simply stated the **generic** advantages and disadvantages of each model rather than **applying** these to the **scenario**

- Failed to identify that the main tangible asset in the proposed acquisition was **inventory** and therefore the **FV** of the landbank was a key issue

- Failed to consider the impact of **synergy gains** on the valuation

- Made **basic errors** in the calculation and **failed to compare** the prices reported from the models with each other nor commented that some calculation results appeared to be out of line with others

- Failed to **separate** the discussion of financial reporting issues from analysis of financing alternatives – a better approach would have been to use a **separate** page with a clear **heading**, as was done by stronger candidates

Strong answers

- Produced an **initial data table** of ratios in a clearly structured way

- Made effective **comparisons** between companies and regions to explain differences

- Recognised the **importance** of the land bank as a key resource and gave this prominence in the discussion

- Recognised that the **landbank** had been acquired when land values were lower, hence enabling better margins

- Identified **interconnections** between pieces of data

- Produced **structured discussions** of factors to consider based on a structure of "strategic, operational and financial" considerations

- Made reference to the **debt** that would be **brought into the SFP on acquisition**

- Made reference to **horizontal integration**, **synergies** from **cost savings** and/or **specific operational advantages**

- Produced several **different** valuation results drawing on **different** methods, with a range of calculation results

- Developed the discussion of fair value measurement by referring to **IFRS 13**, particularly with respect to the **brand**

- Created a clear **separation** between financial reporting and consideration of financing alternatives, using a **separate** page with a clear **heading**

Task 1 Summary

Here we can see a range of common complaints from the examiner such as a failure to address the question, weaknesses regarding valuations, a failure to separate out elements of the question and problems with listing out generic points rather than applying these to the scenario.

Task 2   Financing alternatives (shares or bonds)

This Task involved the familiar SBM requirement to consider different forms of financing: this time the comparison was not between 2 different loans but between the use of shares and a bond.

Weak answers

- Stated the **generic** pros and cons of **equity versus debt** without making their points relevant to the scenario

Strong answers

- Addressed each part of the question **separately**

- Considered relevant issues such as **risk**, **dilution of control**, **EPS** and **gearing**

- Provided **advice** that the share alternative was the preferred option

- Produced **gearing** calculations, showing their ability to apply knowledge

Task 2 Summary

As always, you will do substantially better if you **avoid generic points**. Please make a note of the points which the examiner thought are relevant to analysis of evaluation of financing alternatives i.e. **risk, dilution of control, EPS** and **gearing**. At the same time, please only use these as **headings** and **reminders** – to score well, you must relate the points to the **specific scenario**.

Task 3   Assurance (Risks and Due Diligence)

This Task involved identification of key risks on an acquisition and related DD procedures to apply.

Weak answers

- Used **generic** points such as "legal Due Diligence is required to check contracts"

- Used a **preprepared** list of headings to mention any possible general risk such as price, value of assets, strategic and operational risks

- Relatedly, students produced **any possible** procedures to address these broad risks

Strong answers

- Correctly highlighted the key **risks** and suggested appropriate **procedures**

- Appropriately **structured** their discussion around the various types of DD such as IT, legal, HR and so on

Task 3 Summary

Some fairly typical examiner points here. Note that the examiners do like to have a discussion of DD around certain standard areas but the trick is then to use these headings as a **structuring device** rather than as an opportunity to provide **generic** points. **Use the scenario as much as possible**.

If you have worked through all the examiner comments to this point, you may well be bored of seeing the point that you need to use the scenario … but as we can see from the examiner comments it is clear that candidates are not taking this obvious step in SBM so we will risk your boredom to ensure your best chance of passing!

Task 4   Ethics (Bribery, self-interest threat and integrity)

It is fairly self-explanatory what this Task involved.

Weak answers

- Suggested **extreme** actions

- Did not make the statement that it is **first necessary to establish the facts**

- Failed to appreciate that the acquisition had **not yet taken place** so the ethical issues were future possibilities rather than relating to actual events that had already happened

- Failed to use appropriate **ethical** language

Strong answers

- Used relevant **ethical** language and recognised the potential issues of bribery, self-interest threats and integrity

- Suggested **reasonable actions** that should be taken in response

Task 4 Summary

We have discussed elsewhere in this book how important it is not to take an **extreme position**. Please also do read the data very carefully as the "trick" in this instance was the fact that the potentially ethically dubious actions **had not yet taken place**. We can also see that it will always be worth making a first point that the facts need to be established in full. Finally, make sure you are giving some recommendations on what actions to take.

Question 2   Kinn plc

Task 1   **Financial performance review** (possible sale of the division)

This Task asked candidates to analyse some forecast information in the context of the sale of a particular division of the company.

Weak answers

- Provided only very **brief analysis** of the division which had been sold

- Did not provide any **professional scepticism** in respect of the forecast figures

- Produced very few **calculations**

- Failed to recognise or state that the decision to dispose of the division was appropriate

- Failed to note any **limitations** to the analysis which they had provided

Strong answers

- Presented an initial table of key ratios including **ROCE**, **ROE** (return on equity) and **gearing**

- Made comments on the performance of each **individual** division

- Made specific comments on the **underperformance** of the division which had been sold – only the "strongest candidates" did this

Task 1 Summary

Here we can see that it was quite important to focus in on the division which had been sold – this was after all the major event during the year for the company so it was not surprising to see that the examiners wanted this to be analysed in detail.

Task 2   **Financial reporting** (IFRS 5)

This financial reporting Task was relatively unusual in SBM as it focused on a single IFRS standard rather than looking at a range of different areas. However, note that this single standard does cover the 2 different areas of assets classified as held the sale and, secondly, discontinued operations. There was therefore some opportunity for students to go into different areas of the standard – as we know, the SBM examiners favour range over depth.

Please note that the examiners made a general comment that "candidates did not perform well on this requirement".

137

Weak answers

- Failed to **develop** their answers based on the **facts** in the **scenario**

- Did not mention the **criteria** for an asset to be classified as held the sale and **whether the criteria** were **satisfied** in the scenario

- No mention of the "**disposal group**" concept

- No consideration of the **measurement** implications, including the evidence of **impairment**, in relation to the assets – instead, it was simply stated that the assets were "available for sale"

- Not stating exactly **what** would be disclosed in profit or loss regarding the discontinued operation – rather, it was simply stated that the "discontinued operation would be shown in profit or loss" with no further explanation

Strong answers

- Produced an **initial** data table of ratios in a clearly structured way

- Made effective **comparisons** between companies and regions to **explain differences**

Task 2 Summary

Here it is clear that most weaknesses could be avoided simply by knowing and explaining IFRS 5 properly.

Task 3   Derivatives (interest rate futures)

This Task drew heavily on brought forward Financial Management knowledge of interest rates futures. The calculations would have been straightforward for candidates who followed the advice that we give in our taught courses to ensure that Financial Management is revised well as part of your preparations for SBM. (For a quick method of revising technical content that you have already studied once, please consider purchasing our *Financial Management Q&A 2018* which provides hundreds of short form questions to quickly get you back up to speed in terms of your Financial Management knowledge.)

The examiners commented that some candidates produced entirely correct numbers whereas others tended to have answers which were completely wrong. This probably reflects the fact that some candidates would not have revised this area before the examination.

Weak answers

- Made **few comments** beyond stating that buying and selling 50 contracts was the most appropriate action

- Made **basic errors** in the calculation such as: only considering the 3.75% rate, only considering the 2.75% rate and **not taking into account the 3/12 apportionment**

- Just **presented** the calculations with limited **discussion**

Strong answers

- Produced an excellent **discussion** of how the hedge worked and the benefits to the company

Task 3 Summary

We expect that most weaknesses here could be avoided through some revision of the derivatives calculations from the Financial Management syllabus.

Task 4   **Alternative use of proceeds** (analysis of likely returns)

In this Task, candidates were required to consider the alternatives of purchasing new production equipment or, alternatively, reducing the level of gearing in the company.

Weak answers

- Did not comment that if gearing were **reduced** (one of the options), this would **improve** the company's ability to borrow in the future if different opportunities presented themselves – in other words, the **debt capacity** of the company would be higher in future

- Did not comment on the appropriate **hurdle rate** for the project

Strong answers

- Commented on financial **risk** and the problems with financing investment from increased debt

- Provided **detailed comments** about the fixed or variable rate loan and appropriate advice specific to the scenario

- Made **comparisons** between the 2 alternatives, recognising that investing in new assets is a **higher risk** strategy than the gearing – this was because of the uncertainty of cash flows from the newly purchased assets and the need to finance this from increased debt, increasing risks.

8.6 July 2016 Examiners' Comments

Question 1 Kiera Healy Company plc

Task 1 Pricing strategy

This Task required candidates to analyse the strategic impact of 2 distribution strategies, explain related risks and provide reasoned recommendations.

Weak answers

- Did not consider **exit costs** if the venture failed

- Failed to realise that the decision to expand into the US had **already been taken** and so would happen regardless of whether or not a particular distribution warehouse was acquired

- Assumed that the manufacturing of products would take place in the **US** even though the **scenario** made it clear that this would continue to happen in the **UK**

- Attempted to **force the facts into a standard model** such as PESTEL which was not appropriate to the question

- **Regurgitated knowledge** on cost plus pricing without using information in the question

- Failed to discuss **price skimming** and **price penetration** strategies

- Failed to link **price** and **quality**

- Failed to provide a **recommendation**

Strong answers

- Used the **information** given in the question to provide **different** points on each strategy

Task 1 Summary

The feedback here is very much in line with other questions reviewed above – strong answers will create a scenario-specific response whereas weak answers will leave parts of the Task unanswered and will try to use stock or **standardised** approaches.

Task 2   **Foreign exchange issues** (use of hedging methods)

This Task required candidates to identify and explain issues relating to foreign currency risk and discuss different methods of hedging currency risk. Candidates also had to do some supporting calculations.

Weak answers

- Discussed transaction and translation risk only and **failed to explore the economic risk** related to US expansion, which was probably of a significant risk in the **scenario**

- Failed to understand the different inflows and outflows of currency and how this will impact on **risk**

- Sat on the fence and simply referred to an "adverse movement of exchange rates" without **specifying** which direction of movement would be adverse to the client

- Provided answers which were fairly "**textbook**" and had limited application to the scenario

- Made **basic errors** in the calculation for the **forward contract** including adding the premium, not converting cents into dollars, treating a sterling figure as a dollar amount, mixing bid and offer rates and multiplying the US dollar amounts by the exchange rate rather than dividing

- Made **basic errors** in the calculation of the **money market hedge** including using the annual interest rate rather than pro rating this for 3 or 6 months

- Entered into **extended discussions** on how to do the calculations but never got on with **doing** the calculations themselves

Strong answers

- Mentioned **Brexit** and how this could impact exchange rates, stating that a **weaker pound** may be **beneficial** in some cases as revenue would be generated in US dollars

- Often scored **full marks** in the **derivatives** calculations

Task 2 Summary

In this feedback, we can see the importance of revising your **brought forward** knowledge from the Financial Management paper in order to perform well in the **derivatives** question. This revision should include not just revision of the calculations but also the different types of currency risk as the examiners noted that people did not discuss **economic risk** in enough depth. We can also see the standard criticism of "textbook" or stock responses and the examiner's dislike of students who sit on the fence and do not make the effort to specify the direction of movements (hedging the nature of their responses in the wrong sense!).

Task 3 **Investment into a warehouse** (financing decision and financial reporting)

Here candidates were required to perform an NPV calculation involving foreign currency cash flows and to consider how the investment would be financed.

Weak answers

- Struggled with the **NPV calculation** due to an inability to deal with the **appreciation** in the US dollar

- Failed to **complete** the **NPV calculation** or provided **disorganised** attempts with a poor layout and lack of workings

- Failed to deal with the **initial outlay of £2 million** and did not do anything with the **probabilities** referred to in the question

- Provided very **generic** discussion of **financing**, rather than providing points applied to the **scenario**

- Did not expand on the **nature** and **terms** of the **loan** that would be appropriate to the client, such as an appropriate **loan term**

- Did not consider the possibility of **leasing** the warehouse in enough detail – this in turn then also meant that candidates lost the available marks relating to the **financial reporting** aspects of **leasing**

- Wasted time discussing the merits of **equity** finance, which had been **excluded** by the question wording

Strong answers

- Recognised the possibility of **leasing** and discussed this in detail from both a strategic and financial reporting angle

- Provided a good answer on the **IAS 21** aspects that needed to be considered

- Considered the importance of **hedging**

- Discussed **IFRS 8** in their answer

Task 3 Summary

A key learning point here would be that if you have a major capital investment project to analyse then you should consider whether the question allows you to discuss **leasing** – this will raise strategic points but then will also open up some potential financial reporting marks, under the "Accountant in Business" approach.

Although the issue of financing is definitely a key or "classic" SBM question, it is important not to answer this on "autopilot" by always comparing debt and equity because as seen in this question, equity was excluded from the potential methods by the question wording.

Note that stronger candidates considered IFRS 8 as the company was a **plc** and was undergoing a major **geographical** expansion. Please look out for these points again in your own exam.

Task 4   Branding and Agreed Upon Procedures

In this Task, candidates had to compare the options of selling a brand versus licensing it. Candidates also had to identify key risks to be addressed by Agreed Upon Procedures (AUP), as well as the benefits of using such procedures.

Weak answers

- Did not use the **numbers** sufficiently in their answer

- Did not **tailor** their answer to the scenario

- Made very **general** points on loss of income and brand damage when discussing the option to sell the brand

- The examiners noted that the AUP element was **by far the weakest area** in candidate responses, with many candidates ignoring this element or simply talking briefly about Due Diligence

- Incorrectly referred to AUP as a type of **assurance**

- Failed to identify that **ISRS 4400** would provide guidance

Strong answers

- Provided a good discussion on the **difference** between **licensing** and **selling** a brand and produced good discussion about the **value** of the brand, **control issues** and brand **damage**

- Discussed a **number** of ways of determining **brand value** in the event of selling the brand

- Recognised how AUP would be **beneficial** to **all parties** involved in the negotiations

143

Task 4 Summary

The above advice provides useful information on how to deal with issues of brand value, something which was also tested in the SBM Sample Paper and so is clearly something important to the examiners.

Agreed Upon Procedures had not previously been tested in a real examination and also are not found in any SBM Question Bank questions so this may explain why performance was very poor. This is in line with feedback on AUP from the previous Business Change paper where the topic was rarely examined and rarely available in practice questions so performance was always bad when the topic was set in the real exam. Make sure you learn from this example of AUP as the model answer is very similar to the model answers required under the Business Change syllabus so it will provide useful guidance (whilst always remembering to tailor your answer to the specific scenario set).

Task 5   Ethics

In this Task, candidates had to provide some advice on a possible conflict of interest, governance problems and confidentiality.

Weak answers

- The examiners commented that candidate answers were **generally poorly attempted compared with ethics questions in previous sittings** – this is surprising to hear as it is clear that ethics will be a key part of SBM

- Provided **limited discussion** of appropriate ethical **principles** and ethical **language**

- Produced very **brief** answers which amounted to a "**knowledge dump**" of the learning materials on ethics, with little consideration of the **scenario**

Strong answers

- Highlighted the **self-interest** threat and issues of **integrity**

- Considered issues of **transparency, effect** and **fairness**

- Suggested sensible **actions**

Task 5 Summary

It is quite surprising to hear that this ethics Task was done so poorly as we would have expected candidates and tuition providers to put in a good amount of work to ensure a good performance. However, it is encouraging that the comments on what constitutes a strong ethics response are very

144

much in line with the advice that we provide in chapter 17 of this book – as we will explain, you must clearly set out the ethical **principles** and use a **framework** such as TEF (transparency, effect and fairness). We have also explained throughout the book that you must always provide **recommendations** or **action points** in SBM as the examiner will be looking for these.

Question 2   **Quinter plc**

Task 1   **Performance analysis** (quarterly operational and financial data)

In this Task, students had to analyse quarterly data on operational and financial performance and carry out data analysis to identify the key factors that differed between quarters. Candidates were also required to identify key operational weaknesses and provide a reasoned conclusion.

Weak answers

- Mainly **copied out** data without doing any sort of **additional analysis** such as analysing performance **by customer** or **by product type**

- Only computed data at the **annual** level, ignoring the **quarterly** nature of the information which was a specific element of the scenario

- Treated the **quarterly** change as expansion rather than considering whether it could simply be quarterly seasonal **variation**

- Provided **bland commentary** that lacked insight, simply **restating** numbers but not **explaining** what was happening by establishing **causal** relationships

- Did not address the requirement to analyse areas of **operational weakness**

- Failed to present their answer in a **report format** as asked for in the Task

Strong answers

Unfortunately, the examiners did not provide any positive comments at all on this Task so we do not have any points to note under this heading.

Task 1 Summary

The learning point here is that if quarterly data is provided then you do need to conduct a quarterly analysis. Please look out for the possibility that variation could be caused by seasonal factors rather than representing growth or declines for other reasons.

The examiners wish you to **explain** causal relationships. This is in line with the examiners' statement (see chapter 18) that if candidates only used the word "**because**" a bit more then many more students would pass the SBM examination.

Task 2   Additional Management Data

Here candidates had to identify and justify additional data which it would be useful for the Board to have in relation to sales and customer management and inventory management.

Weak answers

- Provided very **general** points which focused on the different methods of inventory control such as JIT and EOQ without explaining **why**, and **if**, these methods would be relevant to the **specific scenario**

Strong answers

- Used the underlying **issues**, referred to in the **question**, in producing their answers

- Thought carefully about how the **pattern of orders and frequency** could be used to the advantage of the client and how more detailed returns information would allow the Board to identify how **quality** could be dealt with throughout the supply chain

- Recognised the key points on **inventory management** such as monitoring of inventory levels and matching with changes in demand

Task 3   Financial reporting (inventories)

In this Task, candidates had to consider the scope for misstatement in the SFP and P&L in relation to inventories. Candidates had to consider the application of IAS 2 and IAS 21 for this purpose.

Weak answers

- Failed to deal with issues relating to the **write-down of inventories** to the **lower** of **cost** or **market value**

- Discussed irrelevant issues such as **revenue recognition** and the treatment of the business **premises** as well as other costs which were **outside the scope of the Task**

- Omitted the elements of the question on providing **appropriate information** to ensure inventories were valued appropriately

146

Strong answers

- Also considered the relevance of **IAS 21** based on the fact that inventories were purchased in **foreign currency**

Task 4   Corporate governance improvements

Here candidates had to discuss some of the key aspects of corporate governance which needed to be reviewed by the client.

Weak answers

As a rare exception, the examiners were very pleased with answers to this Task so no particular weaknesses were mentioned.

Strong answers

Although most answers were to a good standard, the examiners noted that full marks were awarded only to candidates who linked the relevance of each committee back to the facts in the question and provided a rationale for improvements.

A good answer required candidates to be comfortable with the fundamental principles of corporate governance and to discuss the various subcommittees recommended by the UK Corporate Governance Code that would benefit a company seeking an AIM listing.

Task 5   Sustainability Policy

Candidates were required to evaluate how a sustainability policy could make a positive contribution to the public profile of the organisation. As a second element, candidates also had to explain how the data gathered from implementing a sustainability policy could generate additional useful management data for other purposes such as identifying possible sales opportunities.

Weak answers

- Focused only on the **recycling** element of the question rather than considering any of the **wider** environmental aspects

Strong answers

- Identified that the **environmental** angle was only one aspect of **sustainability**

- Considered the "**Integrated Reporting**" element of the scenario

- Identified that one of the benefits of gaining additional management data from a sustainability policy would include allowing management to identify **potential new sales opportunities** when customers contacted them to recycle

- Displayed **professional scepticism** and **questioned** whether the motive behind recycling was for environmental reasons or was actually purely commercial in nature

8.7   November 2016 Examiners' Comments

Question 1   Wooster Ltd

Task 1   Contract evaluation

This Task required students to perform and compare 2 alternative NPV calculations, review the company's supply chain and analyse foreign currency risks.

Weak answers

- Made an **inappropriate comparison** between a 2 year contract and a 3 year contract by failing to adjust for the **different time periods** involved

- Failed to consider **opportunity cost**

- Provided a **very limited response** to the **discussion** element of the question, failing to **evaluate** the underlying assumptions or other issues affecting the **validity** of the calculations

- Failed to identify that one contract involved "**natural hedging**"

- Spent far **too long writing** about different **hedging** strategies

Strong answers

- Used a **variety** of effective techniques to allow for the different timescales (2 year versus 3 year comparison)

Task 1 Summary

Here there is clearly a learning point – the examiners definitely want you to try to make a reasonable adjustment if you are comparing projects with different lifespans.

Note too the remark by the examiners that most candidates spent too long writing about different hedging techniques – there are unlikely to be a huge number of marks available here.

Task 2   Environmental Assurance (including KPIs)

For this Task, candidates had to explain some potential environmental and sustainability KPIs to be included in a Service Level Agreement with an external provider.

Weak answers

- Inappropriately suggested **commercial or financial KPIs** or suggested a **vague** KPI that would therefore be very **difficult to measure**

- Provided **generalised** or "**textbook**" assurance procedures which scored few marks – these were insufficiently **applied** to the scenario

- Failed to give **any assurance procedures** whatsoever and instead discussed **auditing** rules, **types of assurance** that could be given and general issues surrounding **Due Diligence**

Strong answers

Unfortunately, the examiners did not have anything positive to say about strong answers to this Task. This is in line with the fact that Assurance is normally done very badly by students. For this reason, we provide detailed notes on specialist Assurance areas in chapter 10 to chapter 14 inclusive of this book.

Task 3   Evaluation of a further production proposal

In this Task, candidates had to perform further NPV calculations in relation to 2 different proposals. Candidates also had to review the wider benefits and risks of outsourcing compared with automation, providing a reasoned recommendation on the best approach for the client.

Weak answers

- Provided **poor attempts** at the calculations or **did not even attempt** the core NPV calculations

- Provided **simplistic calculations** that failed to reflect the **different possible useful lives** of the machines and their respective **annuity** factors

Strong answers

- Allowed for **opportunity cost** – this was rewarded, even if the candidate did not include this point **within** the NPV pro forma

- Reached a **reasonable conclusion** on the basis of a good discussion of **benefits and risks**

Task 3 Summary

We can see here again that you should look out for issues such as opportunity cost in the NPV calculation. This was also noted by the examiners in their review of Task 1 of this paper.

The examiners also noted that knowledge of annuity factors was poor – as we explained elsewhere in this book, and particularly in chapter 15, the SBM examiners do like annuity and perpetuity approaches so there is no excuse for not performing well in this area.

Task 4   Financial reporting issues of the proposed projects

Here candidates had to explain how the potential projects might affect the financial statements.

Weak answers

- Struggled to identify the **key** issues

Strong answers

- Noted that **forex issues** were relevant and also spotted that there could be implications under **IFRS 5** (Assets Held for Sale and discontinued operations).

Task 4 Summary

The discussion by the examiners was very brief. We would note that the topics tested are potentially very common in SBM papers as they concern foreign currency and discontinued operations: therefore, please ensure that you familiarise yourself with the model answer.

Task 5   Analysis of financial and operating data

Here candidates had to analyse performance by looking at a range of standard and company-specific performance indicators.

Weak answers

- Provided only **basic calculations** such as gross profit and operating profit margins

- Merely **stated by what percentage** a ratio had moved without **developing the discussion** any further

- Failed to present data for **all relevant time periods**

- Presented just a **small number** of relevant ratios

- Demonstrated **errors** in the ratios presented

- Provided a **limited number** of **qualitative** comments, often restricted by the relatively **minimal calculations** performed

- Missed the point of the **difference** between **management performance** and **company performance**

- Failed to provide an **additional short paragraph summarising performance**, despite being **required** to do so by the **question wording**

Strong answers

- Provided a **range** of **specific ratios** such as revenue per employee, production per employee, ROCE and gearing

- Used the **information in the question** such as changes in profit mix, production capacity and the impact of investment in new assets

Task 5   Summary

This feedback clearly demonstrates what we have said elsewhere many times in this book – you must provide scenario-specific, rather than generic, answers. This means that whenever possible you should try to develop indicators which are more specific to the company in the question than measures such as gross profit margin which can be applied to almost any company.

We can also see that the examiners want to see an **explanation** of movements – simply listing out movements and changes with supporting numbers will not attract credit. This is in line with the examiner comments which we will review in chapter 18 – if candidates would only use the word "because" a bit more than grades in SBM would improve.

Additionally, note the interaction between calculations and narrative discussion – if your calculations and ratios are generic and limited in number, then it is likely that your narrative discussion (which is likely to carry more marks than the calculations) will also be viewed negatively by the marker.

SBM is all about distinctions and differences – this could be reflected in the examiners wanting you to make different points about different products or divisions within the company. In this examination, the point was that management performance and company performance are different things. Make sure you revise the model answer to see the distinction required in this case.

As with any examination, do read the question wording carefully so that you do not miss out key requirements such as the provision of an additional short paragraph summarising performance which appears to have been missed by many candidates in this examination.

Task 6   Ethics

Candidates had to discuss and analyse ethical issues in relation to redundancies and share options.

Weak answers

- Discussed the **financial reporting** implications of share options or provided an extended discussion of **redundancy** in a legal context – such answers were irrelevant because it was clear that the question was about **ethics**

- Provided limited discussion of appropriate **ethical principles** and demonstrated little use of **ethical language**

Strong answers

- Described a **number** of issues that could arise from the scenario and recognised the potential for illegality around **dismissals/redundancies**

- Made good use of the "**transparency/effect/fairness**" framework and used appropriate **ethical language** to describe the main issues

- Demonstrated **professional scepticism** regarding the information provided

Task 6

This feedback is in line with our discussion of the importance of an ethical framework in chapter 17 of this book. It was surprising to see students waste time on financial reporting and legal issues within a Task that was indeed very clearly about ethics.

Question 2   Phantom West Airlines plc

Task 1   Revenue calculation

In this Task, candidates were required to perform a revenue calculation for 2 different seat configurations on an aircraft. A reasoned recommendation as to which seat configuration should be used was also required.

Weak answers

- Failed to correctly address the potential of **upgrading** the customer's seat on a Saturday

Strong answers

- Provided a **competent discussion** and recognised the **distinction** between business class and premium economy customers which would generate extra costs in terms of service, food and drink

Task 1 Summary

Unusually for a calculation Task, the examiners were fairly positive here and only had 1 type of weakness to specifically mention.

Task 2   Alternative seat configurations

Here candidates had to compare 2 methods of financing the acquisition of new aircraft, providing supporting calculations and explanations, together with a reasoned recommendation and statement of further information that would be needed.

Weak answers

- Failed to produce any **calculations** at all for this Task

Strong answers

- Made **reasonable comments** on the **comparison** between 2 methods and the additional information required

Task 2 Summary

Here the examiner feedback was relatively brief so there are not a huge number of learning points.

Task 3   Financial reporting of financing methods

For this Task, candidates had to explain the financial reporting consequences of each of the 2 proposed financing methods.

Weak answers

- Based their **depreciation** calculations on the original cost rather than the depreciable amount

- Failed to deal correctly with the **lease**, stating that it was a **finance lease**

- Failed to address the **break clause** and potential for **grounding** the aircraft well

- Did not clearly **distinguish** their answer to **this Task** from their answer to the **previous Task**

Strong answers

The examiners did not have anything positive to say regarding stronger answers on this occasion.

Task 3 Summary

Leases are a very common question area in SBM so it is important that you understand the distinction between a finance lease and an operating lease – but also, and most importantly, how these tend to be tested in SBM. We strongly recommend that you work through all examples of leases in SBM so that you can start to see the clues that the SBM examiners leave.

Task 4   Financial reporting of a cash flow hedge

This Task involved explanation of the financial reporting implications of a cash flow hedge.

Weak answers

- Were unable to clearly and simply **explain** the main principles

- Provided **incorrect** calculations on how the **loss** on the forward contracts had impacted the **recognition** of 2016 fuel costs in the financial statements

- Had the **principles the wrong way round**, suggesting that a gain had been recognised and that underlying fuel costs had risen – in fact, the question Exhibit indicated the opposite relationship

- **Netted off** the 2 items going through OCI, demonstrating a lack of understanding of the principles

Strong answers

The examiners did not have any particular points of strength to note here.

Task 4 Summary

We would note here that cash flow hedge accounting was done very poorly, which is slightly surprising as it is obviously a core element of the new Advanced Level financial reporting syllabus. We would recommend that you revise this area well as you will need to know it for Corporate Reporting anyway and since it has been done so badly in SBM then it is likely to be tested again in future.

Task 5   Fuel price hedging

In this final task, candidates had to explain whether the company should use fuel price hedging. If it was recommended to use hedging, the candidate had to go on and provide reasoned advice on the most appropriate hedging strategy.

Weak answers

- Did not analyse the **extent** to which fuel made up a significant proportion of the total cost of the company and therefore that **variability** could cause significant risks

155

- Spent **too much time discussing options**, despite the question wording clearly stating the **only futures and forwards** should be considered

- Did not clearly **distinguish** their answer to this Task from their answer to the **previous** Task

Strong answers

- Discussed the **risk appetite** of the company

- Reached a **conclusion** on the appropriate **action** to take

- Considered the **implications** of **doing nothing**

- Provided some good discussion on the **purpose** and **advantages** of **forward contracts** and **futures**

- Made sensible comments about **timeframes** and the proportions of fuel cost to hedge

Task 5 Summary

Issues relating to hedging appear to have been a major theme in recent SBM examinations. These comments therefore provide important learning points.

We would note again the concern of the examiners that many candidates simply list out standard points and answer questions on "autopilot" – for example, here the question did not ask anything regarding options but candidates appear to have tried to force points on options in because they have revised and preprepared them.

Finally, we would note that the examiners criticise the fact that candidates did not clearly distinguish their answer from this Task from the answer to other Tasks in the same question – this criticism was made regarding Tasks 3 and 6 in this question. As explained elsewhere in this book, the SBM examiners do favour the use of clear headings in your answer in order to divide up the discussion and make it clear which element you are attempting to address. We would recommend that you start each Task on a fresh page, with a new and clear heading, for this reason. (See also the comments on this matter in relation to Q1 of the July 2014 paper which we have already reviewed above.)

8.8 July 2017 Examiners' Comments

Question 1 Best Baked Bread plc

Task 1 Contract evaluation

This Task required students to estimate the likely impact on operating profit and cash flows of a new contract.

Weak answers

- Did not time apportion the impact of the contract for the three month and nine month periods within the financial year

- Provided only very brief explanation of the financial impact

- Failed to prepare a basic cash budget

- Did not use the information provided fully enough

Strong answers

- Applied scepticism to the 10% volume growth assumption proposed by the customer

- Noted that there would be a reduction in profit margin

- Gave detail about the impact on receivables days and whether there was enough headroom in the overdraft facility

- Explained that the predicted increase in volume was broadly within the capacity of the company

- Considered whether there could be a capacity constraint on particular days when the company was already a capacity

- Discussed the broader declining market for traditional breads

- Identified the opportunity cost of using spare capacity for low margin sales

- Discussed the importance of the customer to the company

- Considered the relative bargaining strengths of the company and its customer

- Considered whether a price reduction might also be expected by other existing customers

Task 2 Hedging

For this Task, candidates had to discuss whether the company should hedge its wheat costs.

157

Weak answers

- Failed to connect their points to the specific circumstances of the company in the question

- Failed to provide a conclusion on whether hedging should be used or not

- Lacked a clear explanation of the link between volatility and option prices

- Stated that the risk to be hedged was that wheat prices might fall … but wheat was a raw material (not a sales product) for the company so such a price fall would have been beneficial and would not require hedging!

- Provided a poor explanation of the financial reporting treatment due to a lack of certainty as to the nature of the hedge – such candidates therefore described all possible accounting treatments in a generic way

- Failed to distinguish between a firm commitment and a highly probable forecast transaction

- Mixed up gains and losses or had debits and credits the wrong way around

Strong answers

- Set out the answer in a logical manner and considered materiality, volatility and timeframe issues in a way that was specific to the question

- Used information from the question in their answer

- Referred to the variables in the Black-Scholes-Merton model

- Identified counterparty risk in the hedges

- Understood that there were both commodity and currency risks to hedge

- Identified the hedge as either a fair value hedge or a cash flow hedge

Task 3   Forecast operating profit and longer-term sustainability

In this Task, candidates had to estimate the expected operating profit for a future year and assess any potential impact on going concern status.

Weak answers

- Failed to get the multiplier correct, using 1.01 instead of 0.99

- Applied probabilities for 1 year instead of for 2 years

- Misinterpreted the Task as being about environmental sustainability – the Task was rather about the sustainability of the business model

- Provided disappointing financial reporting responses which were often limited in length and focused on Corporate Social Responsibility disclosures rather than going concern and liquidity

- Failed to consider financial reporting at all

- Provided extensive comments on the impact in relation to the statutory audit (including ISAs) when this was not asked for in the question wording

Strong answers

- Described declining profit as problematic for business sustainability

- Noted that a high chance of losses meant there were significant concerns for the future of the business

- Identified the competitive market environment and used other information from the scenario relating to alternative strategies

- Identified that it may be appropriate to prepare the financial statements on a breakup basis

- Considered the possibility of impairment of assets or provisions for potentially onerous contracts

Task 4   Ethics

For this Task, candidates had to look at the transparency and confidentiality issues arising from an email which proposed that lower quality raw materials were used in production.

Weak answers

- Ignored the issue of confidentiality relating to the email sent in error to the engagement partner – candidates should realise that SBM ethics questions are widely-scoped and therefore candidates should never just focus on the first issue identified

- Did not consider all stakeholders

- Provided limited comments on Actions or Recommendations

- Suggested excessive actions such as contacting the police or speaking to the MLRO

159

Strong answers

- Noted that transparency was a key issue

- Used a TEF framework to answer the question

- Used appropriate ethical language to describe the main issues

Question 2   Moonbeam Marine Yachts Ltd

Task 1   Due Diligence

In this Task, candidates were required to identify the key risks facing a potential target (MMY) and Due Diligence procedures that a potential investor should consider when evaluating such risks.

Weak answers

- Provided vague responses rather than identifying specific procedures

- Failed to identify the possibility of inventory being impaired

- Failed to mention the relevance of IAS 10

- Described an event, rather than explaining the risks arising from the event – for example, candidates said "there is a legal dispute with the manufacturer" without stating the resulting risk to the business

- Provided "shopping lists" of Due Diligence procedures which had no relevance to the risks specific to the scenario

Strong answers

- Identified the need for a provision

- Discussed the possibility of disclosing a contingent asset

Task 2   Evaluation of current financial position

For this Task, candidates had to appraise the debt position of the company.

160

Weak answers

As the examiners stated that most answers to this Task were "very good", no points specific to weak answers are noted in the examiner comments.

Strong answers

- Discussed the implications of a range of issues

- Calculated financial indicators, including the 2 most relevant to the debt covenants

- Discussed the overall picture and concluded on the ability of the business to continue as a going concern

Task 3   Corporate recovery plan

For this Task, candidates had to analyse the feasibility of a corporate recovery plan.

Weak answers

- Often got confused in the narrative discussion regarding which company they were commenting on and incorrectly discussed the risks to MMY rather than the risks to the investing company, as required by the question wording

Strong answers

- Made an attempt at calculating the return to the investor and provided an approximate NPV

- Questioned the sustainability of the cash flows and the validity of the information provided, applying professional scepticism

Task 4   Financial reconstruction

Here candidates had to review 2 proposals for the financial reconstruction of the target company (MMY).

Weak answers

- Did not provide enough detail on the implications for each separate group of stakeholders

- Failed to identify the possibility of negotiating to buy the target's trade and assets under approach 2 or the annual interest return for the investor, should they purchase a loan under approach 1

- Did not conclude which would be the preferred option

- Made no attempt to calculate the amount that the target's bank would receive

- Failed to address the factors to be considered

Strong answers

- Recognised the split between fixed and floating charges

- Provided an assessment of the impact of each approach for each of the different stakeholders

8.9   November 2017 Examiners' Comments

Question 1   Gemstone Jewellery Ltd

Task 1   Valuation

For this Task, candidates had to prepare a valuation of a potential target at 2 specific future dates.

Weak answers

- Demonstrated basic errors in knowledge and approach

- Overlooked the narrative element of the requirement

- Failed to take into account the potential use of surplus cash to repay debt

- Included 2017 free cash flows in the valuation despite the benefits only arising from 1 January 2018 (the date of the proposed MBO)

- Failed to adjust the depreciation figure for a reduction in owned shops from 20 to 15 as a result of the operating sale and leaseback

- Ignored the sale and leaseback proceeds or placed these into the wrong year

- Placed other elements of the calculation into the wrong year

- Incorrectly included interest cashflows in their calculations

- Calculated an equity valuation but ignored enterprise value

- Failed to calculate a terminal value

- In cases where a terminal value was calculated, some candidates failed to discount back correctly to 31 December 2017

- Provided no explanations whatsoever despite the clear requirement for such explanations in the question wording

- Provided very general explanations which tended to focus only on the disadvantages of the valuation method

Strong answers

- Recognised the need to remove depreciation and then add it back

- Recognised the need to apply a perpetuity calculation for 2021 cashflows onwards

- Arrived at an enterprise value and made an adjustment for debt

Task 2   Benefits and Risks of an MBO

This Task required a discussion of the proposed MBO for 3 different groups of stakeholders.

Weak answers

- Made no reference to the specific individuals involved as part of the management team

- Provided few comments on the future governance structure

- Provided few comments on future business strategy and the risks involved

- Did not comment in detail on financial gearing

- Failed to comment that a payment of £250,000 could be a substantial amount for an individual

- Failed to calculate any numbers or look at the potential return to the MBO team

Strong answers

- Structured the answer into separate subheadings for each of the 3 stakeholder groups and provided a range of benefits and risks that applied to the scenario

- Commented on the acquisition price and made reference to the ownership percentage, interest rates on loans and the strategic ideas of the buyout team

Task 3   Due Diligence

Here candidates had to review potential financial, commercial and operational Due Diligence issues.

Weak answers

- Did not provide specific procedures and instead talked generally about the difference between financial, commercial and operational procedures

- Did not provide the specific procedures required by the scenario

Strong answers

Although the examiner stated that this part of the question was "usually well attempted", no specific statements in relation to strong answers are provided in the examiner comments.

Task 4   Financial reporting

For this Task, candidates had to discuss the financial reporting implications of 4 specific issues relating to the strategy of the target company.

Weak answers

- Did not scope their response widely enough and failed to address any financial reporting issues other than the sale and leaseback

- Discussed IFRS 5 in too much depth

- Missed straightforward points such as not stating that the profits of £3 million should be recognised or that the improvement costs should be capitalised

- Tended to ignore the refurbishment in favour of overlong discussions about inventory management – again, the problem here is that candidates did not identify a sufficiently wide range of financial reporting issues

Strong answers

- Discussed the lease and correctly identified that it was an operating sale and leaseback – many candidates then went on to show the correct financial reporting treatment

- Considered the timing of the disposal and the fact that some aspects of IFRS 5 might not be relevant for the period under consideration

Task 5   Ethics

This Task concerned some potentially non-transparent actions by one of the members of the Board of the target company.

Weak answers

- Gave equal emphasis to each of the TEF parts of the framework rather than selecting and emphasising those most relevant to the specific question

- Focused too much on the TEF framework and therefore missed the fact that other ethical principles were important to the scenario

- Failed to separately identify the ethical actions for the advisory company and 2 named individuals as required by the question – instead, weak answers provided a general list of ethical actions, without specifying to whom they were applicable

- Provided thin coverage of Actions or Recommendations

Strong answers

- Identified and emphasised that a conflict of interest and transparency were the key ethical issues in the specific scenario

- Considered Actions from each stakeholder group's specific perspective

Question 2   Hayfield plc

Task 1   Profit reconciliation (variance analysis)

In this Task, candidates had to analyse actual profit performance compared to budget.

Weak answers

- Failed to structure the answer as a reconciliation of budgeted profit and actual profit – instead, many candidates showed the movement, line by line, in each item in the management accounts

- Failed to correctly calculate sales volume or foreign currency variances

- Identified a price variance on EU sales when in fact the movement was due entirely to foreign currency changes

- Failed to apply time apportionment to the figures

- Provided generic narrative answers which were not particularly well applied to the scenario

- Completely omitted the requirement to prepare explanatory notes

Strong answers

As the examiners commented that answers to this element of the question were "generally weak", the examiners did not make any specific comments in relation to strong answers.

Task 2   Currency hedging

Here candidates had to calculate the loss on certain foreign currency derivatives and explain the related financial reporting treatment.

Weak answers

- Made vague and ambiguous statements such as "the loss was due to a change in exchange rates" without further explanation of the direction and consequences of the change – open statements of this type received no credit

- Failed to realise that a net loss on forward contracts means that there must have been a net gain on the underlying business transactions, and vice versa

- Failed to comment on the different scale and time-periods involved in each of the 2 hedges which candidates were required to evaluate

- Got the direction of change wrong in stating that the pound sterling had strengthened in value

- Stated that the strengthening of overseas currencies had the same effect on revenue and costs

- Provided very generic answers about how forward contracts work with limited application to the scenario

- Simply regurgitated different hedge accounting treatments

- Misclassified the hedge as a fair value hedge or did not attempt to classify it at all

- Stated the normal financial reporting treatment of derivatives when these are held outside of a hedging arrangement – this was not relevant to the question at all

- Failed to provide any answer at all to this Task

Strong answers

- Correctly identified that the loss was due to the hedging arrangement in place and therefore arose because of the hedging instrument rather than because of the underlying hedged transactions

Task 3   Overseas expansion strategies

In this part of the question, candidates had to evaluate 2 alternative strategies for international expansion.

Weak answers

As the examiners noted that most candidates provided "good quality, applied answers" to this Task, there are no points specific to weak answers in the examiner comments.

Strong answers

- Covered both the joint arrangement and subsidiary options and reached a relevant conclusion

- Provided reasonable discussion of the benefits and risks of each option

- Provided very well-structured answers, separately discussing the financial, commercial and operational risks of a joint arrangement and of a subsidiary

Task 4   Financial reporting of overseas expansion strategy

In this part of the question, candidates had to look at the financial reporting implications of one of the proposed overseas expansion strategies.

Weak answers

- Made no mention of the subsidiary being an overseas subsidiary and did not refer to IAS 21

- Did not state that the joint arrangement was a joint operation for financial reporting purposes

- Did not explain the correct financial reporting treatment for a joint operation – many stated that it should be accounted for using the equity method and/or identified it as an Associate

Strong answers

- Gave a full explanation of the issues involved in the financial reporting of a foreign subsidiary

Task 5   Assurance in relation to overseas expansion strategy

In the final part of the question, candidates had to discuss how Assurance procedures could help reduce the risks of one of the proposed overseas expansion strategies

Weak answers

- Were quite general in nature, rather than being related to the specific scenario

- Identified only 1 or 2 risks, together with some basic assurance procedures – many of these procedures were only tangentially relevant to the scenario

Strong answers

- Focused on specific risks and the resulting assurance procedures which should be undertaken for each risk

8.10   Strengths and Weaknesses: Summary

Based on the above review, some **key general strengths in student scripts** can be summarised as:

- Provision of a **table of data** at the start of the answer

- Usage of **client-** or **industry-specific** indicators

- Recognition of **interconnected** factors

- Provision of a **bespoke solution/recommendations** based on the specific client scenario, supporting this with an appropriate amount of reasoning and explanation

- Usage of **headings**

- Polite and gentle **scepticism** of the data

- Used an **appropriate structure** for the **calculations** and **presentation**, separating out different elements or stakeholders

- First **explored** ethical principles and then **applied** them to the scenario

- Discussion of relevant **practical** factors

Based on the same review, some **key general weaknesses in student scripts** can be summarised as:

- Not **making enough use of the data**, thereby not including **scenario-specific metrics**, and concentrating too much on standard points to do with revenue, gross profit etc

- Provided **random**, **mixed in** calculation results rather than a **clear table** at the start of the answer

- Not providing enough information on **causes** of the changes

- **Reproduction** of a general section **from the learning materials**

- **Limited discussion** of valuation methods and alternatives

- **Errors** in application of **foreign currency rates** and **discount rates**

- **Sitting on the fence** and not providing clear advice (remember that there is often not "a" right answer but rather answers that can be justified in different ways so be brave!)

- **Failed to keep ethics issues separate** from financial reporting issues

- Provided **extreme ethical positions**, rather than nuanced approaches

- **Did not separate out the explanation into different sections** (e.g. for different stakeholder groups) and therefore did not provide a balanced approach

- Did not apply **professional scepticism**

- **Failed to spot** Tasks/requests which were **mixed in** with the main Introduction text

8.11   Enough Analysis! Time for Part 2

Over the previous 8 chapters we have undertaken a **very** detailed review of the nature of the SBM examination, the Case Study "lenses", our MAP approach and the recent examination papers. Based on this theoretical review of how to plan, it is now time to turn towards our advice on what to write into your answer. In Part 2 of the book we will concentrate more on the kind of content you should include, based on a review and revision of key technical issues. We will cover the areas of practical business advisory (PBA), Specialist Audit & Assurance and ethics: unfortunately, financial accounting issues are too numerous to review neatly in this book[57]. We then conclude the book with some comments from the examiners at SBM Workshops at recent ICAEW Tutor Conferences and provide some final advice for your exam day.

---

[57] See instead our *Advanced Level Financial Reporting Q&A 2018* and *Financial Accounting and Reporting Q&A 2018* for relevant self-test questions.

Part 2 – Potential Scenario and Technical Content

Chapter 9   The Mini-Case Study: What To Do and What Not To Do

---

Learning Points

After reading this chapter, you must be able to:

1. understand the characteristics of a strong answer to Q1
2. understand how to avoid the characteristics of weak answers to Q1
3. understand the likely format and nature of the Tasks in Q1

9.1   The "Mini-Case" Study

Although it is not marked in a way remotely similar to the unusual way in which Case Study is marked[58], SBM Q1 is informally termed the "mini-Case" study by both the examiners and the tutor community. This is presumably because of the large amount of information to absorb and the fact that there is likely to be a financial performance review at the start of the question (just as in Requirement 1 of the Case Study).

The examiners have confirmed (see chapter 18) that SBM Q1 may range between 55 and 65 marks. If Q1 is worth 65% of your attempt then it is hard to see how it will be possible to pass SBM without a good performance whilst even if the question is "only" worth 55 marks then this will still be the single most highly rewarded ACA question you will ever do.

In short, your SBM Q1 needs to be good! For this reason, we have decided to create a chapter dedicated to Q1. To some extent, this chapter will be a reiteration and reemphasis of points collated from various other chapters in the book so **apologies for any repetition** – however, **we would rather ensure that you definitely have seen this advice** because as stated this really is a "make or break" question.

9.2   The Likely Structure of Q1

Chapter 3 reviewed the typical structure of SBM papers in significant detail. Here are some useful reminders:

There will generally be **6 or 7 Exhibits** and a total of around **7 pages** of information to absorb, which will be tested by **9** total Tasks and sub-Tasks.

Exhibits 1 to 3 will often tend to "**cluster**" into becoming the background information for Task 1, which will generally involve a financial review of performance.

As a result of the fact that **3 different Exhibits may need to be used just for Task 1**, that Task is, in our opinion, a potential **time-trap**: the amount of material that needs to be absorbed, processed

---

[58] See our book *Cracking Case™ – How to Pass the ACA Case Study* for further explanation of the Case Study marking approach and the reasons why this needs to be taken into account in your approach to Case Study.

and used is high relative to the rewards obtained (conversely, subsequent Tasks may only have half a page or two thirds of a page of data but plenty of marks available): you need to read around 50% of the Exhibit material for around 25% of the marks.

The general format will be that Exhibit 1 looks at the industry, Exhibit 2 describes the client in more detail and Exhibit 3 provides some financial information, **including some client- or industry-specific measures which you must use (even if they are not familiar)**.

Additionally, we noted in chapter 7 that Task 1 will not always be the most highly rewarded Task in Q1 – therefore, do not just assume that Task 1 is the "big one" and therefore that if Task 1 is done well that you will be okay.

9.3   Do Not Forget the 4 Case Skills "Lenses"

Remember that the 4 Case skills "lenses" (translated into useable language: see chapter 4) basically involve **identifying** the key data, **using** the key data, **Applying Judgement** and offering **Conclusions & Recommendations**. Note that a typical Q1 will not always remind you to **Apply Judgement** or offer **Conclusions & Recommendations** so it remains up to you to remember to do so. Here is a reminder from chapter 4 of some of the ways that Applying Judgement and Conclusions & Recommendations have been rewarded in Q1:

Applying Judgement (Professional Scepticism)

- **Stripping out particular activities or events enables underlying activities to be analysed** but judgement is required and errors could be made (July 2014 real paper Q1)

- **Allocation of overheads** in the management accounting system has a significant impact on results (July 2014 real paper Q1)

- There is a **lack of information** to determine whether price discounting or a change in product mix has affected results (July 2014 real paper Q1)

- **Ability and knowledge of staff at client is unknown** and may not be specialised enough (July 2014 real paper Q1)

- The difference between an 8% and 5% interest rate is **material** but the reasons for the difference need to be confirmed (November 2014 real paper Q1)

- A reconstruction scheme requires shareholders to inject funds and it is **not known** if this will occur (November 2014 real paper Q1)

- **Assurance over the projected profit figure should be obtained** because this will make a crucial difference to whether the scheme will work (November 2014 real paper Q1)

- There is **no supporting evidence for the figures provided** and management have a strong incentive for optimism to persuade shareholders to invest (November 2014 real paper Q1)[59]

- The client company should consider a **range of currency fluctuations** and not just the fluctuation between sterling and a single foreign currency (July 2015 real paper Q1)

- Not **all** costs will be incurred in sterling (July 2015 real paper Q1)[60]

- Various points raised regarding the data provided as part of a set of **forecasts**, to be reviewed as an assurance exercise under ISAE 3400 (July 2015 real paper Q1)

- Uncertainty of the ability to **repay a loan** and therefore the going concern basis of the client company (July 2015 real paper Q1)

- There may be unexpected **costs of integration** and **synergy gains** are not confirmed or **guaranteed** (November 2015 real paper Q1)

- Due Diligence is very useful but **may not identify all issues** (November 2015 real paper Q1)

- It is **not known** how certain stakeholders with **high shareholding percentages** will react (November 2015 real paper Q1)

- Incorrect estimates of fair value would be particularly significant in respect of a "**landbank**" if the relevant company is a **property developer** – this is likely to be one of its main assets (November 2015 real paper Q1)

- Further **market research** on the target market is needed before reaching a final decision (July 2016 real paper Q1)

- All NPV figures are dependent on the accuracy of **assumptions** (July 2016 real paper Q1)

- Debt and equity are not the **only** alternative financing methods – others should be considered (July 2016 real paper Q1)

- The implication of a **perpetuity** (constant renewal of a contract) cannot be assumed in reality (July 2016 real paper Q1)

- A **casual conversation** may not be a **reliable** source of information and information obtained from such a source would need to be **verified** independently (July 2016 real paper Q1)

- Data on some key operating costs is **missing**, **preventing an analysis** of operating margins (July 2016 real paper Q2)

- Profit data has not been provided on several **key product lines** so the analysis is necessarily limited in nature (July 2016 real paper Q2)

---

[59] In relation to this point, the term "professional scepticism" is even used in the model answer – this is definitely not something to do in Case Study as the term itself should not be written into your answer (instead you should just apply professional scepticism as a skill).
[60] Again, in relation to this point, the term "professional scepticism" is even used in the SBM model answer.

- There is no information on the **rate of returns** and product **quality** (July 2016 real paper Q2)

- The data currently being gathered by the Board is **too aggregated** to be of use (July 2016 real paper Q2)

- The final part of Q2 asked candidates to indicate which **additional data** would be required for a better analysis – this was effectively an opportunity to exercise **scepticism of the data already provided** (July 2016 real paper Q2)

- The results of the different alternative financial models are **very close** so **additional** financial and non-financial information needs to be considered (November 2016 real paper Q1)

- Certain key factors are **not adjusted for** in the models and some form of **averaging** over different years is probably also advisable (November 2016 real paper Q1)

- It is **unreasonable** to compare 2 NPV calculations if the projects cover **different time periods** (November 2016 real paper Q1)

- The **useful life assumption** makes a huge **difference** to the results of the calculation and so should be checked carefully (November 2016 real paper Q1)

- An evaluation of **management performance** over a particular time period must factor in the impact of variables **outside** the control of management as these may have **interfered** with the efforts of management (November 2016 real paper Q1)

- The **first step** in an **ethical** evaluation is to **establish the facts accurately** (November 2016 real paper Q1)

- The decision to invest must **not** be taken **purely on the results of the NPV calculation** – there may be **other** factors to consider (November 2016 real paper Q2)

- Further information should be obtained on **how the discount rate has been calculated** and **how sensitive** the NPV is to the discount rate (November 2016 real paper Q2)

- The **price reduction** is **certain** if the agreement is made whereas **volume** increases are only an **estimate** which could have been made by the customer in a **self-interested** way to persuade the client to accept new contract conditions (July 2017 real paper Q1)

- Forecasts **exclude** important elements such as tax, interest and investment in PPE – a more comprehensive cash flow forecast is advised (July 2017 real paper Q1)

- **Opportunity cost** may not have been considered correctly in the model (July 2017 real paper Q1)

- Extent of **counterparty risk** is **not known** (July 2017 real paper Q1)

- An ethical concern relates **only to one member of the Board** and there is **no evidence** that the Board in general has done anything wrong (July 2017 real paper Q1)

- The **limited period of time** available is unlikely to be sufficient to establish evidence to support the projections – market research would be needed as to the likelihood of the projected sales being achieved (July 2017 real paper Q2)

- The valuation depends on the **forecasting being reliable** and the **discount rate being appropriate and stable over time** (November 2017 real paper Q1)

- The revenue growth rate is a **fundamental assumption** that **drives** much of the increase in the value of the equity from the MBO – therefore, this growth rate needs to be **substantiated** (November 2017 real paper Q1)

- The valuation model **assumes that surplus cash can be distributed to shareholders** and does not need to be **retained for investment** to generate future cash flows (November 2017 real paper Q1)

- There may be **unrecognised** asset values in **intangibles** (November 2017 real paper Q1)

- The forecast's working assumptions made by the management team may not be **realistic** – the assumption that cash flows are **indefinite** needs to be evaluated carefully, given the relatively **short-term strategy** proposed (November 2017 real paper Q1)

- The management team is subject to various **conflicts of interest** and may **lack commitment** to the MBO – other members of the team appear to **lack suitable finance expertise** (November 2017 real paper Q1)

- Financial, commercial and operational Due Diligence is strongly advised to **substantiate** key facts (November 2017 real paper Q1)

- Although the joint arrangement offers modest and temporary benefits, there may **only be a five-year horizon** to the activities (November 2017 real paper Q2)

- Assurance over the proposed joint arrangement is strongly advised to **substantiate** key facts (November 2017 real paper Q2)

- **Manipulation of accounting policies and estimates should not be reflected in valuation models** as this will overstate growth (Sample Paper Q1)

- There may be **unrecognised** assets, liabilities and provisions which should be included in a valuation (Sample Paper Q1)

- Financial Due Diligence procedures can only provide **limited assurance** (Sample Paper Q1)

- **Statutory accounts should not be used directly for valuations** – they are not prepared for this purpose (Sample Paper Q1)

- An **effective tax rate of 25%** used in all working assumptions is a "**crude assumption**" as it does not separate current tax from deferred tax (Sample Paper Q1)

- The **perpetuity** assumption appears **unrealistic** (Sample Paper Q1)

- Not realistic to assume constant prices and costs assumed into **perpetuity** (Sample Paper Q1)

- **Not clear how the cost of equity has been arrived at** and whether this is a real or money rate (Sample Paper Q1)

- The **proposal** to integrate companies of such different sizes and with such different strategies is **questionable** (Sample Paper Q1)

Conclusions & Recommendations

- Examine **capacity** in more detail – temporarily reduce output and activities until demand recovers (July 2014 real paper Q1)

- Reduce **price** provided that demand is elastic (July 2014 real paper Q1)

- Increase advertising and marketing **expenditure** (July 2014 real paper Q1)

- Consider **rebranding** (July 2014 real paper Q1)

- Set up a **contingency plan** to deal with similar issues if they reoccur in future (July 2014 real paper Q1)

- Undertake a **public relations** exercise (July 2014 real paper Q1)

- Improve **quality** (July 2014 real paper Q1)

- Continue to use an existing supplier as this supplier is reliable but undertake **negotiations** on price and service, perhaps raising the possibility of moving to a different supplier to encourage a better deal (July 2014 real paper Q2)

- **Negotiate** an approach under which the commitment to the existing supplier is made conditional on service levels being achieved (July 2014 real paper Q2)

- **Improve operating efficiency** and review operating management procedures and productivity (November 2014 real paper Q1)

- Raise production **capacity** by investing in new assets (November 2014 real paper Q1)

- Increase **prices** until excess demand is removed (November 2014 real paper Q1)

- **Renegotiate** the existing contract with the customer (November 2014 real paper Q1)

- Strategy 1 should be preferred because it is superior in terms of **satisfying customer needs**, even though it has a higher **cost** than Strategy 2 – it also has **higher revenue** and allows for **local** supply methods (July 2015 real paper Q1)

- The company should take a **selective** approach, rather than expanding **too rapidly** in an unfocused manner (July 2015 real paper Q2)

- A market segment with **high levels of competition** and **low barriers to entry** is unlikely to be very **profitable** (July 2015 real paper Q1)

- **Threats** should be adequately **reviewed** and **assessed** (July 2015 real paper Q1)

- A **share for share** exchange could be a **lower risk option** as it does not increase **gearing** – this also preserves **liquidity** and **debt capacity** (November 2015 real paper Q1)

- Finance Method A is preferred **despite its higher cost** because it has **better currency matching with Australian operations, a longer loan period which helps liquidity and avoids a mismatch in loan periods** as would happen under Finance Method B (July 2015 real paper Q1)

- Sell **directly from the UK** when **initially** entering the market but then **revise** this if sales take off significantly (July 2016 real paper Q1)

- Perform **market research** before deciding on a **final strategy** (July 2016 real paper Q1)

- A **positive NPV appears good** but bear in mind the **40% probability of the result being negative** if a different outcome happens (July 2016 real paper Q1)

- **Invest** in the warehouse but any **commitment should be delayed as long as possible** to gain the maximum amount of **information** from market entry (July 2016 real paper Q1)

- In addition to confirming the **valuation** in a proposed brand sale, consider **strategic factors** such as the **loss of the ability to benefit from the brand in future** and the **impact** of the actions of **other companies** if the brand is any way shared with other entities (July 2016 real paper Q1)

- Consider **risk**, including renegotiation risk, as well as the **NPV result** (November 2016 real paper Q1)

- Consider **flexibility** of the options – purchasing one aircraft and leasing a second aircraft may provide a good blend of **affordability** and **flexibility**, compared to purchasing or leasing **both** aircraft (November 2016 real paper Q2)

- The **amount of hedging** used will depend on the **risk appetite** of the Board (November 2016 real paper Q2)

- An advantage of **not hedging all** fuel purchases is that this is more **flexible** if demand is not as high as expected (November 2016 real paper Q2)

- Something needs to be done regarding the relevant customer, given their **importance** to the business (July 2017 real paper Q1)

- The client should develop alternative strategies to **reduce dependency** on a particular customer in future (July 2017 real paper Q1)

- Alternative strategies to deal with problems facing the business could involve seeking **new products** and **new markets** – **speciality** breads with **high margins** may be an opportunity to **expand** or the company could look at **non-bread baked items** – the company could also look at **new geographical markets** (July 2017 real paper Q1)

- Any doubts over the **short-term viability** of the company resulting from the change in credit terms should be considered (July 2017 real paper Q1)

- A **detailed cash flow forecast** is needed (July 2017 real paper Q2)

- The client should consider acquiring the **equity** of its target as well as the target's **debt** (July 2017 real paper Q2)

- **All assumptions should be re-evaluated** in order to reduce the key risk of overpayment for the target (November 2017 real paper Q1)

- It may be advisable for the **client** (investor) **to appoint at least 1 member of the Board** of the target to represent its **interests** and to gain **access to information** (November 2017 real paper Q1)

- The proposed joint arrangement appears to offer modest and temporary benefits but also involves **major risks** such as a short five-year horizon – therefore the preferred recommendation is to set up a **subsidiary** rather than become involved in a **joint arrangement** (November 2017 real paper Q2)

- Even **after** Due Diligence has been undertaken, there should be **ongoing monitoring** of any joint arrangement (November 2017 real paper Q2)

- **Recommendation to proceed** with a particular financing option, based on cost and other factors (Sample Paper Q2)

- **Recommendation of an alternative financing option** if the preferred option is not ultimately possible (Sample Paper Q2)

9.4   What Pleases and Annoys the Examiners in Q1?

In the previous chapter, we detailed some of the common examiner complaints regarding Q1 as well as some of the points that made the examiners happy when reviewing Q1 answers. We recommend that you revisit the relevant sections of the previous chapter but focusing only on the Q1 comments in order to learn more about how to attempt this question specifically.

9.5   Remember MS²

As always, the key to a good answer is going to be to make **scenario-specific points**. This is not something specific to Q1 but it is just so incredibly important that we are repeating it once more!

Something which will be specific to Task 1 in Q1, however, is that there will be client- or industry-specific indicators to use in addition to standard accounting figures – these must be used to secure a good score (see chapter 18).

9.6 Other Reminders

Use headings – Tasks 2 and later are very likely to have several sub-Tasks so if you clearly head these up then not only will it make the job of the marker easier, it will also ensure that you allocate sufficient time to each area and can also see whether you have a balance between the different elements. See chapters 6 and 18 for more on this.

Ethics can appear in Q1 – the examiners have stated that ethics can be tested in either question or both so do not assume that this area will or will not appear in Q1. For revision of ethics, including relevant frameworks, please see chapter 17.

Chapter 10   Specialist Audit & Assurance Topics: Summary

Learning Points

After reading this chapter, you must be able to:

1. understand which Specialist Audit & Assurance areas are most examinable within SBM
2. understand the difference between "statutory audit" and "Specialist Audit & Assurance" topics
3. understand how Specialist Audit & Assurance has been tested in SBM past papers and Mocks

---

10.1   The Importance of Specialist Audit & Assurance to SBM

We know from our taught courses that some students believe that Specialist Audit & Assurance (Specialist A&A) topics are not really worth spending too much time on: the examiners have stated that Specialist A&A will only account for around 10% of the marks available so why bother spending much time on this area?

We would disagree. A&A is definitely worth revising well: there will be no real way for the examiner to test these concepts via numerical work, meaning that there is less chance of losing time or confidence (or both!) by getting lost in the figures and calculations: the **narrative points should be fairly consistent** from exam to exam so provided that you prepare well (using the following chapters of this book) and then of course apply the general points/framework to the specific scenario set (see chapter 3 for the importance of this) then there is an opportunity to score very well. Although there will not be a huge number of Specialist A&A narrative marks available, even so those marks could make all the difference between a score of, say, 45 and a score of 50.

The examiners have stated that, just as in the old Technical Integration paper in Business Changes, Specialist A&A questions continue to be done poorly by candidates (see chapter 18). Since many failing candidates get close to the 50 marks required (there are apparently a **large number of students in the 45-49 range**, according to the examiners) then it follows that just a **little more effort** on this area could make a big difference to your chance of passing.

We find that many students tend to "disrespect" the narrative marks at Advanced Level, either because they assume that there will be more marks for numerical work (definitely not the case in SBM) or because they assume that narrative marks will be easy to get by "making something up on the day". In fact, in relation to Assurance, the ICAEW markers are looking for you to make **very specific points in your narrative answer**, using appropriate headings and **mentioning points very similar to those contained in the Study Manual** rather than just making up "commonsense" material: doing all of this under time pressure is much harder than you may think.

The topics we will revise in the next few chapters to help you gain the Specialist A&A marks are taken from the relevant content in the SBM and Corporate Reporting Study Manuals and past papers, falling under 4 broad areas:

1. Corporate Governance

2. Assurance and Related Services (including Due Diligence)

3. Environmental and Social Audits and Assurance

4. Internal Audit

To help you revise well for these marks which could potentially make the difference between passing SBM or not, in the following 4 chapters of the book we will revise the key points relating to the above Specialist A&A areas. We will also look at how these topics have been tested in the 8 real SBM examinations, ICAEW SBM mocks and the ICAEW SBM Sample Paper.

In our original plan for this book, we were also aiming to review the testing of Specialist A&A areas as tested in the preceding Business Change paper for the old Technical Integration (TI) level: as mentioned elsewhere in this book, the Business Change paper remains a very valid source of guidance in cases where the evidence regarding SBM is relatively light. However, in the interests of preventing *Smashing SBM™* from becoming too long a book, we have not included our analysis of the Business Change paper in our final text for this book but rather have added points into our *SBM Exam Room Notes*. Please therefore refer to our *SBM Exam Room Notes* for further ideas relevant to Specialist A&A areas.

10.2   The Difference Between "Statutory Audit" and "Specialist A&A Areas"

By "Statutory Audit" topic areas we mean the kind of topics examined at the Professional Level in the Audit & Assurance paper and then again at the Advanced Level in the Corporate Reporting paper: in other words, checking that you would be able to assist in the performance of a statutory audit by determining the risks of misstatements in the financial statements and designing appropriate tests to minimise these risks.

By "Specialist A&A" topics we mean assurance areas such as a review of prospective financial information or non-statutory auditing areas such as internal audit. **As the Corporate Reporting paper provides full opportunity for the examiner to test statutory audit areas, we would expect SBM to favour the Specialist A&A areas so that both elements are tested in some way within the Advanced Level overall**. Based on the Advanced Level syllabus, this means:

1. Corporate Governance

2. Assurance and Related Services (including Due Diligence)

3. Environmental and Social Audits and Assurance

4. Internal Audit

In this chapter we will provide a brief review of these areas so that you understand the key points. We will also provide a review of how these topic areas have been tested in the 8 real SBM papers and the SBM Sample Paper.

10.3 Summary of Specialist A&A Areas Tested in Real SBM Examinations to Date

Based on the 8 real papers available at the time of writing, Specialist A&A areas have been tested as follows:

Examination	Question and Marks[61]	Topic	Notes
July 2014	Q1 (5 marks est.)	Due Diligence	Explain the benefits of Due Diligence
July 2014	Q2 (6 marks)	Corporate Governance	Explain the issues relating to a director's personal interest
November 2014	Q2 (5 marks)	Due Diligence	Explain the procedures and benefits of Due Diligence when shares are used as consideration
July 2015	Q1 (10 marks)	Prospective information	Apply ISAE 3400 to forecasts to help lenders evaluate a business
November 2015	Q1 (9 marks)	Due Diligence	Explain the procedures and benefits of Due Diligence in an acquisition
July 2016	Q1 (14 marks)	Agreed Upon Procedures	Identify risks to be addressed by AUP, suggested procedures to be used and benefits to both parties
July 2016	Q2 (5 marks)	Corporate Governance	Suggest improvements in Corporate Governance
November 2016	Q1 (9 marks)	Environmental and Social	Identify environmental KPIs and suggest assurance procedures
July 2017	Q2 (8 marks)	Due Diligence	Identify key risks and appropriate Due Diligence procedures
November 2017	Q1 (7 marks) & Q2 (6 marks)	Due Diligence & Contract Assurance	Identify financial, commercial and operational Due Diligence procedures Identify Assurance procedures (including Due Diligence) in respect of a proposed joint arrangement

Based on the above review, we can see that Specialist A&A areas have accounted for between 5 and 14 marks in the 8 real papers available at the time of writing. As such, Specialist A&A areas are not as important as other aspects of SBM … but 5 marks could come in handy (whilst 14 marks definitely will!) and therefore do consider revising the topics in the following few chapters. You should also note that the 2015 and 2016 papers contained a higher number of marks for this area – if we exclude the

---

[61] As some markschemes do not provide a precise split of marks within each Task, in cases where the Specialist A&A issue was contained in a bigger question we have estimated this based on our review of the amount of text included in the ICAEW model answer and our knowledge of the number of marks that used to be awarded for similar areas under the old Business Change syllabus. We include the text "est." to indicate this in the tables above. In other cases, the Specialist Audit & Assurance issue was contained in a separate Task and therefore our statement of the marks is precise.

abnormally low number of marks in the November 2014 paper then in fact the average would be more than 10 precious marks for Specialist Audit & Assurance per paper.

We can see that Due Diligence has been tested five times (or six times if the couple of marks on Due Diligence in November 2017 Q2 are also included: most of the Assurance marks in this question were for issues other than Due Diligence) so this topic has been tested more frequently than any other Specialist Audit & Assurance area: this is not surprising as this area fits well with the business change and valuations aspects of SBM. However, do not assume that Due Diligence will **always** be tested.

10.4   Summary of Specialist A&A Areas Tested in the SBM Sample Paper

Here is a summary of the ways in which Specialist A&A areas were tested in the SBM Sample Paper:

Examination	Question and Marks[62]	Topic	Notes
Sample Paper	Q1 (4 marks est.)	Due Diligence	Set out Due Diligence procedures regarding an acquisition
Sample Paper	Q2 (7 marks)	Corporate Governance	Review proposed changes to structure of the Board, including NEDs

In the Sample Paper, we can see a fairly standard weighting to Specialist Audit & Assurance areas with an estimated 11 marks available. The Corporate Governance issue received a relatively long write up (we have integrated the key points into our notes in the next chapter) and required a careful analysis of the percentage shareholding figures that would exist following the proposed changes. Overall, then, the Sample Paper included the 2 most common Specialist Audit & Assurance areas considered in our review of papers: Due Diligence and Corporate Governance.

10.5   ACA Simplified *Exam Room Notes*: Contribution to Your Specialist A&A Marks

As you may be aware, we provide 3 sets of *Exam Room Notes* which are relevant to Advanced Level Audit & Assurance questions:

---

[62] As the markschemes do not provide a precise split of marks within each Task, in cases where the Specialist Audit & Assurance issue was contained in a bigger question we have estimated this based on our review of the amount of text included in the ICAEW model answer and our knowledge of the number of marks that used to be awarded for similar areas under the old Business Change syllabus. We include the text "est." to indicate this in the tables above. In other cases, the Specialist Audit & Assurance issue was contained in a separate Task and therefore our statement of the marks can be precise.

Advanced Level Audit & Assurance Exam Room Notes 2018

The first part of this book provides an alphabetical listing of all key risk areas on statutory audits seen in Advanced Level papers, together with lists of relevant audit procedures to apply. We do not expect that most SBM papers will cover statutory audit in great detail … but you never know what could be tested in SBM and, particularly if you are not an auditor in your day to day job, then this book could get you out of a difficult position. **It was also the case that risks and procedures questions came up fairly regularly in the previous TI Business Change paper**: the Business Change Question Bank in particular is full of questions with 7-10 marks for tests and procedures to apply within the context of strategic change, such as acquisitions and disposals. So if you have purchased our *Advanced Level Audit & Assurance Exam Room Notes 2018* book for use in Corporate Reporting then we would still recommend that you bring it into your SBM examination for safety.

The second part of our *Audit & Assurance Exam Room Notes 2018* contains alphabetical summaries of all key Specialist Audit & Assurance areas (the areas discussed in this chapter and the following 4 chapters of this book). We have added these notes because Assurance has recently been tested more frequently in the Corporate Reporting paper so students have been asking for a single resource that they can easily access relating to both statutory audit and Specialist A&A areas.

Please note that the Specialist Audit & Assurance notes in our *Audit & Assurance Exam Room Notes 2018* are the same notes as in our *SBM Exam Room Notes 2018* (see below) – this is because the content is the same for both papers. We have included the same content in our *Audit & Assurance Exam Room Notes 2018* so that we can have a standalone book just for Corporate Reporting but if you are taking both Corporate Reporting and SBM then you could use **either** our *Audit & Assurance Exam Room Notes 2018* or *SBM Exam Room Notes 2018* to access the relevant reminders on Assurance.

Advanced Level Financial Reporting Exam Room Notes 2018

Based on popular demand, we launched this publication in 2016 to provide a set of summaries of all key financial reporting standards tested in the ACA, together with reminders of likely mark allocations and standard points to ensure that you always address in your answers. Given the importance of brought forward knowledge at the Advanced Level, our *Financial Reporting Exam Room Notes 2018* contains summaries of important Professional Level topics from the FAR examination.

Our *Financial Reporting Exam Room Notes 2018* are organised using the same popular alphabetical listing, as used in our *SBM Exam Room Notes 2018* (see below). This will allow you to find the relevant material very quickly indeed.

SBM Exam Room Notes 2018

Our *SBM Exam Room Notes* are organised alphabetically by topic area and include both practical business advisory and Specialist A&A areas. As such, our *SBM Exam Room Notes* will provide a very easy, quick reference method of finding the information you need. All the Specialist A&A areas which are introduced at the Advanced Level are covered in our *SBM Exam Room Notes* so we would advise you to obtain a copy and work through a few questions to practice your technique in using the book (this can only be done by practising full questions under time pressure, using our *SBM Exam*

186

Room Notes as a reference resource in a realistic scenario). See Appendix 4 for a sample from our *SBM Exam Room Notes*.

10.6   Further Practice: ACA Simplified *Advanced Level Audit & Assurance Q&A 2018*

For further interactive practice of Specialist A&A areas, we would recommend our *Advanced Level Audit & Assurance Q&A 2018* which contains hundreds of short form questions to help you learn via a self-test format. This Q&A is relevant to both Corporate Reporting and SBM as it contains questions on both statutory audit and Specialist A&A areas: in particular, the Q&A contains many short form questions on the 4 main Specialist A&A areas that we will consider in the next few chapters.

We will now move onto our first chapter dedicated to a specific Specialist A&A issue, Corporate Governance. The next 4 chapters all follow the same format of **briefly reviewing the relevant material from the Study Manual** and then **analysing how the topic has been tested** in the real SBM examinations, SBM mocks and/or SBM Sample Paper.

Chapter 11   Corporate Governance: Revision Notes and Examination Analysis

---

Learning Points

After reading this chapter, you must be able to:

1. understand what Corporate Governance is and how it should be defined
2. understand how Corporate Governance has been tested in SBM examination papers
3. recognise that Corporate Governance is a topic which has been tested fairly often

---

11.1   Corporate Governance: Revision Notes

The examiners have stated that Corporate Governance (CG) will be tested from the point of view of **understanding the best management and governance structure to ensure that the company is run well and achieves its aims for all stakeholders**: CG will not be tested via pure knowledge questions on the details of the UK Corporate Governance Code, UK Stewardship Code, OECD Code or Sarbox issues – it will be tested more "practically" via questions which look at the operational implications and potential problems of different management structures[63].

Corporate Governance has been of increasing importance in recent years as a result of issues concerning **financial reporting**, **corporate scandals and collapses** and **concerns regarding excessive director remuneration**.

Corporate Governance can be defined as "the system by which organisations are directed and controlled". We would advise you to start your answer with this definition, before applying this to the scenario given.

CG is used to:

- Reduce risk

- Specify distribution rights and responsibilities between different stakeholders

- Specify rules and procedures for corporate decisions

- Provide a structure through which objectives are set

- Provide a framework for ethical and other safeguards

- Promote new investment and confidence in companies

---

[63] Nevertheless, certain UK and international codes do provide some useful analytical frameworks to consider. Note that (as discussed in more detail below) the testing of CG in the SBM Sample Paper did require some knowledge of UK Corporate Governance Code rules.

188

Fundamentally, as a matter of good governance the Board should have clear strategic objectives

The Board should also establish its risk appetites and framework for considering risks

11.2 Features of Poor Corporate Governance

When reading the scenario and looking for CG problems, consider the following features of poor CG, as specified in the Corporate Reporting Study Manual:

Indicators of CG problems

- Domination by a single individual

- Lack of involvement of the Board

- Lack of an adequate control function, including internal audit

- Lack of supervision due to systems deficiencies or a lack of segregation of key roles

- Lack of independent scrutiny by the external auditors

- Lack of contact with shareholders

- Emphasis on short-term profitability rather than long term investment

- Misleading accounts and information

- Persistent Board disagreements between Executive Directors and NEDs

As these are the potential warning signs or "**red flags**" highlighted in the Study Manual, the examiner could reasonably expect you to be able to identify these in the scenario data.

Remember that the SBM examiners love headings (see chapter 8 and chapter 18 for discussion) so perhaps use the above potential problem areas as headings.

11.3 Corporate Governance Concepts

The below list of concepts indicates what corporate governance should, ideally, involve – as such, **look for any lack of these concepts in the SBM scenario given**. As just mentioned above, the SBM examiners love headings (see chapter 8 and chapter 18 for discussion) so perhaps use these concepts as headings:

Fairness – decisions are taken after considering different interests

Openness/Transparency – appropriate disclosures are made

Independence – independent Non-Executive Directors (NEDs)

Probity/Honesty – information is not misleading

Responsibility – corrective action and penalisation of mismanagement

Accountability – directors and the organisation are answerable for their actions

Reputation – a good reputation will result from following the other concepts

Judgement – decisions are made that enhance the prosperity of the organisation

Integrity – straightforward dealing and completeness, demonstrating high moral character

Note that all the principles are considered to be of **equal importance**: you should be able to find something in the scenario to say regarding these.

Another useful framework to apply would be the 5 main principles contained in the UK Corporate Governance Code. Although we do not expect you to be tested on the details of the UK Corporate Governance Code (see chapter 18), the Code framework does cover a wide range of potential scenario issues. The 5 main principles of the Code, together with related considerations, are[64]:

---

[64] See the Corporate Reporting Study Manual for a full explanation of these concepts: here we are only creating short revision notes to act as reminders.

Leadership	The role of the Board
	Division of responsibilities
	The Chairman
	NEDs
Effectiveness	Composition of the Board
	Appointments to the Board
	Commitment of time
	Development
	Information and support
	Evaluation
	Re-election
Accountability	Financial reporting
	Risk management and internal control
	Audit committees and auditors
Remuneration	The level and components of remuneration
	Procedure
Relations with stakeholders	Dialogue with shareholders
	Constructive use of the AGM

11.4   The Roles of the Board

In an SBM question, you are likely to be engaged as an adviser to the senior members of the Board, whether directly or working through your partner. As such, it is helpful to revise what the Board should be doing so that you can again detect any problems in the scenario.

According to the Study Manual, the roles of the Board should include:

- **Decisions on fundamental matters** to the business such as mergers and takeovers, acquisitions, investments, capital projects, bank borrowing facilities and loans

- Monitoring the **Chief Executive Officer**

- Overseeing **strategy**

- Monitoring **risks and control systems**

- Monitoring the **human capital aspects** of the company in regard to succession, morale, training and remuneration

- Ensuring that there is **effective communication of its strategic plans**, both internally and externally

11.5   Non-Executive Directors (NEDs)

NEDs are given significant importance in the Corporate Reporting Study Manual, accounting for 2 pages of bullet point lists on their roles, advantages and disadvantages – **highly examinable lists**!

Non-executive directors can be defined as **directors with no executive or managerial responsibilities**. NEDs should **provide a balancing influence**, particularly in reducing conflicts of interest between management and shareholders. Effective NEDs provide reassurance to shareholders that management is acting in the interests of the organisation.

The **roles** of NEDs are:

- **Strategic** – NEDs contribute to, and challenge, strategy

- **Performance** – NEDs scrutinise performance of management in meeting goals and objectives

- **Risk** – NEDs should ensure that financial information is accurate and that controls are robust

- **Remuneration and succession** – NEDs should be responsible for determining appropriate levels of remuneration for executives and should be key figures in the appointment and removal of senior managers and in succession planning

Some **advantages** of having NEDs on the Board include[65]:

- Possess **external experience and knowledge** which executive directors do not have

- Can provide a **wider perspective**

- **Provide comfort to third parties** such as investors or creditors

- Can play **certain important roles** such as father-confessor (being a confidant for the chairman and other directors), oil-can (making the Board run more effectively) and acting as high sheriff (removing the chairman or chief executive if necessary)

- **Dual role** as full Board members but also having a strong, independent element

---

[65] If your SBM client is relatively small and perhaps family-owned, then the client will be missing out on these advantages so this should give you something to discuss.

Some **problems** with having NEDs on the Board include:

- May **lack independence**

- May not include people **other than those proposed by the Board**

- The **best candidates for an NED role might naturally work at the best-run companies** anyway i.e. companies that do not need any input from good NEDs

- May have **difficulty in imposing their views** on the Board

- May not **pay enough attention** to preventing trouble or advising on the early warning signs of a problem

- **Limited amount of time** to devote to the role

Note that the final issue of "limited time" is stated in the Study Manual[66] to be "perhaps the biggest problem" with NEDs.

Independence is another important topic to consider regarding NEDs – the examiners in fact make this very clear indeed by stating that "**whenever a question scenario features non-executive directors, watch out for threats to, or questions over, their independence**". Here are some factors to consider regarding independence[67]:

- Whether the NED has been an **employee of the company in the last 5 years**

- Whether the NED has had a **material business relationship** with his or her company as a result of serving in a senior role with another company

- Whether the NED receives **additional remuneration** apart from a director's fee or participates in share options or pension schemes

- Whether the NED has any **close family ties** with the company's advisers, directors or senior employees

- Whether the NED holds **cross-directorships** or has significant links with other directors or through involvement in other companies or bodies

- Whether the NED is a **significant shareholder**

- Whether the NED has **served on the Board for a substantial period of time**

---

[66] See p169 of the 2018 edition of the Corporate Reporting Study Manual.
[67] The Corporate Reporting Study Manual provides specific time periods here which appear to be based on the UK Corporate Governance Code: we have not included these specific rules in our summary notes above because we are following the examiners' statement (see chapter 18) that the specifics of different codes will not be tested in SBM.

11.6 Evaluation of Corporate Governance Mechanisms

In our final element of CG revision notes we include a brief summary of **how an auditor might investigate and evaluate client Corporate Governance mechanisms**: we include these notes because there is a substantial section in the Corporate Reporting Study Manual but as it would appear to relate more closely to audit testing we believe that these aspects of CG are **less examinable** than the points already reviewed above.

The auditor may have responsibilities under relevant sets of listing rules to review certain disclosures on matters such as remuneration on share options, details of long term incentive schemes and pension.

Procedures could include:

- **Reviewing minutes** of the meetings of the Board of directors

- **Reviewing supporting documents** prepared for the Board of directors

- **Making inquiries of certain directors** and the company secretary

- **Attending meetings of the audit committee** at which the annual report and accounts are considered and approved

The auditor may have to test and examine the annual review of the effectiveness of the company's system of internal controls if this is required under the relevant listing rules (it is under the UK Corporate Governance Code).

Key Points in the April 2016 update to the UK Corporate Governance Code

The audit committee is required to have "competence relevant to the sector in which the company operates"

The audit committee report within the annual report must provide "advance notice of any retendering plans"

The provision that FTSE 350 companies are expected to put the audit out to tender at least every 10 years has been removed – but note that this has been replaced with the EU Audit Regulation and Directive requirements for mandatory tendering and rotation of the audit firm.

Procedures could include:

- **Making appropriate enquiries** and reviewing the statements made by the Board

- **Reporting by exception** if problems arise such as the Board summary not reflecting the auditors' understanding of that process or there has been a failure to disclose or conduct an annual review

194

The auditor should indicate in the audit report that the auditor is not required to consider whether internal controls cover all risks or to form an opinion on the effectiveness of the company's corporate governance procedures.

The auditor may have to communicate with those charged with governance. Two ISAs (ISA 260 and ISA 265) then become relevant. In brief, these ISAs require the auditor to:

- Communicate the responsibilities of the auditor, as distinguished from those charged with governance

- Obtain relevant information from those charged with governance

- Provide those charged with governance with timely observations arising from the audit

- Promote effective 2-way communication between the auditor and those charged with governance

The auditor should communicate the expected scope and timing of the audit, including materiality issues. Significant findings that might be communicated could include:

- Matters relating to significant accounting policies

- The impact of any risks and exposures such as potential litigation

- Significant difficulties encountered during the audit

- Material deficiencies in the design, implementation or operating effectiveness of internal control

- Written representations that are being requested

Some matters to evaluate when determining whether "significant deficiencies in internal controls" exist are specifically highlighted in the Study Manual: these are worth revising to see whether the SBM scenario you are given includes such problems:

- Susceptibility to fraud

- Subjectivity and complexity of determining estimated amounts such as FV estimates

- The volume of activity in the account balance or class of transactions

- The importance of controls to the financial reporting process

- The case and frequency of exceptions detected

- The interaction of the deficiency with other deficiencies in internal control

As part of the "Risk management and internal control" disclosure requirements of the UK Corporate Governance Code, the Directors must explain how they have assessed the prospects of the company, the period of assessment and why that period of assessment is considered to be appropriate.

The directors should state whether they have a reasonable expectation that the company will be able to continue in operation and meet its liabilities as they fall due over the period of their assessment.

The expectation is that the period of assessment for these purposes will be significantly longer than the 12 months required to determine whether the going concern basis of accounting is appropriate.

We have also included the above areas in our *SBM Exam Room Notes* so ensure that you can quickly locate the relevant pages and then ensure that you look at the specific scenario given to identify the relevance of the above points in the Study Manual.

11.7   Corporate Governance: How Has It Been Examined in SBM?

Having reviewed CG points **in theory**, based on a review of the Study Manual, we will now review how CG has **actually been tested**: this should give you a good insight into how the examiners think and how your points should be connected to the specific examination data.

SBM real examinations

In the July 2014 examination, Q2 Task 4 asked candidates to explain the CG issues arising from the fact that the Finance Director had a personal interest in a contract with a particular supplier.

The model answer was very brief on the issues arising:

- The **Board of Directors is a key stakeholder** in an entity and therefore **fundamental to CG**

- The **Finance Director can potentially influence** whether the other party becomes a supplier and, if so, the terms on which the contract is made and the service monitored

- This results in a **CG risk that contracts undertaken or continued may not be in the best interests of the company**

- A **safeguard** would be to **exclude the Finance Director** from any decisions in respect of the relevant supply cases. If this is not possible, then the Finance Director should at least be excluded from voting on affected issues

This testing of CG was thus very brief. The issue of acting in the **best interests of the company** and the **pivotal role of the Board of Directors as a stakeholder** are points that we expect you will often be able to make in many CG answers so do bear these in mind.

In the July 2016 examination, Q2 Task 4 asked candidates to suggest improvements in CG that could assist the Board to manage and control performance to a better extent. Key points included:

- **Non-Executive Directors** should have the right **skills** and **experience**

- **Subcommittees** should be set up

- An **Audit Committee** could help to monitor performance and information flows (rather than **simply dealing with external auditors**)

- Information flows and management controls would be enhanced by an **internal audit** function reporting to the Audit Committee
- The Audit Committee would consist of **Non-Executive Directors** who would monitor the performance of the company and its executive directors

- It may be suitable for the **Chairman** to **chair** the **Audit Committee**

- A **Remuneration Committee** may also be advisable as otherwise the Directors can simply award themselves **excessive** pay rises (**self-interest threat**)

- A Board of **4** members is likely to be **too small** and may have the full spectrum of skills necessary – an **Appointment Committee** may be able to help here.

In this second testing, a number of useful practical points were made. We would definitely bear these in mind again in future.

SBM mock examinations

July 2014 Mock 1 and November 2014 Mock 1 both featured marks for CG issues (5 and 4 marks, respectively).

In July 2014 Mock 1, 5 marks were available for identification of the reasons why 2 different Boards were finding it hard to work together effectively and recommendations of measures which could therefore improve governance. Governance problems identified included:

- **Lack of clarity about the respective authority** of each Board: one Board believed it could make investment and financing decisions without reference to the other Board

- **Poor communication** between the 2 Boards with no shared directors

Recommendations to improve the position included:

- **Making a clear statement of matters that should be decided or approved** by each Board of Directors

- **Decisions on investing and financing** above a certain amount of money **should require approval of both Boards**

- There should at the same time **not be interference in other minor matters** that have been appropriately delegated

- **Appointing a director from each Board to serve as an NED on the Board of the other company** – this might improve communication and allow the 2 Boards to gain a better understanding of each other

The interesting thing about this CG question is that it does not relate to the usual **ethical** aspects of CG – rather, it is a very practical matter of **running the business effectively**. This is an additional dimension to the way that CG is tested (whilst bearing in mind our caveats about the July 2014 SBM mocks as representative of real examinations: see Appendix 5).

In November 2014 Mock 1 Q2, 4 marks were available for identifying the CG issues that arise when a takeover offer is received by a Board. Points noted include:

- The offer is a "**friendly**" approach in that the acquirer was hoping for an agreed takeover deal, enabling it to gain access to information for the purposes of Due Diligence

- As the **target is a UK-listed company**, the proposed acquisition would be subject to the rules of the **UK Takeover Code**

- As the bid is a "**friendly**" approach then the directors **are entitled to reject the bid**

- **There might be a requirement in the company's Articles of Association or in a shareholder agreement** which requires that friendly bids from a potential acquirer should be referred to the shareholders.

- If the target were to reject the bid and a "**hostile**" bid was then launched, then **this would have to referred automatically to shareholders under takeover rules**

- The acquirer in a "hostile" bid would have to base its bid on **public information** rather than detailed access to internal information

In our view, this question required quite detailed knowledge of "friendly" and "hostile" bids so would have been a difficult question to answer without that knowledge. This bid language is not included in the Corporate Reporting Study Manual sections on CG nor in the Strategic Business Management Study Manual so something to be aware of (again, as this is a mock examination then it may not be as indicative of the SBM syllabus: see Appendix 5).

SBM Sample Paper

In Q2 of the Sample Paper, there were 7 marks available for considering 2 proposed changes to CG arrangements. The first change was suggested by a lending bank and involved the removal of an employee representative from Board committees, the appointment of 2 additional independent NEDs and the separation of the roles of Chairman and Chief Executive. The second change related to the creation of share options which would potentially change the percentage shareholdings of different stakeholder groups.

With respect to the proposal by the bank, the model answer could be summarised as follows:

- **Tabular presentation** of the shareholdings of different stakeholders

- Analysis of the number of executive and NEDs

- **Definition of CG**: the set of processes, customs, policies, laws and institutions affecting the way in which an entity is directed, administered or controlled. CG is designed to serve the needs of shareholders and other stakeholders by directing and controlling management activities towards good business practices, objectivity and integrity in order to satisfy the objectives of the entity

- Explanation that CG involves both a **service/strategy role** and a **control role**

- Proposals by the bank may only represent **one stakeholder group** (the bank itself) and may not be appropriate for other stakeholders. At the same time, renewal of financing may be very important to the company and benefit all stakeholders.

- **Removal of the employee representative from the Board to disenfranchise the employee stakeholder group** – in future, the Board may be less likely to represent the legitimate interests of employees

- The existing Board has **more executive directors than NEDs** but this is not in line with best practice according to the UK Corporate Governance Code which states that there should be an equal number of both types of director

- Some existing NEDs may in fact **not be independent** as they are aligned with particular stakeholder groups (professional scepticism skill)

- According to the UK Corporate Governance Code, the audit committee should have **at least 3 independent NEDs** – the existing Board does not reflect this

- The company has an **AIM-listing only**, rather than a full listing, so it is **not required to comply with the UK Corporate Governance Code**

- However, **stakeholders may expect compliance with the Code**

- **Combining the roles of Chairman and Chief Executive may give one individual too much authority to run the company** and dominate the Board – therefore the UK Corporate Governance Code regards **the separation of these roles as best practice**

- Furthermore, the Chairman/Chief Executive in this case has a **35%** shareholding as well, making him potentially dominant in both shareholder meetings and Board meetings

199

- It seems reasonable, therefore, to **split the roles** but the company would need to identify a suitable and highly skilled candidate

- The separation will only be effective if the new chairman has enough **independence and skills**

We can again see the need to **define CG and then apply it to the specific scenario**. It also appears that some basic knowledge of the UK Corporate Governance Code will be beneficial. It seems that the examiners will view the Code as important guidance even in cases where the company is not required to apply the code (e.g. AIM-listed or perhaps even an unlisted family-owned company). We do not expect that the question wording will ever **remind** you to apply the Code so it will be up to you to remember to do so[68].

With respect to the proposed share options and their impact on CG, the model answer could be summarised as follows:

- The proposal **does not on its face** appear to **require Board representation** from the external party funding the business but **in practice a party in such a position is likely to request Board representation**

- If the options were to be exercised, the **balance of power would change significantly**

- A **tabular analysis** of the new distribution of shares was then provided

- If the options were exercised, the **external party would become the largest shareholder** and this would have a significant impact on the balance of power within the Board

- At the same time, the **external party would not have a controlling interest**

- The new shareholding structure **would not apply until 31 December 2016** and only then if the share price exceeded a particular target level

- Some stakeholders would **no longer have the 25% shareholding needed to block a special resolution** whereas under the current shareholding they do have the necessary shares, representing a substantial change in their position

- The external party **might exercise their options but then sell the shares**, leading to a **further unknown impact on CG**

Overall, the points here involve looking carefully at the **precise shareholdings before and after exercise** as well as practical business advisory points such as the **timing of the exercise** and the **likelihood of exercise based on the share price**. We would note that consideration of the **75% shareholding needed to pass a special resolution was a very common theme under the old Business Change paper**.

---

[68] Our MAPs include a relevant reminder and the Code is incorporated into our *SBM Exam Room Notes* book.

We would therefore advise you to always look at the key barrier holdings of 50% and 75% in all CG-related SBM answers.

11.8   Changes to the Corporate Governance Syllabus Content in the 2016 Materials

Whilst the SBM Study Manual sections on Corporate Governance was relatively unchanged for 2016, the 2016 edition of the Corporate Reporting Study Manual did contain quite a few tweaks with respect to Corporate Governance (but not other areas) so we will quickly review the main changes here: as with all additions to the syllabus, we recommend that you ensure you understand the changes in case the examiners have added these sections with a specific intention to examine them.

For the much more minor syllabus changes on Corporate Governance in the 2017 and 2018 Corporate Reporting Study Manual, please see the following sections later in this chapter.

Additional Corporate Governance rules and content added to 2016 syllabus

A section was added to state that in the UK, s439A of Companies Act 2006 requires a quoted company's director remuneration policy to be approved by a binding shareholders' vote at least every 3 years. The actual amounts of remuneration to be paid will be subject to an annual advisory vote on the remuneration report (p141).

A new revised version of the UK Corporate Governance Code was published in September 2014. The changes have been controversial with companies and investors – in particular, the changes regarding going concern have been criticised for failing to address investor concerns and placing a heavy risk management and reporting burden on Boards.

Some key changes introduced by the latest update include:

- Companies should disclose whether they consider it appropriate to apply the going concern basis and should identify material uncertainties

- Companies should perform an annual review of the effectiveness of their risk management and internal control systems and then report on the review in their annual report

- Companies should implement arrangements to withhold or recover variable pay where appropriate and consider the appropriateness of the vesting period for deferred remuneration
- Companies should explain how they intend to engage with shareholders when a significant percentage of shareholders have voted against any resolution

Several changes were made to the table sections entitled "the level and components of remuneration" and "procedure". In particular:

- It is now stated that executive director remuneration should be designed to promote the long-term success of the company and any performance-related element should be transparent, stretching and rigorously applied

- Performance-related schemes should include provisions allowing the company to recover sums paid or withhold the payment of any sum and specify the circumstances in which this can be done – presumably here the aim is to recover or withhold payment in the case of actions which are discovered to be damaging to the company later in time

- Non-Executive Directors should not generally be given share options or other performance related elements. If, as an exception, options are granted, shareholder approval should be sought in advance and any shares acquired by exercise of the option should be held until at least 1 year after the NED leaves the Board. If share options are held, this could affect the determination of an NED's independence

- Notice or contract period should be set to 1 year or less

- Shareholders should be invited specifically to approve all new long-term incentive schemes as well as significant changes to existing schemes, except in the circumstances permitted by the Listing Rules

In a section on the disclosure requirements of the UK Corporate Governance Code, a statement was added indicating that the impact of any changes to the other significant commitments of the chairman during the year should be explained.

With respect to going concern, a sentence was added in the 2016 edition to emphasise that the directors of **listed** companies must specifically report on the going concern status of the company under the UK Corporate Governance Code. The directors must include a detailed "viability statement" within the **Strategic Report**: this must provide a broad assessment of the solvency, liquidity, risk management and viability of the entity.

11.9   Changes to the Corporate Governance Syllabus Content in the 2017 Materials

Although no changes were made to the Corporate Governance sections in the 2017 edition of the SBM Study Manual, the Corporate Reporting Study Manual 2017 does make some important additions in relation to the April 2016 update to the UK Corporate Governance Code (p158):

> The audit committee is required to have "competence relevant to the sector in which the company operates"

> The audit committee report within the annual report must provide "advance notice of any retendering plans"

> The provision that FTSE 350 companies are expected to put the audit out to tender at least every 10 years has been removed – but note that this has been replaced with the EU Audit Regulation and Directive requirements for mandatory tendering and rotation of the audit firm.

The other changes in chapter 4 ("Corporate Governance") of the Corporate Reporting Study Manual 2017 relate more to the duties of statutory auditors and hence are not very likely to be examined in

SBM. However, for completeness, please ensure that you have carefully read through the following pages to which updates have been applied (particularly if you have already used the 2016 or earlier edition of the Advanced Level syllabus): p163, p164, p172, p182, p183, p184, p185, p186 and p187. [2018 update: these page numbers are the same in the 2018 edition of the Corporate Reporting Study Manual.]

11.10 Changes to the Corporate Governance Syllabus Content in the 2018 Materials

There have been minimal changes in relation to Corporate Governance in the 2018 materials. One key point to be aware of (as already added in our discussion above) is that the 2018 materials clarify that as part of the "Risk management and internal control" disclosure requirements of the UK Corporate Governance Code, the Directors must explain how they have assessed the prospects of the company, the period of assessment and why that period of assessment is considered to be appropriate.

The directors should state whether they have a reasonable expectation that the company will be able to continue in operation and meet its liabilities as they fall due over the period of their assessment.

The expectation is that the period of assessment for these purposes will be significantly longer than the 12 months required to determine whether the going concern basis of accounting is appropriate.

11.11 The Examination of Corporate Governance Concepts: Summary and Conclusions

In this chapter, we have reviewed in significant detail both the textbook sections regarding CG and the ways in which CG has been tested. **We strongly recommend that you re-read the chapter several times to learn the necessary information**[69] but as a short summary of the key points, we would note the following:

- Ensure that you can offer a **brief definition of CG** and **explain why it is necessary**

- Ensure that you can spot the **warning signs** or "**red flags**" which could indicate a **CG problem**

- Revise the **basic aspects of the UK Corporate Governance Code** but check whether this will apply in the scenario (if not, then just apply the same concepts but state that the Code would be guidance that many stakeholders may wish to see followed)

- Revise the **roles of the Board and NEDs** (including **advantages and disadvantages of NEDs**)

- Learn some **procedures** relating to the **testing of CG at the Board level**

---

[69] As noted on page 163, our *Advanced Level Audit & Assurance Q&A 2018* is available if you require a more interactive, self-test method of learning CG concepts.

- Consider **stakeholders and their interests**, applying **scepticism to any proposed changes** (see in particular the Sample Paper here)

- Look at the **existing and potential balance of power**, always considering the **key cut off points of 75% and 50% shareholdings**

- Prepare some possible ways of **improving CG** and the **operation of Boards**

- Ensure that you can **identify different stakeholder groups** and try to provide some **different points for each group**, perhaps under headings, to show the impact of a CG change

- **Purchase our *SBM Exam Room Notes*** and ensure that you are familiar with CG points – ideally you should use the *Exam Room Notes* in at least one full SBM mock exam attempt

In the next chapter, we will apply the process used in this chapter to the next Specialist A&A area of "Assurance and Related Services", again starting by providing some revision notes from the Study Manual and then looking at how these areas have been tested in examination papers.

Chapter 12   Assurance and Related Services: Revision Notes and Examination Analysis

---

Learning Points

After reading this chapter, you must be able to:

1. understand which areas are contained within the Assurance and Related Services topic
2. appreciate the importance of a good understanding of Due Diligence
3. understand how Assurance and Related Services have been tested in SBM examination papers

---

12.1   Assurance and Related Services: Revision Notes

The chapter in the Corporate Reporting Study Manual on Assurance and Related Services is relatively long and therefore covers a large number of topics. It is helpful to list out at the start of our notes the 6 different specialist areas that fall under the "Assurance and Related Services" topic:

1.   Engagements to review financial statements

2.   Due Diligence

3.   Reporting on Prospective Information

4.   Agreed Upon Procedures

5.   Compilation Engagements

6.   Forensic Audits

We have organised our notes around these 6 headings. As in the previous chapter, for each heading/topic we will first summarise the Study Manual material and will then look at how the areas have been tested in SBM examination papers (if at all).

You should note that only Due Diligence, Reporting on prospective information and Agreed Upon Procedures have been tested to date in the available set of SBM papers (past papers and ICAEW SBM Mocks).

12.2   Engagements to Review Financial Statements

This type of review is similar to an external audit but it gives a reduced degree of assurance based on a **negative assurance** statement that **nothing has come to the attention of the auditor which causes the auditor to believe that the statements have not been prepared in accordance with the relevant financial reporting framework**.

Often relates to review of **interim financial information**

ISRE 2400 provides the rules and relevant guidance for this type of review. Note that this standard has not been adopted in the UK.

ISRE 2400 contains guidance on compliance with ethical standards including independence requirements, planning and performing the engagement with professional scepticism, exercising professional judgement and the role of the engagement partner.

Materiality should be applied in the same way as for a statutory audit.

The practitioner should also obtain an understanding of the business including a review of the relevant industry, the nature of the entity, the accounting systems and accounting records, and selection and application of accounting policies.

Procedures include **inquiry and analytical procedures** to obtain sufficient appropriate audit evidence to come to a conclusion about the financial statements as a whole.

Specific inquiries could include:

- How management makes significant accounting estimates

- Identification of related parties and related party transactions

- Consideration of significant, unusual or complex transactions

- Actual or suspected fraud

- Whether management has identified and addressed events after the reporting period

- The basis of management's assessment of going concern

- Material commitments, contractual obligations or contingencies

- Material non-monetary transactions or transactions for no consideration in the reporting period

Analytical procedures should be used to help the practitioner to:

- Obtain or update an understanding of the entity and its environment

206

- Identify inconsistencies or variances from expected trends, values or norms

- Provide corroborative evidence in relation to inquiry or other analytical procedures

- Serve as additional procedures when the practitioner becomes aware of matters that indicate that the financial statements may be materially misstated

The practitioner should also determine whether the data available is adequate for the above purposes.

A typical practitioner's review report should contain the following headings/report sections:

- **Report on the financial statements** – statement regarding which set of statements have been reviewed

- **Management's responsibility for the financial statements**

- **Practitioner's responsibility**

- **Conclusion**

The conclusion can be **qualified**, **adverse** or a **disclaimer** of a conclusion based on the usual rules applicable to a statutory audit and considering whether the matter is pervasive or not.

One particular financial statement review mentioned in this section of the Study Manual is the **review of interim financial information** performed by the independent auditor of the entity. As this is given its own section, we recommend that you treat this as a very important sub-type of financial statement reviews.

Reviews of interim financial information are governed by **ISRE 2410**. This differs from ISRE 2400 reviewed above in that ISRE 2410 assumes that the practitioner (the entity's auditor) will have information available from its work on the statutory audit which would not be available to an independent practitioner under ISRE 2400 engagements.

Reviews of interim financial information should use the same procedures as a standard audit but they can be **performed to a lower level of assurance**. As usual, then, you can refer to the generic types such as inquiries and analytical procedures in your answer. Procedures could include:

- reading last year's audit file and considering any significant risks identified

- reading the most recent and comparable interim financial information

- considering materiality

- considering the nature of any corrected or uncorrected misstatements in last year's financial statements

207

- considering significant financial accounting and reporting matters of ongoing importance

- considering the results of any interim audit work for this year's audit

- considering the work of internal audit

- reading management accounts and commentaries for the period

- considering any findings from prior periods

- asking management what their assessment of the risk of fraud in the interim financial statements may be

- asking management whether there have been any significant changes in internal controls or business activity

- reading the minutes of meetings of shareholders, those charged with governance or other appropriate committees

- considering the effect of matters giving rise to a modification of the audit or review report and accounting adjustments

- communicating with other auditors that audit different components of the business

- performing analytical procedures designed to identify relationships and unusual items that may reflect a material misstatement

- reading the interim financial information and considering whether anything has come to the auditors' attention indicating that it has not been prepared in accordance with the applicable financial reporting framework

- agreeing the interim financial information to the underlying accounting records

- reviewing consolidation adjustments for consistency and reviewing relevant correspondence with regulators

- inquire with the members of management responsible for financial and accounting matters regarding issues such as the applicable reporting framework, changes in accounting policies, significant misstatements, fair value assumptions, compliance with debt covenants and fraud issues, amongst others

Comparative information should be considered to determine whether this is consistent with that presented in the interim financial statements.

Written representations should be obtained from management in which management recognises its responsibility for the design and implementation of internal control and that significant facts relating

208

to frauds or non-compliance with law and regulations have been disclosed to the auditor and that all significant subsequent events have been disclosed to the auditor.

The format of report should be very similar to the above noted format for review engagements: relevant sections to include in the report would be:

- **Introduction**

- **Directors' Responsibilities**

- **Practitioner's Responsibilities**

- **Scope of the Review**

- **Conclusion**

Changes have been made to ISA 250 *Consideration of Laws and Regulations in an Audit of Financial Statements* by the IAASB following the conclusion of its NOCLAR (non-compliance with laws and regulations) project – this has resulted in "conforming amendments" to ISRE 2400.

The amendments provide guidance regarding the reporting of identified or suspected non-compliance with laws and regulations to an appropriate authority outside the entity.

If the professional accountant suspects fraud or non-compliance with laws and regulations, the following 5 steps should be followed:

1. Communicate the matter to the appropriate level of management/those charged with governance

2. Request management's assessment of the effects, if any, on the financial statements

3. Consider the implications for the practitioner's report

4. Determine whether law, regulation or ethical requirements require that the matter should be reported to a third party outside the entity

5. Determine whether law, regulation or ethical requirements establish responsibilities under which reporting to an authority outside the entity may be appropriate

The professional accountant should also consult internally, obtain legal advice and consult with the regulator or professional body in order to understand the implications of different courses of action.

12.3 Engagements to Review Financial Statements: How Has This Topic Been Examined in SBM?

As indicated above, we unfortunately do not yet have an example of a how a review engagement has been tested in SBM.

12.4 Due Diligence

We suggest that this topic is **highly examinable in SBM** as it relates to **acquisitions and disposals**, a classic SBM (and Business Change) topic. Our review of SBM examination papers supports this view as **Due Diligence has already been tested several times in SBM**.

Due Diligence (DD) can be defined as the **attestation of information by an external party, normally on behalf of a prospective bidder**. It aims to confirm the accuracy of information, identify and quantify areas of commercial and financial risk, provide assurance to providers of finance, provide the bidder with an independent review of the target business and, overall, assist the bidder with placing a valuation on the target company.

DD can take place at different stages in the negotiations: it could be pre-acquisition DD or could be retrospective DD. **Note that not all types of DD are carried out by accountants**.

You should always mention in an examination response that DD does **not** involve the **same level of detailed testing that would be carried out in a statutory audit** and so provides only **limited** assurance.

If DD is not performed correctly then those involved could face legal proceedings, including being held liable for damages. Corporate Governance requirements could mean that the directors are held personally liable if adequate DD has not been carried out.

A key concept relating to the DD process is that of a **warranty**. This is a type of promise/commitment which acts as insurance given by the seller regarding issues that cannot be definitively answered by the DD: if the information contained in the warranty proves not to be correct then the buyer may be able to claim back some of the sale consideration paid. Common warranties include:

- A commitment that the details of all relevant employment contracts have been disclosed

- A commitment that contracts are current and truly exist

- A commitment that all liabilities, including contingent liabilities, have been disclosed

- A commitment that tax has either been paid or appropriately accrued for

Types of Due Diligence Report

This particular element of the DD process is highly examinable: you could be asked to explain which types of DD should be applied to the scenario in question.

The possible examinable types of DD are as follows:

1. Financial Due Diligence

2. Commercial Due Diligence

3. Operational Due Diligence

4. Technical Due Diligence

5. IT Due Diligence

6. Legal Due Diligence

7. Human resources Due Diligence

8. Tax Due Diligence

We provide some brief notes on the types of Due Diligence below.

1. Financial Due Diligence

Financial DD reviews the **financial position, risk and projections of the target company**.

The information which could be reviewed includes financial statements, management accounts, projections, assumptions underlying the projections, detailed operating data, working capital analysis, major contracts by product line, actual and potential liabilities, detailed asset registers, debt/leave agreements, current/recent litigation and property and other capital commitments.

2. Commercial Due Diligence

Commercial Due Diligence **reviews the markets and external economic environment of the target company**. Information can be taken from the target company, business contacts or external sources. Accountants can often carry out commercial Due Diligence but they must have a good understanding of the industry in which the target company operates.

Information which is relevant to commercial Due Diligence is likely to include analysis of the target's main competitors, marketing history and tactics, competitive advantages, analysis of resources, strengths and weaknesses, integration issues, supplier analysis, market growth expectations, ability to achieve forecasts, critical success factors, KPIs, exit potential, management appraisal and strategic evaluation.

An advantage of commercial Due Diligence is that it **not only helps to value the target company but also helps with the advance planning of an appropriate post-acquisition strategy**.

3. Operational Due Diligence

Operational Due Diligence considers the **operational risks and possible improvements that can be made to a target company**. The process will validate the assumptions within projections and will also attempt to identify any operational upsides that could increase the value of the deal. Operational Due Diligence considers the supply chain, logistics and manufacturing processes: as such, it is potentially examinable since several of these topics have been added to the SBM syllabus following the "evolution" from the previous Business Change paper[70].

Operational Due Diligence will typically cover procurement costs, cost synergies, growth drivers, potential risk areas, business relationships, supplier and distribution channels, sales networks, inventory levels and flexibility, size of the operational footprint, utilisation of business assets and the effectiveness of back office functions.

4. Technical Due Diligence

Technical Due Diligence looks at the **potential for technological development as this can be the key to the future profitability of certain types of industry such as electronics, IT, pharmaceuticals, engineering, biotechnology and product development**. Technical Due Diligence will therefore reach a judgement as to whether the proposed technological benefits are likely to be delivered. Unfortunately, even though this aspect must be taken into account in a valuation, accountants are unlikely to be able to reach a reasonable conclusion on a project's technological merits and therefore will have to rely on the work of relevant experts.

We would advise you to check whether the target/SBM scenario falls into one of the specified industries (electronics, IT, pharmaceuticals, engineering, biotechnology and product development) as this will determine whether technical Due Diligence is important – it may also indicate matters that should be considered in your valuation of the target. Scepticism of the work of experts may be merited, particularly if there is any indication of bias on either side.

5. IT Due Diligence

IT Due Diligence assesses the **impact, including the impact on risks, of IT factors in the target company**. These issues can arise whether or not the target operates specifically in the IT industry as all businesses use IT to some extent. However, the issues will be more significant if the target is an IT company.

The process of IT Due Diligence could include a risk assessment of IT systems, IT security, evaluation of synergies and duplication, compatibility of IT systems after the acquisition, an audit of IT skills and a review of process management.

---

[70] See chapter 18.

6. Legal Due Diligence

Legal Due Diligence involves **review of potential legal risks in the acquisition**. This could involve looking at the valuation of the target company and determining whether this fully reflects any potential or hidden liabilities, uncertain rights or onerous contractual obligations. Legal Due Diligence can also involve establishing the terms of the takeover within the investment agreement, contingent arrangements, financial restructuring and the rights, duties and obligations of various parties. There may also be consideration of the legal composition of the new group i.e. the Articles of Association which will apply, affecting the rights of finance providers and restructuring.

Accountants will have to place **reliance on the work of lawyers as part of this process**.

7. Human Resources Due Diligence

This type of Due Diligence **examines the rights and interests and human resources and associated legal obligations**.

Human Resources Due Diligence could include a human resources audit, employment contracts review, review of personnel files, analysis of pension obligations, review of training processes, assessing synergies and duplications in numbers and skills to inform redundancy arrangements and review of compliance with legal issues.

8. Tax Due Diligence

Tax Due Diligence is designed to **help the purchaser form an assessment of the tax risks and benefits associated with the company to be acquired**, including an appropriate review/assessment of the potential assets and liabilities involved.

Information and processes considered within tax Due Diligence include analysis of the explanation for the disposal structure being used (including an analysis of the case cost position) and a full technical analysis of the tax position, corporation tax reference details, copies of all previous tax computations, copies of HMRC correspondence on Corporation Tax and VAT, details and proof of the pre-disposal VAT grouping position, details of corporation tax group payment arrangements, details of any transactions with connected parties (including outside the UK) and details of payroll arrangements including PAYE and NICs.

Due Diligence Procedures for an Acquisition

- identify legal title

- confirm accuracy and assumptions of financial data and projections

- commercial review – order book, contracts, realism of growth rates assumed and projected

- identify and quantify areas of commercial and financial risk

213

- identify possible areas of synergy

- identify key personnel

- give assurance to providers of finance if required

Due Diligence and Valuation Models

Clearly, some valuation models are very sensitive to changes in variables so these should always be part of the financial and commercial Due Diligence process

Ensure you make some points explaining or querying specific model variables

You may wish to note that the acquisition will change the risk profile of the combined company so previous cost of capital/discount rate figures may be out of date

Financial Due Diligence – some procedures

- Test forecasts against industry trends and recent sales patterns
- Test assumptions on production process and costs
- Verify projections of expenditure to suitable evidence e.g. independent evidence
- Assess costs and prices against plans
- Review marketing plans
- Determine capacity for further borrowing
- Test projected capital expenditure
- Discussions with management – reasons, alternatives, contingencies and Plan B

Income Statement Due Diligence

Note – these are simply examples taken from the SBM QB – you must ensure that they are applicable to your exam scenario

Issue	DD Procedures
Revenue	Verify price and volume changes including timing of the price change Confirm that policy is consistent with IAS 18
Cost of sales	Procedures to verify volume changes Verify reasons for changes
Depreciation	Confirm treatment fits with IAS 16 Confirm useful economic lives Confirm that depreciation policy reasonable Determine if assets incorrectly grouped
Impairment	Determine if impairment needed If impairment already proposed, determine if there are other assets that need writing off Confirm value in use and impairment methods used

Provisions	Professional scepticism if provision being reversed – why? Can relate to aggressive earnings management Consider causes and consequences Review the measurement of the original provision and the necessity of the reversal – has there been an intentional effort to distort profit?
Financing costs	Determine if changes are in line with other business changes such as loans and capital expenditure
PBT	Check for unusual movements such as increased PBT but falling GP or margins

SFP Due Diligence (Asset-based valuations)

Note – these are simply examples taken from the SBM QB – you must ensure that they are applicable to your exam scenario

Issue	DD Procedures
PPE	Inspect any relevant valuer's reports Check whether depreciation rates are low Check FV of assets
Inventory	Physical inventory count at the acquisition date with attention to cut off Determine if any impairment is needed, especially if a technology company with high risk of obsolescence Determine inventory turnover rates
Receivables	Investigate returns and impairment Verify title to receivables
Cash	Probably low risk as an objective item but confirm whether cash is included as part of the deal
Loans	Determine carrying amount in accordance with IAS 38/IFRS 9 Review terms of the loan agreement
Pension obligation	Could be either over or understated Determine competence of actuary if used Assess discount rate – rate should be rate on AA corporate bonds Confirm that entries appear in IS, especially if errors made
Tax liability	Consider under and over provisions from last year and any tax payments needed Confirm whether a deferred tax balance is included and whether needed
Trade payables	Assess cut off issues Review whether trade payables days appear reasonable

12.5   Due Diligence: How Has It Been Examined in SBM

SBM real examinations

Both the July 2014 and November 2014 real examinations tested Due Diligence concepts, with 5 marks being available in each case. The topic was tested again in the November 2015 real examination, with 9 marks being available. Due Diligence marks were also available in both examinations in 2017: 8 marks in July 2017 and 7 marks (plus potentially a further 2 marks: see below) in November 2017.

In the **July 2014 examination**, Q1 Task 3 asked candidates (amongst other sub-Tasks) to explain the **benefits of carrying out Due Diligence on a potential target** and also to **recommend whether this should be completed by the client's own staff or by an external assurance provider**. The model answer emphasised the following points:

- The acquisition would be material to the client

- Definition of DD: attesting of information, normally on behalf of a prospective bidder

- Objectives of DD:

    - To confirm the accuracy of information and assumptions on which a bid is based

    - To provide the bidder with an independent assessment and review of the target

    - To identify and quantify areas of commercial and financial risk

    - To give assurance to providers of finance

    - To place the bidder in a better position to determine the value of the target

The above points are, in our view, **very closely** related to the text in the Study Manual: therefore you should develop your own concise and neat explanation of DD and its objectives as the model answer is too lengthy to be written in the time available.

The July 2014 answer then listed out various headings for different types of DD and identified scenario-specific information which could make each type of DD advisable. Again, you need to find a quick summarised way of doing this as the model answer is not achievable in the time available.

With respect to who should conduct the DD (the client internally or an external set of advisers) the answer varied depending on the type of DD: internal staff, external advisers and then external experts were all considered to be feasible for different types of DD.

In the **November 2014 examination**, Q2 Task 4 asked (amongst other elements) candidates to explain the DD procedures that should be carried out when shares are being used as consideration in an acquisition. As the November 2014 Q2 had a relatively unpleasant numerical aspect relating to overhead allocation, the Specialist Audit & Assurance marks would have been particularly valuable for candidates. Unfortunately, the examiner commented (see chapter 8) that candidates did not give a specific enough answer and just discussed DD in general: this is perhaps because a general discussion was exactly what was required in the preceding July 2014 paper. Therefore, as always, **check what you are being asked to do very carefully**.

With respect to DD on the use of shares as consideration, the model answer contained the following points:

DD could be used to obtain evidence from market transactions as the "best source" of information. Information to consider would include:

- Any recent acquisitions of a bundle of shares or any credible offers for the same

- Comparable trades for companies of the same size or industry

DD should also provide assurance that an exit route is available (i.e. that the shares were easy to dispose of).

Legal DD was also noted as a good idea in order to understand the rights of a minority investor within the shareholder agreement, rights to dividends and rights to a seat on the Hexham Board.

Particular risks, which made DD even more important, included: the shares being in an unlisted company and the shares being for a holding of less than 25%, meaning that majority shareholders could change the Articles of Association of the company.

In the **November 2015 examination**, Q1 Task 3 asked candidates to determine the risks involved in an acquisition and to provide appropriate DD procedures to address each risk. The model answer begins with a brief, one sentence definition of DD as the "attesting of information, normally on behalf of a prospective bidder". It was then noted that DD can take place at various times in the negotiations but that the DD findings could then influence those negotiations.

This definition was then applied to 4 specific risks areas, with procedures being briefly listed within each area:

1. Bid price and forecasts – procedures included examining the order book of forward purchases/sales, researching demand in the sector and region, using the forecasts of similar companies as a benchmark, operational Due Diligence over the capacity of the company to achieve growth through a **resource audit** including physical and human resources, analysing peaks and troughs in forecast demand and reviewing historic issues relating to capacity

2. Valuation of assets – procedures included identifying maximum and minimum fair values for assets, investigating impairments, using an expert in residential property and land valuation and analysing recent sales by the company to test the ability to achieve a price comparable to the attributed fair value

3. Ownership and rights over assets and relevant legal obligations – procedures included legal Due Diligence to establish rights and restrictions, analysis of possible unforeseen costs and related legal obligations (such as in relation to ground rent, obligations to repair any environmental damage, obligations to maintain the property in good order, other hidden liabilities and owner's contractual obligations)

4. Costs and uncertainty over integration – procedures included an assessment of the compatibility of the operations, governance and Information Systems of the 2 different companies and an operational assessment of commonalities in procurement and methods as part of operational Due Diligence

In the **July 2017 examination**, Q2 Task asked candidates (amongst other sub-Tasks) to identify the key risks of a **potential acquisition** and the additional Due Diligence procedures that should be carried out by the **prospective purchaser**.

The model answer emphasised that the main risks included the costs and reputational damage in relation to possible faulty yacht engines.

Due Diligence procedures to deal with such risks mentioned in the model answer included:

- Ascertaining the number of faults claimed to have occurred

- Examination of documentation of customer complaints and repair scheduling

- Examination of correspondence with the engine manufacturer to gain further evidence of the nature of the dispute and cause of the faults

- Examination of any legal correspondence concerning claims against the engine manufacturer

- Examination of any legal claims against the target company by customers

- Review of the per engine cost calculated by the target company

- Identification of any unrecognised costs

- Extrapolation of potential future claims experience

- Examination of evidence of faults with the same engine for other yacht manufacturers

- Consideration of the extent of reputational damage

Linked financial reporting implications included potential impairment of inventories, provisions for repairs in relation to future claims, a possible contingent asset in relation to claims against the engine manufacturer and provisions for returns of yachts with major faults.

This example of a Due Diligence model answer is noteworthy because there was **no definition of Due Diligence offered** – instead the answer just goes straight into the risks and tests.

We would recommend making a note of the **financial reporting** issues arising from this kind of scenario (**potential acquisition of a target in distress** due to a manufacturing fault) as we can definitely see such a situation being tested again in SBM.

In the **November 2017 examination**, Q1 Task 3 allocated 7 marks for financial, commercial and operational Due Diligence procedures within the context of a proposed management buyout (MBO). As with the July 2017 examination, there was **no initial definition of Due Diligence provided** in the model answer but at the end of the Financial Due Diligence section the model answer reviews some of the **differences between Due Diligence and statutory audit** (Due Diligence does not involve the same level of detailed testing, only limited assurance is provided by Due Diligence). **Definitions** of

Commercial Due Diligence and **Operational Due Diligence** were also offered at the start of the relevant sections.

Financial Due Diligence points included:

- An FCF valuation depends on the validity of revenue and cost cashflows and the discount rate assumed – financial Due Diligence could therefore validate the underlying revenue assumptions and proposed cost savings to determine whether they are consistent with forecasts. Commercial Due Diligence could then be used to determine whether the forecasts are credible.

- Staff cost savings would need to be evidenced in terms of wage rates and the number of staff reductions needed – redundancy costs would have to be investigated

- Due Diligence could attest the fair value of assets subject to sale and leaseback arrangements and the security involved in a loan

- The discount rate could be assessed against market interest rates by comparison to listed companies (but an adjustment should be made to allow for the unlisted status of the company involved in the scenario)

Commercial Due Diligence points included:

- A definition of commercial Due Diligence was provided: work which complements that of Financial Due Diligence by considering markets and the external economic environment

- Information could come from the management team or from external information sources

- Work could be done to test the revenue growth assumptions for future periods – the Due Diligence team could look at likely changes in demand, using market data

- Historic data could also be used in relation to the previous time that a price increase was applied, to determine the likely customer response

Operational Due Diligence points included:

- Operational Due Diligence considers the operational risks and possible improvements which can be made

- Operational Due Diligence would validate the implications of assumed operational cost savings (e.g. determining whether cost savings are possible whilst maintaining a reasonable level of service)

- Operational Due Diligence could be used to identify operational upsides that might increase the value of the company

Rather unusually, Q2 of the November 2017 examination provided some **further** marks on Due Diligence within a second Assurance Task focusing on how assurance procedures could be used to monitor a joint arrangement. The relevant Task allocated marks to discussion of **both Due Diligence prior to commencement of the project** and **also** to assurance over the **ongoing** operations of the arrangement.

Points in relation to Due Diligence concentrated on the **initial investigation phase**. Investigations could review the joint arrangement agreement, ensure that the purpose of the arrangement is clear, ensure a clear separation from the other operations of each company, review the tax status of the joint arrangement entity, establish that any initial capital has been contributed in accordance with the agreement and that legal rights to fixed assets and labour have been established, establish the creditworthiness, going concern and reputation of the proposed partner, ensure that the terms of disengagement are clear in the initial agreement, establish the fair value of assets transferred, determine if the revenue sharing arrangements are clear and establish any health and safety responsibilities and possible liabilities.

In short, the Due Diligence procedures in this example were very much of a **legal Due Diligence type**.

SBM mock examinations

Both **July 2014** mock examinations contained marks for DD issues. As explained in Appendix 5, **July 2014 Mock 1** was unusual in including DD within a numerical question and therefore the 13 marks available are not perhaps representative.

In **July 2014 Mock 1**, Q2 Task 1 asked for a review of issues raised by DD regarding an acquisition. No definitions of DD were provided in the model answer making this answer very different to the other narrative-type answers reviewed here. We would ignore this answer as an example of typical SBM-style narrative DD points.

In **July 2014 Mock 2**, Q1 Task 2 asked for some relevant remarks on DD issues in relation to historical and forecast information within the context of (you guessed it!) an acquisition. Answers were provided in brief bullet point format:

- Financial DD procedures over historical financial statements

- Valuation of key assets to determine their fair values

- Legal Due Diligence to discover any undisclosed potential liabilities

- Assurance over the projections of future revenue growth and underlying assumptions such as the order book, contracts in place, records of discussions with major customers

- Commercial DD to establish the business model and any synergistic cost savings and surplus assets

- Details of transfer prices to establish whether these are at arm's-length or not

- Validity of the discount rate used by considering market conditions and necessary risk adjustments

This style of answer on DD was almost a mixture of the style seen in the real July 2014 and real November 2014 SBM examinations: the model answer works through the list of different types of DD (as in the July 2014 paper) but is very brief in nature and does not define DD from a theoretical point of view (as in the November 2014 paper).

In **July 2017 Mock 1**, Task 3 of Q2 allocated 8 marks for discussion of Due Diligence in the context of a proposed merger. Points in the model answer included:

- Due Diligence helps to narrow the information gap between the parties

- Procedures can identify legal title, confirm the accuracy and assumptions of financial data and projections, provide a commercial review of the order book and contracts, identify and quantify areas of commercial and financial risk including use of a risk register, give assurance to providers of finance, enable a more precise bid price to be ascertained, identify possible areas of synergy and identify key personnel to tie in for post-merger operations

The model answer then provides definitions and examples of Financial Due Diligence, Commercial Due Diligence, Technical Due Diligence, IT Due Diligence, Legal Due Diligence, HRM Due Diligience and Tax Due Diligence.

Overall, this is a very useful model answer which is well worth reviewing.

Sample Paper

In the SBM Sample Paper, Q1 briefly referred to some limitations of DD by stating that financial DD can provide limited assurance but it does not involve the detailed level of testing that would be carried out in a statutory audit – therefore it may be advisable to delay the acquisition (if this is practical) until after a statutory audit can be performed.

The following specific procedures were then noted within the review of the financials:

- Revenue – procedures to verify price and volume changes, including timing

- Cost of sales – procedures to verify volume changes

- Depreciation – review of PPE policies and calculations

- Impairment – investigation of the reasons for the impairment to determine if further writeoffs are needed

- Finance costs – investigation of reasons for a lack of increase

- Taxation – investigation of the rate applied, aspects of the computation and confirmation of the reasons for the absence of a deferred tax balance

- Financial instruments (loans) – review of carrying amount and determination of whether the treatment of the loan arrangement is appropriate under IFRS

- Pensions – review of the discount rate and comparison to good quality corporate bonds

As we can see, **the model answer "tests" are nowhere near as detailed as would be expected regarding a statutory audit in your Corporate Reporting** paper so ensure that you do not write too much on tests: it is better to save time so that you can give a very broad review over a wider range of issues to impress the examiner.

12.6   Reporting on Prospective Information

A **forecast** is prospective financial information based on assumptions as to future events which management expects to take place and the actions which management expects to take: it is a best-estimate

A **projection** is based on hypothetical assumptions and scenarios, rather than events which management necessarily expects to happen

ISAE 3400 governs the reporting of prospective financial information. Under this standard, there should be agreement with the directors regarding the intended use of the information, whether the information will be distributed generally, the types of assumptions used, the elements to be included in the information and the period covered by the information

The opinion expressed should be in the form of a **negative and limited assurance opinion** that nothing has come to the practitioner's attention to doubt the assumptions and proper preparation of the information – caveats should be indicated – assurance given is not to the same standard as for historical statements – as with any forecast, it is important to recognise that assumptions may subsequently prove incorrect even if they were completely reasonable at the time of formulation

The practitioner/auditor must have sufficient knowledge of the business. The assurance provided is **limited** and **negative** in nature.

The options of a **qualified**, **adverse** or **disclaimer of opinion** are available

The procedures for reporting on prospective information noted in the Corporate Reporting Study Manual can be split into 2 types: general and specific

General procedures involve obtaining sufficient appropriate evidence regarding whether management's best-estimate assumptions are not unreasonable and consistent with the purpose of the information. It should also be determined whether the prospective financial information is properly prepared and presented and whether the information is consistent with the historical financial statements

Specific procedures are provided for the areas of profits, capital expenditure and cash flows.

Review of profit forecasts: procedures

- verify projected income figures to suitable evidence, including comparison of the basis of projected income to similar existing projects in the firm

- reviewing competitor prices for the relevant product or service to determine whether projected information is reasonable

- verify projected expenditure figures to suitable evidence, such as quotations or estimates, current bills, interest rate assumptions or costs such as depreciation

- check assumptions about annual revenues based on market prices and estimates of costs and how these have been divided into fixed and variable elements

Review of capital expenditure forecasts: procedures

- check capital expenditure for reasonableness by ensuring that all relevant costs are included and that costs estimated are reasonable

- verify projected costs to estimates and quotations

- review projections for reasonableness by examining the prevailing market rates

- verify that there is evidence that the required capital assets can be located and purchased

Review of cashflow forecasts: procedures

- review cash forecasts to determine whether the timings involved are reasonable

- check the cash forecast for consistency with profit forecasts, looking at both the expenditure and income side or undertake some other method of verification if there is no relevant or comparable profit forecast

12.7   Reporting on prospective information: How Has It Been Examined in SBM?

We have noticed that many model answers on this area have a very similar format or "skeleton outline" (this is also the case when the topic is examined in the Business Planning: Banking Professional Level paper which shares identical syllabus content on ISAE 3400 with SBM). We summarise this "skeleton" below.

Skeleton Outline of ISAE 3400 Points to Include

Statement that reporting on prospective information is covered by ISAE 3400 *The Examination of Prospective Financial Information*

Statement that ISAE 3400 highlights that prospective information is based on assumptions about the future and is therefore highly subjective – judgement is required in its preparation

Definition of a "forecast" and of a "projection"

Procedures must be used to obtain sufficient appropriate evidence that

> management's best-estimate assumptions are not unreasonable and that any hypothetical assumptions are consistent with the purpose of the information. Then apply these points by referring to the scenario.

> the information has been properly prepared on the basis of the assumptions. Then apply these points by referring to the scenario.

> the information is properly presented and all material assumptions are adequately disclosed, including a clear indication as to whether they are best-estimate assumptions or hypothetical assumptions. Then apply these points by referring to the scenario.

> the information is prepared on a consistent basis with historical financial statements, using appropriate accounting principles. Then apply these points by referring to the scenario.

Statement that as prospective financial information is subjective, it is impossible to give the same level of assurance regarding forecasts as can be provided regarding historical information e.g. may be over a significant future time horizon, which creates uncertainty

Procedures are used to support limited assurance in the form of a negatively expressed opinion in relation to whether

> the assumptions provide a reasonable basis for the prospective financial information

> the information is properly prepared on the basis of the assumptions and relevant reporting framework

Appropriate caveats should be given as to the achievability of any forecasts, together with examples from the scenario as to why they may not be achieved.

Testing of ISAE 3400 in SBM papers

ISAE 3400 was examined for the first time in a real examination paper in the **July 2015** examination. Task 3 in Q1 provided 10 marks in relation to ISAE 3400 issues. The context was a question asking students how assurance over forecasts could help the providers of financing (i.e. a bank).

The model answer starts by setting out the 2 main risks facing the bank (the risk that the client business may not be viable or have sufficient cash flows and, secondly, the fact that the client business may not have sufficient assets to realise on liquidation if loan repayments are not made). The model answer then explains that assurance in respect of forecasts is subject to ISAE 3400. The model answer explains that prospective financial information means "financial information based on assumptions about events that may occur in the future and possible actions by an entity". It is also stated that a forecast is defined as "prospective financial information based on assumptions as to future events which management expects to take place and the actions management expects to take (best estimate assumptions)".

After these definitional aspects, the model answer moves on to provide examples of areas where sufficient appropriate evidence would be useful:

Management's best estimate assumptions – it would need to be confirmed that these are not unreasonable and that assumptions are consistent with the purpose of the information: the realism of all assumptions and related research would need to be assessed

Translation of assumptions into a model – it would need to be confirmed that the financial information produced is consistent with the value and timing variables within the assumptions

Disclosure of assumptions and presentation – it would need to be confirmed that the prospective financial information is properly presented and that all material assumptions had been adequately disclosed: in particular, it should be clearly stated whether they are best estimate assumptions or hypothetical/working assumptions

Consistency with the financial statements – it would need to be confirmed that the forecasts are prepared on a consistent basis with historical financial statements, using appropriate accounting principles. In this case, this was stated to be a key risk area as there seem to be a lack of historical information to support assumptions and forecasts.

Given the limitations, the model answer then goes on to state that prospective financial information is subjective and does not give the same level of assurance as is possible with respect to historical financial information. Therefore limited assurance, in the form of a negatively expressed opinion, is the best that can be provided.

SBM mock examinations

The **November 2014 Mock 2** features 8 marks for a question on the requirements involved in carrying out an assurance engagement on financial forecasts, which were to be published by a listed UK company. Points made in the answer include:

- A **lack of information from the client** on exactly what level of detail will be published (and therefore on the subject matter of the assurance engagement)[71]

- The **terms of the engagement should be agreed in advance** – the terms would probably involve an arrangement to test the assumptions that management has used in making the forecast

- **ISAE 3400 provides the guidelines** for this sort of assurance engagement

---

[71] This is perhaps an example of the use of the SBM skill of scepticism: see chapter 4 for further detail.

- **Forecasts will be based on assumptions**, generally including historical information

- The practitioner needs to satisfy itself about the **reliability of any historical information** that has been used as the basis of the forecasts

- The practitioner should consider the **reasonableness of the assumptions** that have been used to prepare the forecast and whether the forecast has in fact been prepared on the basis of those assumptions (and correctly so)

- The **assumptions must be stated as part of the published forecast**

- **Predicting the future is a speculative matter** and can lead to errors if events turn out differently

- Therefore the assurance provider's task cannot be to say whether the results will be "correct" or turn out as planned – rather **the practitioner's role is instead to consider whether the assumptions are free from any material misstatement or weakness**

- If the **assumptions appear to be unrealistic**, then the assurance provider **should not accept or continue with the assurance engagement**

- If historical information has been used as the basis for making the forecast then it would be necessary to **check whether the information has been audited** or to obtain other evidence of its reliability

- The report provided at the end of the engagement should include a **statement of negative assurance** as to whether the assumptions used provide a reasonable basis for making the forecast

- The report should **contain an opinion as to whether the forecast has been properly prepared** on the basis of these assumptions

- **Caveats should be included regarding the prospective nature of the results** and therefore the fact that the figures included may not necessarily be achievable

As we can see, the answer does include many of the standard points in our revision notes but with a little tailoring to the question scenario (e.g. the point that the client had not been very specific about the information required): that said, **there were not a huge amount of tailored remarks here, supporting our view** (indicated by the very fact that we have provided extensive specialist Audit & Assurance revision notes provided here) that **learning the "standard" list-type points for each type of engagement is very important**. The above list is fairly long but at 10 marks this was a key element of Q2[72].

---

[72] As noted, this analysis relates to a mock examination so please bear this in mind as our own caveat here.

The review of forecasts is also covered in 3 mock exams released in 2015: **July 2015 Mock 2** Q1, **November 2015 Mock 1** Q2 and **November 2015 Mock 2** Q2. This amount of testing again emphasises the importance of this topic to the examiners.

In **July 2015 Mock 2** Q1 Task 9 (this question is an amended Business Change question, hence the very large number of Tasks compared to a normal SBM question), there were 5 marks available for explaining the difference between assurance over prospective financial information and the audit of historic financial information. The main points were:

- Reviews of prospective information are governed by ISAE 3400 rather than ISAs.

- A review of prospective information is necessarily subjective in nature and requires judgement.

- In a review of prospective information the aim is to obtain sufficient evidence that the assumptions are not unreasonable and that the information is properly prepared on the basis of those assumptions – the aim is not to pronounce on whether the information is "true and fair".

- In a review of prospective information there will not be production of a statutory report and only negative assurance is given. The opinion will be limited to saying that nothing has come to the attention of the practitioner to suggest that the assumptions used in the forecasts do not provide a reasonable basis for the forecasts and that nothing has come to the attention of the practitioner to suggest the forecasts have not been properly prepared on the basis of those assumptions.

- In a review of prospective information the addressee of the report will not be the shareholders but rather a specific client (e.g. a bank) and will be private in nature – on the other hand, a statutory audit report is produced for the shareholders and is included in published financial statements.

In **November 2015 Mock 1** Q2 Task 3, there were 10 marks for explaining the nature of the key assurance procedures to be performed in respect of forecasts. The points made were almost word for word identical to the points noted above regarding the November 2015 real paper. This included the structure of the answer, which starts with a definition of prospective financial information and forecasts (based on the same wording as the November 2015 real paper). The application to the scenario based on considering whether the assumptions are not unreasonable and whether the model is then based on the assumptions, together with the reference to historical financial information, is almost identical to the wording of the November 2015 real paper.

The only additional point to note is that, in addition to the usual points that an opinion under ISAE 3400 is negative in nature, in this answer it was stated that under ISAE 3400 there should be a clear statement of appropriate caveats as to the achievability of the forecasts.

In **November 2015 Mock 2** Q2 Task 4, there were 7 marks for discussing the value of an assurance report over forecasts. The points made were almost identical to the examples reviewed already above. Similarly, the structure of starting with definitions, making points in relation to the reasonableness of assumptions and preparation of the model based on those assumptions and then noting that only negative assurance is given was the same as usual and as seen above.

The only additional point to note is that the model answer states that a "consultancy engagement" could be more useful than mere assurance over a specific forecast. This is because a consultancy engagement could involve preparing an alternative forecast based on different assumptions and work to assess the reliability of the original forecast (rather than simply stating, as in an assurance engagement, that the assumptions do not appear unreasonable). It was noted that an accountancy firm could undertake such an engagement but equally the client may be able to perform this role itself.

The final Task in Q1 of **November 2017 Mock 2** allocated 10 marks to an explanation of the Assurance that can be obtained from a review of prospective information. The model answer applies the very standardised ISAE 3400 skeleton approach seen in various other model answers: the answer first defines the term "forecast", explains that the Assurance process will determine whether the assumptions are not unreasonable and that, in the case of hypothetical assumptions, that such assumptions are consistent with the purpose of the information. The model answer then reviews various assumptions that are critical to this particular example: the nature of agreements with suppliers, costs of fixtures and fittings, ability to obtain the necessary premises, advertising assumptions and cost estimates.

The model answer then explains that the process will also involve checking the figures for mathematical accuracy. Tax assumptions should be checked and sensitivity analysis should be carried out.

The model answer then ends with some standard ISAE 3400 points:

- Prospective financial information is subjective so it is impossible for the Assurance provider to give the same level of assurance regarding forecasts as can be provided regarding the financial statements

- A five-year horizon for an entirely new enterprise creates material uncertainty

- Limited assurance is given in the form of a negative opinion

- The opinion should provide a statement of negative assurance as to whether the assumptions provide a reasonable basis for the prospective financial information and whether the prospective financial information is properly prepared on the basis of the assumptions and relevant reporting framework. The opinion should also provide appropriate caveats as to the achievability of the forecasts

We would note that the final set of points is also made towards the start of the answer so you should be careful to make these points only once in your answer in order to save time.

Although the above points are very standard indeed for an ISAE 3400 model answer, an interesting aspect of this question is that the model answer then goes on to discuss ongoing Assurance because the bank which provided finance to the project wished to receive updates once the project was underway.

The model answer then states that assurance over historical information would be needed to the extent that separate disclosures are not already made in the financial statements. There might also be a need for revised forecasts based on revised assumptions as more evidence becomes available over time.

The answer ends by stating that reasonable assurance could be provided for actual results but limited assurance is all that is possible for forecasts (even revised forecasts and even if these are based on improved assumptions and new data).

We can conclude that prospective information has been tested in a number of SBM papers: if you carefully review the above points, you should be able to spot some patterns in terms of what you need to say each time. This does seem to be a quite formulaic area.

12.8   Agreed Upon Procedures

Agreed upon procedures are procedures of a standard audit nature but which have been **specifically agreed upon by the auditor, entity and any appropriate third parties for a purpose other than preparation of a statutory audit**.

A difference with statutory audit is therefore that there must be **agreement on the procedures to be applied** (hence the name "agreed upon" procedures) whereas in a statutory audit it is the auditor who determines which procedures to use.

A second difference is that the recipients of the report containing the "agreed upon" procedures are **left to form their own conclusions – the auditor/practitioner does not offer a conclusion**, unlike in a statutory audit (or other types of assurance).

Agreed upon procedures are governed by **ISRS 4400**. Note that ISRSs have not been adopted in the UK.

In setting up the agreed upon procedures, agreement should be reached on the following matters:

- Nature of the arrangement as not constituting an audit or review i.e. no assurance is expressed at all

- Purpose of the engagement

- Identification of the financial information to which the agreed upon procedures will be applied

- Nature, timing and extent of the specific procedures to be applied

- Anticipated form of the report

- Limitations on distribution of the report

The report of factual findings should contain:

- Identification of specific financial or non-financial information to which the agreed-upon procedures have been applied

- Statement that the procedures performed were those agreed upon with the recipient

- Statement that the engagement was performed in accordance with the ISRSs applicable to Agreed Upon Procedure engagements or with relevant national standards or practices

- If the auditor is performing the agreed upon procedures, a statement that the auditor is not independent of the entity

- Identification of the purpose for which the agreed upon procedures were performed

- A listing of the specific procedures performed

- A description of the auditor's factual findings including sufficient details of errors and exceptions found

- A statement that the procedures performed do not constitute either an audit or a review, and, as such, **no assurance is expressed**

- A statement that had the auditor performing additional procedures or an audit/review then other matters may have been arisen and reported

- A restriction on use of the report to only those parties that have agreed to the procedures which have been performed

- A statement that the report relates only to the elements, accounts, items or financial and non-financial information specified and does not extend to the entity's financial statements taken as a whole

Again, **no assurance or opinion is offered** – there is only a reporting of **factual findings**.

12.9 Agreed Upon Procedures: How Has This Topic Been Examined in SBM?

Agreed Upon Procedures was tested for the first time in the July 2016 real paper. We are not aware of any other examples in the SBM materials. Key points from the July 2016 real paper example include:

In an AUP engagement, the practitioner provides a report on factual findings from procedures agreed in advance with the relevant party or parties.

Procedures and tests should be sufficiently detailed so as to be clear and unambiguous and discussed in advance to ensure that they are useful for the purposes.

The practitioner is required to comply at a minimum with ISRS 4400 *Engagements to Perform Agreed Upon Procedures on Financial Information*

The AUP report does not express a conclusion and is therefore not an assurance engagement – it will not provide recommendations based on the findings – the relevant parties are instead requested to review the procedures and findings and to use the information to draw their own conclusions

The value of the AUP process is in providing objective testing by a practitioner with relevant expertise – testing is independent and also protects confidentiality (practitioner is bound by the Code of Ethics for Professional Accountants under ISRS 4400) – saves one of the parties carrying out the procedures themselves (time and money saving)

Example of AUP performed on a licensing agreement

Procedures on the contractual terms such as number of bags sold, number of customer complaints about product quality and the number of customer complaints about service quality

Benefit is that the engagement provides evidence of compliance with the terms of the licensing contract: ensures correct royalty payments and monitoring of quality control issues

The confidential nature of AUP might be the only way to give the parties enough confidence to allow the procedures to be carried out at all

Although there are no other examples of AUP in the SBM materials, we would note that the skeleton of the above response is almost identical to the November 2013 Business Change paper. At the SBM Workshop at the 2014 Tutor Conference, the examiners discussed this Business Change paper (since there were no SBM exams to discuss) and noted that candidate performance regarding Agreed Upon Procedures was very poor indeed. Please therefore ensure you can outperform the average by revising AUP properly.

12.10   Compilation Engagements

Collection, classification and compilation of financial information. In this type of engagement, the accountant is using his or her **accounting** expertise rather than **auditing** expertise. The process is governed by **ISRS 4410**.

Example outputs from this process include historical financial information, pro forma financial information and prospective financial information including financial budgets and forecasts.

There should be agreement on:

- the intended use and distribution of the financial information and any restrictions on its use or distribution

- identification of the applicable financial reporting framework

- the objective and scope of the engagement

- the responsibilities of the practitioner, including the requirement to comply with relevant ethical requirements

- the responsibilities of management for the accuracy and completeness of the information and records and documents

- the expected form and content of the practitioner's report

The practitioner works to **obtain an understanding of the entity's business and operations**, including the accounting system and records and the applicable financial reporting framework. **The specific nature of the work varies considerably, depending on the nature of the engagement.**

If the practitioner becomes aware that the information provided by management is incomplete, inaccurate or otherwise unsatisfactory then the practitioner must bring this to the attention of management and request additional or corrected information. The practitioner must withdraw from the engagement and inform management/those charged with governance if management fail to provide this information and the engagement cannot be completed or if management refuse to make the amendments proposed by the practitioner.

The practitioner obtains an acknowledgement from management/those charged with governance that they take responsibility for the information in its final form. The practitioner's report should contain the following elements:

- a statement that the practitioner has used the information provided by management

- a description of the responsibilities of management or those charged with governance

- identification of the applicable financial reporting framework and any special purpose financial reporting framework

- identification of the financial information, including the titles of each element of the financial information

- a description of the practitioner's responsibilities in compiling the financial information

- a **description** of what a compilation engagement entails

- explanation that the compilation engagement is **not an assurance engagement** and therefore the practitioner is not required to verify the accuracy or completeness of the information provided by management

- explanation that the practitioner does not express an audit opinion or a review conclusion on whether the financial information is prepared in accordance with a financial reporting framework

- an explanatory paragraph which describes the purpose of the financial information and which draws the attention of readers to the fact that the information may not be suitable for other purposes, if it is the case that a special purpose framework has been used

Changes have been made to ISA 250 *Consideration of Laws and Regulations in an Audit of Financial Statements* by the IAASB following the conclusion of its NOCLAR (non-compliance with laws and regulations) project – this has resulted in "conforming amendments" to ISRS 4410.

The amendments provide guidance regarding the reporting of identified or suspected non-compliance with laws and regulations to an appropriate authority outside the entity.

If fraud or non-compliance with laws and regulations is suspected, the professional accountant should consult internally, obtain legal advice and consult with the regulator or professional body in order to understand the implications of different courses of action.

12.11   Compilation Engagements: How Has This Topic Been Examined in SBM?

As already noted, this topic has not yet been examined in SBM.

12.12   Forensic Audits: Revision Notes

Defined as "the process of gathering, analysing and reporting on data for the purpose of finding facts and evidence in the context of financial or legal disputes and giving preventative advice in this area".

A key aspect of forensic auditing is therefore that the issue must arise in the context of a financial or legal **dispute**.

Applications of forensic auditing include:

- Fraud

- Negligence

- Insurance claims

- Shareholder and partnership disputes

233

- Contract disputes

- Business sales and purchase disputes

- Matrimonial disputes

- Investigation of terrorist financing

- Expert witness services

When providing expert witness services, the duties of the witness are set out in the Civil Procedure Rules (CPR):

- experts owe a duty to exercise reasonable skill and care to those instructing them but their overriding duty is to the court to help the court judge the matter justly

- experts should provide opinions which are independent

- experts should confine their opinions to matters which are material to the dispute between the parties

- experts should only offer opinions on matters which lie within their expertise

Planning a Forensic Audit

As with a statutory audit, there should be a planning stage, an evidence-gathering stage, a review process and a report to the client provided at the final stage. There are some differences to a statutory audit:

- there will be no materiality threshold

- the timing of the report will be more variable – there will not be a standardised reporting date

- documentation needs to be reviewed more critically than on a standard audit

- interviews may be required, and these will need a high level of experience and skill

- there may be greater use of sophisticated data mining techniques

- the environment could be one defined by conflict such as in a fraud of matrimonial dispute

Example procedures for a Fraud investigation could include[73]:

- developing a profile of the entity/individual under investigation

---

[73] As forensic audits/investigations vary considerably in nature, always ensure that you include points which are relevant to the scenario set.

- identifying weaknesses in internal control procedures and record-keeping

- performing trend analysis and analytical procedures to identify significant transactions and variations

- identifying changes in patterns of purchases/sales

- identifying significant variations in consumption of raw materials and consumables

- identifying unusual accounts and account balances

- reviewing transaction documentation for discrepancies and inconsistencies

- tracing the individual responsible for fraudulent transactions

- obtaining information regarding all responsibilities of the individual involved

- inspecting and reviewing other transactions of a similar nature conducted by the individual

- considering all other aspects of the business which the individual is involved with and performing further analytical procedures

12.13   Forensic Audits: How Has This Topic Been Examined in SBM?

As already noted, this topic has not yet been examined in SBM.

12.14   ISAE 3402: November 2017 Mock 1

As a final point in relation to Assurance in SBM, we would note that an area that is very rarely referred to in the Advanced Level question resources (past papers, Mocks and Question Banks) was tested in **November 2017 Mock 1**. Task 4 of Q2 allocated 9 marks to discussion of Assurance over systems, operations and processes under **ISAE 3402, *Assurance Reports on Controls at a Service Organisation***. The background to the scenario was that a company called Domstore had approached a company called Rammond Paints (the company being advised as part of the question) to discuss the offer of a contract to supply Domstore with paint. Rammond Paints already had in place an online ordering system for the use of its regular customers and Domstore required assurance regarding this system.

Key points made in the model answer include:

- When a company acts as a service organisation for another company (in this case, Rammond Paints would be a service organisation for Domstore), then guidance is provided by ISAE 3402.

- ISAE 3402 states that the objectives of an assurance provider reporting on the systems of a service organisation will be to obtain assurance whether, in all material respects, and based

235

on suitable criteria, the service organisation's description of its systems fairly presents the systems as designed and implemented, the controls related to the control objectives stated in the service organisation's description of its system are suitably designed and that the controls operated effectively to provide reasonable assurance that the control objectives stated in the service organisation's description of its system are achieved

- A Type 1 report would provide an opinion on the design and existence of the control measures in place over the service organisation's systems

- A Type 2 report will provide an opinion on these aspects as well as on the operating effectiveness of the controls – therefore a Type 2 report covers **all** the points in the paragraph regarding ISAE 3402 above, whereas a Type 1 report is more limited

- The assurance conclusion and related recommendations can then be used by the management of the service organisation to improve the quality of systems and controls, if this is deemed necessary

- Domstore would be looking in particular for assurance over the integrity and quality of the service organisation's information technology systems in terms of processing orders completely, accurately and on a timely basis

- Domstore would be concerned that Rammond Paint's systems will be available for use as required, protected against unauthorised access and that any confidential information provided is protected in a secure database

- As the ordering system is an online system then cybersecurity will be a concern for Domstore – it will want to obtain assurance that Rammond Paints has robust firewalls around its systems, has installed virus and malware/ransomware protection and that all such software is up to date

As this is a rare example of a model answer on ISAE 3402, please do ensure that you look through it carefully.

12.15 The Examination of Assurance and Related Services: Summary and Conclusions

In this chapter, we have reviewed both the textbook sections regarding Assurance and Related Services and the ways in which Assurance and Related Services has been examined as a topic area. We strongly recommend that you re-read the chapter several times to learn the necessary information but as a short summary of the key points we would note the following[74]:

- The main areas tested to date have been **Due Diligence** and **Reporting on Prospective Information**, perhaps because of the easier fit to the classic SBM/BC areas of acquisitions, valuations and forecasts/plans

- **This does not mean that you should assume that only these areas will be tested in SBM**: we know from experience of the BC examination that the same examiner team does

---

[74] As noted on page 163, our *Advanced Level Audit & Assurance Q&A 2018* is available if you require a more interactive, self-test method of learning Assurance and Related Services concepts.

like to **rotate around the specialist areas** and when this happens, student performance is usually poor as students did not expect a topic to come up at all – **therefore, give yourself an advantage over other candidates by preparing properly!**

- Ensure that you are clear about the **different aims, methods and levels of assurance** offered by each of the above 6 Assurance and Related Services areas

- Ensure that you can quickly list out the **8 different types of DD** and then also **apply them to the scenario to make MS^2 points**

- Ensure that you are familiar with the different **responsibilities of the client, practitioner/assurance provider and forms of report** that are involved in the above 6 Assurance and Related Services areas

- **Purchase our *SBM Exam Room Notes*** and ensure that you are familiar with the notes in the various sections of our *Exam Room Notes* in relation to the topics covered in this chapter – ideally you should use the *Exam Room Notes* in at least one full SBM mock examination attempt

In the next chapter, we will apply the process used in this chapter to the next Specialist A&A area of "Environmental and Social Audits and Assurance", again starting by providing some revision notes from the Study Manual and then looking at how these areas have been tested in examination papers.

Chapter 13   **Environmental and Social Audits and Assurance: Revision Notes and Examination Analysis**

Learning Points

After reading this chapter, you must be able to:

1. understand which areas are contained within the Environmental and Social topic
2. understand why this topic is of increasing interest and therefore potentially examinable
3. understand how Environmental and Social topics have been tested in SBM examination papers

---

13.1   Environmental and Social Audits and Assurance: Revision Notes

This is another specialist auditing area which is given its own dedicated chapter in the Corporate Reporting Study Manual: we have tried to summarise the most important points here. Note that the topic of **Integrated Reporting** was specifically added in the **2015 edition** of the Corporate Reporting Study Manual within the Environmental Audits sub-topic so do check this area carefully.

Why apply assurance to social responsibility reports?

Entities are increasingly supplying more information of this type to stakeholders so stakeholders need reassurance that the information is correct – however, the information is not part of the financial statements and so will not be audited as part of a statutory audit engagement.

An independent, external party can verify the data and information – this will increase credibility – the stakeholders can have more confidence the information is drawn from reliable sources and that it has been calculated accurately using a consistent methodology over time.

The assurance engagement should provide assurance as to compliance with certain fundamental standards promised but also more detailed assurance as to whether performance indicators are accurately and consistently recorded.

Difficulties

Often performance will relate mainly to non-financial indicators – these may not be part of standardised information flows and may involve judgement – it is also not possible to apply certain types of assurance procedures to information which is not financial e.g. analytical procedures, ratio analysis or computer analytics

Sometimes questionnaires are issued to the entity and its staff or interviews are conducted – a problem here is knowing whether the information is truthful

The Triple Bottom Line

According to the Study Manual, the triple bottom line in reporting should be to consider the **economic**, **environmental** and **social** impacts of the operations of an entity. You may therefore wish to use this framework in your answer.

Reporting Frameworks

There is currently no single consensus framework on social and environmental reporting so you need to be aware of the following frameworks:

Global Reporting Initiative (GRI)

Designed to promote transparency, accountability, reporting and sustainable development.

Revised in May 2013

Based on the following principles:

- Stakeholder inclusiveness

- Sustainability context

- Materiality

- Completeness

- Balance

- Comparability

- Accuracy

- Timeliness

- Clarity

- Reliability

In October 2016, the GRI launched the new Sustainability Reporting Standards. These Standards replace the previous G4 Guidelines but are based on the previous Guidelines. The Standards are:

GRI 101: Foundation – this sets out the Reporting Principles

GRI 102: General disclosures – this is used to report contextual information about an organisation and its sustainability reporting practices and includes information about an organisation's profile, strategy, ethics and integrity, governance, stakeholder engagement practices and reporting processes

GRI 103: Management approach – this is used to report information about how an organisation manages a material topic

Companies Act 2006

Requires the business review in the directors' report for quoted companies to include information on environmental, social and community issues. The information should include both financial and non-financial key performance indicators.

From 1 October 2013, Companies Act 2006 requires all UK quoted companies to report on their greenhouse gas emissions within the annual Directors' Report. Other companies are encouraged to report this information but it remains a voluntary process.

DEFRA Guidelines

Originally published in 2006 and updated in June 2013

The guidelines help companies to understand what to report in various situations such as when preparing a Business Review, making mandatory greenhouse gas emissions statements and for SMEs who are part of a larger supply chain and who need suppliers to behave responsibly

Accounting for Sustainability (A4S) Connected Reporting Framework

Launched in the UK in 2006 by Prince Charles

Aims to help ensure that sustainability is embedded in the DNA of an organisation

Requires sustainability to be clearly linked to the organisation's overall strategy and requires consistency in presentation to aid comparability between years and organisations

Contains 5 key elements:

- Explanation of how sustainability is connected to the overall operational strategy of an organisation

- Five key environmental indicators to be considered in all reporting: greenhouse gas emissions, energy usage, water use, waste and significant use of other finite resources

- Other key sustainability information should be given where the business or operation has material impacts

- Use of industry benchmark key performance indicators when available

- Upstream and downstream impact of the organisation's products and services

A4S now has the following 3 core aims:

1. To inspire finance leaders to adopt sustainable and resilient business models

2. To transform financial decision-making to enable an integrated approach, reflective of the opportunities and risks posed by environmental and social issues

3. To scale up actions across the global finance and accounting community

The 4 main themes of A4S projects are:

1. Lead the way: developing a strategic response to macro sustainability trends

2. Transform your decisions: integrating material sustainability factors into decision-making

3. Measure what matters: developing measurement and evaluation tools

4. Access finance: engaging with finance providers on the drivers of sustainable value

Advantages of sustainability reporting

- Employee satisfaction with working for a company that behaves appropriately

- Improved stakeholder satisfaction

- Investors may want to see a company adopt sustainable practices

- Abuses of social and environmental issues can damage reputation

- Using resources effectively can save money

Disadvantages of sustainability reporting

- Moves focus away from financial returns, which could be argued to be the main point of the business

- Shareholder value may be reduced if profits are lost

- Costs incurred to become more green

Impact of environmental and social issues on statutory audit

Some possible impacts include:

- Impairment of assets after introduction of new laws and regulations

- Accruals for remediation, compensation or legal costs

- Constructive obligations

- Contingent liabilities and provisions

- Development cost expenditure for new products

- Going concern issues

- Impact on understanding the entity and assessing risks

- Need for the auditor to ask environmental questions such as what laws and regulations are applicable or any history of legal penalties or proceedings

Social Audits

A social audit involves:

- Establishing whether the entity has a reason for engaging in social activities

- Identifying that all current environmental programmes are congruent with the mission of the company

- Assessing the objectives and priorities related to these programmes

- Evaluating company involvement in such programmes past, present and future

13.2   Environmental Audits

An environmental audit involves assessing how well the organisation performs in protecting its environment and whether the company is in compliance with its environmental policies. Procedures could include:

- Obtaining a copy of the company's environmental policy

- Assessing whether the policy is likely to achieve objectives such as meeting legal requirements, meeting British Standards and satisfying key customers/suppliers

- Testing implementation and adherence to the policy by discussion, observation and walk through tests

13.3 Assurance on Sustainability Reporting

This type of service could involve offering assurance over the figures and statements that are stated in the directors' environmental and social report, if these are verifiable.

There is currently no general standard that applies to related assurance assignments but ISAE 3000 and AA1000AS (issued by AccountAbility) could also be relevant. AA1000AS establishes 3 principles for sustainability reporting:

- Inclusivity

- Materiality

- Responsiveness

Under the standard, the objective of engagement should be to evaluate and provide conclusions on the nature of adherence to the AA1000 principles and the quality of publicly disclosed information. There should be a statement regarding any limitation of scope. There is no set wording but the following should be considered:

- Intended users

- Responsibility of the reporting organisation and of the assurance provider

- Assurance standard/s used

- Description of the scope

- Description of disclosures covered

- Description of methodology

- Any limitations on information

- The criteria used

- A statement of the level of assurance provided

- Findings and conclusions relating to AA1000

- Observations and/or recommendations

- Notes on the competencies and independence of the assurance provider

- Name of the assurance provider

- Date and place of preparation

13.4   Environmental Due Diligence (EDD)

EDD has been used for many years within the process of acquisitions and mergers and property transfers, generally considering risks relating to contaminate land and regulatory compliance.

However, EDD now includes a wider range of areas:

Integrated Reporting

As noted above, **this topic was added to the 2015 edition of the Corporate Reporting Study Manual whilst a further detailed real-world example has been added to the 2018 edition of the Corporate Reporting Study Manual** – we therefore recommend that you study it well.

There has been increasing interest in Integrated Reporting (IR) due to a belief that traditional corporate reporting does not "tell the whole story".

Benefits of IR include:

> Streamlined performance reporting with efficiencies found within the organisation

> Reduction in duplication of information and consistency of messaging

> Aligns and simplifies internal and external reporting for consistency and efficiency

> Greater focus on what is material to the organisation and helps identify what is not material

> Less time and effort is wasted on reporting unimportant issues

The International Integrated Reporting Council (IIRC) introduced the integrated reporting framework in 2013. This framework is based around the concept of 6 different "types of capitals":

> **Financial capital** – funds available and obtained from operations, debt, equity or grants

> **Manufacturing capital** – manufactured physical objectives available for use

244

Intellectual capital – knowledge-based intangibles developed by the organisation

Human capital – competencies, capabilities and experience

Natural capital – environmental resources and processes

Social and relationship capital – relationships with stakeholders and networks

These types of capital will interact in positive and negative ways.

Integrated reporting should look at the long term impact and value creation, where value creation is not understood simply in monetary terms.

Some implications of introducing integrated reporting into an entity include:

- IT costs

- Time and staff costs

- Consultancy costs

- Disclosure – the entity may disclose more information about its operational performance than intended

The Study Manual provides ICAEW's own integrated report as an example of integrated reporting: the following sections were included:

- Organisational overview of aims, people, relationships and thinking

- Performance: student and membership numbers, year on year changes and commentary

Auditing Integrated Reports

In reality, performance will depend on a variety of factors rather than separate independent variables. Therefore the auditor may have to adjust for background factors that have changed in the meantime to assess performance correctly. However, this will require substantial professional judgement.

Additionally, look out for any incentive to manipulate the figures, particularly if there is any performance-related element.

The auditor should also look out for any perverse incentives where motivations are not appropriate for the organisation as a whole: if the performance metric for a call centre is "number of calls answered", will this result in good quality responses from operators or will it just result in a lot of short and unhelpful calls, just to meet targets?

Guiding Principles of Integrated Reporting

Strategic focus and future orientation – insight into strategy

Connectivity – holistic and relates to the connections between different elements

Stakeholder relationships

Materiality

Reliability and completeness

Conciseness

Consistency and comparability

Elements of an integrated report

Organisational overview and external environment

Governance

Business model

Risks and opportunities

Strategy and resource allocation

Performance

Future outlook

Implications of an integrated report

Need to be careful what forward-looking information is disclosed – do we want to reveal our strategy?

Should force the business to take a long-term perspective and think about the 6 capitals

Increased use of non-financial information

Report must give insight into strategy

Significantly increased information requirements: need to consider whether systems can provide this, whether non-financial issues can be embedded and any necessary improvements to reporting

Conducting an audit of performance information

- Identify the objectives against which the organisation is to be evaluated

- Plan procedures to determine whether objectives are being achieved: these procedures could include social-scientific research methods as well as more traditional audit-type approaches

- Express a conclusion in the form of a report, either separately or within another document. Ideally, both the performance statistics and the auditor's view will be presented alongside each other within the same document

13.5 Social and Environmental Audits and Assurance: How Has this Topic Been Examined in SBM?

Both 2016 SBM past papers tested the area of social and environmental audits and assurance.

The **July 2016 model answer** made the following points:

Sustainability is about ensuring that development meets the needs of the present without compromising the ability of future generations to meet their own needs.

Recycling is an aspect of sustainability as an organisation should only use resources at a rate that allows them to be replenished. However, sustainability is about much more than simply just recycling. Wider social, environmental and economic issues also need to be addressed to demonstrate genuine corporate responsibility.

Sustainability reporting is considered in the ICAEW publication *Outside Insights: Beyond Accounting* which indicates that sustainability policy in an annual report should include information such as:

- who the report is for
- links to corporate/business strategy
- materiality of issues reported
- validity of indicators
- reliability of indicators
- objectivity of reporting
- transparency of information
- comparability of information
- balance of information
- understandability of the report
- audit/assurance of the report and corporate performance
- external stakeholder engagement
- integration with financial reporting
- addressing true sustainability

(The model answer states that only some of the examples from this list would need to be mentioned by candidates to score the marks relating to the type of disclosures needed for sustainability reporting.)

An integrated report should explain how the organisation creates value, using both quantitative and qualitative information.

Natural capital includes the impact of the company's activities on air, land, water, minerals and forests – recycling could be one element of addressing this area.

The benefit of sustainability disclosures for the company is that such disclosures communicate the company's attempts to demonstrate corporate responsibility by explaining what the proposed sustainability policy is.
Including environmental issues within integrated reporting makes environmental assurance more feasible as it provides a statement of policies which have been implemented – the effectiveness of implementation can then be confirmed as part of the assurance purpose.

The **November 2016 past paper** question was more specifically about the question of how KPIs can be used to monitor environmental issues and how assurance procedures could be used regarding the KPIs. A key point made by the examiners in the question wording is that there is a difference between "environmental impact" and "sustainability" – this was implied by the fact that the examiners wanted to see different KPIs for each of these concepts.

In the model answer, a KPI based on CO2 emissions was considered appropriate in relation to "environmental impact" whilst a "sustainability" KPI related to the proportion of recycled engine parts. The examiners therefore appear to view "sustainability" as relating primarily to resource usage and "environmental impact" as relating to emissions and other types of broader damage.

It is important to bear this distinction in mind as in everyday discussions it is common to conflate the 2 concepts of "sustainability" and "environmental impact" – however, when taking the SBM examination, you need to understand how the terms are treated by the SBM examiners. As mentioned elsewhere in this book, subtle **differences** or **distinctions** do matter in SBM.

In addition to the above 2 past paper examples, we also have 2 examples from the SBM mocks.

November 2014 Mock 1 Q1 provides an example of audit issues relating to environmental or social matters: 10 marks were available for explaining why an ethical purchasing policy might be needed and then structuring an assurance approach to the review of an ethical purchasing policy.

Points made include:

- **Discussion of the reasons why an ethical purchasing policy might be entered into**: recognising responsibilities to other stakeholders, promoting good standards and avoiding negative publicity – assurance over the client's actions will help the client demonstrate its credentials to other stakeholders

248

- The **contents of an ethical purchasing policy** will vary but typically such policies will set standards for the performance of suppliers on matters such as human rights including employee rights, health and safety and environmental protection and sustainability

- **Social responsibility within the supply chain might involve consideration of employee contracts, wages and working hours, health and safety, child labour and discrimination**

- ISO 14001 provides an **international standard on environmental performance** and environmental protection

- **The company should ask its suppliers to agree to ethical standards in its purchasing decisions** and should establish a system of carrying out regular audits of its suppliers

- **Before** the assurance engagement takes place, the client must **establish and set out what its policies and procedures are**

The answer then moved on to consider how the assurance engagement would be run by the assurance provider (accountancy firm): relevant steps would include:

- **Confirming the subject matter of the engagement with the company,** looking specifically at the information or issues to be assessed

- **Identifying the criteria which should be used to evaluate the subject matter** – if suitable criteria cannot be identified, then the practitioner should withdraw from the engagement

- **Identifying the controls which the client has in place** for evaluating its suppliers

- **Verifying that the client has carried out the audit checks on its suppliers,** in accordance with its ethical purchasing policy

- **Inspecting any evidence that policies have been followed** and comparing to the evidence provided by suppliers

- **Considering whether to obtain further additional evidence** from suppliers or other sources

- **Assessing the statement that the client intends to publish** regarding its ethical purchasing policy and **comparing this to the evidence obtained** from the assurance engagement

- **Limited assurance is the most likely type of assurance** that could be provided in this kind of engagement

In this second element, the points made are very similar to the points in the Study Manual (see notes above). Both the procedures indicated and the reference to the type of assurance ("limited") that could be offered are standard points mentioned in the Study Manual.

This again reflects our view that specialist Audit and Assurance topics are not intrinsically difficult – but if you do not know where to find them in the Study Manual or your provider's notes do not provide a good summary then it will be almost impossible to get any marks as **you need to stick closely to what the Study Manual says**.

Overall, in our view this answer was very detailed and it would definitely not have been possible to include all the text in the model answer in your own response: at the same time, the answer was worth 10 marks and so would have been worth investing some time into.

A second example of a question on environmental and social auditing is provided in **July 2015 Mock 1 Q2**. Here 8 marks were available for explaining the objectives of an assurance engagement on the supply chain and explaining why a social responsibility report should be subject to external assurance.

Use of an external assurance provider was considered useful as the company traded on the back of a specific claim that the ingredients used in its chocolate were produced in an environmentally and socially responsible manner. The company also committed itself to a good standard of working conditions and human rights. Using an external provider would give additional reassurance to shareholders and other readers of its social responsibility report. Some key points included:

- The assurance provider would need to review performance indicators but a difficulty is created by the fact that many are **non-financial** in nature – information may therefore be hard to gather

- Indicators may not be **standardised** so comparisons over time and between companies could be difficult

- Assurance could be also be useful in determining if suppliers were likely to **stay in business** and **complying** with **contractual conditions** – it could also be determined whether the company was paying a **fair price** for its supplies

- Assurance could also review whether suppliers were **complying with fundamental standards** e.g. not employing child labour

- Methods to obtain information could include use of a **questionnaire** but this would not provide **independent** verification of facts – an **independent auditor** might be needed

With respect to the second part of the question on the need for assurance over social responsibility reports, the following points were made:

- Organisations are sharing an **increasing** amount of CSR information and this is becoming part of **business strategy**

- However, this kind of information is **not part of the financial statements** and so will not be audited as part of a routine audit engagement even though stakeholders need to be confident that they can trust the information and claims made about CSR in reports

- Having an **independent, external party** to verify the data and information will enhance the credibility of the reports

- An external assurance engagement can increase the **confidence** of stakeholders that information is drawn from **reliable sources** and that the calculations are accurate and consistent in methodology over time

13.6 The Testing of Environmental and Social Audits and Assurance: Summary and Conclusions

In this chapter, we have reviewed in significant detail both the textbook sections regarding Environmental and Social Audits and Assurance and the ways in which this topic has been tested. We strongly recommend that you re-read the chapter several times to learn the necessary information, particularly as there are in fact several sub-topics to this area[75], but as a summary of the key points, we would note the following:

- Ensure you are familiar with **different potential reporting frameworks** (GRI, Companies Act, DEFRA, Connected Reporting Framework)

- Ensure you can list some **advantages** and **disadvantages of sustainability reporting**

- Revise the **forms of report and levels of assurance** possible in environmental and social audits and assurance

- Ensure that you understand the concept of **Integrated Reporting** (a new addition to the 2015 Corporate Reporting Study Manual): in particular, **ensure that you can list out and apply the different forms of "capitals"**

- **Purchase our *SBM Exam Room Notes*** and ensure that you are familiar with Environmental and Social Audit and Assurance points – ideally you should use the *Exam Room Notes* in at least one full SBM mock exam attempt

In the next chapter, we will apply the process used in this chapter to the next Specialist A&A area of "Internal Audit", again starting by providing some revision notes from the Study Manual. Unfortunately, this area has not been tested to date in any SBM resources so we will not be able to give an examples of how the examiners approach this topic.

---

[75] As noted on page 163, our *Advanced Level Audit & Assurance Q&A 2018* is available if you require a more interactive, self-test method of learning Environmental and Social Audits and Assurance concepts.

Chapter 14   Internal Audit: Revision Notes and Examination Analysis

---

Learning Points

After reading this chapter, you must be able to:

1. understand which areas are contained within the Internal Audit topic
2. understand the different types of Internal Audit engagement
3. understand the 3 Es applied in Value for Money (VFM) Internal Audits
4. appreciate that Internal Audit topics have not yet been tested in SBM examination papers

---

14.1   Internal Audit: Revision Notes

Internal Audit was tested fairly regularly under the old Business Change syllabus and we had expected this to continue into SBM: testing Internal Audit allows the examiner to test whether you have understood the difference between statutory audit (which forms the basis of most audit questions/papers in your ACA studies) as compared to Internal Audit. Also, internal auditors can have an advisory role, promoting improvements in processes and efficiencies, giving their work more of a "business change", and hence SBM, aspect. However, to date, internal audit has not been tested in any SBM real papers or mock examinations. Perhaps your exam will be the time for it to return?

Internal Audit is defined in the Corporate Reporting Study Manual as "an appraisal or monitoring activity established by management and directors for the review of the accounting and internal control systems as a service to the entity".

14.2   Objectives of Internal Audit

The objectives of internal audit include:

- Review of accounting and internal control systems

- Examination of financial and operating information

- Review of the Economy, Efficiency and Effectiveness of operations

- Review of the safeguarding of assets

- Review of the implementation of corporate objectives

- Identification of significant business and financial risks

- Special investigations such as fraud investigations

14.3   Differences to Statutory Audit

The following table provides some useful reminders of the key differences on which you may be tested:

	Internal audit	**External audit**
Purpose	Add value to operations	Express an opinion on the financial statements
Reporting to	Board of Directors or Audit Committee	Shareholders
Relating to	Operations of the organisation	Financial statements
Relationship with the company	Often employees of the entity – can be outsourced	Independent of the company and its management

Therefore, internal audit has a much wider scope than statutory audit as internal auditor considers all the operations and objectives of the entity and is not limited just to the financial statements.

14.4   Does an Entity Need an Internal Audit Function?

Per the Study Manual, a number of factors should be considered:

- scale, diversity and complexity of the company's activities

- number of employees

- cost-benefit considerations

- changes in organisational structure

- changes in key risks

- problems with internal control systems

- an increased number of unexplained or unacceptable events

These factors could be relevant if you have a particularly small or large client in your SBM scenario and the company does not yet have an internal audit function: it may perhaps be too early for the smaller client to implement internal auditing formally.

14.5 How Does the Internal Audit Function Assist the Board?

The internal audit department can act as auditors for Board reports which are not audited by the external auditors. Internal auditors may also be experts in fields such as auditing and accounting standards and can assist in implementing new standards.

Internal auditors can also liaise with external auditors to reduce the time and therefore cost of the external audit. Internal auditors can also check that external auditors are performing their job properly and reporting all relevant facts back to the Board.

Internal auditors also have a two-fold role in relation to risk management:

- monitoring the overall risk management policy to ensure that it operates effectively

- monitoring the strategies implemented to ensure that they continue to operate effectively

14.6 Types of Internal Audit Assignments

In our view, this element is **highly examinable** – it would be an easy way for the examiner to test your understanding of how a struggling company could be assisted by effective internal audit services.

Value for Money (VFM) Audits

A VFM audit tests for the 3 Es: **economy**, **efficiency** and **effectiveness**, where these concepts are defined as follows:

Economy – obtaining the appropriate quantity and quality of resources at minimum cost

Efficiency – maximising the output from a given set of inputs or minimising the inputs used to produce a given output

Effectiveness – how well an activity achieves its policy objectives or other intended effects

We strongly recommend that you learn the difference between the 3 Es above. Remember to relate them to the scenario by quoting back information in the extracts.

Information Technology Audits

An IT Audit tests the computer systems of a business. Effective IT systems are vital to the functioning of most modern businesses. The internal auditors would look at issues such as:

- the operating system

- e-business

- the database management system

- system development processes

- problem management

- change management

- asset management

- desktop audits

- capacity management

- access controls

Financial Audits

A financial audit involves reviewing all the available evidence (usually the company's records) to substantiate information in management and financial reporting. As such, this role is quite similar to that of external or statutory audit and therefore the Study Manual indicates that it is a minor part of the function of internal audit and one which does not add huge value to the business.

Operational (or Management and Efficiency) Audits

This type of audit involves examination of the operational processes of the organisation. The primary objective is to monitor management performance to ensure that company policy is adhered to.

The internal auditor will ensure that the policies in place are adequate for the purpose and will then also ensure that the policy works effectively in practice.

Examples of operational audits given in the Study Manual include:

Procurement – checks to ensure that the process of purchasing for the business achieves its key objectives and that it operates according to company guidelines.

Marketing – checks to ensure that the process of assessing and enhancing demand for the company's products is managed effectively. This will require that information is freely available to manage demand and to ensure that risks are being managed correctly.

Treasury – checks to ensure that the risks involved (such as interest rate and foreign exchange risk) are managed effectively and in accordance with company procedures. As with marketing, this will require that information is freely available to the treasury department so that they can ensure funds are available when required.

Human resources – check to ensure that processes are in place to ensure that people are available to work for the business and that there is appropriate planning and control of the business. Once again, this will involve ensuring that company polices are maintained and that information is freely available on key risk factors.

14.7 The Standard Internal Audit Process

The standard steps in an Internal Audit assignment are:

- setting the process objective

- determining the audit terms of reference

- reviewing current processes and controls

- analysing risks

- testing and results

- reporting

- management actions and monitoring

14.8 The Standard Internal Audit Report

There are no formal requirements for internal audit reports (unlike with statutory audit): the document can be adapted to suit the relevant purposes. A suggested outline would include:

- Executive Summary – objectives, outcomes, key action points and further work to complete

- audit tests carried out and their findings

- list of action points

- future time-scale and costs

- summary of existing culture of control

- overall opinion on the managers' willingness to address risks and improve

- implications of outstanding risks

- results of control evaluations

- causes of basic problems detected

14.9   The Qualities of Good Internal Audit Recommendations

We have split this section out in our notes since one of the key skills required in SBM is to be able to make appropriate recommendations to the client. Perhaps, therefore, you might be asked to indicate what kinds of recommendations are made by internal auditors or perhaps to formulate your own recommendations, having been given the results of internal audit work.

Internal audit recommendations should consider:

- the available options, emphasising the internal auditor's preferred solution

- the removal of obstacles to control such as poor communication or lack of management willingness to enforce controls

- resource issues: how much will recommendations cost and what are the costs of poor control?

- the terms of reference of the internal audit report, the work performed and the results

14.10   Internal Audit: How Has This Topic Been Examined In SBM?

As already noted, this topic has not yet been examined in SBM. However, as the topic was tested several times in the old Technical Integration paper in Business Change we have been able to build some of the relevant points into our *SBM Exam Room Notes* book.

14.11   The Testing of Internal Audit: Summary and Conclusions

In this chapter, we have reviewed both the textbook sections regarding Internal Audit. We strongly recommend that you re-read the chapter several times to learn the necessary information but as a short summary of the key points we would note the following[76]:

- We are **currently waiting for the first test of this within SBM** but it was **popular** under the predecessor paper Business Change

- Ensure you are familiar with the **definition and objectives of Internal Audit**

---

[76] As noted on page 163, our *Advanced Level Audit & Assurance Q&A 2018* is available if you require a more interactive, self-test method of learning Internal Audit concepts.

257

- Ensure that you can clearly explain the **difference between Internal Audit and statutory audit**

- Ensure that you can analyse a scenario to determine whether a client **could potentially benefit from an Internal Audit function**

- Ensure that you can list out the **various different types of Internal Audit assignment** (Value for Money, IT Audits, Financial Audits, Operational/Management/Efficiency Audits)

- Ensure that you are familiar with the **3Es** – ensure that you can provide a definition of each E and then also apply it to the scenario given

- Learn the format of a **standard Internal Audit report** and ensure that you understand what good Internal Audit recommendations would look like

- **Purchase our *SBM Exam Room Notes*** and ensure that you are familiar with Internal Audit points – ideally you should use the *Exam Room Notes* in at least one full SBM mock exam attempt

14.12   Enough Assurance – Time for Some PBA

We have now completed our review of Specialist Audit & Assurance topics. Hopefully the review and examination analysis contained in the last 5 chapters will put you in a better position to attack the valuable 5-10 narrative marks on Specialist A&A issues which could easily make the difference between passing and failing your SBM examination.

In the next chapter we move on to consider typical topics in the area of practical business advisory, looking at SBM examinations to determine some key points that the examiners wish you to make.

Chapter 15   Practical Business Advisory: Revision of Key Topics

---

Learning Points

After reading this chapter, you must be able to:

1. understand some typical practical business advisory topic areas
2. understand common technical concepts and calculations within typical PBA topic areas
3. understand how a Case Study perspective can be useful to generating appropriate points
4. understand how to achieve a good range of MS^2 points in PBA questions

---

15.1   Practical Business Advisory – What Do You Mean?

Practical business advisory or "PBA" is our own term for the aspects of SBM which are **not** financial reporting, **not** Specialist A&A and **not** ethics. The official ICAEW terminology for what we term PBA is "Strategy" but we have adopted the term PBA as a reminder that many points that you will need to make to advise the client are not necessarily at a high or Board level but will often involve day to day operational issues – hence the term "practical". Secondly, in this aspect of SBM there will often be **numerical or technical points** to consider and, to us, "Strategy" sounds more like a purely narrative topic.

Within PBA, based on the SBM past papers and our knowledge of the predecessor Business Change paper, we would expect to see some of the following topic areas:

1.   Reviewing Financial Information and Commenting on Performance

2.   Investment Appraisal Techniques

3.   Company Valuation Methodologies

4.   Bond Valuation Methodologies

5.   Cash Flows versus Accounting Profits

6.   Foreign Currency Issues and Derivatives

7.   Operational Decisions to Deal with Problems

8.   Financing Business Change: Loans versus Equity

9.   Financial Reconstruction and Liquidation

10. Marketing Strategies

11. Analysing Risks (SOF Framework)

12. Change Management

13. Remuneration Strategies

For further review of relevant concepts and topics, please see chapter 16 which includes selected questions from our *Business Strategy and Technology Q&A 2018* and our *Financial Management Q&A 2018*, providing a self-test method of reviewing the materials. For more detailed revision, please see the full-length book versions of these Q&As.

We have included more detailed notes on this PBA area (as well as other SBM topics) in our *SBM Exam Room Notes* book. See Appendix 4 for a sample. **In this chapter, we have included the points which we think are most important but clearly we cannot cover as much material as in our dedicated *SBM Exam Room Notes* book.**

This chapter also provides some advice on answering style for PBA Tasks.

15.2   Overview of PBA Topics in Recent Examinations

To help you appreciate a little more what we mean by PBA, here is a list of some of the PBA topics tested in the SBM real exams, mock exams and Sample Paper:

Topic 1   Reviewing Financial Information and Commenting on Performance

Some Tips on Answering Style and What To Look For

The first Task in Q1 will generally involve analysis of management accounting information (usually looking at least at the Income Statement (and probably also at the Statement of Financial Position) for recent years, possibly with future projections). Look out for the specific verbs mentioned (such as "**analyse and explain**" in July 2014: **you must do both**) to guide your answer.

Based on our review of SBM papers, here are some other tips for areas you may consider writing about (see also our Q1 MAP):

- Use tables of figures, particularly if comparing different years or different business streams, and present such tables at the **start of your answer before the narrative**: the examiners really seem to like this (see chapter 8) and it also automatically gives you an overview of the position, as well as a range of points to look out for

- Look out for **exceptionals** – are there any unusual events in only one of the years considered or only one of the business streams considered? If you do not have time to make the adjustments numerically then at least still comment on the issue to get some partial credit

- **Do not forget the obvious** – mention that revenue declined by X% and mention that profit increased by Y% – just because this is one of your last few examinations, do not assume that every point has to be rocket science

- Suggest **causes** – look for reasons for the changes: you do not have to be certain here as anything sensible, based on the scenario data, should score some credit

- Compare **volume versus price changes** (if the data allows) – still on the theme of causes, try to assess whether it is a change in price or the change in sales volumes which is driving the overall change (note that this may not always be possible if you do not have price information but you could look at margins)

- If **price has changed**, look at the "**elasticity**" or responsiveness of demand to the changes – was the price change a good decision?

- Consider the **product mix** and any changes

- **Look for any missing figures/provisions etc – but do not go too crazy as there will always be plenty of factors not considered!** Try to stick to **MS²** points – if there has been a legal dispute in the year but there is no provision then this is relevant but mentioning that the gross profit margin has moved from 15.4% to 15.3% is probably not important. If CAPEX has increased funded by loans then a lack of change in finance charges is significant but only if the scenario puts some emphasis on CAPEX spend, and so on

- Comment on **margins** but ensure that you add narrative – do not just say that the margin has gone up or down, give some reasons **why**

- Look for **patterns** – are all costs up? Was there only one business stream which suffered a loss? Recognising these patterns will help you to understand the big picture

- **Exceptions** – is there only one revenue stream that is growing? Is operating profit down, even though gross profit is up?

- **MS² indicators (scenario-specific indicators)** – make sure you include plenty of points on these, moving beyond the typical accountant's figures such as gross profit margin and operating profit margin to consider the unique forms of data that are specific to the company in the scenario[77] (for example, revenue per passenger, profit per staff member etc)

- Try to identify the **major drivers of the changes** and also specifically comment that these are the main drivers

- Look for **interdependencies** between streams

- Comment on **particularly high and low margins**

- **Compare changes in monetary figures with absolute underlying numbers** e.g. revenue changes versus changes in passenger numbers

---

[77] In the July 2014 paper, company-specific "operating data" was provided below the P&L: weaker candidates concentrated too much on the P&L as this was more familiar territory. Familiar/typical information is of course at the other end of the spectrum to scenario-specific points so you will not be getting as much credit for generic points.

- Consider **fixed costs**, **operating gearing** and **marginal costs**

- Analyse **different cost categories** (but only if there are material changes – see page 111 regarding the July 2014 examination)

- Consider **cash flows versus financial reporting treatment** (providing the perspective of the "Accountant in Business")

Topic 2   Investment Appraisal Techniques

Investment appraisal was a very popular question in Business Change Q3, a question style which the examiner has said will be closely related to SBM Q2 (see chapter 18). Setting students an NPV calculation (or more than one!) is a very easy way for the examiner to quickly set a large number of numerical marks and should also give you plenty of narrative points to make. On the more cynical side, it is also an easy way for the examiner to trick you into a **time trap** by spending too long on this first part of the answer as you attempt to get the numbers spot on (very hard to do under time pressure). **Always remember the 33:66 Rule and ensure that you have enough narrative points based on your NPV.**

In this section we review some key tips on NPV and other investment appraisal techniques.

Use round thousands in your calculations

The model answers show the answer to the nearest £1 but this is because the model answers are calculated in Excel and with plenty of time available. In your answer, round thousands should be fine and will save a lot of time.

Foreign currency effect – calculate this at the end of the NPV

In SBM it is highly likely that you will have to perform calculations involving foreign operations. Wherever possible, **try to leave all figures in the foreign currency until as late as possible in the calculation** so that you can then translate the figures for a particular year in one calculation rather than having perhaps 5-6 more calculations per year by translating revenue, variable costs, fixed costs, disposal costs/proceeds etc.

We find that many students get the exchange rate the wrong way around – this is probably caused by rushing and the "exam room effect"[78]. Generally, you should be told the **number of units of foreign currency per £1 sterling** so you should normally be looking to **divide** the foreign currency figure by the number given (not multiply) … but always check the question wording carefully in case the examiner has decided to try to catch you out.

---

[78] According to the examiners, this happened to a large number of students in both questions in the July 2014 real examination paper. See chapter 8.

Sense check on changes in the exchange rate

Hopefully you should know that if sterling is falling in value or depreciating then this is good for the amount of sterling earned from foreign operations – each unit of foreign currency will be rising in value and will purchase more units of sterling. Put another way, it is good to be a holder of a currency experiencing a rise in value and that is what is happening through our foreign currency operations: we are generating precisely that currency (foreign currency) which is increasing in value and this helps to compensate for the fact that our "home" currency is losing its value in world markets.

If, as is normal, the exchange rate is given as the number of units per £1 sterling (see above) then just be a bit careful – a **rise** in value of the foreign currency (and a decline in sterling) is shown as a **fall** in the quoted number for foreign currency units per £1 sterling. Therefore there is an opposite relationship and it is easy to get confused under examination pressure.

Here are 2 examples, imagining that 1 million units of Ruritanian Rurals (RR$) have been earned:

Appreciation of the RR$

		RR$ per £1	
	100	50	20
£ earned	10,000	20,000	50,000

Here we can see that the quoted number of Rurals per £1 is **falling** as we move to the right and this generates **more** sterling because the value of the Rural is **increasing** (as it takes fewer RR$ to purchase each £1).

Depreciation of the RR$

		RR$ per £1	
	100	200	1,000
£ earned	10,000	5,000	1,000

Here we can see that the quoted number of Rurals per £1 is **rising** as we move to the right and this generates **less** sterling because the value of the Rural is **decreasing** (as it takes more RR$ to purchase each £1).

Scepticism of the model: some possible points

Remember that SBM is designed to be a skills "bridge" to the Case Study: one of the most important Case Study skills to develop is **professional scepticism**. Therefore there is nothing wrong in politely querying the methodology: just as in Case Study, the question will not normally remind you to exercise this skill – it is a type of judgement that you should just know that you should be using as an almost-qualified Chartered Accountant.

As an example, for an NPV then some points to query could be:

Length of model time horizon – often this will be 3-4 years which may not be enough for a major capital purchase such as a factory

Query how revenue and cost figures have been arrived at – this is a particularly useful point if the product or market is new as we will not have any historic figures to use

Query exchange rates assumptions – like any assumptions, these could change: **to make the point more interesting, explain what appreciation and depreciation would mean for the project, rather than just generically saying that exchange rates "can change"**. You can also suggest that exchange rates will vary depending on future interest rates and inflation (and expectations thereof) based on the principle of Purchasing Power Parity: has the model incorporated these aspects? Even if it has, there will always have to be estimated figures used in the model and these can be queried.

What happens after the end of the time horizon? – does the project continue on the same basis or will there be renegotiation? If the latter, suggest some possible impacts.

Query the discount rate applied – the discount rate is a really key variable in an NPV calculation and should always be considered. If the existing WACC has been used, this may not be accurate if the level of gearing changes: we do not know what the new WACC will be (the higher gearing could cause the WACC to fall due to tax-deductible interest payments forming a larger part of the return on capital but the greater risk from gearing could increase the cost of capital). Also the level of business risk may be different in the new project so again the WACC could change.

Narrative analysis on NPV/investment appraisal calculation results

It is likely that you will have more than 1 NPV/scenario to assess. Therefore some standard and important narrative points could be:

- **State the highest NPV, the next highest and so on**: this may appear obvious from the numbers but there are still narrative marks for identifying these differences and any patterns

- **Examine the project with the highest NPV more carefully**: is there a downside such as high fixed costs or dependency on a particular event happening (e.g. are disposal proceeds, to be received in perhaps 5 years, one of the main reasons for the high figure? These could change)? Are any of the other options more flexible, in both positive and negative growth scenarios? **In general, the project with the highest numerical benefit will always have some qualitative drawbacks that you are supposed to spot**.

- Consider if there is a **trend that is not reflected in the figures**: the calculations will have to cease in a particular year but are the revenues for one project continuing to rise quickly, an impact not included in the model? Or is there something to say about the exchange rate trend?

- **Consider other operational and strategic impacts of the project**: note that the question wording may not remind you to do so but it is **a good idea to have a couple of headed sections looking at these aspects**.

  These points must obviously demonstrate **MS²** and will depend on the scenario but consider issues such as:

- Impact on suppliers and customers

- Scale economies

- Collaboration and technological development

- Stability of supply chains

- Impact on Porter's 5 Forces

- Problems in international production: distance, regulations, language, culture

- Exchange rate risk

Other investment appraisal techniques

NPV is likely to be the most commonly tested investment appraisal method (even in an earnings-based valuation model, discounting principles are tested: see below) but we strongly recommend that you also revise the standard advantages and disadvantages of other investment appraisal techniques from your Financial Management Study Manual. Or see our *SBM Exam Room Notes*.

Topic 3   Company Valuation Methodologies

Valuation of an acquisition or disposal used to be a common topic in Business Change and we would expect it to remain so in SBM. This is because it relates to issues of fundamental business change and also requires you to use some **judgement** in justifying your valuation (which will be a subjective issue rather than "a" correct answer): hence the examiner can easily test your advisory and recommendations skills.

This topic also allows the examiner to apply the "Accountant in Business" concept by distinguishing between book or accounting values (which are unlikely to be an accurate representation of current business value) and fair values or cash (which are more important on a day to day or practical level): hence the examiner can ask you to be **sceptical** regarding the ability of the financial statements to indicate business value.

Overall, then, the topic of valuations helps the examiner test several SBM-specific skills and perspectives and we would expect this topic to be examined regularly. In this section we provide some narrative notes on typical things to say regarding a valuation.

Company Valuations: Some Typical Things to Say/Consider

Based on our review of SBM model answers, the examiners seem to like the comment that **the valuation provided by any valuation technique is no more than the starting point for negotiations on a company purchase**.

The final sales price is likely to be determined by negotiations which will be constrained by:

1. The maximum amount a purchaser is willing to pay, which may include alternative uses of the assets/trade, and
2. The minimum amount that shareholders will accept for a sale

In addition to the results of the valuation model, further consideration should always be given to factors such as:

*   The cost of acquiring a similar company

*   The cost of purchasing assets and setting up a similar company

*   The value of brand name and other specific intangible assets

*   Future earnings potential

*   The value of key personnel

*   Nature of the consideration

*   The relative bargaining power of the 2 parties

After you have calculated the range of different values, **do not forget to state which is the highest, which is the lowest and the reasons for the differences**. There will be easy narrative marks for these points and remember that even if your valuations are wrong then **you will get follow through narrative marks**: if you just state the numbers without any discussion then you are basically relying on the calculations to be correct to get any marks at all.

Note that in July 2014 Mock 2 (which appears to be based on a previous Business Change question rather than being drafted specifically for SBM: see discussion in Appendix 5) the examiners apparently expressed a preference for cash flow based models by stating that an earnings-based model was being used only because "the information provided does not give enough detail to determine cash flows as a basis for valuation".

We will review the specifics of the different calculation methods below but some general narrative points regarding methodologies include:

*   Does the method involve a **perpetuity** calculation? This is a simplification which may not reflect the reality particularly if the market changes in future.

*   Does the method involve an **assumed growth rate**? This may change or not transpire, affecting the calculation.

*   Query the **discount** rate – what is the basis of this crucial variable?

*   Query any **synergistic** savings – how have these been calculated? Are they realistic?

Note that many of the above points may be relevant to discussion of Due Diligence if there are also some Specialist A&A marks floating around. See chapters 11 to 14 to revise the key Specialist A&A areas for SBM.

Valuation methodologies: Dealing with Positive and Negative Growth

If you are asked to provide a present value of perpetuity flows into the future and no growth is expected then the formula is very straightforward – take the cash flows and just divide by the discount rate. In other words, the PV of £10m into perpetuity with no growth, with the first flow starting in one year from today and a discount rate of 10%, is simply **£10m/0.1** = £100m.

If you are asked to show the impact of growth (positive or negative) "for the foreseeable future" then you can use the following formula:

$$\frac{earnings\ or\ cash\ flow\ x\ (1+g)}{(discount\ rate - g)}$$

Note that this formula finds the present value today of **flows which start in one year's time** – therefore you may have to **further discount the value** found from the above formula.

For example, it was quite common in the predecessor paper Business Change for the examiner to provide you with detailed figures for years 1, 2 and 3 (allowing a precise NPV to be calculated for those years) followed by "growth at x% for the foreseeable future, starting in year 4". Hence the year 4 and onwards cash flows are a type of perpetuity but with growth, and therefore the above formula should be used. However, note that the result of the above formula finds the PV of all future flows starting in year 4 in terms of the present value in **year 3**. Therefore you should always have the same discount factor for the final precise year estimated **and for the perpetuity following that year** because in the final year of precise figures you are evaluating both those figures and the subsequent perpetuity. Your pro forma should therefore look like the example below (assuming a 10% discount rate and a perpetuity from year 4 onwards):

	Year 1	Year 2	Year 3	Year 4+
	Precise estimate	Precise estimate	Precise estimate	***Perpetuity formula***
Discount factor at 10%	0.909	0.826	**0.751**	**0.751**
			Identical discount factors for final 2 columns	

If we are looking at positive growth, then there should be a positive sign on the top of the fraction and a negative sign on the bottom of the fraction – so with a growth rate of 5% and a discount rate of 10% we would have:

$$\frac{earnings\ or\ cash\ flow\ x\ (1+0.05)}{(0.10-0.05)}$$

If we are looking at negative growth, there should be a negative sign on the top of the fraction and a positive sign on the bottom of the faction (due to the double minus signs) – so with a negative growth rate of 5% and a discount rate of 10% we would have:

267

$$\frac{earnings \ or \ cash \ flow \ x \ (1 - \ 0.05)}{(0.10 + 0.05)}$$

Valuation Methodologies: Earnings

Having reviewed some important **numerical** aspects, we now review some useful **narrative** points on valuations. For more ideas, see our *SBM Exam Room Notes*.

The **earnings-based method** cannot generally be applied to a loss-making business as this would give a negative value – but perhaps there are **exceptional reasons** as to why losses are being made or there are **synergies on acquisition**: in this case, the method may still be useable.

The **measure of profit is likely to be imperfect** and could include non-cash items such as depreciation which are the result of accounting policy choices.

A multiple of EBITDA can be used as a rough estimate for a cash flow model without going to the trouble of analysing cash flows.

The examiners appear to believe that a cash flow-based model is the optimum (see below) and that an **earnings-based model should only be used if the information is not sufficient to perform a cash flow analysis**.

According to July 2014 Mock 2, **a net assets calculation should be performed as a benchmark against an earnings valuation**: this will show whether the earnings estimate seems wildly optimistic. Also the net assets valuation will give some assurance in case earnings performance is poor and an exit is needed (provided that the net assets have been updated to fair value to accurately reflect the realisable value).

In the same mock exam, an **NPV model was created based on earnings, rather than cash flows**. Therefore it appears that allowing for the time value of money is permitted even when the figures are accounting earnings rather than strictly cash flows. This method was used with respect to a company that did not have any current profits but which was projecting good levels of growth in future. The same approach was used in Q1 of the SBM Sample Paper.

Another simple method if you are given a discount rate, and are told that earnings will not grow, is to use the **perpetuity formula (with no growth)** by dividing the profit after tax/earnings by the discount rate e.g. £2m earnings at a discount rate of 10% are equivalent to a perpetuity of £2m/0.1 = £20m in PV terms. The same process can be used if there are synergies quoted as annual savings/income: simply divide these by the discount rate to find the PV of the synergies or cost savings. Then look out for any surplus assets that can also be added into the value of the acquisition: this should not be treated as a perpetuity as they are a one-off flow realised now so discounting should not be used.

Valuation Methodologies: Asset-Based

The net assets method is unlikely to be relevant if the company has a **low realisable value or assets are approximately equal to liabilities** – this would give an incorrect value if an acquisition would yield future cash flows.

Always look out for **anything which has not been included in the net assets valuation** – for example, is there a large item of PPE or a brand that has been omitted? Generally there will be something missing. For services companies, there will be a lot of positive value that is not recorded on the SFP for assets such as staff skills, experience and knowledge and other internally-generated competitive advantages of the business. **Try to make this point more interesting by applying an MS^2 approach and finding something relevant from the scenario**.

An asset-based method using **fair values** is always likely to be more accurate than a book value approach – the requirement to update to FV was always mentioned in the predecessor Business Change paper. After making this point, some further issues then follow:

- Establishing **fair values may be difficult, costly or time-consuming** – fair values may also fluctuate between the valuation date and the acquisition date

- Some types of **fair value are subjective** and there could be widespread disagreement

- Determining a fair value ideally requires an active market and a large number of similar items but in practice many assets (such as specific buildings) are **unique**

- Fair value may also be affected by the **needs of a potential purchaser** and this needs to be taken into account

Brand Valuation (and Valuation of Other Assets Excluded from Net Assets)

Since we know that a common examiner theme is to criticise the net assets approach on the basis that it excludes certain important assets it seems **quite possible that you will have to act practically and suggest a way of valuing these missing assets**: this would extend the question in a logical direction and prevent students simply saying that some assets are not valued correctly – **a client would surely then follow up by asking for help to allocate a value**.

This kind of exercise was in fact required in Q1 of the SBM Sample Paper, focusing on valuation of a brand, but we would expect a similar approach to occur with other assets such as PPE (the predecessor Business Change paper tested this extensively). You should also note that **IFRS 13 has only recently started to form part of the ACA syllabus so this area allows the examiner to check that your understanding is up to date**. Based on the brand valuation exercise in the SBM Sample Paper, some points to consider include:

- Discussion of the **3 Levels** of inputs in **IFRS 13** (Level 1, Level 2, Level 3)

- Correspondingly, discussion of the **market basis**, **income basis** and **cost basis** of the valuation

- The market basis looks at the **market price of similar transactions** – this is unlikely to be possible in the examination question as the asset will be relatively unique

- The income basis looks at the **post tax income generated by the asset, expressed as a perpetuity by dividing the result by the discount rate**

- The cost basis looks at the **costs of establishing a similar brand** – key variables here would be estimates of the annual costs of establishing the brand and the discount factor applied as this would affect the valuation significantly

Following these estimates, **the value to the company should be the highest and best use calculated**.

Valuation Methodologies: Dividend Growth Valuation

If you are given information on dividends, the dividend growth rate and the discount rate then a valuation can be achieved using the following formula:

$$D_0 (1 + g) / (\text{discount rate} - g)$$

Professional scepticism may be possible regarding all 3 variables (D_0, the discount rate and g) – remember that the dividend growth rate cannot exceed the growth in earnings forever or there will not be enough earnings to pay the dividends.

Valuation Methodologies: Free Cash Flows

Various SBM model answers suggest that this model is the best model as it most accurately reflects the business value generated and is not affected by accounting policy choice.

This method cannot generally be applied to a loss-making business as this would give a negative value – but perhaps there are exceptional reasons as to why losses are being made or there are synergies on acquisition: in this case, the method may be still be useable if profits are hypothetically obtained after making the relevant adjustments to the currently-recorded losses figures.

Arguably this is a more objective method because cash flows are not affected by accounting policy choices but like all prospective models there will be uncertainty (a lack of objectivity) regarding future performance.

Valuation Methodologies: EBITDA Multiple

Use of an EBITDA estimate, multiplied up by an appropriate multiple, is **similar in nature to a cash flow model**: the theory is that earnings before interest, taxation, depreciation and amortisation are a good proxy for operational cash flows since non-cash flows and non-operational cash flows are excluded. An EBITDA model can therefore be used if you do not have enough information to perform a full cash flow model or as a suggestion if the client does not want to spend the time to estimate all possible cash flows.

Some points to note based on our review of SBM papers:

- The specific multiple chosen can have a huge influence on the valuation: it is a really **key variable** so you should comment on this and show some **professional scepticism**

- The valuation will be **sensitive** as to what is put through the Income Statement – and the **multiple aspect will further increase this sensitivity** because for every £1 change there will be a multiplied effect

- Look for any **disputed figures** as these will have a significant impact

- Look for any **exceptional** items – should they be excluded and are they genuinely exceptional?

- An EBITDA approach is preferable to an earnings method because it removes depreciation and amortisation as these are **non-cash and subjective in nature**

- EBITDA ignores essential **capital expenditure** for asset replacements and this is a problem with the methodology

- An EBITDA multiple approach **ignores expectations of growth in future cash flows** – a method incorporating future cash flows should be more appropriate

- Remember to note that if a **listed company/industry multiple** is being used as a benchmark then this needs to be **discounted** (reduced) if the entity being valued is a **private company** as a result of reduced marketability of its shares

Using a Multiple to Estimate the Cost of Capital

To explain the principles, we will assume a multiple of 5 and (if needed) growth of 2%, purely for tutorial purposes.

Assuming no growth, then we are saying that the company is worth 5 times its EBITDA. So if the company has EBITDA of £1m then its value will be £1m x 5 = £5m.

To arrive at the same result using a perpetuity formula (i.e. based on the cost of capital rather than a multiple) we would have to divide the EBITDA by 0.20. This is the same thing as saying that the **cost of capital is 1/multiple because 1/5 = 0.20**.

If we assume growth, then things are more complicated because we cannot use the simple perpetuity formula. If we assume growth of 2% purely for tutorial purposes then we can use the following formula based on the dividend valuation model and replacing the future dividend D_1 with future earnings E_1 (which is today's earnings x 1.02 to represent growth to earnings in 1 year):

$$\text{cost of capital} = (E_1 / P_0) + g$$

We know that for every £1 of earnings then the valuation or price (P_0) must be 5 times that figure. Therefore applying the formula:

$$\text{cost of capital} = [(1 \times 1.02) / 5] + 0.02 = 22.4\%$$

Valuation techniques: APV method

This method is covered in Financial Management but, in our experience, is not well understood by students (perhaps because it is not often tested in the Financial Management examination itself). The process is as follows:

1. Calculate an **ungeared** cost of equity

2. Discount cash flows at this **ungeared cost of equity** and find the total PV – keep a note of this total for the final stage

3. Calculate the PV of the tax relief on interest **but using the discount rate of the loan (not the rate calculated in step 1)**

4. Add together the result of steps 2 and 3 to find the APV valuation

Cost of Capital and WACC

Ensure that you have revised all relevant Financial Management formulae, including the ungearing/regearing formula required to translate an industry/comparator company beta into a beta for our client company, by allowing for different levels of gearing: ensure that you are able to manipulate the following equation so that you can extract whichever variable is needed[79]:

$$k_{eg} = k_{eu} + (k_{eu} - k_d) \times V_d/V_e \times (1 - t)$$

We strongly recommend that you revise these aspects of Financial Management as **almost all SBM papers reviewed for this book have used at least one of the cost of capital formulae**.

We already noted above (see section entitled "Using Multiple to Estimate the Cost of Capital") that at the Advanced Level, the examiners may ask you to use a familiar equation in an unfamiliar way: for example, working backwards from a given multiple to find the cost of capital in the example noted above, rather than using a given cost of capital to work out a valuation and therefore a multiple.

---

[79] This formula was used in November 2014 Mock 1 so is definitely potentially examinable in SBM.

In relation to the WACC, please note that the July 2015 real examination required candidates to calculate the cost of equity, **given the value of the WACC and given the cost of debt** – at the Professional Level in Financial Management, you would typically be asked to calculate the WACC, given the cost of equity and given the cost of debt so this is another example where you need to be able to reverse the normal equation/process in SBM. Provided that you correctly enter the variables into the standard WACC formula, this should not be a technically difficult adjustment but of course please do ensure that you practice this before the examination so that a simple mistake is not made on the day. In other words, make sure you are able to work with figures such as (from the July 2015 real examination)

$$0.075 = (ke \times 0.33058) + 0.026777$$

Here the WACC of 7.5% is inserted on the lefthand side and we have completed as much as possible of the equity and debt components of the standard WACC formula (the debt element (furthest righthand term of 0.026777)) can be completed in full as all information was given). To extract ke and therefore answer the question you would need to use the following process

0.075 - 0.026777 = ke x 0.33058   subtracting 0.026777 from both sides

0.048223 / 0.33058 = ke = 14.6%   dividing both sides by 0.33058 to leave Ke alone

Please note that after finding the cost of equity, the July 2015 real examination required you to find an implied PE ratio using the relationship that the cost of capital is equal to 1/multiple (see section above entitled "Using Multiple to Estimate the Cost of Capital"). Based on this, if we know that the cost of capital is 14.6% then the related PE multiple/ratio must be 6.85 (as 14.6% or 0.146 = 1/6.85, where the 6.85 is found as 1/0.146 for the cost of capital as 14.6% (0.146 as a decimal)).

Valuation of a Potential Acquisition: Narrative Points on Post-Integration to Consider

- Which company is larger than the other and how will **control** be determined?

- Is the **market positioning** similar for both entities? Or is one entity at the high quality end and the other at the low quality end?

- Relatedly, what is the **customer perception and interpretation of the different brands**? Will the low quality producer benefit from association with the high quality producer or will the high quality producer be damaged by association with the low quality producer?

- Impact on **location** and **coverage**

- Impact on **product range** and **coverage**

- Impact on **synergies** and **whether these will be realised in practice**

Valuation Methodologies: Examination Technique

We know from our own taught course students that many students are pleased when a valuation is tested in SBM – they immediately see some familiar figures or the opportunity to perform an FCF model across several years and therefore have a **feeling of familiarity with the numerical content, providing reassurance**.

Whilst it is obviously good to be comfortable with the numerical approach, remember that the weighting of marks in SBM is heavily weighted towards narrative analysis (our 33:66 Rule) – therefore, **unless you can develop interesting narrative points, which demonstrate MS^2 and hence are specific to the scenario set, then you will not in fact be accumulating as many marks as you may think through your familiar number-crunching**. The examiner sets a valuation question to test skills of judgement and recommendation, not just to see how quickly you can use a calculator.

Therefore always take a step back and look for interesting, scenario-specific points to note before diving into the calculations. And once the calculations have been completed, try to make points that connect with the specific scenario set.

Similarly with our list of narrative points/criticisms regarding the valuation models: the core of your narrative answer should always be built on these elements **but the key to a good answer is to connect the generic point to a scenario-specific example, rather than just listing out standard points**.

Overall, then, we believe that valuations can be a **false friend** as there is too much potential just to bash out generic content and trick yourself into thinking you are writing a good answer just because you are writing a lot of familiar points.

Topic 4   Bond Valuation Methodologies

Use of bonds with premiums and discounts were a very popular topic in the predecessor Business Change paper. This is probably because, for financial reporting purposes, we apply the Effective Interest Rate method to determine the cost of a bond but the cash flows on bonds are simpler and are based on the nominal or coupon interest rate. **This therefore introduces a difference between accounting treatment and cash flows/business impact, hence allowing the topic to test the "Accountant in Business" perspective.**

Exhibit 4 of Landex plc (Q2) in the July 2014 paper asked candidates to compare 2 different types of bond, which would be issued to raise cash for the construction of a factory. One bond had no coupon but was redeemable at a 17% premium so the 17% premium represented a type of "rolled up" interest rate over the 4 years of the bond. The other bond was more "vanilla" in nature and involved a 5% interest rate and redemption at par.

This kind of question was one of the favourite mathematical areas of the examiner in the Business Change paper under the old Technical Integration syllabus. It was frequently commented under that syllabus that students did a poor job of bond appraisal so it appears that the topic has been retained for testing under the evolved SBM paper.

274

As well as revising the relevant equations and numerical technique, we strongly recommend that you consider our advice to adopt the perspective of the "Accountant in Business" (chapter 3) when appraising bonds: in other words, **look at the differences between the financial reporting treatment and cash flows**.

For example, both the zero coupon bond and vanilla bond will have a finance cost in the financial statements: in the case of the 17% premium, this will be spread on a compound basis over 4 years (so we take the 4th root of the change 117/100 to find the compound annual growth rate) to find the effective interest rate: see the worked example below.

However, there will be **radically different cash flow implications** – under the zero coupon bond there will be **no cash flows (and no associated cash flow risks relating to currency) until the final payment** ... but the final payment will then be a **large** amount including the premium: on the other hand, under the vanilla bond the cash flows are **required earlier but are more regular** and there is no nasty **large cash flow impact all at the end**.

This provides a perfect opportunity for the examiners to test the perspective of the "Accountant in Business" – financial reporting implications are contrasted with cash flow or "practical" considerations. Raising the cash flow issue also raises the practical business analysis issue of **timing.** (See chapter 4 for explanation of why the issue of timing is a key "lens" based on the Case Study.)

We would expect bonds and financing to remain a key area for examination, given the way that this topic can test the difference between the financial reporting treatment and the "practical" aspects of cash flows.

Please find below some worked examples on bond interest rate calculations.

Finding the effective interest rate on a zero coupon bond redeemable at a premium

Example: a £1m bond is redeemable at a premium of 15% in 4 years

We need to find a rate which fairly allocates the 15% (or £150,000) over each of the 4 years, but which also takes into account the effect of compound interest: for example, after year 1, the liability will have increased by the effect of a year of interest and so when the year 2 interest is calculated this will have to be a higher amount than in year 1.

The correct formula to use is to apply the nth root (where n is the number of years) to a fraction of 100 + interest rate/100, and then deduct 1 to find the interest rate.

So for the example bond above the calculation would be $[(115/100)^{0.25 \text{ or } 1/4}] - 1$ or **3.6%**

Ensure that you know how to use your calculator to find roots such as 0.25, 0.33 etc.

Finding the effective interest rate on a standard bond with a transaction fee

If we have **issued** a £20m bond at 5% (i.e. taken on a liability to raise cash) but there are transaction fees of 2% (see July 2014 real paper Q2) then unfortunately the effective interest rate is **not** simply 5%. This is because we will capitalise the bond at £20m x 0.98 to allow for the transaction fees, which are always a debit entry (see below). Therefore the interest rate will have to be **slightly higher than 5% because our initial liability is stated at £19.6m** and so will need to unwind upwards (after cash payments at 5%) so that the liability stands again at £20m just before settlement on the final day.

The correct approach is to set up an equation as follows:

Lefthand side – capital amount of the loan adjusted for transaction costs (e.g. x 0.98 or x 0.95 etc)

Righthand side – series of interest payments based on the coupon value, divided by 1 + i, raised to the relevant power to allow for compound interest

The final figure on the righthand side should be the repayment of the capital amount plus the final interest payment so a large figure. In our example it will be £20m + £1m.

Based on transaction fees of 2%, a £20m capital amount, repayment over 4 years and a 5% coupon rate the equation would be:

$$(£20m \times 0.98) = £1m/(1 + i) + £1m/(1 + i)^2 + £1m/(1 + i)^3 + £21m/(1 + i)^4$$

Note that it is easier to ignore the millions and just use 20, 1 and 21 – you will get the correct result.

The quickest way in the examination to solve for i is to guess a couple of figures slightly higher than the coupon (e.g. 5.5% and 6.0%) and then approximately estimate the right figure once you have used these 2 "educated guesses" in 2 different calculations to understand where the true answer is likely to be: this will be fine for examination purposes and there is no point wasting lots of time to get the correct figure to 3 decimal places – **the examiner will be able to see that you know what you are doing and he or she will not be interested in the precise result**. It is far more important to have correct narrative commentary, based on your answer, than to have a precise result.

Note that if the transaction is the other way around (our client has purchased an asset, being a loan issued by another entity) then the process and equation is largely the same but the lefthand side will be a **higher amount** than the loan figure as we are required to capitalise the transaction costs. Therefore with 2% transaction costs on a £20m loan we would start with 1.02 x £20m = £20.4m. Hence the effective interest rate will have to be lower than 5% to unwind the loan back down to £20m ready for the final settlement day.

Bond transaction fees – always a Debit entry

Since the cash paid on the intermediary or lawyer's fee must result in a Credit entry to cash then it follows that the Debit must be to the financial instrument.

In the case of an issued bond (liability), this will **reduce** the first liability entry in the bond working.

In the case of a purchased bond (asset), this will **increase** the first asset entry in the bond working.

Convertible Bonds

This form of bond is tested extensively in Financial Accounting and Reporting and we would expect to see the topic occur again in SBM: it provides a relatively quick and easy way for the examiner to create perhaps 3-4 marks for calculations[80], based on something that the examiner could argue you should know very well. **Ensure you have revised your understanding of how to split the bond into its liability and equity elements**, perhaps also commenting on the current and non-current liabilities but be careful of falling into a **time trap** regarding this issue – certainly use **round thousands** to make the calculation quicker and consider using **estimates** (indicating the principles involved to the examiner) if you are really running short of time.

In terms of practical business advisory points on convertible bonds[81], consider points such as:

- **Likely take up by the market** – how attractive is the issuer of the bonds? Such bonds will be attractive to investors if there is a likelihood of good growth in the share price between the time the original bond is used and the date when the bonds become convertible into shares

- In return for the opportunity to convert the bonds, investors are willing to accept a **lower interest yield** – comment on the positive impact of this (and always remembering the difference between cash flow and accounting profit)

- **An unusual instrument** – there are relatively few issues of such instruments in the real world (and fewer than one may expect from the emphasis given to the topic in Financial Accounting and Reporting!) so it may be hard to predict demand

- Consider taking **advice from an investment bank** on these complicated instruments

Do not forget to use this as an opportunity to stress the "**Accountant in Business**" concept – **explain the difference between the cash impact and the accounting charge** (and impact on diluted EPS)

If you conclude that, in light of the scenario information, the company will not be able to issue convertible bonds then use this as an opportunity to show the **recommendations** skill by suggesting an alternative – remember that you cannot really be wrong here so go ahead and suggest something else which might work.

---

[80] If this number of marks seems low compared to the reward in Financial Accounting and Reporting then you are quite right: in general, the reward for number work in SBM will be less than at the Professional Level, even for the same topic. This is because the examiners are more interested in testing your advisory ability through narrative advice.

[81] The topic of narrative remarks on convertible bonds was tested in Q2 of SBM November 2014 Mock Exam 2. It is also noteworthy that this topic is tested in the SBM Sample Paper.

Bond Narrative Points

In addition to finding the Effective Interest Rate using technical equations as above, do not forget to add some practical narrative, looking at some of the following factors:

- Discuss cash flows (**business impact**) versus Effective Interest Rate (**financial reporting** impact)

- **Timing** of cash flows: a zero coupon bond has no cash flows until the final redemption amount (but does incur an effective rate of interest for accounting purposes)

- Consider impact of changes in **exchange rates** (if foreign currencies are involved)

- **Interaction of timing of cash flows with exchange rates**: a zero coupon bond has no cash flows until redemption so there is no exchange rate impact until redemption but if there is a premium on redemption (likely to be necessary to generate demand for the bond as it pays no interest) then the exchange rate impact will be amplified, compared to a "vanilla" bond

- Consider **risk versus cost**: perhaps one bond is cheaper on its face but involves more risk

Overall, it is probably unlikely that one bond option will be clearly superior to the other (although this did happen in Q2 of the July 2014 real paper) so look for the **benefits and disadvantages of each type carefully** – if you cannot find any disadvantages of the bond with a lower interest rate, you may have missed something.

Bonds and Quarterly Interest Rates – Important Note from the SBM Workshop at the 2015 ICAEW Tutor Conference

As you will know from your previous ACA studies, looking at issues of time apportionment is a classic examiner "trick" to generate a couple more marks from any particular scenario: you should always be on the lookout for this.

In the November 2014 real paper, one "time apportionment trick" in Q1 involved provision of a 3 year lease over the company's assets to customers with an annual discount rate of 8.24% but **quarterly lease payments**. Therefore the correct approach to determine the present value of these quarterly flows involved **discounting 12 total payments** on a quarterly interest rate.

The examiners expressed disappointment that students did not allow for the quarterly nature of cash flows in the discounting calculation so **we would expect this principle to be examined again in the near future**. Hence we explain it here.

If an annual interest rate is quoted, then the correct equation to convert that rate into a quarterly or 6 month rate (allowing for the effect of compound interest) will be to raise the annual rate to a power of 1/number of periods in a year (e.g. to 1/4 or 0.25 if we are looking at quarterly payments) and then to deduct 1. Hence in the November 2014 paper the equation for an 8.24% annual interest rate and quarterly payments was:

$$[1.0824^{1/4 \text{ or } 0.25}] - 1 = 2\%$$

The **2% figure** should then have been used as the basis of an annuity formula based on **12 payments** (4 quarterly payments per year for 3 years) at **2%** (use your discount tables to find the relevant discount factor).

In the November 2014 paper there was also a final residual value (£4,000) on sale/disposal of the leased asset. **Note that this can be discounted using the normal 8.24% annual rate** because quarterly issues are not relevant to this one off sale at the end of the lease. Therefore use the standard approach of dividing the £4,000 by 1.0824^3. **Hence ensure that you just use a simpler and standard approach for the final disposal amount.**

Topic 5   Cash Flows versus Accounting Profits

It is often said that "Cash is King" – in the case of SBM, cash is not just "King" but also the rest of the Royal Family! **Contrasting cash impact and accounting impact is the perfect way for the examiner to test the "Accountant in Business" concept** as it allows the examiner to test your understanding of the difference between **practical business impact** (cash) and **financial reporting** (accountant's contribution to strategy). Therefore you need to ensure that you are well prepared to comment on cash and cashflow forecasts.

To some extent, this topic will naturally overlap with investment appraisal (reviewed above) since a common technique within investment appraisal is the Discounted Cash Flow (NPV) model. However, cash will be tested in other ways too.

Evaluating Cash Flow Forecasts[82]

- Check for any **material omitted figures**

- Check for any **material underestimates**

- Consider whether the **forecast is full enough** – does it extend beyond gross profit activities or operating activities to include all relevant cash flows (e.g. CAPEX and taxation)?

- Have any **finance costs** been omitted? (e.g. if there is not enough cash to make necessary purchases, credit will be needed but has this been allowed for in the model?) Consider an appropriate interest rate, taking into account the changes being considered (e.g. a higher gearing rate may increase the interest rate charged)

- Has **enough been allocated to key categories** such as the advertising spend, administrative costs, new staff costs and CAPEX, etc?

- Do **cost savings and synergies appear unrealistic**?

- Do **variable costs change in line with activity** (e.g. staff costs, material costs, taxation figures)?

---

[82] See, for example, July 2014 Mock 1 for an example question on cash flow forecasts.

- **Use your professional scepticism** – are there any reasons to think that the forecast could be biased (intentionally or otherwise)? Has the forecast been prepared by a manager who is keen to retain his or her job, for example, and has therefore been estimated too generously?

Topic 6   Foreign Currency Issues and Derivatives

Derivatives

The financial reporting aspects of derivatives, including hedge accounting, will clearly be covered by financial reporting marks (as discussed on page 23, we do not cover financial reporting rules in this text). When approaching derivatives from the perspective of PBA, we are more interested in the **practicalities, costs, cash flows and rationale** for using derivatives.

For example, in the July 2014 examination paper, the client faced the unusual situation of **receiving its foreign currency payments in advance**. Therefore the model answer rehearses some of the reasons for using derivatives but ultimately concluded that they may not be relevant to the scenario. **This is an example of MS² so always look out for ways that the examiner is stopping you from just listing out the standard narrative on derivatives**.

Derivatives such as swaps, foreign currency cash balances, forwards and options can reduce exchange rate risk by locking in agreed exchange rates and avoiding future fluctuations.

Hedging does not protect against long term economic risk (the risk that exchange rate movements might reduce the competitiveness of a company in a particular country).

If a company receives its foreign currency in advance of providing a service then there is less transaction risk than in a normal international sale where costs are incurred first followed by a risk that the value of the receipt in foreign currency could change.

Key concepts to remind yourself about here include the 3 types of currency risk (translation, economic and transaction) – see the Financial Management Study Manual or *our Financial Management Q&A 2018*, which contains hundreds of short-form questions to help you rapidly revise via an active, self-test format.

Foreign currency interdivisional balances: How to calculate the net payments due

Q1 in the July 2014 examination paper contained an interdivisional analysis in 3 different currencies. The Treasury department had decided that settlement would be net in sterling so all amounts needed to be translated into sterling first before solving for the relevant amounts.

The correct approach to solving this kind of question is therefore:

Step 1   Convert all amounts into the net settlement currency (probably sterling)

Step 2   Add up all receipts for each division by moving across (down) the receivables division row (column)

Step 3   Add up all payments for each division by moving across (down) the payables division row (column)

Step 4   Enter the total receipts and total payments into their respective columns

Step 5   Find the net receipt or payment for each division

As an example, in the July 2014 examination, the following table was presented:

			Payables	
		UK	France	US
	UK (Sterling)		£2.4m	
Receivables	France (Euro)			EUR1.8m
	US (Dollar)	$6.4m	$3.6m	

In this presentation, the UK's **payments** are found by adding up everything in the UK **column**, France's payments are found by adding up everything in the France column and so on. **Receipts** are found by **adding across the relevant row**.

Therefore (ignoring the translation into a single currency which you should actually do first), the UK will be paying $6.4m and receiving £2.4m. France will be paying £2.4m and $3.6m and receiving EUR 1.8m.

Once you have added up these receipts and payments and put them into columns (all translated into the net settlement currency: we have skipped the performance of this step for simplicity) then you should have a table that looks like the following:

		Payables					
		UK	France	US	Total receipts	Total payments	Net receipt/ (payment)
	UK (Sterling)		£2.4m		£2.4m	(£4.0m)	(£1.6m)
Receivables	France (Euro)			£1.5m	£1.5m	(£4.65m)	(£3.15m)
	US (Dollar)	£4.0m	£2.25m		£6.25m	(£1.5m)	£4.75m

This will show you which divisions are net payers and which divisions are net receivers so the final stage is to add in your write up that the UK division should pay £1.6m to the US division and the France division should pay £3.15m to the US division.

Topic 7   **Operational Decisions to Deal with Problems**

Obviously, it is hard to develop a list of points which will apply in all cases and you should always ensure that your points fulfil the **MS²** criterion but to give you a flavour of the types of point that the examiners have in mind, here are some ideas[83]:

Dealing with reputational damage following an incident (July 2014 real paper)

- Reduce the scale of operations/output to reflect the new lower demand, either permanently or on a temporary basis

- Sell off assets, including assets under construction

- Reduce pricing – this will only work if demand is price sensitive or "price elastic"

- Increase advertising and marketing expenditure

- Rebrand activities

- Set up a contingency plan to deal with similar outbreaks in future

- Improve quality overall and ensure that the market knows about the improvements

- Public relations exercise

Topic 8   **Financing Business Change: Loans versus Equity**

The choice between different funding methods was always a classic question in the predecessor paper Business Change and we expect this to continue.

Arguments in favour of a fixed rate loan

- The amount provided is guaranteed – less uncertainty than raising funds via sale of assets or issue of equity (since we are not sure if the market will accept the equity price set)

- Repayment schedule is fixed and known in advance – helpful for planning cash flows

- Loan could be set to match with the period in which new revenues/cash will be raised

Arguments against a fixed rate loan

- Impact on gearing and commitment to further interest payments (which will have to be made regardless of performance)

---

[83] See also our *SBM Exam Room Notes* for other scenario-based practical ideas.

- Terms may require provision of a fixed or floating charge to an external party, meaning that the external party will have a position of power over the company

- The company may make a mistake when seeking to match revenues and repayments

Comparing financing packages

It is likely that there will be different financing options in the scenario (e.g. at least 2 different loans, perhaps with one being a convertible bond or zero coupon, or a comparison of loans and equity). In this case, here is a suggested framework for aspects to consider:

- The **length of the time period involved**

- **Cash** interest payable (interest rate) versus **Effective Interest Rate** (EIR) and diluted EPS issues (for convertible bonds), again showing the difference between cash and accountancy impact

- **What is the catch with the lower cost option?** Normally there will be a drawback with the loan that has a lower interest rate which prevents it being the obvious and easy best choice – **look carefully for this catch**. If the loan is a zero coupon loan then there is likely to be a large cash outflow on redemption when the premium (effectively a form of "rolled up" or delayed interest) is paid in the final year

- **Covenants** – are there any differences here? Who has the power to affect the way the company is run? Is the lower interest rate counterbalanced by greater covenants?

- Loan payments **must be made** whereas equity payments (dividends) are **optional**

- For convertible bonds, **what would be the impact on corporate governance (shareholdings) if the debt is converted into equity? What interest savings are possible if conversion happens?** What is the cash benefit if the shares are converted (and therefore the loan principal does not have to be repaid)?

Financing an acquisition through debt – some considerations:

- Consider the **current debt to equity (gearing) ratio** of the company and how this may be altered

- Consider whether there are **fixed assets such as PPE to provide security** over the debt

- Consider **interest cover** and how this may be affected by the acquisition

- Consider the **potential earnings** of the target – adding these into the consolidated earnings will affect ratios such as interest cover and even gearing through increases in retained earnings over time

- Consider the **impact on finance costs** if funding is hard to obtain or gearing changes to such an extent that providers of debt require a higher interest rate

- Consider the **debt of the target** – how will this affect the consolidated SFP? How will any extra interest payments affect the consolidated IS and related ratios?

- **Cash may be used up in the acquisition**, affecting the ability to meet obligations when due

- The **growth prospects** of the target are particularly important if a risky strategy is being followed

See also our *SBM Exam Room Notes* for further ideas in relation to this area (and all other PBA areas) based on our review of SBM examinations, the SBM Question Bank and also our notes from the predecessor paper Business Change.

Topic 9   Financial Reconstruction and Liquidation

Q1 in the November 2014 real examination allocated 17 of the 60 marks towards a challenging liquidation scenario. Hence this topic is worth revising well.

In a liquidation, the main stakeholders to comment on are likely to be:

- A bank or provider of funds (which probably holds a charge over property)

- Shareholders

- Suppliers and other creditors

Try to find some different points to make under the above 3 specific headings for these groups.

The funds generated should be based on a pro forma, probably involving PPE, inventories and trade receivables. The liquidator's fee should then be deducted, together with any **fixed** charge due.

Once the remaining net amount after the liquidator's fee and fixed charge(s) ("Remaining funds") is known then we can estimate what we can potentially repay to any creditors with a **floating** charge – this is found by dividing the Remaining funds by the floating charges due to find how much per £1 of floating charge will actually be repaid (it will probably be less than £1 due to the difficulties the company is facing).

Overall the proforma should look like that below:

Funds generated
      PPE
      Inventories
      Trade receivables
      Total proceeds
Less liquidator's fee
Less paid to holder's of a fixed charge
Remaining funds   R

Floating charges
      Loans
      Overdraft

                                        F

Amount paid to holders of a floating charge (per £1 of floating charge) = R/F

For example, if the company has been lent amounts subject to floating charges of £10m but the R figure is only £5m then holders of floating charges will only receive back 50% (5/10) of their original investment.

After this, you should make some standard narrative points (see next section).

Note that if the result of the fraction R/F is less than 1, then this means that floating chargeholders will not receive back the full amount of their investment – it follows that unsecured creditors and shareholders (neither of whom have any charges at all) will not receive anything back at all.

The calculation steps to follow again are:

Step 1   Calculate proceeds received based on assets

Step 2   Deduct liquidator's fee and fixed charges

Step 3   Arrive at Remaining funds (R)

Step 4   Calculate Floating charges (F)

Step 5   Find amount repayable per £1 of Floating charge (R/F) (probably to a bank)

Step 6   Make standard narrative points (see below)

Based on the November 2014 real exam, you can ignore the "prescribed part" in your calculation but should comment on this: effectively, this preserves a small amount for the unsecured creditors.

Financial reconstruction and liquidation: Narrative points

Unsecured creditors and shareholders will receive nothing if the ratio of R/F is less than 1 – if the ratio is less than one, then we are saying that even floating **charge**holders are not receiving all of their money back so there is clearly nothing further available to those **without any charges** recorded at all (unsecured creditors and shareholders).

In some cases, it may be that you need to **compare a liquidation against an alternative option** (such as keeping the business going, but on revised terms – this would be a financial reconstruction). Again, try to consider the matter from the perspective of different **stakeholders** such as the funding bank, shareholders and creditors.

Points to consider could include:

Bank

The bank receives **certain cash back under a liquidation** but could be subject to **further risk if the money is left invested under a financial reconstruction**.

Consider the **interest rates** under the financial reconstruction – these will probably be higher than before in order to give the bank an incentive to continue to invest.

Consider **whether other stakeholders would invest** under the financial reconstruction or **will the bank remain the main funder** and therefore subject to the most risk?

Consider the **potential return** under the financial reconstruction – is this probable and/or attractive to the bank?

Shareholders

The shareholders **may get nothing back under a liquidation** but at least have some **voting power** to determine what happens.

You may wish to comment on what **shareholders are being asked to do** under the financial reconstruction option.

The amount invested in the original shares could be considered to be a sunk cost if liquidation is an active option: in other words, if the financial reconstruction does not happen then that money is lost anyway so the cost of the original investment is not a relevant or incremental cost – only the new capital injected under the financial reconstruction is a relevant cost.

Use the **forecast returns** for calculation purposes but **apply professional scepticism** as the projections may be optimistic in order to keep the company going (look at the position of the Board of Directors here).

Suppliers

Suppliers **may get nothing back under a liquidation** and, unlike shareholders, have no **voting power** to determine what happens.

Unsecured creditors would only get a small "**prescribed part**" back in a liquidation whereas if a financial reconstruction works then, over time, they may receive the **full** amount back.

As **suppliers are in a weak position**, it may be possible for the client company to negotiate hard and improve its position.

Resorting to court action would be a waste of time if there are other creditors which rank ahead of the suppliers (fixed and floating charge holders).

Financial reporting points

Although it remains outside the scope of this book to discuss financial reporting issues in detail[84], any discussion of liquidation and financial reconstruction is likely to be paired up with some financial reporting marks for points such as:

- IAS 1 and going concern presentation (valuation and also classification of liabilities and assets as current or non-current)

- ISA 570 *Going Concern* issues and the position of the auditor

- IAS 10 *Events after the reporting period*

- IAS 36 *Impairment of Assets*

- IAS 37 *Provisions, contingent liabilities and contingent assets*

Topic 10   Marketing Strategies

The SBM November 2014 Mock 2 Q2 contained a sub-Task on the implications of a change in strategy on a company's marketing strategy. The framework used was the 4 Ps model. This suggests that the Business Strategy models that we will help you to revise in the next chapter are worth revising, to provide a good framework (we know that the SBM examiners love headings: see chapter 8 and chapter 18) and also as a way to generate ideas. For further review of the models, see our *Business Strategy and Technology Q&A 2018*.

The 4Ps are:

- Price

- Product

- Place

---

[84] As discussed on page 23, the financial reporting syllabus is too large to discuss in *Smashing SBM™*. Please see our *Advanced Level Financial Reporting Q&A 2018* and our *Financial Accounting and Reporting Q&A 2018* for relevant revision questions. We also provide our *Advanced Level Financial Reporting Exam Room Notes 2018* as a set of alphabetically-organised, quick reference reminders to take into the examination with you.

- Promotion

Remember to add some **Recommendations** at the end.

Topic 11   Analysing Risks (SOF Framework)

Discussion of risks used to be a standard narrative question in the old Business Change paper and we would expect this to continue in SBM. Generally, the examiners will ask (or expect) you to analyse risks under the headings of **S**trategic, **O**perational and **F**inancial (SOF framework).

We are often asked about the difference between **strategic** and **operational** risks.

In our view, **strategic risks are the risks that the Board of Directors should consider**. Typical examples (see also below) could be decisions whether to enter or exit a market and whether a new project is consistent with the long term aims of the company or the company's image and values.

In our view, **operational risks are the risks that managers would need to consider**, on a day to day basis, when implementing the overall strategy set by the Board. Issues could involve efficiency and under/overutilisation of resources, shortages of staff, staff morale, availability of materials and so on.

Financial risks can relate to the way the project or business is funded so typical points to consider could include debt versus equity, cash flow issues, possible loss of control through covenants, interest rate risk/volatility and so on.

See our *SBM Exam Room Notes* for further examples of SOF risks to apply in different scenarios.

Topic 12   Change Management

Project Lifecycle Model

The SBM July 2014 Mock 1 set out the following useful 4 step model regarding the implementation of a new project: this may provide some useful headings and structure to your answer if you are asked to explain how to plan for implementation[85]:

1. **Define the project** – explain the reasons for the project but also the changes in working arrangements needed

2. **Design the project** – compare with other options and ensure impact has been fully and correctly estimated

3. **Deliver the project** – establish a clear and feasible timetable and resource specification

---

[85] The sub-Task wording in July 2014 Mock 1 Q1 was "I'd also like you to summarise for Lincoln's Board the main areas that the plan for purchasing and implementing the new machinery should cover."

4. **Develop the process** – build a post-set up review into the plan to allow for consideration of whether the change was as efficient as it could be and whether the expected value is being obtained

Please also thoroughly revise the Change Management models within our *SBM Exam Room Notes*.

Topic 13   Remuneration Strategies

Some factors to consider in setting remuneration packages (including share options) include:

Retention of talent – policy needs to ensure sufficient incentives for talented managers and staff to remain at the company

Rolling nature – a rolling set of incentives (with increases and new incentives issued each year) should help as a staff member may lose options or opportunities if he or she leaves the company

Goal congruence – the package should ensure that there is alignment of the interests of managers and shareholders so that what benefits the manager will also benefit the company

Value of share options – must be set in such a way that the exercise price is below the market price at the end of the vesting period: otherwise there is no benefit to the employee

Controllability – the employee/manager must have some control over the variable which is the basis of the incentive or the employee/manager will not have a reason to improve performance

Cash savings – some incentives such as share options or bonuses payable in several years' time will preserve cash in the short run whilst still improving performance and therefore generating cash

Impact on EPS – this will need to be considered – for example, share options need to be included in the calculation of diluted EPS

Chapter 16   Revision of Key Business Strategy and Financial Management Topics

---

Learning Points

After reading this chapter, you must be able to:

1. complete our short form Q&A questions to a high standard
2. recognise which key topics have been included in our selection of short form Q&A questions
3. understand your next port of call if you require further practice
4. recognise that FAR topics will also need to be revised very thoroughly

---

16.1   Revision of key Professional Level Concepts (ACA Simplified Q&A questions)

As you will hopefully already be aware, we provide short form, self-test revision question banks for all Professional Level ACA papers. In this chapter, we are pleased to reproduce some of the most relevant questions to SBM taken from our *Business Strategy and Technology Q&A 2018* and our *Financial Management Q&A 2018*. To revise these topics in more detail, please purchase the relevant Q&A book.

Unfortunately, for reasons of space and given the detailed syllabus for Financial Accounting & Reporting (the examiner can really draw on any FAR issues whereas certain Business Strategy and Financial Management issues can be ignored for SBM purposes), **we have not reproduced any questions from our *Financial Accounting & Reporting Q&A 2018*.**

We therefore strongly recommend that you separately purchase our *Financial Accounting & Reporting Q&A 2018* – it provides an ideal way to quickly refresh your financial reporting knowledge in a self-test format. You do not need to know FAR topics in as much depth as when you sat the Professional Level exam but you do need to have revised all areas in at least some detail or you risk being caught out by the financial reporting marks in SBM.

Sorry for the sales pitch but we do believe that some quick "refresher revision" of the Professional Level will put you in a great place for your attempt at the Advanced Level: certainly, you will be in a better position than other students who (understandably) prioritise their revision into the new Advanced Level topics only.

16.2   Selected questions from the ACA Simplified *Business Strategy and Technology Q&A 2018*

The following short form questions are reproduced from the 2018 edition of our Professional Level Q&A. We have concentrated on the following chapters and topic areas from the Business Strategy and Technology Study Manual:

You can see that we have focused on the areas of new strategic developments, the industry environment, strategies for change, acquisitions and ethics. These will hopefully be relevant areas for SBM and will give you some appropriate "lenses" through which to look at the stimulus material given in the examination.

We have included some revision of key Business Strategy models. Please note that in SBM you will not be given credit just for reproducing these models so you do not need to learn them perfectly or to the same standard as for the Business Strategy and Technology examination. We provide the models merely because they are useful ways of **generating ideas** – it is those ideas, and the related application to the scenario, which will get the marks in SBM rather than the quoting of the model or its specialised terms.

16.3   Selected Revision Questions from ACA Simplified *Business Strategy and Technology Q&A 2018*

What are the 3 levels at which a strategy can be operated within a company?

1. Corporate – head office or Board level, determining overall mission and major investment decisions

2. Business – at strategic business unit level, determining marketing and strategy versus competitors

3. Functional/operational – day to day operational level, looking at production, purchasing, finance, human resources and marketing

---

What are the 4 main characteristics of the positioning approach?

1. Focus on customer needs

2. Gaining of superior position versus rivals

3. Assessment of relations with stakeholders

4. Seeking to gain preferential access to resources

What is the overall belief of the positioning approach regarding successful strategy?

The business must adapt to its environment

Which leading writer is associated with the positioning approach?

Michael Porter

State 4 criticisms of the positioning approach.

1. Products become obsolete so future possibilities need to be anticipated ahead of time

2. Stakeholders decline in power

3. Technology will eventually eliminate cost advantages or technical superiority

4. Continually changing the company's skill base and products is disruptive and will lead the company into fields where it has little expertise

---

The alternative resource-based view looks at 3 aspects of strategic capability. State these. (Hint: FSL)

1. Fit

2. Stretch

3. Leverage

What does the resource-based view say companies should do in relation to customer needs?

The business should not merely satisfy needs – the company should "create" needs

---

Complete the following table:

Factor	Positioning-based view	Resource-based view
Profitability		
Approach		
Diversity		
Key focus		

Factor	Positioning-based view	Resource-based view
Profitability	5 Forces determines profits Company position determines profits	Sustainable competitive advantages from exploitation of unique resources
Approach	Outside-in – consider markets and then determine approach	Inside-out – determine key resources first, then determine how to exploit available markets
Diversity	Diversify to spread risk	Focus only on products where a company has a sustainable competitive advantage
Key focus	Positioning in the market	Focus on core competences, which are difficult to copy

Porter's Five Forces constitute the basis of the industry environment. This is surrounded by the macro environment. What are the 6 elements of the macro environment?

Basically, the PESTEL model

1. Political

2. Economic

3. Social

4. Technological

5. Environmental

6. Legal/regulatory

Political factors lead to political risks. Give some examples. [4]

1. Ownership risk – state may expropriate a company's assets

2. Operating risk – may be required to take on local partners; may be a guaranteed minimum shareholding

3. Transfer risk – may be restrictions on transfers of funds

4. Political risk – host government may change taxes or seek a stake in the business

Also consider:

- Stability of the government

- International relations

- Ideology of the government, especially in relation to economics

- Informal relations and connections with government officials

- Suspicion of foreign ownership

- Opposition politicians and appeals to nationalism

- Government can change its position and want a different deal later

- Restrictions on profit repatriation

- Cronyism and corruption

- Arbitrary changes in taxation

- Pressure group activity

State some ways in which political risk can be reduced. [9]

1. Detailed risk assessments

2. Seek protection via legal agreements

3. Partner with local businesses

4. Raise finance for projects from within the host country

5. Operate underneath an international body

6. Share a project with other firms to spread risks

7. Avoid total reliance on any one particular country

8. Lobby for political support from the home government

9. Gain support for political groups in the host country

Sketch Porter's Five Forces model.

**Potential
entrants**

| **Suppliers** | Bargaining power of suppliers | **Industry competitors** | Bargaining power of customers | **Customers** |

COMPETITIVE
RIVALRY
BETWEEN
EXISTING
FIRMS

Substitutes

According to Porter, which force is driven by the other 4 forces?

Competitive rivalry between existing firms depends on the other 4 forces

---

State 8 factors which would tend to increase buyer power in an industry.

1. Customer buys a large proportion of output of the industry

2. Product is not critical to customer's business – take it or leave it

3. Low switching costs

4. Products are standard items and easily copied

5. Low customer profitability

6. Ability to bypass or acquire a supplier

7. Skills of the customer's purchasing staff

8. High degrees of price transparency

State 6 factors which affect the bargaining power of suppliers.

1. 1 or 2 dominant suppliers

2. Threat of new entrants or substitutes to the supplier's industry

3. Suppliers do not rely on this industry for sales

4. Importance of product supplied to the customer's business

5. Whether supplier has a differentiated product

6. Switching costs

Sketch the Boston Consulting Group matrix.

		Market share	
		High	*Low*
% rate of market growth	*High*	Star	Problem child/ Question mark
	Low	Cash cow	Dog

297

The BCG concept can be extended by mapping it onto a product life cycle diagram. This gives 7 types of product (including the above 4 categories).

State the 7 types.

On or above the industry growth line

- Infants – introduction stage
- Stars – growth stage
- Cash cows – maturity stage
- War horses – decline stage

Below the industry growth line

- Question marks – growth stage
- Dogs – maturity stage
- Dodos – decline stage

According to Johnson, Scholes and Whittington, management must make choices on 3 types of strategy. State the 3 types.

1. Competitive strategy

2. Product/market strategy

3. Development strategy

Sketch Ansoff's matrix.

		Product	
		Existing	**New**
	Existing	Market penetration	Product development
Market			
	New	Market development	Diversification

State some advantages of vertical integration. [11]

1. Economies of combined operations such as reduced handling costs

2. Economies of internal control and co-ordination

3. Economies of avoiding the market

4. Tap into technology

5. Safeguarding proprietary knowledge

6. Assuring supply and demand

7. Reduction in bargaining power of suppliers and customers

8. Enhanced ability to differentiate

9. Stronger relationships

10. Share of profit at all stages of the value chain

11. Creation of barriers to entry

State some disadvantages of vertical integration. [9]

1. Increases fixed costs and therefore operational gearing

2. Reduced flexibility to change partners

3. Higher capital investment needs

4. Cut off from suppliers and customers e.g. now has to develop its own technology

5. Dulled incentives

6. Differing managerial requirements

7. Avoids transaction costs arising from external relationships

8. Overconcentration

9. May fail to benefit from economies of scale e.g. better to subcontract to larger firm

---

What is a financial conglomerate? What is a managerial conglomerate?

Provides a flow of funds to each segment of its operation, exercises control and is the ultimate risk taker

Provides managerial counsel and interaction on operating decisions

---

State some advantages of conglomerate diversification. [10]

1. Risk-spreading

2. High profit opportunities

3. Ability to grow quickly

4. Escape from reliance on present business

5. Better access to capital markets

6. Could be only way to grow

7. Use for surplus cash

8. Exploit under-utilised resources

9. Obtain cash or other financial advantages such as accumulated tax losses

10. Use a company's image and reputation

State some disadvantages of conglomerate diversification. [6]

1. Dilution of shareholders' earnings if EPS of acquired company quite low (high P/E ratio)

2. Failure in one of the businesses may drag down the rest

3. Lack of management experience

4. Poor return for shareholders – shown to occur in practice, based on datasets

5. No synergy

6. Earnings of conglomerates appear to be particularly badly affected by economic recession

---

State 4 circumstances when withdrawal from a market may be a completely rational strategy.

1. Products have reached the end of their life cycles

2. Weed out underperforming products

3. Sale of business for strategic reasons

4. Sale of assets to raise funds and release other resources

Explain some exit barriers which may make exit difficult or costly. [6]

1. Redundancy costs, termination penalties on leases and contracts, difficulty of selling assets

2. Managers may want to go on, having spent a lot of money already

3. Political barriers such as government attitudes

4. Marketing considerations

5. Psychology – failure to admit failure

6. Assumption that carrying on is a low risk strategy

Note – there are often marks for considering withdrawal – do not just assume that the business must always battle on

---

State some reasons for divestment and demerger. [5]

1. Rationalise a business as a result of strategic appraisal e.g. portfolio appraisal

2. Sell off subsidiaries at a profit or as an exit for shareholders

3. Allow market valuation to reflect individual company prospects – an average P/E, based on the mixed companies, can make a takeover easier, and the predator may then split up the acquisition

4. Satisfy investors who dislike conglomerates, given recent research that conglomerates do not perform well

5. To raise funds to invest elsewhere or to reduce debt

State the 7 Ps of the marketing mix.

1. Product

2. Price

3. Promotion

4. Place

5. People

6. Physical

7. Process

Plot a Positioning Matrix.

		High	Cowboy brands		Premium brands	
Price						
		Low	Economy brands		Bargain brands	
	Very poor	**Poor**	**Reasonable**	**Good**	**Very good**	
			Perceived quality			

State some disadvantages of a very authoritarian entrepreneurial structure (e.g. the entrepreneur takes charge of everything). [6]

1. Other directors may fear the sack and become demotivated

2. The leader may lack of the time and knowledge to make all decisions effectively

3. Less discussion so decisions are worse

4. Prevents team working on individual tasks and projects

5. Institutional investors may be concerned about the arrangement

6. Entrepreneur uses up all time on day to day decisions so not enough time for strategic decisions

---

Sketch Lynch's Matrix of possible expansion methods.

		Internal development	**External development**
	Home	Internal domestic development	Joint merger Acquisition Alliance Franchise
Location	**Abroad**	Exporting Overseas office Multinational	Joint merger Acquisition Alliance Franchise

Note – external development methods are the same, regardless of whether location is home or abroad.

State some advantages of organic growth. [9]

1. Process of developing a product gives good understanding of the market

2. May be only way to pursue technological innovations

3. No suitable target for acquisition

4. Planned and financed from current resources

5. Same style of management and corporate culture

6. Hidden or unforeseen losses

7. Career development

8. Could be cheaper

9. Less risky

State some disadvantages of organic growth. [5]

1. Does not reduce competition (buying a competitor reduces competition)

2. Can be too slow

3. Does not gain access to knowledge and systems of an established operator

4. Initially lacks economies of scale

5. There may be prohibitive barriers to entry

Give some reasons for expanding abroad. [16]

1. Happens by chance

2. Life cycle

3. Competition at home

4. Reduce dependence on the home market

5. Economies of scale

6. Variable quality i.e. might be lower demand for quality abroad

7. Finance

8. Familial

9. Aid agencies

10. Profit margins

11. Sales volume

12. Even out seasonal fluctuations

13. Dispose of excess production

14. Spread risk

15. Sell off products which are obsolescent in the domestic market

16. Enhance image and prestige

State some reasons to avoid engagement in external markets. [5]

1. Profits are even more dependent on events outside the entity's control

2. Adaptations to the product will diminish the effects of economies of scale

3. Extending the product life cycle is not always cost effective

4. Resources better used at home

5. Anti-dumping duties might be imposed

State some strategic issues for management to consider in deciding whether to expand abroad. [5]

1. Financial return good enough?

2. Fit with overall mission and objectives

3. Enough resources

4. Impact on risk profile

5. Method of entry

State some tactical issues to consider in deciding whether to expand abroad. [4]

1. How can the company understand needs and preferences?

2. Knowledge to conduct business abroad

3. Foreign regulations and associated hidden costs

4. Necessary management skills and experience

These considerations may mean that overseas expansion is more easily achieved through some form of acquisition or share arrangement, rather than by organic growth.

State some general reasons for mergers and acquisitions. [7]

1. Marketing advantages

2. Production advantages

3. Finance and management

4. Risk-spreading

5. Retain independence

6. Overcome barriers to entry

7. Outplay rivals

State some advantages under the production advantages reason. [5]

1. Economies of scale

2. Technology and skills

3. Greater production capacity

4. Safeguards future supplies

5. Bulk purchase opportunities

State some advantages under the finance and management reason. [4]

1. Management team

2. Cash resources

3. Gain assets

4. Tax advantages (e.g. use losses brought forward)

State 3 reasons for diversification.

1. Objectives cannot be met without diversification

2. More cash available than needed for expansion

3. Promises to be more profitable than expansion or activity in current industry

---

What 2 tests did Porter propose when evaluating an acquisition?

The cost of entry test

The better off test – does it leave shareholders better off than if they undertook their own action?

State 6 factors which a potential acquirer should evaluate.

1. Prospects of technological change in the industry

2. Size and strength of competitors

3. Reaction of competitors

4. Likelihood of government intervention and legislation

5. State of the industry and long-term prospects

6. Synergies available

State 4 sources of synergy.

1. Marketing and sales

2. Operating

3. Financial

4. Management

Give some examples of marketing and sales synergies. [3]

1. Brand impact on the other company's products

2. Common sales and advertising

3. Wider product range

Give some examples of operating synergies. [4]

307

1. Economies of scale

2. Economies of scope

3. Rationalisation

4. Capacity smoothing

Give 5 examples of financial synergies.

1. Risk spreading leading to cheaper costs of capital

2. Reduction in market competition

3. Shared benefits from same R&D

4. Possibly more stable cash flows

5. Sale of surplus assets

Give 3 examples of management synergies.

1. Managers now involved in fixing a company, not just running a successful one

2. Transfer of learning

3. Increased specialisation in a larger firm

What are the differences between acquisitions via an agreed bid and hostile/contested takeover?

Agreed bids involve prior discussions and a recommendation by the Board of the target to shareholders to accept the offer.

A hostile/contested takeover does not involve prior discussion, either because the acquirer did not ask to discuss or was turned down. The acquirer will gradually build a shareholding over many months at lower prices.

Give some reasons why many acquisitions are not successful. [6]

1. No management audit by acquirer

2. Major implementation problems including morale, performance assessment and culture

3. Excessive price paid due to overvaluation of synergies

4. Lack of actual strategic fit

5. Failure of new management to retain key staff and clients

6. Failure by management to exert corporate governance and control

---

Given the above problems, why do acquisitions still take place? [5]

1. Many acquisitions are successful

2. There may be a loss of value on combination but this may still be smaller than the loss without a combination

3. Vested interests of corporate finance advisers

4. Empire building by CEOs

5. Short-term need for Boards to give the impression that there is a long-term strategic plan and active intervention

---

State some advantages of joint ventures. [10]

1. Attractive to smaller or risk averse companies

2. Attractive in relation to very expensive technologies

3. Increased coverage of countries

4. Reduced risk of government intervention

5. Provides close control over operations

6. Provides local knowledge

7. Learning exercise

8. Provide funds for technology and research projects

9. Cheaper alternative to buying or building a wholly owned operation

10. Access core competences of 2 parties

State some disadvantages of joint ventures. [6]

1. Major conflicts of interest over profit shares, amounts invested, management of joint venture, marketing strategy

2. Problems in protecting IP

3. Partner might leave JV suddenly if priorities change

4. Lack of management interest

5. Unclear exit routes

6. Hard to enforce contractual rights across boundaries

State 3 reasons why firms might enter a long-term strategic alliance. How do such alliances differ from joint ventures?

1. Shares development costs

2. Regulatory environment prohibits take-overs

3. Complementary markets or technology

Alliances have looser contractual arrangements than joint ventures and no separate company is formed. There is generally less commitment/effort than in a joint venture.

State 3 limitations of strategic alliances.

1. May not create new core competences

2. Loss of flexibility due to handing over a key aspect to a partner

3. May be less commitment by the parties than in the case of a joint venture

---

Explain the 5 basic elements of a franchise operation.

1. Franchisor grants a licence to a franchisee allowing use of name, goodwill, systems

2. Franchisee pays a fee for these rights and subsequent support services such as advertising, research and development, technical expertise, management support

3. Franchisee runs the operation day to day but franchisor may stipulate quality control standards

4. Capital is supplied by both parties

5. Franchisor may support the franchisee in applications for capital

---

State 5 advantages of a franchise for the franchisor.

1. Rapid expansion and increased market share, possibly leading to economies of scale

2. Franchisee can provide local knowledge and supervision

3. Franchisor concentrates on core skills of management and marketing

4. Low capital invested in any one unit

5. Franchisee has strong incentives to perform well

State 4 advantages of a franchise for the franchisee.

311

1. Receives a lot of assistance in the start up phase, which is where most businesses fail

2. Provides an instant brand name, trading format and tried and tested product specification

3. Minimises the learning curve

4. Receives immediate training and guidance on how to get started

---

State some disadvantages of franchises (for both parties). [5]

1. Franchisee has day to day influence over quality and impact on reputation

2. May be disagreements over strategy

3. Franchisee may be slow to accept changes or may not want to write off inventory after a change

4. Franchisees could become very successful and break away to set up as a competitor

5. Franchisees will gain access to exclusive IP

When might an agency arrangement be appropriate as a distribution channel?

Where local knowledge and contacts are important e.g. exporting.

Other examples include sales of cosmetics, holidays, financial services

---

What is the main drawback of an agency arrangement?

Company is cut off from direct contact with the customer

State 2 fundamental questions in a buyout decision.

1. Can the buyout team afford the buyout?

2. Can the bought out operation generate enough earnings to pay the interest on the borrowings?

State some reasons for divesting of a subsidiary/business stream. [5] (Dec 2011 Business Strategy mock exam)

1. Good price offered

2. Poor performance

3. Staff problems

4. Concentrate on other markets

5. Wish to engage in a joint venture or partnership

State some arguments for growth by acquisition. [8] (Dec 2011 Business Strategy mock exam)

1. Existing companies have stronger brands making it hard to grow organically

2. Quicker method of growth

3. Reduces competition

4. Combined operation may take a large market share

5. Might acquire strong brand name and reputation

6. Access to suppliers, contacts and networks

7. Economies of scale

8. Gives rise to future opportunities and other real options

State some advantages of a partnership arrangement. [8] (Dec 2011 Business Strategy mock exam)

1. Might internationalise a brand

2. Might allow brand to become better known

3. Market access

4. Improved presence and network

5. Synergies

6. Opportunities to learn from partner, including knowledge and experience

7. Reduces competition

8. Lowers barriers to entry

State some advantages for both a university [13] and an engineering company [12] in establishing a joint venture. (Sep 2011 Business Strategy real exam)

Advantages for university

1. Revenue from sales

2. May attract further funding, investors or grants

3. Increase in publications

4. Attracts more students

5. Publicity

6. Placements for university students

7. Practical commercial applications

8. Technology transfer

9. Access to knowledge and resources

10. Teaching and training

11. May counterbalance a cut in research funding in current climate

12. New opportunities for staff in terms of personal development

13. Shared costs/risk

Advantages for the engineering company

1. Cheaper R&D

2. May increase speed of development

3. Increase value of R&D output

4. Access to wider pool of expertise

5. May learn about new research areas

6. Shared costs/risk

7. May help with benchmarking

8. May help retain research staff

9. Offers a talent pool

10. Promotes image of company

11. May satisfy certain corporate social responsibility objectives

12. May allow access to further government funding

State some potential benefits of an acquisition. [6] (June 2010 Business Strategy real exam)

1. Diversification

2. May give multinational access

3. Able to compete better

4. Reduced variable costs

5. Economies of scale

6. Potential to acquire customers

What is the single most important question in relation to an acquisition? (June 2010 Business Strategy real exam)

Is the acquisition price value for money?

State some benefits of:

1. **strategic alliances [4]**
2. **licensing [6]**   **(March 2010 Business Strategy real exam)**

Strategic alliances

1. Faster growth than via organic approach

2. Access to capital

3. Synergy

4. Access to wider markets, including international

Licensing

1. Faster expansion than under own resources

2. Opportunity for greater worldwide coverage

3. Reduces risks

4. May enhance brand names

5. May guarantee revenues

6. Cash flow injection from sale of licences and revenues

State some disadvantages of:

1. **strategic alliances [6]**
2. **licensing [3]**   **(March 2010 Business Strategy real exam)**

Strategic alliances

1. Unclear responsibilities

2. Gives away share of benefits of technology

3. Likely to lead to some loss of control

4. Disputes may arise over rights and obligations

5. Access to know-how is given away

6. Could be an element of exchange risk

Licensing

1. Growth may be slower than some options (other than organic growth)

2. Involves sharing profits and know-how

3. May not give the group a large role in the market

State 6 reasons why change may be needed or triggered.

1. Change in the environment

2. Changes in the products/services made

3. Changes in technology and working practices

4. Changes in management and working relationships

5. Changes in organisation structure or size

6. Post-acquisition changes

State a fundamental division between types of change and a related fundamental division in management's response options.

Change can be incremental or transformational.

Therefore management response can be reactive or proactive.

Briefly define the following types of change.

1. **Incremental**
2. **Transformational**
3. **Step**
4. **Planned**
5. **Emergent**

Incremental – a series of small steps, gradual

Transformational – major, significant change which is introduced quickly

Step – unexpected jump upwards or downwards in the pace of change, caused by an unexpected event

Planned – following a series of pre-planned steps

Emergent – continuous open-ended adjustments to the environment

---

Sketch the Johnson, Scholes and Whittington model of change.

		Nature of change	
		Incremental	**Transformational**
	Pro-active	Tuning	Planned
Management role			
	Reactive	Adaptation	Forced

At what 3 levels of a company might change occur?

1. Individual

2. Organisation structure and systems level

3. Organisational climate and interpersonal style

State the 8 stages of the change process, per the Business Strategy and Technology Study Manual.

1. Determine need or desire for change

2. Prepare a tentative plan

3. Analyse probable reactions to the change

4. Make a final decision (participative, coercive)

5. Establish a timetable

6. Communicate the plan

7. Implement the change

8. Review the change

State the 3 stages of the Lewin & Schein model of change management. Which is the most difficult stage?

1. Unfreeze

2. Move

3. Refreeze

Unfreezing is usually the most difficult stage. Often a crisis will be an unfreezing method.

State 5 problems with a coercive approach.

1. Underestimation of the forces of resistance

2. Failure to muster forces in favour

3. Failure to attack root causes of resistance

4. Management shifts their attention too quickly elsewhere

5. Failure to ensure implementation

What is a "change agent"?

Individual (Champion of Change), group or external consultancy with the responsibility for driving and selling change.

State some roles for a change agent. [4]

1. Define the problem

2. Suggest solutions

3. Select and implement a solution

4. Gain support from all involved

What 4 skills/attributes should a change agent have?

1. Communication skills

2. Negotiation and "selling" skills

3. Awareness of organisational "politics"

4. Understanding of the relevant processes

What are the 4 steps in the activities of a change agent in driving through change?

1. Senior management agree on need for change

2. Appointment of the change agent: management supports the agent, reviews and monitors progress, endorses and approves changes

3. Change agent works to win support from functional and operational managers*

4. Change agent galvanises managers into action and gives them any necessary support*

*Note – the original change agent may cause others to become additional change agents at their own level. Indeed, this may be necessary to ensure that something actually happens.

What are the 4 Rs within the Gemini 4 Rs framework?

Reframing – vision and mobilisation

Restructuring – changing infrastructure and plans

Revitalising – achieving market focus, inventing new business, exploiting technology

Renewal – create a reward system, build individual learning, develop the organisation

---

State 3 areas in which change affects individuals.

1. Physiological

2. Circumstantial

3. Psychological

State 2 general types of barrier that can emerge in relation to a change process.

1. Cultural

2. Personnel

The "psychological contract" is a deal between employer and employed. State 2 important pressure points which can develop during the change process.

1. Lack of appropriate skill levels

2. Declining staff morale

What should a staff development plan include, within a change management process? [5]

1. Communication of implications for jobs

2. Communication of required jobs

3. Discussions about individual development needs/options

4. Learning and training opportunities

5. Opportunities for making a contribution to changes

What 3 factors can management vary when introducing change? (Hint: PMS)

1. **P**ace of change

2. **M**anner of change

3. **S**cope of change

What is the ideal "manner" in which to introduce the change, per the Business Strategy and Technology Study Manual? [5]

1. Recognise and confront resistance – do not try to ignore it

2. Free circulation of information

3. Sell the change to people concerned

4. Individuals must be helped to learn

5. Involve people in the process, to lessen insecurity, helplessness and therefore resentment

---

What is Forcefield Analysis?

An attempt to analyse the forces which will drive change and the forces which will resist change. The balance of these will determine if, overall, there is movement towards or away from the ideal position.

Change managers should attempt to weaken resisting forces and strengthen the driving forces.

Driving forces	Strength	Current state	Strength	Restraining forces	Ideal position
1	→				
			←	a	
2	→				
			←	b	**Aim**
3	→				
			←	c	
4	→				
			←	d	

Note – the driving forces and restraining forces can be completely different – hence they are drawn above in different rows and using numbers versus letters – they are not necessarily 2 parts of the same force/issue.

Complete the following table in relation to the communication of change:

Stakeholder	Needs	What they want to know	How to communicate
Shareholders			
Press			
Suppliers			
Customers			
Senior managers			
Staff			
Line managers			

Stakeholder	Needs	What they want to know	How to communicate
Shareholders	Reassurance	Strategy is well thought out	Press Financial statements AGM Website
Press	A good story	What is happening, rationale	Briefings
Suppliers	Information	How changes will affect working relationship	Meetings face to face Letters/emails
Customers	Motivation	Service will continue without interruption	Press Advertisements
Senior managers	Acknowledgement and involvement	How they will be involved, opportunities	One-to-one meetings
Staff	Help to adapt	Training and support Job security	Briefings One-to-one meetings with line manager
Line managers	Involvement	Opportunities to be involved, opportunities to learn	Briefings One-to-one with senior manager/HR

State 3 levels at which to consider ethics.

1. Personal ethics

2. Business ethics

3. Corporate responsibility

The difference between business and corporate is that business ethics relates to the way that the firm as a whole behaves whereas corporate responsibility is the belief that a firm owes a responsibility to society and its wider stakeholders.

State 3 possible stances that an organisation can adopt with regard to ethics.

1. Meet minimum levels and concentrate on short-term shareholder interests

2. Do more than the minimum, recognising the possible benefit for long term shareholder wealth

3. Go well beyond the minimum and use ethics as a key element of the business (e.g. The Body Shop)

Where will the ethical stance of an organisation often be reflected?

In its mission statement

What 2 ethical standards were published by the APB?

Ethical Standards for Auditors

Ethical Standards for Reporting Accountants

State the 5 principles of the ICAEW Code of Ethics.

1. Integrity

2. Objectivity

3. Professional competence and due care

4. Confidentiality

5. Professional behaviour

State the 5 potential ethical threats to an accountant in his or her work.

1. Self-interest

2. Self-review

3. Advocacy

4. Familiarity

5. Intimidation

What types of safeguard does the ICAEW Code state might be applied in the work environment? [10]

1. Employer's oversight systems

2. Employer's ethics and conduct programs

3. Recruitment procedures in the employing organisation

4. Strong internal controls

5. Disciplinary processes

6. Leadership that stresses the importance of ethical behaviour

7. Policies to implement and monitor the quality of employee performance

8. Timely communication to employees

9. Policies and procedures to empower and encourage employees to communicate

10. Consultation with another professional accountant

What simple, 3 element test does the Institute of Business Ethics propose in relation to ethical issues?

Transparency

Effect

Fairness

State some points in the strategy process where ethics may have an influence. [4]

1. Formulation of strategic objectives – rule out certain lines of business

2. Ethical expectations which the company has set

3. Internal appraisal

4. Strategy selection

State 6 areas where ethics and business strategy may potentially conflict.

1. Cultivating and benefiting from relationships with legislators and governments

2. Fairness of labour contracts

3. Privacy of customers and employees

4. Terms of trade with suppliers

5. Prices to customers

6. Managing cross cultural businesses

State some ways in which ethical issues can impact on the 4Ps of the marketing mix.

Product	Dangerous or harmful products such as tobacco, alcohol Some products are wasteful Ceasing to provide some products such as drugs has an impact on people
Price	Some people cannot afford products Price discrimination means discriminating between people Low pricing can encourage excessive consumption e.g. alcohol
Promotion	Possible "brainwashing" Some adverts can be distasteful Some adverts can be upsetting Possible false claims
Place	Encouraging or denying access Encouraging excessive consumption e.g. placing sweets in children's eyeline Premium rate telephone lines Branch closures to save costs affect people Move towards websites may exclude those not competent with computers

---

What 4 arguments do marketing experts use to defend their actions/profession?

1. Improves personal choice

2. Codes of Practice are used to curb abuses

3. Marketing follows people's needs and wishes, it does not create them

4. Recently marketing has increased interest in ethical investment funds

---

State 6 possible ethical issues in relation to manufacturing.

1. Pollution and environmental issues

2. Manufacture and sale of potentially dangerous items

3. Use of child labour

4. Technological issues such as GM food, health concerns

5. Product testing ethics

6. Scrappage and disposal

Note that by avoiding these issues and making a point of this avoidance, companies can gain a competitive advantage in advertising.

State some aspects/considerations of ethical purchasing. [7]

1. Human rights of workers in supplier firms

2. Proper health and safety standards

3. Environmental protection

4. Fair contracting terms and conditions

5. Transparency in negotiations with suppliers

6. Fraud and corruption

7. Zero tolerance of gifts/bribes

Define "sustainable development", as defined by the Brundtland Report.

Development which allows us to "meet the needs of the present without compromising the ability of future generations to meet their own needs".

What 4 types of strategy can a company adopt in relation to "sustainable development", in terms of the level of engagement of the company?

1. Defence

2. Reactive

3. Accommodation

4. Proactive

State 7 different mechanisms which have been proposed as part of global sustainable development initiatives. (Note – the question is not about specific policies, just generic types of policy)

1. Corporate policies

2. Supply chain pressure

3. Stakeholder engagement

4. Voluntary codes

5. Rating and benchmarking

6. Taxes and subsidies

7. Tradable permits

State 3 general types of view on the merits of sustainability as a concept/aim.

1. Essential consideration

2. Fad

3. Greenwash

State 7 justifications for a company to consider corporate responsibility to an extent beyond that needed just to meet the minimum needed for its everyday operations.

1. Source of opportunity

2. Self-regulation now is better than inflexible regulation later

3. Improves relations with key stakeholders

4. Good for PR

5. Develops managers and staff more fully

6. Helps create a value culture and a sense of mission

7. In the longer-term, upholding community values

State some common tangible benefits of active corporate responsibility activities. [6]

1. Lower cost base

2. Opportunities to enter new markets and attract ethical customers

3. Provide new solutions

4. Protect company's licence to operate and its reputation

5. Opportunity to build core competences

6. Enhance a firm's reputation and attract more finance

16.4   Selected Revision Questions from ACA Simplified *Financial Management Q&A 2018*

The following short form questions are reproduced from the 2018 edition of our Professional Level Q&A. We have concentrated on the following topic areas in Financial Management:

1. Investment appraisal

2. Valuations

3. Hedging and overseas risk issues

As with your revision of Business Strategy and Technology, when revisiting Professional Level Financial Management the really key topics to focus on are those which relate to new strategic developments, the industry environment, strategies for change, acquisitions and ethics. These will hopefully be relevant areas for SBM and will give you some appropriate "lenses" through which to look at the stimulus material given in the examination. Remember that SBM is an evolution of the old **Business Change** examination, and has been largely put together by the same examiner team, so you need to be focusing on the same general areas that came up in Business Change.

State 9 possible political risks.

1. Government stability

2. Economic stability

3. Inflation

4. Degree of international indebtedness

5. Financial infrastructure

6. Level of import restrictions

7. Remittance restrictions

8. Evidence of expropriation

9. Special taxes or investment incentives

State 4 sources of cultural risk.

1. Different practices of customers and consumers in target markets

2. Media and distribution systems in overseas markets

3. Different business practices in target markets

4. National cultural differences

State 5 possible ways to deal with political risk.

1. Negotiations with the host government

2. Insurance e.g. Export Credits Guarantee Department

3. Production strategies e.g. outsource, produce locally

4. Management structure e.g. JVs, sharing control with locals, local investment

5. Finance e.g. obtain finance locally so that local banks are stakeholders

---

State 5 possible considerations when financing an overseas subsidiary.

1. Local finance costs and subsidies

2. Taxation

3. Restrictions on dividend remittances

4. Possibility of flexibility in repayments

5. Access to capital – may be easier in local markets to optimise gearing

---

State 5 advantages of organic growth.

1. Spreads costs of growth over time

2. Often cheaper than an acquisition

3. Slower rate of change prevents disruption to behaviour, culture and systems

4. The synergies claimed to result from acquisitions often fail to occur so organic growth may not actually miss out on these

5. Slower rate of change so less disruption

State 6 advantages of acquisitions over organic growth.

331

1. Synergies

2. Risk reduction through diversification

3. Reduces competition/eliminates a competitor

4. May be vertical or horizontal integration

5. Quicker method of growth

6. Can increase market share (see point 3)

State 4 possible restructuring mechanisms.

1. MBO

2. MBI

3. Spin off/demerger

4. Sales of shares/assets to a third party

State 4 possible valuation methods and related problems.

1. **Net assets** – based on out of date book values (can use revalued amounts)

2. **P/E multiple** – hard to estimate earnings: is industry P/E applicable to the company we are looking at?

3. **Dividend yield model** – is it reasonable to use industry average yield with respect to this company? Ignores dividend growth over time. Not useful for valuing a controlling interest because then dividend could be changed at will and the controlling shareholder will often take out cash in other ways anyway

4. **Discounted Cash Flows** – probably best methods but problems in estimating future cash flow, especially if there are synergies. Problems with estimating the correct discount rate and the number of years to apply to

---

State the 3 basic ways of paying for an acquisition (mnemonic: CSL). State 3 advantages and 3 disadvantages for each one (only 2 advantages for L).

1. **C**ash

2. **S**hare for share exchange

3. **L**oan stock for share exchange

Cash – Advantages

1. Guaranteed amount received
2. May be an appropriate use of surplus cash
3. No dilution of control

Cash – Disadvantages

1. More cash may need to be found
2. May be tax issues
3. Shareholders of the target reduce their proportionate shareholding interest so may be opposed

Share for share exchange – Advantages

1. Preserves cash and liquidity
2. Shareholders of the target retain their interest
3. No immediate tax issues

Share for share exchange – Disadvantages

1. Issues costs may be high
2. Existing shareholders in the purchasing company have their shareholdings diluted
3. Unknown value received

Loan stock for share exchange – advantages

1. Does not dilute control of purchasing company's shareholders
2. Loan holder gets more certain return than if held shares

Loan stock for share exchange – disadvantages

1. Obligation to pay interest
2. May prefer equity
3. Increased gearing (could be an advantage if brings nearer to optimum)

State some disadvantages of organic growth. [3]

1. May be more risky than acquiring an established company

2. Process may be too slow

3. May be barriers to entry in the new market

333

Give some examples of synergies in acquisitions. [5]

1. Administrative savings

2. Economies of scale

3. Use of common investment in marketing, new technologies, R&D

4. Leaner management structures

5. Access to underutilised assets

What does the empirical data state generally happens in the case of acquisitions? [4]

1. Synergy does not automatically result and must be actively pursued

2. Shareholders in the target are the only consistent winners

3. Shareholders in the bidder often lose out by paying too much and/or incurring high professional fees, where these costs are not offset by synergies

4. Often takes place in the interests of managers, not shareholders

---

State 6 reasons to divest or sell off a company.

1. Lack of fit with existing companies

2. Subsidiary is small and so does not warrant management time

3. Individual parts may be worth more than the combination if the combination is being discounted (conglomerate discount)

4. One part is trading poorly and selling it is cheaper and quicker than putting it into liquidation

5. Parent may need to improve liquidity

6. Some companies buy and sell as risks and rewards change over time

---

State 7 reasons to use an interest rate swap.

334

1. **Gain lower interest rate than possible alone**

2. Better match of assets and liabilities

3. **Access to market rates which may not otherwise be possible**

4. Hedge exposure by switching between fixed and floating

5. Restructure debts without incurring new loans/fees

6. Speculation

7. **Available for lower periods than other hedging methods**

Points in bold are the most significant.

State 3 risks of interest rate swaps (mnemonic: DUT)

1. **D**efault – other party may default

2. **U**nfavourable movements in rates – one side will lose out as rates change

3. **T**ransparency risk – may undermine the clarity and transparency of company's financial statements

---

State some issues to consider with respect to interest rate options. [8]

Premium may be high

OTC options

1. Can be tailored

2. Used over longer periods

3. May only be exercisable at a particular time

4. Not transferrable

Traded options

1. Exercisable at any time

2. Straightforward to use

3. Can be sold early if exit is needed

State some drawbacks of currency options. [4]

1. Cost is about 5% of the total foreign currency covered

2. Must be paid for as soon as bought

3. Tailor-made options lack negotiability

4. Not available for all currencies

Outline the key characteristics of:

Forward contracts [4]
Futures contracts [8]

Forward contracts

1. Fix the amounts involved in advance
2. Binding contract – this could be a problem if one side fails to pay or money not needed
3. Customised contract tailored to the user's needs
4. An OTC forward involves risk that other side will default

Futures contracts

1. Binding contract
2. Standardised amounts – so values and maturity may not match requirements precisely (i.e. basis risk is involved)
3. Lower transaction costs due to standardisation
4. Deposit required is small and lower than a tailored forward or option
5. Ready market – no need to identify a particular counterparty
6. Only a limited number of currencies are available
7. Can be complex if neither currency is the US$
8. No counterparty risk as the exchange guarantees that both sides will honour their agreements

---

State and define the 3 currency risks (mnemonic: TET).

1. **T**ransaction risk – adverse short term movements during ordinary business e.g. fixed prices

2. **E**conomic risk – effect of exchange rates over the longer term

3. **T**ranslation risk – risk of exchange losses when translating foreign branches/subsidiaries into the home currency

---

State 5 potential ways in which to manage economic risk.

1. Diversification of operations worldwide

2. Marketing and promotional management, to promote diversification

3. Product management – do not release a high risk product if there is uncertainty over economic risk

4. Pricing

5. Production management – set up production in countries with lower relative production costs

---

What does the value of an option depend on? [5]

1. Price of underlying security

2. Exercise price of the option

3. General level of interest rates* – higher rates reduce the value of a call option

4. Time to expiry – a longer time period makes a call option more valuable

5. Volatility

*If interest rates are high, it is not so good to have money tied up in the premium which is payable upfront – it would be better to keep the cash and then buy the underlying asset later. As an alternative way of looking at things, the future value is being discounted to a greater extent, reducing present value.

It is usually assumed that hedging will take place. State 5 reasons why it may make sense not to hedge.

1. Costs too high

2. Immaterial amount to be hedged

3. Company may want exposure to upside risk

4. Portfolio effect – company may already have products/shareholdings which reduce risk

5. If shareholders are fully diversified, no need to hedge

State 6 methods of hedging without use of forwards, futures or options

1. Change invoicing currency

2. Match payments and receipts

3. Match assets and liabilities

4. Leading and lagging payments

5. Maintaining currency accounts

6. Use money market hedging

State 4 risks involved in overseas trade, other than currency risk.

1. Physical risk

2. Credit risk

3. Trade risk – customer cancels or refuses to accept the goods

4. Liquidity risk

State 5 institutions that can help reduce the risks of overseas trade.

1. Banks

2. Insurance companies

3. Credit reference agencies

4. Government agencies – e.g. UK Export Credits Guarantee Department (ECGD)

5. Risk transfer to logistics company – i.e. contract with the courier to ensure that courier shares part or all of the losses

---

Complete the following summary table on 3 types of hedging technique.

Characteristic	Forward	Money market	Futures
Tailored			
Secondary market to unwind			
Transaction cost			
Complexity			
Management costs			
Volume/popularity			

Characteristic	Forward	Money market	Futures
Tailored	Yes	Yes	No
Secondary market to unwind	No	Yes	Yes
Transaction cost	Via spread	Via spread	Brokerage fees
Complexity	Low	Medium	High
Management costs	Low	Medium	High
Volume/popularity	Small/medium	Banks	Growing usage

Explain how the 7 components of shareholder wealth affect that wealth.

Mnemonic is:

Stupid **P**eople **T**ake **F**ar **L**onger **W**ith **C**rosswords

Sales growth rate –
Higher sales generate more cash

Profit margin (operating profit) –
The higher the margin, the more profit generated per sale and so the higher the cash flows generated

Corporation **T**ax rate –
Tax drains cash

Fixed asset investment –
Cash is drained into CAPEX but can enhance wealth

Life of cash flows –
The longer the life of the cash flows the higher the value contributed

Working capital –
Ties up cash

Cost of capital –
Cheaper sources of long-term finance will enhance value

Explain the following "real options". State the related mnemonic.

Flexibility
Abandonment
Timing

Follow on
Growth

Mnemonic is FLAT FoG

Flexibility –
A more expensive option may give increased flexibility e.g. a machine could run off electricity or gas, allowing the company to pick the better option as appropriate

Abandonment –
Some projects allow assets to be sold at a good price if abandoned
Some projects have inbuilt options to reduce capacity and to suspend operations temporarily
These rights are similar to put options

Timing –
Projects with options to delay are more attractive – allows company to wait and see
However, this is only valuable if it more than offsets the loss of business/profits to competitors during the delay
Can be seen as a type of flexibility option

Follow On –
Launching this project gives an opportunity to launch a second and third project
This is similar to a call option

Growth –
Project provides an ability to start small and expand if market conditions are good: JVs and strategic alliances
Also relates to follow on options

State 3 key considerations in determining whether to invest overseas.

1. Market attractiveness – forecast demand, growth rates

2. Competitive advantage – prior experience, understanding, language barriers

3. Risk – political stability, government intervention and similar external influences

---

Define "political risk".

The risk that political action will affect the position and value of a company.

State 6 measures which a foreign government could implement to prevent exploitation of its country by multinationals.

341

1. Quotas

2. Tariffs

3. Non-tariff barriers

4. Restrictions

5. Nationalisation

6. Minimum shareholding

State 4 techniques to deal with political risk.

1. Negotiations with host government – obtain concessions and agreements

2. Insurance – e.g. UK Export Credit Guarantee Department

3. Production strategies – control patents which can be enforced internationally; produce locally to give local enterprise "buy in"

4. Management structure – JVs or ceding control to local investors

---

State 4 sources of cultural risk.

1. Cultures and practices of consumers and customers in individual markets

2. Media and distribution systems in overseas markets

3. Different ways of doing business in overseas markets

4. Degree to which national cultural differences matter for the product concerned

---

State 5 factors to be considered when determining the choice of finance for an overseas subsidiary.

1. Local finance costs and subsidies

2. Taxation systems

3. Restrictions on dividend remittances

4. Possibility of flexibility in repayments which may arise from parent/subsidiary relationship

5. Access to capital

State 9 factors which could be taken into account when assessing political risk.

1. Government stability

2. Political and business ethics

3. Economic stability/inflation

4. Degree of international indebtedness

5. Financial infrastructure

6. Level of import restrictions

7. Remittance restrictions

8. Evidence of expropriation

9. Existence of special taxes and regulations on overseas investors or investment incentives

---

Give 4 examples of the main categories of loan covenant.

1. Restrictions on issuing new debt

2. Restrictions on dividends

3. Restrictions on merger activity

4. Restrictions on investment policy

State 2 advantages of organic growth.

1. Costs are spread over time

2. Rate of change is slower, avoiding disruption and behavioural problems

---

State 4 disadvantages of organic growth.

1. May involve higher upfront costs

2. May be more risky

3. May be too slow, so fails to exploit the opportunities available

4. May be barriers to entry in new markets

State 4 reasons why acquisitions take place.

1. Synergy

2. Risk reduction

3. Reduces competition

4. Vertical integration

State 7 possible reasons to undertake a valuation.

1. To establish merger/takeover terms

2. To help in making share purchase/sale decisions

3. To value companies listing on the stock exchange

4. To value shares sold in a private company

5. For tax purposes

6. For divorce settlements

7. To value subsidiaries for disposals, MBOs etc

Which is regarded as the best valuation approach? State 3 problems with this approach.

Discounted cash flow (DCF) model

Problems include:

1. Estimating future cashflows (particularly synergy)

2. Estimating the discount rate (risks)

3. Time horizon – how long do we assume the cash flows last? Do we use a perpetuity calculation?

Purchaser Ltd is about to acquire Target Ltd. State whether the following should increase or decrease the price which Purchaser Ltd should be willing to pay:

1. **Target's head office would not be needed and can be disposed of immediately for £10m**

2. **Synergistic benefits of £500,000 per year are expected**

3. **Target has loan stock worth £2m**

344

1. Increase

2. Increase (assuming that predicted synergies prove to be accurate)

3. Decrease – be careful with the phrase "worth" – this just means that the market value of liability is, in this case, £2m

---

State one very common adjustment when valuing an unquoted company using a P/E model.

It is necessary to adjust the P/E downwards for non-marketability of the shares. Typically one third to one half is deducted.

State 4 problems with the dividend valuation model.

1. Estimating future dividends and growth

2. Estimating the cost of equity (risk)

3. Adjustments for non-marketability – these are arbitrary

4. Not very useful for valuing controlling interests as value of these is not based solely on dividend flows

---

State some further considerations in relation to valuations under the following headings:

Quoted companies [2]

Income valuations [8]

General [4]

Quoted companies

1. Existing market value should normally be established as a minimum – why would a shareholder accept less than the current market value?

2. Premiums for bulk buying/control

Income valuations

1. Estimated NRV of surplus assets should be added

2. Trade investment income should be included in earnings but not non-trade investments

3. Dividends should be excluded from income

4. Market value of investments should be added at the end

5. Charge market rent on freehold premises as an adjustment

6. Add on the value of the freehold separately at the end

7. Ensure director remuneration reflects a market approach (in practice, it may be set up based on tax considerations but this may inflate earnings)

8. Deduct market value of preference shares and debt to derive equity value

General

1. Will key employees leave after acquisition?

2. Do key staff have long notice periods or high payoff clauses?

3. Any restrictive covenants?

4. Are there several bidders? This will push the price up

State 5 reasons for divestment.

1. Lack of fit

2. Subsidiary is too small

3. Subsidiary is trading poorly

4. Parent may need to improve its liquidity position, particularly when a good offer is forthcoming

5. Highly acquisitive organisations view companies as portfolios of assets and dispose of companies as risk and returns change

---

State the 2 most common ways of financing MBOs.

1. Junk bonds

2. Mezzanine debt – allows debt holder to gain some equity participation, either through an option to convert or by attaching warrants (right to buy shares in the future)

State 3 reasons for a company to purchase its own shares.

1. Enhancement of share price

2. Escape route

3. Gearing – reduce equity and so increase gearing

State 2 advantages and 1 disadvantage of outsourcing.

1. Access to specialist skills at a lower cost

2. Business can use its investment capital for its core activities

1. Potential loss of control

You are presented with the following valuations of a business.

State and explain which are most relevant to (a) the current owners and (b) a prospective purchaser of the business.

Discounted cash flows	**£3.0m**
Net realisable value	**£2.8m**
Balance sheet value of assets	**£1.8m**
Cost of establishing a new business of same type	**£2.9m**

Current owners –

The current owners should not accept anything less than the net realisable value because this is the amount they could get themselves by breaking up the business.

The current owners cannot realise the discounted cash flows/economic value immediately so they cannot expect to necessarily receive this amount immediately – the net realisable value is the minimum they will definitely receive (if the purchaser bids less than the NRV, the bid should be rejected and the business broken up). However, the current owners might be able to use the discounted cash flows/economic value as a bargaining chip, highlighting to the purchaser the value they could be buying over the long term.

Prospective purchaser –

The purchaser will be interested in the discounted cash flows/economic value as this is the amount which the company will generate. However, the purchaser will also need to consider the cost of establishing an alternative business – if this is lower than the discounted cash flows/economic value, then this lower amount is the maximum that should be offered, provided that the purchaser is certain that the new alternative business will be just as good (of course, it could end up being better).

In this case, the economic value is £3.0m but there is no point paying more than the cost of establishing a similar business of £2.9m – why pay £3.0m for something that can be obtained for £2.9m?

The balance sheet value is unlikely to be of interest to either party.

A target company owns a freehold building which is carried at £2m in the statement of financial position. The building could be rented out at £200,000 per year if sold, providing a 5% return per year to the purchaser.

State the value of the property which might be included in a valuation for the purposes of a potential acquisition. State a problem with using this figure.

Assets and liabilities should be updated to market values if possible.

If the asset can generate £200,000 per year into perpetuity, discounted at 5% per year, then the flows are worth £200,000 / 0.05 = £4m to the purchaser.

This provides some evidence that the market value of the property is £4m, not the £2m at which it is carried in the accounts.

However, if the property is required for the running of the target business, it cannot be sold so the £4m would not in fact be realisable.

What adjustment should always be made (but is never mentioned in the exam question) when valuing a private company? (Mar 2010 Financial Management past paper)

Apply a discount of, say, 30% to the value found to allow for risk and reduced marketability.

Make sure you say that this percentage is relatively arbitrary yet it is a really crucial variable as it can affect the valuation significantly.

You have to calculate an earnings valuation. How, if at all should you adjust for the following?

1. **Corporation tax**
2. **Preference dividends**
3. **Ordinary dividends**
4. **Exceptional income on a contract which will not be renewed next year**
5. **Quoted or unquoted status of the company**

1. Deduct corporation tax – "earnings" are profit **after** tax

2. Deduct preference dividends – these are a type of financing

3. Do not deduct ordinary dividends – these are paid out of earnings, but do not reduce earnings

4. Deduct non-recurring income as you need to work on a maintainable earnings basis

5. Apply a percentage of 25% to 50% to reduce the value of unquoted shares, to reflect risk and reduced marketability

---

You are required to prepare a cash flow statement from income statement and statement of financial position information. Set out the 2 parts of the pro forma.

1. Calculate the change in net current assets

2. Adjust profit, including the change in net current assets found in stage 1

1. Change in net current assets

	2008 Actual	2009 Actual	2010 Forecast
Inventories			
Receivables			
Payables			
Dividends payable			
Increase/(decrease)	-	A	(B)

Use A and (B) in the next stage. Note that you need to reverse the signs in stage 2 – if there has been an increase in net assets – e.g. A – then this is an outflow of cash as cash has been used to enhance the asset base.

2. Adjust profit to cash flows

Retained for the year		
Add depreciation		
Change in net current assets	(A)	B
Expenditure on non-current assets		
Surplus/(deficit) for the year		
Cash b/f		
Cash c/f		

Note that we need 3 years' worth of figures to get a result for current year and forecast year as both the current year and forecast year figures require a comparison to prior year.

Purchaser plc is considering buying Target plc. Purchaser plc has 500 50p shares in issue and Target plc has 150 £1 shares in issue. The terms of the potential takeover are that shareholders in Target plc will be given 3 shares in Purchaser plc for each Target plc share they currently own.

Calculate the correct number of shares to include in an EPS calculation.

Leave the shares of Purchaser plc in their original form as 50p shares as this will form the basis of EPS calculations for the combined entity.

Convert the shares of Target plc into 50p shares (i.e. double the number of shares).

However, when calculating the number of new Purchaser plc shares to be issued, continue to work with a £1 figure for the Target plc shares – this is because Purchaser plc is offering 3 shares in itself for every **existing** share in Target plc.

Therefore number of shares

Original Purchaser plc 50p shares	500
New Purchaser plc shares (3 x 150)	450
Target plc shares transformed into 50p shares	300
Total shares for EPS	1,250

Purchaser plc has PAT of £200m and 500m shares in issue, valued at £3 each.

Target plc has PAT of £50m and 100m shares in issue, valued at £2 each.

What would be the P/E ratio of the combined company if the price of Purchase plc shares doubles after the acquisition?

Earnings will be £250m. There will be 600m shares so EPS will be £0.42 per share.

If Purchaser plc's share price doubles to £6 this is a P/E ratio of £6 / £0.42 or 14.3.

This could also be found by finding the total value of the company and dividing it by the total earnings:

Total value of 600m shares at £6 is £3,600m. Total earnings are £250m. So the ratio of total share price to earnings is 3,600 / 250 or 14.4 as above, allowing for rounding.

The owners of a business estimate that the business will generate £5m in discounted cash flows over the next 5 years. The breakup value of assets is £4m.

What is the minimum the owners should accept if they wish to realise their investment now?

£4m

Discounted cash flows cannot be realised immediately so there is no guarantee that the owners will get this sum from a purchaser. Therefore the £5m is not the minimum but rather a potentially good deal.

Given the following representation of valuation data, create an equation that shows the maximum that the shareholders of Purchaser plc should pay to acquire Target plc.

Earnings of Purchaser plc	**A**
P/E ratio of Purchaser plc	**Z**
Synergy benefits from the merger	**S**
Earnings of Target plc	**B**
P/E ratio of Target plc	**Y**
Estimated P/E ratio of the combined entity	**P**

Group earnings are given as (A + S + B) x P

This value should be compared to the current value of Purchaser plc on its own, which is A x Z. The difference will then be the additional value attributable to acquiring Target plc and therefore the maximum that should be paid for that value.

Hence the full result is:

((A + S + B) x P) – (A x Z)

A plc has a valuation of £25m and B plc has a valuation of £5m.

A share for share exchange takes place, giving the shareholders of A a holding of 65% of the merged company and the shareholders of B a holding of 35%.

The combined company is able to sell a surplus office building for £10m immediately and can invest £2m of the proceeds in a project yielding £5m NPV.

Show the wealth of the shareholders of each original company before and after the merger. Comment on the results.

The shareholders of A plc originally had wealth of £25m.

The shareholders of B plc originally had wealth of £5m.

The merger increases the value of the company by the £10m disposal and £5m NPV. Be careful not to deduct the £2m investment in the project – the £5m NPV generated is already after the deduction of cost (**net** present value) so you would be double counting to deduct the £2m again.

The new company is therefore worth 25 + 5 + 10 + 5 = £45m.

The shareholders of A plc now have wealth of 65% x 45m = £29.25m
The shareholders of B plc now have wealth of 35% x 45m = £15.75m

Shareholders of A contributed 25 / 25 + 5 = 83% of the original value versus the 5 / 25 + 5 = 17% for the shareholders of B.

However, shareholders of A only hold 65% of the wealth of the new company versus the 35% held by the shareholders of B.

This means that the deal is good for the shareholders of B – their wealth has increased by (15.75 / 5) – 1 = 215% versus (29.25 / 25) – 1 = 17% for the shareholders of A.

The shareholders of B can also block special resolutions as they hold at least 25% of the combined shares.

Chapter 17   Ethics: Revision and Application to SBM

Learning Points

After reading this chapter, you must be able to:

1. understand the potential importance of ethics marks to your SBM script
2. utilise some helpful ethical frameworks, based on our analysis of ICAEW marking approaches
3. understand what to revise in your ethics revision

17.1   The Importance of Ethics Marks in SBM

According to the examiners, ethics will always account for **5-10% of the marks in SBM**. Again, we are left with the same position as Specialist Audit & Assurance areas (see chapter 10): seemingly a relatively low number of marks but at the same time **some of the most straightforward and standard marks (with no number work required)** and therefore potentially a vital source of "Plan B"-type marks in case the numbers side does not go so well.

In this chapter, we will review the ways in which ethics has been tested in the SBM papers available at the time of writing. **We will try to understand any patterns in this testing**. Before doing so, we will review some examiner comments on ethics and we will suggest some useful frameworks. As an appendix to this chapter, we have also included some relevant ethics questions from our *Financial Management Q&A 2018*: since Financial Management is very relevant to the practical business advisory issues which we know will be tested in SBM, and since ethics has recently been added as a syllabus area in Financial Management, we believe that this will be a relevant set of questions. We have also included selected ethics questions from our *Business Planning: Taxation Q&A 2018*[86].

17.2   SBM Ethics: The Importance of a Nuanced Approach

At the SBM Workshop at the 2015 ICAEW Tutor Conference, the examiners harshly criticised the approach of students who took a "black and white" or "all or nothing" approach to ethics at the Advanced Level: the examiners suggested that many candidates described SBM ethical issues as either entirely acceptable or the worst form of unethical action imaginable. Similarly, at the first sight of any ethical problem, many candidates state that the advisory firm should withdraw from the engagement and that all interaction with the client should cease immediately: the ICAEW Ethics Helpline is then mentioned all too often.

The examiners have stated that all SBM ethical issues will be more "nuanced" than this so that candidates can offer more **interesting and intelligent Recommendations** (one of the 4 Case Study skills "lenses") rather than just saying "withdraw" every single time – **issues will not normally be clearly right or clearly wrong: there will be different issues to consider**. Therefore, the marks

---

[86] Although UK taxation is not examinable in SBM (as discussed on page 29, "fictional" taxation may be tested) some of the topics covered in Business Planning: Taxation ethics questions are relevant. We have obviously deleted any *Business Planning: Taxation Q&A 2018* questions which are too specific to ethics in connection with taxation specifically.

will not really be for concluding whether the ethical issue is right or wrong: rather, **the marks will be for the quality of argument** and the number of different issues considered in determining what actions the advisory firm and, just as importantly, the client should take.

The examiners were also keen to indicate that they will sometimes include an issue which appears to be an ethical problem initially but which, after further analysis, is in fact not a problem at all. A good example of this occurred in Q2 of the real July 2014 paper where at first sight it may have appeared that the client had a moral commitment to a particular stakeholder group but the model answer in fact argues that, with the passage of time, this commitment will have changed in nature.

Finally, the examiners were **very strongly critical** of candidates who attempted ethics first – this was not perhaps for the reason you may expect (i.e. examiner frustrations at apparent "mark-grabbing" from the easier elements) but rather because, based on the previous 2 points, the examiners do not believe that it is possible to write a good enough and nuanced answer if you just dive in and make the most obvious points. **You should instead become more familiar with the scenario and the interactions between different elements**.

We would actually argue for a **hybrid** approach – we agree with the examiners that, given the need to find the nuances, it is a mistake to write ethics first … but at the same time **we would not leave ethics until last** (and it is often tested in the final Task) because these are some relatively easy marks. Instead, we would encourage you to look at the ethical issues, **make initial notes** and then get on with some other Tasks whilst having it in mind to **add to your plan on ethical issues as you go along** – you should then ensure that you do not write up your ethical element last but perhaps **two-thirds of the way through your attempt**. Therefore just as you **should not overreact to ethical issues in the scenario** you **should not overreact to this advice of the examiners** and always do ethics in the place indicated by the Task list because **you could end up rushing a relatively easy section**.

Therefore the 3 main rules for SBM issues are:

---

1. Do not **overreact** – not all ethical issues will be moral disasters or require immediate resignation and with the correct **Recommendations** it may be possible to move forward positively

2. Look out for matters which are ethical problems at first sight but which are **ultimately not necessarily huge concerns**

3. **Do not do your ethics section first but also do not do it last** – you need to "warm up" to the scenario and appreciate the nuances fully before you start writing but leaving the ethics section to the point at which it is mentioned in the Task list is not necessarily a good idea and could represent a "time trap" trick by the examiners

---

Overall, in SBM ethics responses, try to look for the nuances and consider the position of different stakeholders, using the analytical frameworks discussed below.

17.3   Ethics Analytical Frameworks for SBM

To help you find the nuances and structure your answer under appropriate headings, here are a few frameworks to use (see our MAPs for reminders):

Framework 1 – Case Study Approach: IIR Framework

Given the skills "bridge" to Case Study, using our recommended Issue-Impact-Recommendations (IIR) framework developed for Case Study[87] should give you a relevant approach in SBM and has the added advantage of getting you used to an approach that you **must** use in Case Study.

> **Issue** – clearly explain why there is a potential ethical problem, using moral language such as "breach of confidentiality", "breach of distrust", "lack of integrity" and so on

> **Impact** – clearly explain how significant the issue is, considering the different stakeholder groups (and considering that there will likely be differential impact on different groups)

> **Recommendations** – clearly explain how the client should deal with the issue (demonstrating the **Recommendations** Case skills "lens")

Framework 2 – Institute of Business Ethics: TEF Framework

The following 3 issues should be considered under the TEF approach:

Transparency – is the client being open, honest and upfront with affected parties or is information being unethically withheld for self-interested reasons?

Effect – who is impacted by the issue and how serious is the impact? (Consider different stakeholders and recognise the likelihood of differential impact/effect on each group of stakeholders.)

Fairness – would a reasonable, informed but independent third party view the action as fair to all parties?

We suggest that you consider this approach as we know that the Business Strategy and Technology Professional Level paper frequently invokes **TEF** – some of the SBM examiner team also work on the Business Strategy and Technology paper and a Business Strategy and Technology perspective is of course relevant to practical business advisory points.

Framework 3 – ICAEW Ethical Conflict Resolution: The 6 Steps

According to several Professional Level Study Manuals, the following 6 steps should be applied – therefore you may wish to use these 6 ideas to help guide your own answer:

---

[87] See our book *Cracking Case™ – How to Pass the ACA Case Study* for a detailed explanation of IIR: there is not really any choice over framework in Case Study – IIR is what you **must** use so why not get practising for this future challenge in your preparations for SBM?

Establish the:

1. Relevant **facts**

2. Relevant **parties**

3. Ethical **issues** involved

4. Fundamental **principles** related to the matter

5. Established **internal procedures**

6. **Alternative** courses of action

Framework 4 – ICAEW Code Principles: The 5 Core Principles

By now you really should be able to remember the 5 ICAEW Code principles by heart – you can use this ability as a framework because an SBM ethical issue will generally involve **at least 2-3 of these principles** – therefore working methodically through the 5 principles should yield some different and nuanced points:

ICAEW Code Principles

1. Integrity

2. Objectivity

3. Professional competence and due care

4. Confidentiality

5. Professional behaviour

Framework 5 – Threats and Safeguards

This framework works particularly well when looking at ethical issues involving the advisory firm (something that does tend to crop up in SBM: see discussion below). Essentially, you work through a checklist of potential threats, using the terms that should be familiar from the Professional Level (particularly Audit & Assurance), and hopefully find 2-3 different areas together with **Recommendations** on how to deploy **safeguards** to reduce the ethical problem. Typical threats include:

- **Self-interest** threat (very common in SBM)

- **Self-review** threat

- **Advocacy** threat

- **Familiarity** or **trust** threat

- **Intimidation** threat

Safeguards are various and depend on the situation. Essentially, think of a reasonable solution to each of the above threats. Be careful of giving too much of an "auditor ethics approach" to your answer: generally the SBM paper will indicate that the **advisory firm is not the auditor of the client** so **conflicts and threats** will be of a different nature.

17.4   It is Great to Have 5 Frameworks – But Which One Is Best?

You should choose the framework which you feel allows you to write up the matter most convincingly – but also do have a look at the time remaining when deciding what to do (the IIR and TEF frameworks are much quicker to write up as there are only 3 elements rather than 5 or 6 issues under the ICAEW frameworks – however, if you do have the luxury of plenty of time, then there will probably be more marks available using the ICAEW 5 and 6 element frameworks). Ideally, the framework you choose will generate some meaningful Recommendations to fulfil this Case Study/SBM marking "lens".

At the same time, the frameworks are merely there to stimulate ideas – and it is these **ideas which will be rewarded regardless of whether you have used all elements of a framework or have perhaps even mixed points from different frameworks: purity of framework usage is not what is being assessed so do not worry**. At the same time, attempting an SBM ethics writeup with no framework at all is a very bad idea indeed and will quickly lead you into a low scoring and directionless waste of time.

17.5   Ethical Issues in SBM Papers

Having reviewed the ethical frameworks that you could deploy, we will now look at some of the ways in which ethics has been tested in SBM papers. Remember that, according to the examiners (see chapter 18), one of the key themes in SBM ethics issues will be the need to take a **nuanced or careful approach, avoiding extreme positions**. The examiners have also confirmed (see chapter 18) that some examination papers may set scenarios that, after careful consideration, are **not in fact serious ethical issues at all** (despite how things may seem on the surface) – therefore do not always assume (as you can at Professional Level) that there is something problematical in the scenario.

As we will see below, this concept of nuance is definitely evident in the 8 papers set to date but less so in the SBM Sample Paper.

July 2014 Real Examination Paper: Ethical Issues

Changing Supplier: The Status of a Previous Commitment

In this scenario (part of Q2), the client company had made a promise 10 years ago to use a particular supplier: the client company had offered several employees a lower level of redundancy payment on the understanding that the client company would provide continuing business to the supplier and therefore the employees affected could move to the supplier and achieve job security. The ethical dilemma was whether now, 10 years later and with a change in circumstances, it would be acceptable to use an alternative supplier. Aspects of the model answer to note include:

- The answer starts by commenting on what the ethical principle is (honesty).

- The principle is then applied: was it honest for the chairman, 10 years ago, to act in the way that he did?

- The next consideration was that this commitment was made a long time ago, on commercial terms and therefore the passage of time has changed the position, with the commitment becoming less binding. At the same time, there could be an argument that a reduced level of obligation is now owed to employees who were made specific promises at the time.

- In fact, maintaining this supplier (if they are not considered to be the best choice on commercial grounds) could be a breach of an ethical duty to act in the interests of the shareholders of the company.

Hopefully you can see that the challenge here was to **unpick the issue carefully** and **identify the different stakeholders** and the different ethical issues affecting each set (supplier, ex-employees, shareholders). The model answer provides some value added advice by considering the shareholders: we can consider this to be value added advice because it extends beyond the most obvious stakeholders indicated in the question (supplier, ex-employees).

The structure of the answer is to first set out the ethical principle and then apply it to the question, just as we have advised above with our reference to ethical frameworks. The answer also applies the **Conclusions & Recommendations** skills lens (see chapter 4) by advising the client on what it should do (such as considering making payments to ex-employees).

Changing Supplier: The Finance Director's Brother and Related Party Issues

In this scenario (also part of Q2), the Finance Director of the client company had declared a conflict of interest due to her brother being on the Board of one of the suppliers that she was proposing.

Again the answer starts by setting out the ethical principle (this time a potential conflict of interest).

This time a clear ethical concern was found and therefore the answer next moved on to consider safeguards:

- Transparency by declaring an interest openly to the Board (as has in fact already been done)

- Minimisation of the decision-making role of the affected party (as has in fact already been implemented as other proposals from other directors are being actively considered)

The answer then ends with consideration of a possible intimidation threat against the Chartered Accountant if the arguments of the Finance Director were resisted. Again, the safeguards of transparency and openness were mentioned.

In this answer, the structure was again to start with the ethical principles and then to apply these to the scenario. Notice that the nuance in this case was the fact that safeguards were in fact already being applied so again there was no need to resort to extreme points such as "sack the Finance Director".

Overall, on the basis of the above 2 issues from the real July 2014 examination, we might say that **calm description of principles and impact** would be an appropriate approach.

November 2014 Real Examination Paper: Ethical Issues

Inappropriate Use of Forklift Trucks

In this scenario (part of Q1) a journalist indicated to the client company that he had evidence that forklift trucks were being used indoors, causing harm to workers. The client company was alleged not to give clear warnings that the trucks should not be used indoors.

Once again we can see a nuanced or complex position: arguably, it could be considered to be common sense not to use a diesel-powered vehicle in a confined space and therefore it was the actions of others, rather than the direct actions of the client, that were a problem.

On this occasion, the ethical framework used appears to have been the ICAEW's own approach: it was stated that the first action should be to establish the full facts of the situation by checking the instructions and procedures issued. There should also be checks of the client's legal liability as this would depend on the country being considered: therefore legal advice should be sought. It was also stated that the client company should consider the impact on the perceptions of all stakeholders.

Role of the Adviser Company

Related to the same Q1 scenario, the second ethical issue to consider involved the implications for the advisory company (i.e. you and your Partner) of being asked to give advice and support to the client regarding the potential publication of the journalist's information.

The framework applied was the same as above, with the first point being mentioned in the answer being to **establish the facts**. The ethical principles of **transparency** and **honesty** were then mentioned.

Other points to note regarding the specific issue of being an advisory firm in the middle of this issue include:

- The advisory firm must not act outside its areas of expertise

- The advisory firm must consider whether an illegal act has been committed and must investigate its duty to disclose this to the appropriate authorities in the relevant jurisdiction. This will require the advisory firm to take its own legal advice

- Supporting the client could lead to an advisory threat and this would not be appropriate

You should note these kinds of points and the style of answer as it seems likely that the advisory firm could again be put in a difficult position in future questions: surely the advisory firm will be asked to help the client company within another future ethical issue?

Important Note on the 2014 Real Examinations

From the above, we can see that each ethical scenario has tended to have 2 different dimensions to assess. In the July 2014 paper, the scenario was whether to change supplier and the different dimensions were (1) the previous commitment to employees and (2) the conflict of interest involving the Finance Director. In the November 2014 paper, the scenario was the inappropriate use of forklift trucks and the different dimensions were (1) whether appropriate instructions had been issued to users and (2) the extent to which the advisory company could offer support regarding the potential publication of information by a journalist.

Therefore, you should try to look for at least 2 different elements to the issue. In our view, being conscious of the **different stakeholders** who could be affected should usually generate an appropriate set of points.

July 2015 Real Examination Paper: Ethical Issues

Use of confidential information

In this scenario (part of Q1), an ex-member of the client staff became aware of a deal between a potential collaborating company and a specific individual. This was a relatively black-and-white answer with a breach of confidentiality occurring and possible disciplinary procedures if the individual was a member of a professional body such as the ICAEW.

The only element of "nuance" required was to check what the terms of the employee's employment contract said.

Possible intimidation threat?

In this element of the question, the "nuance" was that a particular offer to purchase goods in specified circumstances was an offer made to a **company** rather than an individual: for this reason it could not reasonably be considered to be an intimidation threat whereas it might have been such a threat if the same offer had been made to an individual. Here we can see that the examiners are trying to suck you into saying that the threat level is too high or withdrawing from the opportunity, based on a "black-and-white" approach.

In fact, the ethical risk in this scenario was that the share deal would not be at market value – this was a less obvious point than the potential intimidation threat so make sure you look beyond the obvious.

Possible self-interest threat?

Various other aspects of Q1 in this examination related to possible favourable terms for particular individuals. Students were required to state that this could be to the detriment of the company and this would make it unethical. The solution each time was to use "transparency" and to disclose the way in which information has been acquired. The Board or Chairman should also have been informed.

Finally, there was brief reference to the fact that the Bribery Act could be relevant and legal advice should be acquired once the facts were established. However, there was no need to go into any further detail on the Bribery Act than this: just one sentence was enough.

November 2015 Real Examination Paper: Ethical Issues

In this paper, ethics was again tested in Q1, this time for 7 marks.

Before looking at the answer itself, we would note that the "skills assessed" stated in the model answer markscheme serve as a very useful general summary of what you are trying to do with ethics in SBM:

> "Set out the ethical principles in a structured argument"
>
> "Consider a range of actions and use judgement to recommend the most appropriate"

The above 2 sentences really do put it very well.

Possible inducement

Candidates were supposed to say that it was first necessary to establish the facts and to understand that the claims made by one party would probably be denied or resisted by the other party. It was then stated that it is particularly difficult to establish the facts if the matter has been oral rather than written in nature.

It was then stated that the Bribery Act could be relevant and there could also be a fraud taking place if the inducement leads to a decision that favours the Directors rather than other stakeholders.

It was then advised to take legal advice and it was noted that no inducement had yet been given so the issue was only a **potential** problem in the future.

The key ethical issue was self-interest: i.e. the Directors would be acting in their own interest rather than for the shareholders to whom they owe a fiduciary duty.

The TEF framework was then applied under separate headings. The issue of "honesty" was also then discussed in addition to the TEF elements.

Finally, a "Response" section was provided to offer a clear recommendation. This section contained 3 paragraphs and was fairly detailed, showing the importance of giving recommendations in SBM. The initial action was to speak to the Board and then to consider not acting for the company if there

362

were reasonable grounds to suspect that an inducement had been given. The advisory firm was also told to seek legal advice as to whether they should disclose the matter to the police.

Although this looks like a relatively strong approach to take (above we have seen examiner comments that resigning from the engagement is too rash an action to take), the decision to withdraw was only mentioned after various other ways in which it may be possible to continue to act. In fact, the very final point mentioned was that if the negotiations for the takeover were completed before the start of negotiations regarding Director remuneration contracts, then this would again be a way for the advisory firm to continue to act – it would suggest that negotiations on the takeover would not be influenced by simultaneous negotiations regarding Director remuneration.

July 2016 Real Examination Paper: Ethical Issues

Favourable treatment to a supplier

In this scenario (part of Q1) concerns were raised regarding certain transactions between the client company and a supplier linked to the nephew of the owner of the adviser's client company. The owner had refused to discuss the matter with other Board members.

The first point noted in the model answer related to professional scepticism: The source of some of the information was simply a casual conversation with a personal assistant of the business owner, rather than something that had been verified.

The model answer then went on to say that if the family relationship was substantiated, then there could be a conflict of interest as the business owner may be promoting personal family interests ahead of the interests of the company. The model answer then reviewed issues such as director responsibilities, governance issues in not permitting discussion of the issue, intimidation threats caused by the business owner and issues of confidentiality – certain Board members had passed on information about the matter to the company's advisers.

The ethical framework used was the TEF (Transparency, Effect, Fairness) framework. Action points included obtaining advice from the ICAEW helpline, avoiding tipping off, raising the issue formally at a Board meeting and recording the response in the minutes and potentially outvoting the business owner if it was the considered view of the other Directors that the supplier should be removed. There were also concerns that legal advice should be obtained in case the transaction was illegal.

November 2016 Real Examination Paper: Ethical Issues

In this scenario (part of Q1) the non-executive chairman of the client proposed to make a significant number of share option-holders redundant to prevent the future dilution of the company's share capital upon exercise of the options. The non-executive chairman suggested providing 2 different reasons for the redundancies based on recent changes in the number of staff being supervised and financial performance. The non-executive chairman said that he wished to make enough redundancies to prevent around 60% of the options vesting.

The model answer begins by explaining that ethics is all about "doing the right thing" and that it is first necessary to establish the facts in full. The model answer then explains that any action not in compliance with employment law would be unethical. The answer notes that the chairman appeared to be acting in the interests of a particular section of the shareholders (those who could be affected by a dilution of their shareholdings) rather than acting in the interests of the company or shareholders as a body – this is stated to be a breach of his fiduciary duty as a director.

The ethical framework used was the TEF (Transparency, Effect, Fairness) framework. Action points included insisting that the client took full legal advice and informing the client that the adviser firm would cease to act for the client, explaining to the Board the reasons for its resignation, if the legal advice suggested that the actions could be illegal. It was also highlighted in the model answer that the adviser firm must be clear that its report on performance would be an objective assessment and would not be affected by any particular purpose that the non-executive chairman wished to use the information for (in this case, the non-executive chairman was suggesting that redundancies could be made because financial performance was not acceptable, thus implying that the advisers should provide a negative appraisal of recent performance).

We would note that the answer here is very detailed and therefore potentially a good example to follow for your own answer if you wish to use the TEF approach. At the same time, it would be difficult to include all points in the model answer in the time available, given that there were only the usual 7 marks available for ethics issues in this instance.

As always, you should consider the impact on **all** stakeholders and make the point that directors have a fiduciary duty to promote the interests of the company as a whole and must not act for any particular section of stakeholders. You should also point out, on behalf of the adviser firm, that advisory work will be objective at all times and will not be affected by any specific purpose for which it appears the client needs the information i.e. the adviser firm will resist any intimidation threats fully.

July 2017 Real Examination Paper: Ethical Issues

Use of low quality raw materials

In this scenario (part of Q1), the client company was proposing to use lower quality wheat in its bread in order to save costs. The relevant contract said that the company would make products "using high quality wheat" but the Production Director argued that the statement did not say that the products had to use "entirely high-quality wheat". The Production Director also suggested that the company could exploit the vagueness of the term "high-quality". Finally, the Production Director suggested that it would be possible to change the ingredients used in producing the bread without consumers noticing.

Accidental receipt of a confidential email

As a second element to Q1 in the same paper, a confidential email from the Production Director regarding the proposed change in ingredients had accidentally been sent to the partner of the advisory firm for which the candidate worked.

The model answer begins by stating that ethics pertains to "whether a particular behaviour is deemed acceptable in the context under consideration". The model answer then states that it is first necessary

364

to establish the facts. In this case, the facts are stated to be fairly clear as the content of the email is straightforward.

In relation to the use of low quality raw materials, the model answer indicates that the key ethical issue is one of transparency. The answer states that the problem is not that lower grade materials are being used in itself – rather, the problem is that this fact has not been disclosed and there are indications that the Production Director is trying to deceive its customer and also the market generally. The model answer notes that this could amount to fraud if there is a deliberate attempt to deliver something which was not agreed. The model answer states that the wording of the contract is relevant but there could be an implied understanding which goes beyond the legal conditions. The model answer notes that there could still be a negative "effect" even if there is no change in the quality of the bread because business trust could be damaged through actions that are not transparent.

Action points on the use of low quality raw materials included: checking the terms of the contract are clear regarding the quality of the wheat in use, who is to decide the appropriate level of quality and any disclosure of changes. If the contract terms are clear then compliance with the terms of the contract may be an appropriate ethical defence for the company. There should be consideration of the quality of the bread produced as this is ultimately what the company's customer needs to provide to its own customers (the ultimate consumers of the product): the quality of one input used in making the bread is not the final output and therefore potentially not something that the ultimate consumers of the product may be interested in. If there is any doubt, then disclosure would ensure transparency.

In relation to the accidental receipt of a confidential email, the model answer states that the mistake has been made by the client company rather than by the advisory firm. The answer also notes that the advisory firm may have inadvertently read the email because it may not be obvious that the email was meant to be read only by the internal management team (although the email is marked as "CONFIDENTIAL", it would not be possible to determine who the email is directed to without reading the email itself i.e. the email was not marked as "CONFIDENTIAL – use of BBB Board only", for example). This means that there was probably no deliberate attempt to breach confidentiality by the advisory firm.

Action points on the accidental receipt of a confidential email included informing the company that the advisory firm had received and read the email. Given that the partner had read the email, the partner should confront the Board of the company about how it intends to respond to the suggestions of the Production Director and whether there is any intention to deceive and defraud the customer. If this is the case, then the advisory firm should consider resigning.

November 2017 Real Examination Paper: Ethical Issues

In this examination, Q1 concerns a potential management buyout (MBO) scenario. The Finance Director of the client company had informed the other 3 Directors that, after the MBO, he would only want to work part-time as the Finance Director. The same individual had stated that, like the other 3 directors, he would be willing to contribute £250,000 to acquire shares in the company. The Finance Director had not informed the other Directors of any of the roles he would be taking up. Following this the Chief Executive of the company subject to the proposed MBO had held informal discussions with the CEO of the company's parent. The CEO had informed the Chief Executive that the Finance

Director was in the process of arranging a new contract with the parent company which would use up all of his working time not spent at the company subject to the proposed MBO. The CEO stated that the Finance Director intended to announce his new contract with the parent company but only after the MBO deal had been signed.

The model answer states that ethics pertains to "whether a particular behaviour is deemed acceptable in the context under consideration". In short, it is therefore about "doing the right thing". The model answer then states that it is first necessary to establish the facts. In this case, some of the information is received from the CEO of a company with whom the management team is negotiating a deal so the CEO may not be an entirely reliable source in this instance. Other elements of the facts to be verified include the stage which the negotiations of the Finance Director's contract have reached: it is possible that the contract may be a long way away from being agreed or there may be other reasons why the Finance Director is interested in the role. Overall, it would be better to confirm what the facts actually are.

If it is determined to be true that the Finance Director does intend to sign the contract with the parent company, then the primary ethical issues will be transparency and a conflict of interest. In the current context, any dealings with the parent company should be disclosed fully to the other Directors because the management team as a whole is negotiating with that same parent company for the MBO. It would probably be advisable to disclose the matter to all other interested parties as well, as a matter of business trust. There will also be a conflict of interest because the Finance Director's income would come partly from the success of the MBO but also partly from work for the parent company: the Finance Director might feel that he would be jeopardising the potential contract with the parent company by seeking the very best deal for the MBO team. If the Finance Director engages in any deliberate conduct to change the value of the consideration in return for payments from the parent company, this may be illegal and legal advice should be taken.

Other ethical issues to consider include: "Effect" – if the terms are unduly favourable to the parent company then some stakeholders may lose out, including the MBO team and the banks financing the deal; "Fairness" – if the terms are affected by the personal interests of the Finance Director then this may not be fair as it does not satisfy any arm's-length conditions – it would also be unfair to the other Directors who have placed trust in the Finance Director as a future colleague.

The model answer mentions the following action points or recommendations: as an ICAEW Chartered Accountant, the Finance Director is bound by the ICAEW ethical code. The advisory firm should obtain advice such as from the ICAEW helpline but should not speak to the Finance Director as this could constitute "tipping off". The matter should be raised formally at a Board meeting and the Finance Director should be asked for an explanation, which should be recorded in the Board minutes. It may be that the MBO team no longer wants the Finance Director to remain part of the team after the deal takes place but this would need to be discussed further with stakeholders. The Board should inform stakeholders such as its bank, in the interests of business trust and transparency.

The final point in the model answer relates to action points or recommendations for the candidate themselves. As an ICAEW Chartered Accountant, the candidate should consider reporting the Finance Director to the ethics committee if, on the basis of the established facts, there is reasonable suspicion that there has been an ethical, legal or other disciplinary breach by the Finance Director.

SBM Sample Paper: Ethical Issues

Valuation of a Pension Fund Deficit

This scenario related to a request from the client company to accept a valuation engagement regarding a pension fund deficit within a potential acquisition target.

The model answer this time used the ICAEW Code as the ethical Framework and identified 2 key principles which could be threatened:

- **Professional competence and due care** – the advisory firm may not have the skills necessary for such a specialist engagement: this applies particularly to defined benefit funds where various expert estimates are required on investment returns, mortality, wage inflation and so on

- **Independence (conflicts of interest)** – the advisory firm would be acting for both the target and the bidding company: this would place it in a conflict of interest because it would have access to confidential information that could be used to the benefit of the bidding company. This provides such a severe risk that the engagement could not be accepted

In the Sample Paper, then, the issue of ethics was a **more traditional "serious issue"**, resulting in a conclusion which is more in line with the "withdraw" from the engagement type points which are typical of Professional Level papers. **This is a noticeable difference from the more nuanced SBM past papers.**

17.6   Ethics Appendix: Selected Q&A Questions

Useful Ethics Questions from Our _Financial Management Q&A 2018_

State 4 types of adviser that a business could turn to.

Accountants, including firms with a corporate finance department

High street banks

Investment banks

Solicitors

What are the 5 fundamental principles of ICAEW ethical guidance with respect to corporate finance?

Integrity

Objectivity

367

Professional competence and due care

Confidentiality

Professional behaviour

Note that these are the standard principles referred to under the ethics sections of other papers.

What is meant under the heading of Integrity?

Honesty and fair dealing, with behaviour that is not corrupted by self-interest and will not be influenced by the interests of other parties.

A member must not be associated with information that is false or misleading or supplied recklessly.

What is meant under the heading of Objectivity?

The state of mind which has regard to all considerations relevant to the task in hand but no other with no bias, conflict of interest or undue influence of others.

What 6 elements are mentioned under the heading of Professional competence and due care?

Having appropriate professional knowledge and skill

Having a continuing awareness and an understanding of relevant technical, professional and business developments

Exercising sound and independent judgement

Acting diligently i.e. carefully, thoroughly, on a timely basis and in accordance with the requirements of an assignment

Acting in accordance with applicable technical and professional standards

Distinguishing clearly between an expression of opinion and an assertion of fact

---

What elements are included under the heading of Professional behaviour? [6]

Complying with relevant laws and regulations

Avoiding any action that discredits the profession

Conducting oneself with courtesy and consideration

Being honest and truthful regarding marketing

Avoiding making exaggerated claims about what the accountant can do or the qualifications and experience they possess

Avoiding making disparaging references to the work of others

What 4 categories of activity are stated to be covered by ethical guidance?

General corporate finance advice

Acting as adviser in relation to takeovers and mergers

Underwriting and marketing or placing securities on behalf of a client

Acting as sponsor or nominated adviser under the Listing Rules and the AIM Rules respectively

---

What 4 issues are mentioned under the heading of Statutory and other regulatory requirements under the section on General principles applicable to all professional accountants (in practice and in business)?

Must be aware of and comply with current legislative and regulatory measures and professional guidance governing corporate finance assignments

Required to comply with the City Code on Takeovers and Mergers

Must draw attention at the outset to the legislative and regulatory responsibilities which apply to the client or his employer

Should draw attention to his own responsibilities under professional ethical guidance

---

Professional accountants should always have regard for all shareholders when advising on corporate finance: true or false?

False – this will normally be the case but the accountants may be specifically acting for a single or defined group thereof in which case they can focus on this specific group.

What 2 rules in relation to the preparation of documents are mentioned in the Study Manual?

Any document must be prepared in accordance with normal professional standards of integrity and objectivity and with a proper degree of care

Must ensure that roles and responsibilities are clearly described in all public documents and circulars and that each adviser is named

---

Which particular threats are mentioned in connection with provision of corporate finance advice? [5]

Self-interest threat

Self-review threat

Advocacy threat

Familiarity or trust threat

Intimidation threat

Which type of work is more likely to lead to acute instances of the above threats: work for a non-assurance client or work for an assurance client?

Work for an assurance client – here the self-interest and advocacy threats are likely to be particularly concerning.

An audit firm can never provide corporate finance advice to an assurance client: true or false?

False – there is nothing improper necessarily in this and it may be in the best interests of a company for corporate finance advice to be provided by its auditor.

Which particular corporate finance activity contains an extremely strong element of advocacy and hence will be incompatible with the objectivity required for the reporting roles of an auditor or reporting accountant?

Marketing or underwriting of securities

State 4 safeguards which can be used where a professional accountant in public practice acts or continues to act for 2 or more clients having obtained consent?

Use of different partners and teams for different clients with each having separate internal reporting lines

All necessary steps being taken to prevent the leakage of confidential information between different teams and sections within the firm

Regular review of the situation by a senior partner or compliance officer not personally involved with either client

Advising the client to seek additional independent advice, where it is appropriate

---

Which type of accounting practice will be unable to apply many of the above safeguards?

A sole practitioner

An accountant can always accept an engagement if all relevant clients consent: true or false?

False – it is possible that there is a fundamental conflict which cannot be measured effectively and the accountant must therefore decline the engagement, even if clients are happy to proceed

---

What 2 rules are mentioned regarding documents prepared for client and public use?

For documents prepared solely for the client and its professional advisers it should be a condition of the engagement that the document should be disclosed to other parties without the prior written consent of the firm.

A professional accountant in public practice must take responsibility for anything published under his name provided that he consented to such publication – the published document should make clear the client for whom the accountant is acting.

What may an auditor or reporting accountant do in respect of dealing in, underwriting or promoting shares for their client?

None of these activities would be permitted – this would give rise to an advocacy threat, self-review threat and self-interest threat which could threaten the professional accountant in public practice.

A professional accountant can never act as a sponsor or nominated adviser (as defined under the UK Listing Authority's Listing Rules or the London Stock Exchange's Alternative Investment Market (AIM) Rules): true or false?

False – it is possible that no conflict will arise but at the same time there could be a threat of objectivity as the auditor or reporting accountant could owe different duties to different parties.

A separate broker should be appointed to take responsibility for any underwriting or marketing of the company's shares.

Useful Ethics Questions from Our *Business Planning: Taxation Q&A 2018*

State the 5 principal threats in accountancy engagements.

1. Self-interest

2. Self-review

3. Advocacy

4. Familiarity

5. Intimidation

State the 2 fundamental types of safeguards (i.e. the basic sources of safeguards, not safeguards themselves).

Safeguards created by

1. the profession, legislation or regulation

2. the work environment

State the 6 fundamental elements of the conflict resolution process.

Consideration of

1. Relevant facts

2. Relevant parties

3. Ethical issues involved

4. Fundamental principles related to the matter

5. Established internal procedures

6. Alternative courses of action

Note – this would be an effective structure to use in your examination answer.

State 6 safeguards created by the profession, legislation or regulation.

1. Educational, training and experience requirements

2. CPD

3. Corporate governance regulations

4. Professional standards

5. Professional or regulatory monitoring and disciplinary procedures

6. External review by a legally empowered third party of the reports, returns, communications or information produced by a professional accountant

---

State 2 safeguards designed to deter unethical behaviour.

1. An effective and well publicised complaints system

2. An explicitly stated duty to report breaches of ethical requirements

---

State the 3 situations in which a professional accountant is permitted to disclose confidential information.

1. Disclosure is permitted by law and authorised by the client or employer

2. Disclosure is required by law

3. Professional duty or right to disclose, when not prohibited by law

---

State 4 factors to take into account when considering disclosure.

1. Whether the interests of any third parties could be harmed by disclosure

2. Whether the information to be disclosed is known and substantiated

3. Type of communication that is expected and to whom it is addressed

4. Whether or not information is privileged, for example under Legal Professional Privilege

---

Give 6 examples of potential conflicts of interest in accounting/taxation work.

1. Client has specific interests which conflict with those of the firm

2. Financial involvements between the client and the firm

3. Husband and wife in a divorce settlement

4. Company and its directors in their personal capacity

5. Partnership and its partners in their personal capacity

6. Two competing clients

Give 8 examples of safeguards which might be deployed in the case of potential conflicts of interest.

1. Notify the client

2. Notify all relevant parties

3. Notify the client that the accountant may act for other clients in the same market or sector

4. Use of separate engagement teams

5. Procedures to limit access to information

6. Clear guidelines to members of the team on security and confidentiality

7. Use of actual and perceived confidentiality agreements

8. Regular review of safeguards by an independent senior individual

---

State 7 procedures in respect of anti-money laundering.

1. Register with the appropriate supervisory authority

2. Appoint a Money Laundering Reporting Officer and implement internal reporting procedures

3. Train staff

4. Establish internal procedures relating to risk management to deter and prevent

5. Carry out customer Due Diligence

6. Verify the identity of new clients

7. Report suspicions to NCA, using a suspicious activity report (SAR)

How long do the following records need to be kept?

1. **Records in relation to client identification**

2. **Records in relation to transactions**

1. 5 years from termination of the client relationship

2. 5 years from when all activities in relation to the transaction were completed

---

Who has legal obligations to protect information under the Data Protection Act 1998?

Anyone who handles personal information

Generally, every organisation that processes personal information must notify the Information Commissioner's Office (ICO) unless it is exempt from notification. According to the Study Manual, what is the only exemption applicable to practising firms of accountants?

Where computers are not used in any way to process or store any client information, records or correspondence

---

What type of offence is a failure to notify under Data Protection Act rules?

A strict liability criminal offence

State the maximum penalties for the following, assuming that they are tried in the Crown Court:

1. **Tipping off**

2. **Contravention of systems requirements**

3. **Failure to report**

4. **Main money laundering offences**

1. 5 years

2. 2 years

3. 5 years

4. 14 years

In addition, in all 4 cases an unlimited fine is possible.

Which set of regulations governs the matter of supervisory bodies with respect to anti-money laundering?

The Money Laundering Regulations 2007 (the Regulations)

According to the Study Manual, which 2 aspects of the Regulations are particularly relevant to accountancy firms with respect to anti-money laundering?

1. Firms must determine the extent of customer Due Diligence measures which are appropriate, applying a risk-sensitive basis depending on the type of client, business relationship and services

2. Firms must be able to demonstrate to their anti-money laundering supervisory authority that the extent of their customer Due Diligence measures is appropriate in view of the risks of money laundering

---

If a matter involves a conflict with or within an organisation, what should the professional accountant do?

Consider consulting with those charged with governance e.g. the Board

---

In addition to the above, what else should the professional accountant do when trying to resolve a conflict? [5]

- If the matter remains unresolved following the above 6 procedures, consult with other appropriate persons within the firm

- Document the issues and details of any discussions held

- Consider obtaining professional advice from the relevant professional body or legal advisers without breaching confidentiality

- Consider using the ICAEW confidential ethics helpline service

- Consider refusing to remain associated with the conflict if it still cannot be resolved based on the above

---

Chapter 18   Comments from the ICAEW Tutor Conferences

Learning Points

After reading this chapter, you must be able to:

1. understand the key points made by the examiners at recent ICAEW SBM workshops
2. integrate this advice into your own answering style
3. annotate your own personalised MAPs with reminders not to fall into any of your own bad habits

---

18.1   Comments from recent ICAEW Tutor Conferences

Every February, ICAEW holds a conference for all tuition companies with ICAEW-approved Partner in Learning status. A specific half day SBM workshop is held at each event. These workshops provide invaluable insights into what the **examiners are trying to do** with the examination and what both **strong** and **weak** candidates tend to do in their answers. In this chapter we therefore provide some highlights for you to **absorb** and **integrate** into your answering style.

18.2   SBM and the "Accountant in Business" Concept

The examiners have been very keen to emphasise that SBM is not designed as a **pure strategy or consulting examination**. The intention is that an "MBA student" should **not** be able to pass SBM as such a student would lack the necessary accounting knowledge. Instead, the paper is designed to test the role of the "**Accountant in Business**".

What does this mean in practice? It means that all SBM answers must try to adopt 2 perspectives:

1. **The strategy angle** – Does the relevant business change scenario work for the company? What are the strategic and operational risks that the company faces? What is the impact on cash?

2. **The financial reporting**[88] **angle** – What are the implications of the strategy for the financial statements (including reported profit, the SFP and earnings per share)? Does a change which is good from the "strategy angle" also have a good impact on the financial statements or is there a tension between the two?

The examiners were keen to stress that one of the best ways to adopt both angles in your answer is to start with the strategic aspects but then always consider whether there is a tension or not from a financial reporting perspective: in other words, go back to consider one of the very first tensions that

---

[88] The examiners generally use the term "corporate reporting" to refer to this angle or perspective but because we think this may lead to confusion with the separate Corporate Reporting ACA paper, we have adopted the term "financial reporting" to refer to this perspective. By "financial reporting" we do **not** just mean the lessons that you learned in the Financial Accounting & Reporting paper but also the new IFRS corporate reporting rules that you learn at the Advanced Level. (In some elements of the presentation, the examiners used the term "financial reporting" rather than "corporate reporting" which confirms the shared meaning of the term.)

you studied as an ACA student – the difference between **cash flows** and **accruals-based accounting**.

For example, does the project involve a large purchase of fixed assets at the start of the project life? If so, then that can cause an immediate one-off strain on **cash flow** (strategy angle) but will only affect the financial statements **slowly over time** as the assets are **depreciated gradually**.

Alternatively, does the strategy involve a finance lease? In this case, from the strategy angle it will **preserve cash** in the business but from the **financial reporting angle** there will now be several impacts on the SFP and also a finance cost IS charge which could affect interest cover (or other ratios) and therefore the valuation placed on the company could change, depending on how analysts respond to the changed IS position.

The same tensions can then also be given an ethical angle if there is some kind of pressure to adopt a particular financial reporting choice – for example, over revenue recognition or treatment as an operating versus financial lease.

The examiners stated that these additional financial reporting considerations are what the "Accountant in Business" can uniquely contribute, as compared with an MBA student or a student of business strategy in general.

Therefore always try to think of this difference between the way a businessperson may analyse cash flows and strategic impacts and the way a reporting accountant would highlight the impact on the financial statements.

At the same time, after advising tutors to instil this perspective in students, the examiners were careful to point out that **there will not** always **be a tension or conflict between the perspectives**: students should be equally prepared to say that something is good for cash flows **and** good for Earnings per Share, for example.

Despite this comment, we would predict that more scenarios will suggest a tension or conflict as this makes for a much more interesting scenario and is a better test of your ability to adopt the 2 different perspectives.

18.3 The Marks Range and Differences in Question Style

At the 2014 Tutor Conference, the examiners stated that the marks for Q1 could range from a minimum of 55 marks to a maximum of 65 marks – Q1 will therefore always account for more than half of the marks and in some examinations will carry **substantially** more weight.

This would mean that, based on allowing 2.1 minutes per mark[89], the amount of time to allocate to Q1 should range from a **minimum of 1h55** to a **maximum of 2h16**.

---

[89] As indicated in chapter 5, we recommend a multiple of less than 2.1 when calculating the **writing** time for a question but 2.1 can be used when allocating **total** time between Q1 and Q2. Alternatively, you can simply weight each question by the percentage of marks available i.e. if Q1 has 60 marks available then 60% x 210 minutes = 126 minutes should be allocated to Q1 (which is the same as 2.1 x 60).

Correspondingly, the marks range for Q2 will have to lie in the range of a minimum of 35 marks to a maximum of 45 marks. The time allocation would thus lie in the range of a **minimum of 1h14** to a **maximum of 1h35**.

At the same Tutor Conference, the examiners asked tutors to emphasise to candidates that Q1 should not just be regarded as the "bigger question" – the **style will be different**, with Q1 being a much more **integrated** question, with all requirements focusing on a single underlying problem, whilst Q2 can be looser in format **with requirements which may not all be as closely connected as Q1 and which can therefore cover a broader range of areas**. Q2 was stated to be very similar to the 40 mark questions in the previous Business Change examination under the old TI syllabus (Business Change Q1) but the SBM versions of this question style will have a wider topic range per the examiners' comments.

At the 2014 conference it was also indicated that the mini-Case SBM Q1 would generally involve providing candidates with one or more **problems to solve**: therefore solutions and recommendations will be expected. Q2 will then be used to **balance** the marks on the paper overall to ensure that the different topic areas of practical business advisory, financial reporting, Specialist Audit & Assurance and ethics reflect the intended mark allocation (see discussion below).

As we have explained with our balancing rule (Rule 8), you should take this into account in your mark estimations: if Q1 has very minimal financial reporting elements, for example, it is likely that any financial reporting issues in Q2 will contain a disproportionate amount of marks.

18.4   Reminders on How SBM is Marked

As indicated elsewhere in this book, SBM has been purposefully designed as a "bridge" to the final Case Study examination. In line with this philosophy, examiners will be using the standard 4 Case Study skills areas when designing and marking the SBM examination:

- **Assimilating & Using Information** – using information, providing analysis and appreciating the significance of the information

- **Structuring Problems & Solutions** – calculating or developing new information to solve a problem or to promote understanding

- **Applying Judgement** – identifying significant factors or issues and applying a sceptical or critical approach

- **Conclusions & Recommendations** – setting out advice, options and reservations based on the evidence (Conclusions skill) and formulating reasoned recommendations (Recommendations skill)

Although the above standard 4 skills areas will not be assessed in the highly unusual and specific way that they are in the Case Study examination[90], it is still helpful to think about these skills. We

---

[90] Please see our book *Cracking Case™ – How to Pass the ACA Case Study* for a detailed explanation of how the complex and unique Case Study competency-based marking approach works. This marking approach is completely different to SBM: however, the **skills** areas being assessed are common to SBM and Case Study.

have included reminders on our MAPs and we use simpler, short reminders as follows (see also chapter 4):

- Assimilating & Using Information: **use** and **analysis**

- Structuring Problems & Solutions: **developing new information** to **solve problems**

- Applying Judgement: identifying **important** issues and applying **scepticism**

- Conclusions & Recommendations: **concluding** and **recommending**!

At the Tutor Conference, the examiners reminded tutors that SBM has been purposely designed to leave it up to candidates to identify and structure the problem and solution: the question paper will not make it entirely clear what is required and candidates must use their judgement as to what to do and what to leave out.

The examiners explained that the difference between "Assimilating & Using Information" and "Structuring Problems & Solutions" is that the "Assimilating & Using Information" skill will involve **using information already given to candidates** whereas the "Structuring Problems & Solutions" skill will involve **calculating and using new numbers based on existing figures**.

Again, SBM does not apply these standard 4 skills areas as directly in the marking as in the Case Study examination but the framework does provide useful guidance as to what the examiners are expecting you to do, every time, in your answers. This is why we provide ample reminders of the skills involved on our MAPs. It is also why other chapters of this book use certain aspects of the Case Study approach to generate useful ideas for the kinds of points to write about in SBM.

You should also bear in mind that in SBM the marking does not work on the basis of a **half mark or full mark per point approach** (unlike at the Professional Level). Instead, the markers will apply "**holistic**" marking: this means that each Task has a "pool" of marks available as well as a "banding" system based on the standard of the answer e.g. strong, average, weak. The marker will read the whole Task and form an opinion as to whether the answer is strong, average or weak. Marks will then be allocated depending on how strong or how average the answer is: for example, if the marker decides that the answer to a 15 mark Task is fundamentally strong then they may have discretion to award a mark between 11 and 15 marks (say).

As a result of using this "holistic" approach, there is clearly an element of judgement: the marker will not look at each individual sentence and determine if it is worth a mark or not but will instead look at all sentences, the overall standard, whether all elements are covered to an equally good standard and then perhaps will look back at the above 4 standard skills areas. **Therefore, a good answer will have to have a good range of points across the different skills areas even if the question wording does not make this wholly clear**. This is another reason to bear in mind and memorise the 4 skills areas because they basically tell us what we should be doing in any given question.

The final standardised markscheme which is used by the markers to allocate the final marks, and therefore to determine whether you pass the examination, will be based on an initial assessment of student performance in the actual examination: in other words, **the examiners will take into account what the average student appears to be capable of and what that student tends to discuss when determining the final mark allocation**. Therefore, try to bear this in mind as a further perspective when deciding what to write about: there is no point going for any "Hollywood" or show-off points if most of the marks are going to be based on the average student.

As this section is quite dense yet contains vital clues on how to approach your writing, here is a brief summary of the key points:

- **Bear in mind the 4 skills areas** and try to ensure some coverage of each of them in your answers for each Task (except perhaps in the Tasks with a relatively small number of estimated marks and where guidance is very specific)

- **Holistic marking is subjective** and therefore you need to **impress** the examiner with a broad range of relevant points, covering the standard 4 skills areas – do not assume that if you have estimated that a Task has 10 marks then as long as you say 10 sensible things you will score full marks: **you must ensure that you are doing everything asked by the Task**

- **The markscheme is based on standardisation and the approach of the average student** – you do not need to do or say anything heroic to pass, you just need to cover the basics of the requirements well

18.5 New SBM Topics (Compared to the Old TI Paper in Business Change)

At recent Tutor Conferences, the examiners have provided a useful list of topics which have been **specifically added into the SBM syllabus**. As always, there does not seem to be any point for the examiners to add in syllabus content unless it is going to be tested so we recommend that you pay particular attention to these elements of the SBM learning materials:

- Strategic marketing and brand management

- Supply chain management

- Operations management

- Corporate governance[91] (meaning the appropriate governance structure for a business rather than testing the detailed rules of the UK Corporate Governance Code or similar rules)

- Human Resources Management

- Information strategy

- Performance management

- Treasury and working capital management

---

[91] The examiner team stated that Corporate Governance is a very important subject which is "close to the hearts" of the team. This topic was also extensively examined in the old Business Change paper, an examination set by the same team. Therefore we recommend that you revise corporate governance issues very well. See also chapter 11 for revision notes.

18.6   Financial Reporting Issues Will Be Given More Importance than Assurance

The examiners reminded tutors of the standard weighting of different topic areas in SBM:

Topic	Standard weighting
Strategy	35-45%
Finance, valuations & investment appraisal	30-40%
Financial reporting[92]	15-20%
Assurance	10%
Ethics	5-10%

We can see that financial reporting issues could potentially account for **twice** the number of marks as Specialist Audit & Assurance matters[93]. The examiners further indicated that financial reporting issues would normally be tested in several different sub-Tasks within a question rather than in one "lump" whereas **Assurance issues will tend to be just a single sub-Task**. This is consistent with the fact that there will be potentially double the number of marks for financial reporting as for assurance.

There will be an approximately equal weighting to strategy (meaning narrative points) and calculations (finance, valuations and investment appraisal): since there will be marks for narrative analysis of the calculations then we can conclude that there will be, overall, more marks for narrative aspects than numerical within these first 2 topics (see also our section on **Marks Balance Between Numerical and Narrative Marks** below).

At the 2015 SBM workshop, the examiners stated that ethics can feature in either question or both – **candidates should not assume that "Q2 is the ethics question"**, or vice versa.

The examiners offered some further expansion of the above topic areas to indicate to tutors which are the priority areas for revision:

Strategy (35-45%): Key Topics to Revise

- Business strategy
- Performance management
- Strategic marketing and brand management
- Business risk management
- Corporate governance
- Information strategy
- Human Resources Management
- Supply chain management
- Operations management

---

[92] See footnote 88 on our use of the term "financial reporting" to refer to corporate reporting issues.
[93] The term "Assurance" is used in the table as this is the standard ICAEW terminology: we use the term "Specialist Audit & Assurance".

On the strategy part of the syllabus, the examiners made the following observations:

- Corporate Governance issues should be studied under 2 areas: (1) How does Corporate Governance **help** a business to perform well? and (2) How is Corporate Governance used to **control** the performance of a company and its management?

- Information strategy now includes the use of Big Data, which was an addition to the 2015 Study Manual.

- Candidates should assume that there will always be an international aspect to every paper. Therefore any topics with an overseas element should be studied carefully: the risks of operating in overseas markets would be one such topic.

- Most strategy topics have been studied before in the Business Strategy and Technology and Financial Management papers but supply chain management and operations are considered to be "big new additions" at the SBM level and are also new compared to the predecessor Business Change at the Technical Integration level.

We always advise students to keep a close eye on any additions to the study materials – as an examiner, surely you do not add material unless you mean to **test** it in some way? This should hopefully give you some guidance as to what you should definitely look at in the somewhat mammoth SBM Study Manual: once again, Corporate Governance, Big Data, supply chain management and operations management are topics to start with.

In addition to the above syllabus topics, the examiners advised candidates to practise their data analysis skills, **meaning the ability to look at both financial and non-financial information, determine the key "big picture" changes and succinctly summarise these for the client**. The examiners summed up this skill as "making the numbers talk" or "bringing the numbers to life".

Finance, valuations & investment appraisal (30-40%): Key Topics to Revise

- Business and securities valuation
- Capital structure
- Financial reconstruction
- Small and medium company financing
- Equity instruments
- Fixed interest
- Derivatives
- Financial risk management
- International financial management
- Investment appraisal
- Treasury and working capital management

On the finance, valuation & investment appraisal part of the syllabus, the examiners made the following observations:

- Business and securities valuation should be taught not just on the basis of valuing a full entity/company but also in terms of looking at the valuation of debt and equity instruments specifically. The examiners highlighted that valuation of a bond would be tested as it has tended to be done badly by candidates. Overall, we suggest a thorough revision of Financial Management techniques is in order! (See also chapter 15 for a review of relevant numerical techniques and narrative points.)

- Additionally on the valuations topic, the examiners stated that the question data should be used by candidates to understand which valuation method is being requested. Inclusion of a discount rate would be a strong indication that a free cash flow model is needed whereas statements in relation to accounting profits would suggest that an earnings model was being requested.

- Candidates should assume that there will **always be an international aspect** to every paper. Therefore, revision of exchange rate risk management is definitely advisable.

Financial reporting (15-20%): Key Topics to Revise

- Leases
- Financing issues
- Group accounting methods and rules
- Any financial reporting issues that could impact on valuation matters

On the financial reporting part of the syllabus, the examiners made the following observations:

- Financial reporting issues will always stem from the underlying interest of the SBM paper in **business and financing issues**: therefore candidates should also think through the above lists for the previous 2 topic areas and consider which IFRSs are likely to be relevant.

- Two different types of financial reporting questions will be set and candidates should be prepared for both. The first type ("specific" or "closed" question) will ask a specific question on a particular financial reporting issue. For example, "explain the financial reporting consequences of the lease entered into by Example plc". The second type ("open") will not give a hint as to what the financial reporting issues are: candidates will have to actively identify these issues themselves and then discuss the financial statement impact. Candidates should be broadly familiar with this approach from the Financial Accounting & Reporting (FAR) paper: some FAR questions just ask for "the IFRS reporting treatment" of a series of issues whereas other questions are much more specific and assist the student to understand the target of the question more easily.

- The financial reporting narrative and explanation required from the candidate will be of "limited scope". By this, the examiners mean that most of the marks will be for identifying the issue, making it clear that you know the rules and then moving onto the next financial reporting (or other kind of sub-Task): the examiners do not want to see whole pages or even half pages of text copied out from the standards book or your own notes. **Therefore the amount of detail given should probably be less than in FAR**.

- The candidate should adopt the perspective of the "Accountant in Business" meaning that the **impact on the financial statements should be clearly, thoroughly but concisely explained: this is after all what the accounting profession can contribute regarding a**

385

strategy. The examiners emphasised that the financial reporting impact will not always necessarily be a key decision factor in the strategy – it could be that the benefits and risks or cash flows heavily weigh in favour of the project and it should definitely proceed but the accountant would merely note that EPS may fall due to higher depreciation charges etc. However, in other questions, it may be the case that the financial reporting impact is so significant that it determines whether the project takes place or, perhaps, helps the company to decide between 2 different options which have similar cash flows: perhaps one of these involves a high finance charge (based on a finance lease?) and therefore it harms interest cover and so is not as appropriate as another option with similar strategic impact (cash flows, risks and benefits etc).

- There will not necessarily be "a" correct financial reporting treatment that candidates are supposed to identify. The examiners gave the example of a lease question in November 2014 Q1 where the information was not sufficient to identify definitively whether the lease was an operating lease or a finance lease. Therefore candidates should not assume that they are being asked for "**the**" right answer as matters may deliberately be left vague.

Overall, in this section the examiners were definitely trying to emphasise to candidates that there are many different approaches that the exam paper could take: projects where the financial reporting implications must be noted but are not significant to the decision (or the opposite!); questions where the financial reporting has to be a certain specific way and therefore the directors are potentially acting unethically (or the opposite!). Whilst this may not therefore seem particularly helpful, it is always better to be prepared and therefore to realise that this is an **open examination and it could be that any particular exam paper is designed to direct you down one of several different alternative routes**.

Assurance (10%): Key Topics to Revise

- Avoid statutory audit and instead focus on specialist assurance areas
- Due Diligence
- Forecast financial information (e.g. a share issue or loan request)
- Agreed Upon Procedures

On the Assurance part of the syllabus, the examiners indicated that the Assurance points and scenario will arise from the business or finance scenario. Therefore, like the financial reporting topics, **the assurance questions will be driven by the scenario**. This means that you need to think about how assurance can arise in the context of business change, financing and valuations.

The good news is that there are **fewer of these specialist Assurance areas than there used to be under the old Business Change paper**. We would strongly recommend that you thoroughly revise chapters 10 to 14 of this book which review the following assurance areas from the Corporate Reporting Study Manual:

- Corporate Governance (treated as a Strategy topic by the SBM examiners: see above)
- Assurance and related services
- Environmental and social considerations
- Internal auditing

You can avoid the 4 chapters headed up as "The statutory audit" in the Corporate Reporting Study Manual for SBM (although obviously these areas will need to be known for the Corporate Reporting paper).

We would also recommend that you remember a very important difference between the **statutory audit material** which you need to know for the Corporate Reporting paper and the **specialist audit and assurance** material which you need to know for SBM: you may well be able to get through the statutory audit questions in Corporate Reporting by drawing largely on your Professional Level knowledge of procedures and risks (perhaps supplemented by our *Advanced Level Audit & Assurance Exam Room Notes 2018* book) whereas for the assurance areas of SBM you will probably need to put in **more effort to learn new material specific to SBM** (or to organise your notes effectively so that you can draw on these in the exam: our *SBM Exam Room Notes* will also assist here).

In other words, and particularly if you work in audit on a day to day basis, do not let the fact that the **audit** material in Corporate Reporting seems relatively straightforward (and perhaps more like "revision" than anything particularly new) lull you into a false sense of security regarding the **Assurance** material which you need to know in SBM – **this will be relatively new material**.

Ethics (5-10%): Key Skills to Revise

We have termed this section "Key **Skills** to Revise" rather than "Key Topics to Revise" because, other than the ICAEW Code and the (by now hopefully) familiar threats and safeguards approach, there are no real technical areas to revise for ethics: instead you need to understand the **skills** required.

The examiners made the following observations in this regard:

- Ethics can arise in any question so candidates should not assume that "ethics are a Q2 issue" or vice versa.

- Candidates should identify and explain the ethical problem but also consider appropriate **actions** to take – **candidates should mention the actions to take even if the question does not explicitly ask for discussion of actions**.

- Candidates should use ethical language and principles (breach of confidentiality, fraudulent reporting, lack of integrity, dishonesty) rather than just talking in a generalised way.

- Candidates should refer to ethical codes where appropriate.

- Candidates should exercise professional scepticism: they should query what they are being told by looking at who is providing the information and therefore it is always worth suggesting that the information **must be substantiated** before any serious actions are taken. Candidates should also look at key things which they have not been told and build these into their assessment of the ethical issue and potential actions.

- Candidates should adopt a **balanced** approach and not automatically assume that the issue is definitely a significant ethical problem, requiring extreme measures such as resignation from the engagement – there may well be scenarios where all candidates have to do is

387

explain why there is no ethical issue or the circumstances/additional information which may mean that there is no issue.

- **The ethical sub-Task may not be specifically listed out at the end of the information** and could be **mixed into the background information** – this happened in the November 2014 paper where many candidates appeared to look only at the final Exhibit to Q1 on page 9 of the question paper which contained a bullet point list of Tasks: lurking at the end of the introductory background information on page 3 of the question paper was a request on an ethical issue for the advising firm. This effectively created a **fifth** sub-Task but many students completely missed this and unfortunately this was one of the main causes of failure of the paper as a whole.

All the above advice is obviously very useful but we would definitely highlight in particular (1) the comment that candidates should **always discuss the ethical actions to be taken even if the question does not specifically ask for this** (some valuable marks could thus be unlocked[94]) and (2) the fact that the ethical sub-Task **may be hidden away** in the main narrative rather than being clearly indicated with a bullet point marker at the end of the text.

Knowing these 2 facts will definitely give you an edge over other candidates.

According to the examiners, weak ethical answers will contain the following flaws:

- **Only one issue** is identified – there will be more things to consider than this

- **Unbalanced** (one-sided or extreme) view is taken

- No ethical **framework** is used (issue, ethical principles, actions)

- Ethical **language** (dishonest, breach of trust, breach of confidentiality, exceeds powers of Directors) is **not used**

18.7 Taxation

The examiners reminded tutors that whilst no detailed knowledge of UK taxation will be tested, the examiners do have the power to set questions on a fictional non-UK jurisdiction: if they do so, then all the necessary taxation rules will be given in the question. If so, then such a question would be driven by a business or finance scenario such as an investment appraisal, with the taxation issues affecting cash flows or perhaps the extraction of profits. In other words, the taxation issues will be **a further dimension to consider rather than the focus of a whole question** and therefore you should be able to accumulate enough marks through effective use of normal practical business advisory points … but a few more marks from the taxation "icing on the cake" will of course always be helpful.

---

[94] We therefore recommend that you place a reminder to discuss ethical **actions** somewhere on your planning sheets. Or just use our MAPs which have this reminder by default.

The examiners confirmed that **deferred tax issues will not be tested in SBM**: this will be a Corporate Reporting issue only.

See also page 29 of this book for further discussion of how Taxation can form part of SBM.

18.8 The Importance of Brought Forward Knowledge and What to Revise

The examiners stressed very heavily that the Advanced Level will test whether students can still apply their brought forward knowledge from the earlier examinations. Recognising that this would mean revising a very large amount of material, the examiners provided some useful hints on what to focus on in your revision:

Certificate Level

Here it would be helpful to revise the topics in the **Law** module on insolvency or any other areas that relate to a business change. Candidates will not be expected to have a perfect level of knowledge or a level of knowledge equivalent to that needed to pass the Law paper but there could certainly be some added-value points possible if candidates are aware of some of the legal aspects of business change.

The examiners also indicated that topics from the **Management Information** paper relating to overheads, variances and the pros and cons of different investment appraisal techniques would be useful to revise. (Here we would note that the November 2014 real examination contained a full question relating to overhead absorption methods whilst the November 2017 real examination had a full question on variance analysis.)

Professional Level

Here the key papers are **Business Strategy and Technology**, **Financial Management** and **Financial Accounting & Reporting**. However, candidates should also bear in mind the "**advisory skills element**" of the **Business Planning** papers.

Candidates should be familiar with standard Business Strategy models and particularly any models relating to **business change** (since **change** is a specific topic in Business Strategy and Technology).

From Financial Management, issues relating to investment appraisal (including NPV but covering other techniques as well) and material on overseas businesses including derivatives and exchange rate issues would be the key areas.

In revising brought forward Business Strategy and Technology and Financial Management technical content, **candidates should adopt the perspective of operations management**, looking at practical strategic issues involving production and provision of services. This should be the focus.

The Financial Accounting & Reporting materials should be revised carefully, particularly with respect to the IFRS financial reporting treatment of key topics. Candidates should not assume that the new Advanced Level financial reporting topics such as pensions, deferred tax and share schemes will be the focus: prior knowledge will definitely also be tested. At the 2014 Tutor Workshop, the examiners expressed extreme disappointment with students' knowledge of principles relating to Groups

389

(including consolidation) and stated that this is core knowledge to be expected of newly-qualified accountants with IFRS knowledge – **this may be a hint that Groups will be tested again.**

As for the Business Planning: Taxation brought forward knowledge – do not panic! You will not be tested on complex UK tax issues. What the examiners meant was that BPT also does not give guidance on the mark allocation of relatively open-ended advisory questions: **therefore candidates should remember the techniques that they used to decide what to discuss and what to leave out when answering BPT questions.** As we believe that we have a very strong technique of this type (our MAPs approach) then perhaps you do not have to do too much work on remembering your BPT method but it is still helpful to remember that one of the skills being tested in SBM is the same – identification of the key issues and allocation of the appropriate time/marks to that area.

Helping You to Revise Brought Forward Knowledge

We believe that the above requirements to revise so many earlier papers as well as to study the new Advanced Level topics will place a significant burden on students. We will be providing a number of resources to assist including revision question banks, Exam Room Notes and also online learning materials.

Students may wish to consider purchasing our **Professional Level Q&A** short form question banks for the relevant papers as these provide hundreds of very short form questions to help you self-test yourself in a very rapid-fire, efficient way. As you will already be familiar with the content from passing the relevant examinations, we think that our Q&As would be much more effective than trying to re-read the Study Manual and attempt full questions again – if you learned things properly the first time then it should be just a case of refreshing rather than relearning.

Our final point on revision of brought forward knowledge is that the examiner did stress that you would not be tested to the same level of detail or required to go into complex areas in SBM – you should nevertheless have a command of the basics so that you can at least write something relevant.

18.9   Marks Balance Between Numerical and Narrative Marks

Based on the discussion at the 2015 ICAEW Tutor Conference, in cases where you are faced with a mixed, practical business advisory style sub-Task[95] then we would advise you to assume an approximately **33:66** split between numbers and narrative – **yes, we do have that the correct way around: there are always more marks for narrative than for numerical work.** There was no indication that the numerical marks would ever be more than 50% and the examiners stressed several times that they are interested in **seeing how candidates explain and interpret their results,** rather than in allocating lots of marks for number-crunching.

It is very important to bear this in mind – **working hard to get all the numbers perfect is likely to cause you to lose marks as you will not have enough time for good related narrative analysis.** This may seem counter-intuitive for an accountancy exam but the examiners are not going to pass your script just because you can do calculations well – you have already proven you can do this this

---

[95] As examples, by this we would mean all sub-Tasks in Q1 and sub-Tasks 1 and 2 in Q2 of the July 2014 paper and sub-Tasks 1 and 2 in Q1 and sub-tasks 1, 2 and 3 of Q2 of the November 2014 paper.

at the earlier levels so in SBM the examiners are interested in assessing the "**Accountant in Business**" concept, not just your maths skills.

Remember that the marking has to work on a **follow-through principle** so once you have made your best attempt at the numbers, leave them alone and assume that they are correct – then provide good analysis based on the advice in this text and **even if your numbers are not correct you still have a chance of scoring all available narrative marks in each sub-Task meaning that you have a chance at 60-66% of the marks** … and then do not forget that there will be further narrative-only Tasks (such as ethics or writing about how Due Diligence works), making it even easier to stay well above the 50% that you need to succeed.

18.10   Use of Your Folder of Notes (and/or our *SBM Exam Room Notes*)

The examiners were concerned that some candidates appeared to think that copying out large chunks of the Study Manual or their pre-prepared notes would attract marks. Tutors were told to inform candidates not to write out such large amounts of material and to ensure that the points were always specific to the scenario set.

The marks are awarded primarily for selecting the correct treatment and explaining the detail from pre-prepared notes would also attract some marks because the candidate would be further explaining the rule to the client. However, the examiners asked candidates not to spend so long on this copying out element because most of the marks would be for selecting the right rule in the first place: therefore, candidates would need to preserve enough time to make this selection and then would only attract some (and not a huge amount of) marks for the further detail from notes. **The examiners are aware that candidates have very good exam day folders pre-prepared and therefore they will not award marks just for writing material out but rather for the selection.**

It is for this reason that our *SBM Exam Room Notes* contain only **brief reminder bullet points** rather than huge chunks of text: this means that rather than using up your time to read large chunks of text and then feel like you have to copy them out, we can provide you with reminders or thought-joggers for a large range of potential ideas from which you can then select the right idea and write it up in your own words (our notes do not contain large blocks of text so hopefully there will be no temptation to do too much copying out and you will instead make MS^2 points). If you have a greater reliance on the Study Manual or another provider's notes for your exam room folder then please ensure that you **avoid this problem of writing out blocks of text**.

When we reviewed the 2014 SBM papers and related examiner comments in chapter 8, we saw that the area of **currency derivatives** was one area in the July 2014 paper where the **examiners were particularly keen to note that candidates had done too much copying out of standard points**.

18.11 Important notice on November 2014 Q1 – Look Out for Additional Tasks

During the SBM workshop at the 2015 Tutor Conference, the examiners spent a considerable amount of time advising tutors to warn students to **read the instructions from the partner very carefully**: although the final Exhibit will normally contain a bullet-point list of the main Tasks, students should look out for any additional instructions from the partner that may have been included earlier in the information.

More specifically, near the start of the Exhibit text for November 2014 Q1, the partner asked candidates to respond to the requests contained in Exhibit 7 (at the end of the information) but then also made the following statement:

> "In addition, I am concerned about the implications for our firm of giving advice and support to FFT on its response to the journalist (Exhibit 6). Please provide a briefing note for me explaining any ethical issues arising for our firm from giving advice and support to FFT in this matter."

Unfortunately, this additional request was **not repeated at the end of the Exhibit information** and therefore many candidates did not attempt this aspect. According to the examiners, in many cases this made the difference between a marginal script passing and failing the exam. As the examiners were unhappy with candidate performance in this respect, we would definitely expect them to repeat this "trick" again in the near future.

The examiners felt that candidates had been trained to first read the Tasks before then reading the main information. The examiner stated that they were generally in agreement with this approach because understanding the nature of the Task before reading the information does give some focus and allows candidates to look at key areas in the information: **at the same time, the examiners felt that candidates should be reading the information carefully enough so as to be able to pick out additional Tasks which have been mixed in with the information**. At the 2014 ICAEW Tutor Conference, the examiner did in fact drop the hint that candidates should look throughout the material provided for the question requirements **rather than assuming that a single Exhibit would do the work for them** – the second 2014 examination definitely put this principle into practice[96].

Overall, we recommend that you learn from the above example and base most of your answer on the specific list of points in the final Exhibit of the question but when you start to read the main information please ensure that you are sensitive to any **extra requests that have been "mixed in"**.

18.12 Q1 Answering Style – Use a Table of Figures at the Start of Your Answer

With respect to the November 2014 examination, the examiner stated that candidates who provided a **detailed data analysis table at the start of their answer** tended to perform better than candidates who **mixed their numerical results into their main narrative discussion**. According to the examiners, this was because a clear table at the start resulted in answers which kept the issues separate and addressed things systematically. While some very good answers with mixed in figures

---

[96] This again reminds us of the potential value of carefully reviewing these Tutor Conference remarks – hints are given as to how the examination will develop.

were provided by candidates, it was harder to do a thorough and systematic job in this way and many candidates tended to focus too much on certain areas because they did not have a reminder of each separate issue to look at in the narrative.

Obviously, we suggest that you learn from this advice and use a **separate data table**.

18.13   Some Final Exam Day and Administrative Notes

The examiners requested that candidates should use more **underlined headings** to clearly separate the different Tasks and sub-Tasks being attempted: this will make the life of the marker much easier and we strongly recommend that you do so, given that the marking is likely to be subjective or "holistic" – even the most patient marker is likely to form a negative judgement (to a greater or lesser extent) if your work is very hard to read or work with.

All scripts which score a mark of 48%, 49% and 50% are automatically reviewed by a senior examiner so please be assured that your mark is accurate if you score within this range (and hopefully with a score of 50% rather than the other 2 options!).

The senior examiners mark a few randomly selected scripts and then the same scripts are marked by others in the marking team who are not told that the scripts were assessed at the senior level nor the score awarded. This is done to ensure that the marker's approach is consistent with the senior team. Again, this should give you assurance that your marking is accurate.

18.14   Conclusion: How to Pass (and How to Fail!)

We hope that the above review is a useful insight into how the examiners want tutors to train students for SBM. We strongly recommend that you revisit this chapter several times during your preparation and also just before the examination, in order to remind yourself of what you are really trying to do in SBM.

At the end of the 2015 Tutor Conference workshop, the examiners provided the following useful summary reminders:

- Identify the **big issues**

- Look for **links** between issues

- The marking does not work on the basis of "**half a mark here, a whole mark there**"

- Always look for ways of showing **professional scepticism**

- Look for points which are **embedded** within the Tasks or within the data – try to look beyond the most obvious points

- Apply a test of **realism** – will the project work for the company?

- **Answer the Tasks/requirements in order within Q1 and Q2** – the Tasks/requirements will be included in a specific order for a reason

- Start a **new page for each Task and sub-Task**[97]

- **"It's not so much what you know – it's what you do with what you know"**: the marks are available for demonstrating knowledge and understanding and not just for dumping knowledge onto the page

- If candidates only used the word "**because**" a little more in their answers, their marks would significantly improve – the word "because" is used to introduce a comment which is a **justification or an explanation** and this will attract marks (but students often fail to offer this kind of comment)

- **Read the question wording carefully** – if you are asked to "briefly analyse" then this tells you 2 things: (1) do not go into great detail ("briefly") and (2) you must "analyse", meaning perform some calculations or add some value and do not just describe what you have already been given

- Consider using an **arrowed timeline** so that you can organise dates into the correct order and not become confused or leave an important issue out

Finally, according to the examiners, here are the 10 best ways to fail SBM:

1. **Poor layout** of the answer

2. Workings which are **hard to follow**

3. The student **sits on the fence** and does not give the conclusion or, alternatively, provides a conclusion without a supporting justification ("because" word is lacking)

4. **Generic** answers which are **not specific** to the scenario

5. **Lack of professional scepticism**, accepting face value assertions made by characters in the question

6. **Simply repeating information** already given in the question

7. **Missing out parts of the questions**

8. Not **linking** the issue to a relevant IAS/IFRS

9. Stating the purpose of an audit **test** but not the audit **procedures** required

10. Answering the requirements in a **random order** rather than following the order of the question paper

---

[97] As indicated on page 14 of this book, the terms "Task" and "sub-Task" are our own terms rather than ICAEW terminology.

Chapter 19   Summary of VITAL Magazine Article on SBM

Learning Points

After reading this chapter, you must be able to:

1. understand the examiners' view on the unique nature of SBM as an assessment method
2. understand the proposed differences in Q1 and Q2
3. state and fully understand the 8 key pieces of advice given at the end of the article

---

19.1   Summary of VITAL Article on SBM (April 2014)

As you should be aware, ICAEW publish VITAL, a magazine specifically written for ACA students. Shortly before the first sitting of the new SBM paper, a one page article appeared in the **April 2014** edition of VITAL, designed to help students understand the new format and examination.

As we are aware that many students do not read every edition of VITAL cover to cover (we certainly did not when we were studying …[98]) it is possible that you may have missed the article: therefore we have summarised the main points here.

Many of the points below should be familiar from the other chapters of this book but it is always helpful to take information directly from the examiners. Additionally, **the section in the article entitled "Advice to candidates" and its 8 key tips really is very useful indeed** and should be studied well: see below.

19.2   The Bridge Examination

The examiners confirmed that SBM "forms a **bridge** to the Case Study in terms of exam format and approach, but it has an identity in its own right in developing students' expertise to formulate and implement financial strategy".

19.3   Syllabus focus

Finance, and in particular the areas of valuation and securities, will be an important aspect of the SBM syllabus.

The syllabus will be allocated as follows:

---

[98] Joking aside, VITAL is considered to be the official "journal" for ACA students **so any changes or clarifications regarding the examination must be published in VITAL before they can take effect**. For example, the major changes in the Case Study markscheme with effect from July 2012 were communicated via VITAL – many tuition companies did not make this clear to students who missed the article, damaging student pass rates. Therefore we would strongly advise you to make use of VITAL in the months running up to your examination as it is always better to be prepared than to be surprised.

395

Topic	Weighting
Strategy	35-45%
Finance, financial risks, valuations, investment and distribution decisions	30-40%
Ethics	5-10%
Corporate reporting	15-20%
Assurance	10%

"Strategy" will incorporate a number of disciplines in both business strategy and financial management, including corporate governance and financial strategy.

19.4   Brought forward knowledge

Brought forward knowledge will be mainly based on the Business Strategy and Technology and Financial Management modules.

Further brought forward aspects will be the Financial Accounting and Reporting and Audit and Assurance papers.

19.5   Question format

Question	Mark allocation	Description
1	60	Mini case study Finance, business, corporate reporting and/or assurance
2	40	Scenario-based question Finance, business, corporate reporting and/or assurance.

Ethics may be tested in either question.

19.6   Q1: Mini-Case question

According to the article, this question is considered to be the mini-Case question because most of the information will be provided in the form of Exhibits, like the Case Study[99].

---

[99] Here we would note that Q2 will also contain Exhibits – as such, provision of Exhibits does not seem to be a particularly distinguishing characteristic of the mini-Case but we note this remark anyway.

You will be expected to apply professional judgement and scepticism.

There will usually be some kind of international context to the scenario.

There will not necessarily be a single right or wrong answer but rather several reasonable approaches. The individual requirements may or may not interact.

19.7   Q2: Scenario-based question

This question will be similar in approach to previous Business Change examination **questions but with a wider topic range**.

Q2 will tend to focus on one issue, as opposed to the multi-issue focus in Q1. It is also intended that Q2 will integrate different topics.

19.8   New topics for SBM

The examiners provided the following list of new SBM topics:

- Strategic marketing and brand management
- Supply chain management
- Operations management
- Corporate governance
- Human resources management
- Information strategy
- Performance management
- Treasury and working capital management

Therefore, as noted in chapter 18, please do ensure that you look at these elements of the SBM Study Manual – the Study Manual is huge and contains a lot of revision of earlier papers so **start with the above list to ensure that you have covered the new areas**.

19.9   Ethics

Ethics will be covered in every exam but could feature in either question.

You should ensure that you take a "**balanced approach and offer reasonable solutions**". You should also consider whether any further information or evidence might be provided to support your recommendation – if so, state this in your answer.

19.10 Advice to candidates

The longest section in the VITAL article provides some advice to candidates – in our opinion, this section is the most useful section of the VITAL article as the points contained here are not necessarily already made elsewhere in this book. Remember that we use the term "Task" to refer to what the SBM examiners call a "requirement": as we are reproducing points from the VITAL article below, we use the term "requirement" in this section but not in any other parts of this book.

1. Problem solving and presenting a solution

You will be expected to provide reasoned advice which solves a problem, rather than sitting on the fence and offering a variety of options. The intention is to reflect the real world where a Chartered Accountant would be expected to provide guidance and advice.

2. Identify and prioritise the issues

Look for the really key issues and concentrate on these. Also look out for "embedded" points within the scenario which may be subtle or omitted altogether.

3. Apply professional scepticism

Look at who is supplying the information and consider what their motivations might be. Look at why the information has been provided. Look at the motivations of the supplier of the information. Assess the quality of the information.

4. Answer the requirements in the order they are given in the examination paper

The examiners are not trying to catch students out and there will usually be a flow to the requirements as you move through the examination paper.

5. Start your answer to each requirement on a new page

This is advisable because it means that you can go back and add further points later if they occur to you.

6. Space out your answers

Leave lots of space and it is fine to have blank pages. The markers must indicate on the marking system that they have seen every page of the booklet during the marking process so nothing will be missed just by spacing things out.

7. Full sentences must be used – bullet points are unacceptable

As indicated, use full sentences in your answers.

8. Give each paragraph a subheading

This can help the marker to understand the detail of what you are writing. (As indicated on page 64, we also believe that the act of creating subheadings will keep you focused on writing about the right areas and ensure that you are making enough different points spread across the different parts of the question.)

19.11 Other points to note

Discount tables will not be provided – you should bring these with you and ensure that you are familiar with how they work. (These tables are particularly useful for annuity factors: **the fact that the examiners specifically reminded students to bring the tables into the exam with them may be an indicator that annuity techniques will be required**.)

Chapter 20   Advice for Exam Day

Learning Points

After reading this chapter, you must be able to:

1. understand what to take into the examination with you (and what not to take in)
2. understand the benefits of using a stopwatch and counting your time upwards

---

20.1   What Should I Take In With Me?

As SBM is an "open book" examination, we know that it will be tempting to take in a large amount of materials "just in case". There will naturally be a fear of not bringing something important and regretting it on the day.

Whilst we understand this position, remember that SBM is primarily a **skills-based** examination – the examiner is not particularly interested in technical brilliance or whether you can spot every "prize-winner" point within a complex valuation: the examiner wants to see that you can give reasonable and practical business advice, **based on the numbers that you have calculated** (even if these are wrong). This is reflected in the fact that there will, generally, be a 66:33 split between marks for narrative work versus numerical work (see chapter 5 for more on this). **Spending a long time looking up IFRS rules and related calculations could be self-defeating**, even if you do arrive at the correct answer, since your "looking up" time will mean less time to focus on writing up the narrative points to gain the greater proportion of marks for narrative analysis.

Another danger with an "open book" examination is the temptation to simply copy out the standard, rather than applying it. The examiners have stated that there are no marks at all just for stating what the standard says: you need to apply the standard to the scenario, preferably using what we call "inline definition" (see chapter 6). **The more IFRS or IAS books you have available** (rather than your own more efficient and condensed notes) **then the greater the temptation just to copy out the book**.

Therefore we strongly recommend that you think carefully about what to take into the exam with you and what to leave behind.

We would advise you to spend some time creating your own personalised and condensed summaries of key IFRSs and audit and assurance rules (perhaps in the form of mindmaps). Hopefully you will have some effective notes already prepared for your Corporate Reporting examination. **Since SBM can test any of the same financial reporting issues, we would recommend that you take in your Corporate Reporting notes**, provided that these are not too long.

We also provide titles in our Exam Room Notes series which could be useful to you. Our *SBM Exam Room Notes* contain an alphabetical listing of many key strategic change scenarios, allowing you to quickly locate reminders of both narrative and numerical points to make. Our *SBM Exam Room Notes* also contain summaries of **key assurance areas** such as internal audit or agreed upon procedures as candidates often perform very poorly regarding these areas, which can sometimes be a substantial element of an SBM question (performance of statutory audit and audit procedures are tested extensively in the Corporate Reporting Advanced Level paper[100]). (See chapters 10 to 14 of this book to revise Specialist Audit & Assurance issues.) Although Financial Reporting issues are less important for SBM than for CR, you may also wish to take our *Advanced Level Financial Reporting Exam Room Notes* publication into the SBM examination with you.

We would then also recommend that you take in some **blank MAPs** (remembering that we have specifically designed different MAPs for Q1 and Q2). We have invested quite a bit of time in creating the MAPs to ensure that all the most important timing and structuring information is quickly available to you so please do make the most of this planning method.

You are unlikely to have time to reference or check sections of this book during the exam so whilst we obviously recommend that you study *Smashing SBM*™ very extensively for the exam, we do not think that it is necessary to take the book into the exam with you.

Therefore, our list of recommended items (**bearing in mind our advice to keep things minimal and simple if you can**) is:

- ACA Simplified *SBM Exam Room Notes* and *Advanced Level Financial Reporting Exam Room Notes*

- Personalised summaries of key IFRSs and IASs

- Personalised Corporate Reporting notes (provided that these are not too bulky)

- ACA Simplified SBM MAPs

You should expect to see numerous candidates with suitcases full of books and notes – **do not be intimidated by this**. There is not enough time to make use of such materials and, as explained above, it is possible to reduce your grade through too much use of open books.

Instead, stick to the **minimum amount** of materials recommended above. For a primarily skills-based examination, this is all you will need.

20.2   Use Our MAPS … But Do Not Overplan

Having spent a considerable amount of time explaining how to use our MAPs, as well as explaining the benefits of planning in a way that aims to estimate the mark allocation correctly, it is important that you work very quickly through our 11 mark estimation rules in the real examination: do not spend too long planning and just use the completed MAPs as a rough guide to the marks and what to do – you get nothing for planning unless it is written up. Looking at the example completed MAPs in Appendix 3, we have used short phrases and abbreviations and included reminders of what to say/discuss rather than writing out full points. Depending on how confident you are with certain Tasks (e.g. ethics or a relatively straightforward Specialist Audit & Assurance area) you may wish to write up your answer directly into your answer book, rather than first completing a plan. **Do whatever**

---

[100] If you are sitting Corporate Reporting then check out our *Advanced Level Audit & Assurance Exam Room Notes 2018* book for an alphabetical, quick reference listing of the major audit testing areas to help you quickly generate appropriate tests.

works for you but please do think about the mark allocation and therefore your timing across the paper as a whole.

All we ask is that you **always work through the 11 Rules to fill out your estimated mark and time allocation** even if the answer seems easy – otherwise you will have no idea how to use your time effectively.

20.3   Get a Silent Stopwatch

As a further aspect of time management on the day, we repeat the points made in chapter 5 regarding the measurement of your time. SBM is unique in having only 2 questions, composed of many different Tasks and sub-Tasks, each of which look at very different issues. It is therefore helpful to view the paper as a series of short questions, rather than 2 long questions. This fact, together with our quite detailed MAP planning technique, suggests that you will have to find a way to manage your time efficiently and switch between carefully timed elements without wasting too much time reading the clock.

We are aware that the planning sheets of some other providers suggest that you set timings such as "9.30am – 9.45am: plan answer; 9.45am to 10.15am: financial reporting element" and so on.

We believe that it is much simpler and effective to start your timings at zero and then build upwards as you work down the fourth column of your MAP. You are much less likely to get the timing wrong when working in this way and you will also not have to spend any thinking time at all working out that, for example, at 9.37am you have 38 minutes until 10.15am. This is wasted effort in an examination scenario, particularly when you only have 2 questions to answer, and it can easily lead to a big error in timing if you miscalculate the difference as, say, 28 minutes.

We therefore recommend that you obtain a silent stopwatch and simply start this once your MAP is complete and you are ready to start writing up your answer (including making a start on your calculations). Then simply count upwards from 00:00 based on the timings you have developed by allocating each Task a specified amount of time. This is easier than getting confused or even making costly mistakes while thinking about what the time is out there in the real world.

20.4   Our Final Advice for SBM

Most importantly of all …

Believe in yourself and good luck!

Best wishes

ACA Simplified

PS – Do not forget about our mock exam pack for SBM and if you found *Smashing SBM*™ useful please spread the word or consider leaving a review on Amazon.co.uk.

Appendix 1   MAP for SBM Q1   Planning Page(s)

Primary discipline: PBA

Task	Sub-Tasks	Content	Marks	Time	Stop
		Total			

Mark estimation – the 11 Rules

1. Exhibit length and number of Exhibits	2. Dedicated Exhibit?	3. Financial information?
4. Task wording length and bullets	5. 33:66 (numbers:narrative)	6. Which discipline and which discipline?
7. Multi-discipline?	8. Balancing rule	9. Ethics 6-8 marks
10. Financing comparison 8 marks	11. Narrative risks/strategy 8 marks	

Appendix 1   MAP for SBM Q1   Reminder Page

4 Case Study Skills Lenses

1. Identifying key information

2. Using key information

3. **Applying judgement: scepticism, size of impact**

4. **Conclusions & Recommendations**

[Skills in bold need extra effort]

Scepticism

Lack of information

Capacity and quality of resources (including staff)

Unknown impact, short forecasting period

Obtain independent assurance

Lack of supporting evidence

Manipulation of accounting policies/evidence?

Unrecognised amounts

Financial Analysis Reminders

Start with a data table

Plenty of headings

Use the scenario-specific figures, not just GPM%!

Explain causes and interconnections

MS^2!

Make scenario-specific points at all times

Use scenario-specific performance measures

No copying out!

You are the **Accountant in Business**

Practical/cash impact
versus
Financial reporting

Have you checked our *SBM Exam Room Notes*?

Other reminders

PBA will contain most of the marks

Consider different stakeholders (in sections) and their % holdings

Consider accounting standards (brief explanation)

Balance between numbers and narrative

Use the word "**because**" – causes, financial reporting, reasons, justification

Provide **conclusions** and **recs**

Use **inline** definition if needed

Ethics frameworks

IIR – Issue, Impact, Recommendations

TEF – Transparency, Effect, Fairness

ICAEW 6 steps – facts, parties, issues, principles, procedures, alternative courses

ICAEW Code – integrity, objectivity, professional competence and due care, confidentiality, professional behaviour

Threats and safeguards – self-interest, self-review, advocacy, familiarity/trust, intimidation

Personal reminders (Q1)

Appendix 2   MAP for SBM Q2   Planning Page(s)

Primary disciplines: Look at Q1 first – Q2 will balance across the SBM disciplines

Task	Sub-Tasks	Content	Marks	Time	Stop
		Total			

Mark estimation – the 11 Rules

1. Exhibit length and number of Exhibits	2. Dedicated Exhibit?	3. Financial information?
4. Task wording length and bullets	5. 33:66 (numbers:narrative)	6. Which discipline and which discipline?
7. Multi-discipline?	8. Balancing rule	9. Ethics 6-8 marks
10. Financing comparison 8 marks	11. Narrative risks/strategy 8 marks	

Appendix 2   **MAP for SBM Q2**   **Reminder Page**

4 Case Study Skills Lenses

1. Identifying key information

2. Using key information

3. **Applying judgement: scepticism, size of impact**

4. **Conclusions & Recommendations**

[Skills in bold need extra effort]

Scepticism

Lack of information

Capacity and quality of resources (including staff)

Unknown impact, short forecasting period

Obtain independent assurance

Lack of supporting evidence

Manipulation of accounting policies/evidence?

Unrecognised amounts

Personal reminders (Q2)

MS^2!

Make scenario-specific points at all times

Use scenario-specific performance measures

No copying out!

You are the **Accountant in Business**

Practical/cash impact versus Financial reporting

Have you checked our *SBM Exam Room Notes*?

Other reminders

PBA not necessarily most of the marks

Q2 will be used to balance the marks – **if a discipline was not in Q1 or a small part then will be a big part of Q2**

Balance between numbers and narrative

Use the word "**because**" – causes, financial reporting, reasons, justification

Provide **conclusions** and **recs**

Use **inline** definition if needed

Always consider % shareholdings

Ethics frameworks

IIR – Issue, Impact, Recommendations

TEF – Transparency, Effect, Fairness

ICAEW 6 steps – facts, parties, issues, principles, procedures, alternative courses

ICAEW Code – integrity, objectivity, professional competence and due care, confidentiality, professional behaviour

Threats and safeguards – self-interest, self-review, advocacy, familiarity/trust, intimidation

Appendix 3   Example Completed MAPs: November 2014 Examination Paper – Q1

Primary discipline: PBA

Task	Sub-Tasks	Content	Marks	Time	Stop
1	Explain profit drop	Calcs: data table, use MS^2 indicators	3		
		Narrative: Revenue, Profits, Op Eff	7		
1=**13**	Recommend improvements	Recs: prices, scale, onerous contract	3 **13**	23	23
2	Recon v Liquid calcs	PPE, inventories, Receivables Liquidator fee Fixed charge payment Bank's position	5		
2	Recon v Liquid narrative	Analyse all figures – find impact on bank Other stakeholders: shareholders, suppliers – unsecured Recs	13		
2 2=**25**	FR implications	Going concern (IAS 1) – at least 12 months, disclosures, alternative prep methods Provision? IAS 10 Events after the RP Accountant in Business perspective	7 **25**	44	67
3	Leasing benefits and risks	Calcs – AF and compound interest Compare prices and liquidity impact Promote sales?	5		
3 3=**10**	Leasing FR	IAS 17 – op lease or finance? Indicators x 2-3? Op lease – IS and SFP impacts Revenue recognised? Accountant in Business perspective	5 **10**	18	85
		Total	48		

Mark estimation – the 11 Rules

(Rule reminders not reproduced here due to space constraints – please refer to Appendix 1)

Primary discipline: PBA

Task	Sub-Tasks	Content	Marks	Time	Stop
4 4=**6**	Journalist email	Principles and Ethical Framework (*SBM Exam Room Notes*) Responsibility, honesty, transparency Instructions clear enough? Scepticism: big issue, who is liable? Recs: investigate, discuss with supplier	**6**	11	96
5 5=**6**	Ethics of advising client	Obtain facts and confirm first Must not go outside expertise Principles: transparency, honesty Cannot associate with unethical firm Consider whether illegality – disclose? Advocacy threat is high	**6**	11	**107**
		END OF QUESTION			
		Total	60		

Mark estimation – the 11 Rules

(Rule reminders not reproduced here due to space constraints – please refer to Appendix 1)

Notes on how we have completed the MAP for Q1

In allocating our time, we have assumed **1.75** minutes per mark (with rounding to the nearest minute) – this allows for reading and planning time of 21 minutes (60 marks x (2.1 minutes available per mark - 1.75 minutes per mark allocated for writing up)) followed by a write up time of 105 minutes (60 marks x 1.75 minutes per mark allocated for writing up). (Our answer runs slightly over due to rounding but because we have allowed 1.75 minutes per mark rather than the more normal 2.1 minutes there should be a little headroom.) People read and plan at different speeds so it is important to experiment to find a multiple that works for you.

We have allocated a single "stop" time for each sub-Task (on a cumulative basis working down the page) rather than for each element of the sub-Task – otherwise you will be spending too long looking at your stopwatch and not enough time actually working. The timing does not have to be exact for every single little element: the point is to allocate time across sub-Tasks correctly. We have, however, tried to estimate the marks for the elements within a sub-Task to give ourselves some idea of how much of the time is available to spend on the different elements.

We prefer not to have too many sheets floating around so we have in some cases planned several different Tasks on the same page, just to make use of the space available – if you prefer, feel free to start a new MAP page for each Task within a question.

You will see that we have kept each sub-Task in a separate row even when there was potentially space to plan several sub-Tasks in each row. We have done so because we think that it will be a very good idea to get into the habit of keeping elements separate so that you do not mix your points together: also it will ensure that you reflect on how many marks there may be available for the different elements. Bear in mind that the markers are handed a sheet which does split each Task down very thoroughly into separate elements, based on the question wording, so it makes sense to follow this approach in your own answer (and therefore your own plan).

Please see chapter 7 which reviews this paper fully for our explanation of how to use the evidence available to estimate the mark allocation correctly. We have applied the normal 11 Rules as indicated at the bottom of the MAP.

Most importantly of all, we have prepared this MAP with the considerable benefit of having the markscheme and model answer available – we have also had plenty of time to choose what to write. Therefore you would not be expected to complete as much information in a real examination – we are just trying to illustrate the principles as fully as possible.

Appendix 3   Example Completed MAPs: November 2014 Examination Paper – Q2

Primary discipline: Look at Q1 first – Q2 will balance across the SBM disciplines

Task	Sub-Tasks	Content	Marks	Time	Stop
1 1=**10**	Decline in tender success	Table of data Identify really key factors Tenders, success rate, number of machines, price of machines, MS[2] Compare to PY	3 7 **10**	18	18
2 2=**13**	Profit v budget – Divisional-level Company-level	Contribution v overhead analysis Impact of fixed overheads Contrasts – find different things to comment on Distortions? Labour hours sensible?	6 7 **13**	23	41
3 3=**8**	Overheads, pricing and Industrial Division – impact FR – overhead allocation and inventories	Key cause – revenue fall? Cost per unit analysis – cost increase v material increase IAS 2 – based on normal production level Should only include production overheads Not normal level Cost > sales value? Writedown	4 4 **8**	14	55
4 4=**9**	Strategic, operational, financial – sale of Industrial Division to Hexam Risks and DD – shares as consideration	S – Industrial part of long-term strat, synergies, just one bad year? O – joint processes and assets, under employment of resources? F – price high enough given S and O impact? Costs of non-Industrial? Consider % shareholdings Comparisons to recent sales Discounts Market models for FV Not full list – just for shares as consideration	4 5 **9**	16	71
		Total	40		

Mark estimation – the 11 Rules

(Rule reminders not reproduced here due to space constraints – please refer to Appendix 2)

Notes on how we have completed the MAP for Q2

The process is largely the same as for Q1 and therefore our notes below are similar to the above.

In allocating our time, we have assumed **1.75** minutes per mark (with rounding to the nearest minute) – this allows for reading and planning time of 14 minutes (40 marks x (2.1 minutes available per mark - 1.75 minutes per mark allocated for writing up)) followed by a write up time of 70 minutes (40 marks x 1.75 minutes per mark allocated for writing up). (Our answer runs slightly over due to rounding but because we have allowed 1.75 minutes per mark rather than the more normal 2.1 minutes there should be a little headroom.) People read and plan at different speeds so it is important to experiment to find a multiple that works for you.

We have allocated a single "stop" time for each sub-Task (on a cumulative basis working down the page) rather than for each element of the sub-Task – otherwise you will be spending too long looking at your stopwatch and not enough time actually working. The timing does not have to be exact for every single little element: the point is to allocate time across sub-Tasks correctly. We have, however, tried to estimate the marks for the elements within a sub-Task to give ourselves some idea of how much of the time is available to spend on the different elements.

We prefer not to have too many sheets floating around so we have in some cases planned several different Tasks on the same page, just to make use of the space available – if you prefer, feel free to start a new MAP page for each Task within a question.

You will see that we have kept each sub-Task in a separate row even when there was potentially space to plan several sub-Tasks in each row. We have done so because we think that it will be a very good idea to get into the habit of keeping elements separate so that you do not mix your points together: also it will ensure that you reflect on how many marks there may be available for the different elements. Bear in mind that the markers are handed a sheet which does split each Task down very thoroughly into separate elements, based on the question wording, so it makes sense to follow this approach in your own answer (and therefore your own plan).

Please see chapter 7 which reviews this paper fully for our explanation of how to use the evidence available to estimate the mark allocation correctly. We have applied the normal 11 Rules as indicated at the bottom of the MAP.

Most importantly of all, we have prepared this MAP with the considerable benefit of having the markscheme and model answer available – we have also had plenty of time to choose what to write. Therefore you would not be expected to complete as much information in a real examination – we are just trying to illustrate the principles as fully as possible.

Appendix 4   Sample Pages from ACA Simplified *SBM Exam Room Notes*

Our *SBM Exam Room Notes* are designed to provide reminders and thought-joggers for a wide range of potential SBM scenarios. We have developed the book by reviewing the SBM real papers, SBM mock examinations, SBM Sample Paper and also the predecessor paper in Business Change which had a very similar syllabus to SBM: as noted in chapter 19, the examiners have said that SBM Q2 will be very similar to Business Change Q1.

Our *SBM Exam Room Notes* are organised alphabetically, rather than by Study Manual chapter, so that you can find the information very quickly, saving valuable time. We include plenty of "See also" cross-references so that you can find reminders of how topics link together. We also include plenty of examination tips within the Exam Room Notes, including reminders of what to write about, classic errors, ways to impress the examiner and suggested headings or structures to your answers.

In this Appendix, we provide an example of 2 different pages from our *SBM Exam Room Notes* so that you can see how the notes work. In the full version of the *SBM Exam Room Notes* you would also have 2 different indexes: one organised purely by topic name and the other organised by theme (valuations, overseas investment, financing, ethics etc) to ensure that you do not miss any issues.

(Please note that the sample pages are based on a draft version of the *SBM Exam Room Notes* and therefore the content and formatting may be updated in the final published version which will released after this book. The page references provided are purely for illustrative purposes and may change in the final version of the book.)

Acquisitions – Synergies and Challenges (sample of first page only)

Synergies

Main justification for many acquisitions – but check that will actually happen – if not, shareholder value harmed

Revenue synergies

Benefits
- Higher revenues for acquirer
- Higher return on equity
- Longer periods of growth

Sources
- Increased market power
- Marketing synergies – two parties can combine advertising resources and cross-advertise
- Strategic synergies
- Locational synergies

Dangers
- Revenue synergies are harder to quantify than other synergies
- Hard to know how customers will react – will they actually buy?

Cost synergies

- Normally considered to be substantial – but will they happen and will they outweigh integration/redundancy costs?
- Primary source – economies of scale

Financial synergies
- Diversification – gain to shareholders if not already diversified themselves
- Uses surplus cash that otherwise not being used ("cash slack")

Human resources synergies
- Sharing of skills and expertise
- May be able to buy in access to information, techniques and networks

Accounting impact of an acquisition

Subsidiary – consolidate in debts – affects gearing but could increase profits (100% of subsidiary)

Associate – debts not consolidated in but profits boosted (by lower amount than a subsidiary: lower % owned)

See also   Due Diligence   45
                      Valuations   156 and following

414

Interest Rate Calculations

Importance of Annuity Factors

Most calculations will be "rough and ready" or simple calculations – the easiest way for the examiner to set this style of question is to use an Annuity Factor approach (so that you do not need to do separate calculations for each year of the analysis). So ensure that you are comfortable with using Annuity Tables!

Zero Coupon Bond with a Premium – Effective Interest Rate

Example: a £1m bond is redeemable at a premium of 15% in 4 years

Find a rate which fairly allocates the 15% (or £150,000) over each of the 4 years, but which also takes into account the effect of compound interest

The correct formula to use is to apply the nth root (where n is the number of years) to a fraction of 100 + interest rate/100, and then deducting 1 to find the interest rate.

So for the example bond above the calculation would be $[(115/100)^{0.25 \text{ or } 1/4}] - 1$ or **3.6%**

Exam Tip – this is an excellent opportunity to comment on cash versus accounting principles – no cash flow until the final year (with a large outflow) but finance charges each year under accounting rules

Exam Tip – check whether the loan is in a foreign currency – this further increases risk due to uncertainty regarding the future exchange rate

Implicit Interest Rate on a Sale and Leaseback

Example

The business sells an asset for £150,000 receivable immediately and in return has to pay rentals of £70,000 for 3 years

The entity thus gains £150,000 now in return for paying £70,000 for 3 years.

Solution

The internal rate of return of the transaction is given by finding the Annuity Factor A such that

150,000 – (70,000 x A) = 0

Therefore **A = 2.1429.** Using Annuity Tables, this implies an interest rate of around **19%** (quite a high rate)

See also	Financing – debt versus equity	36
	Option valuation	65

Appendix 5   SBM ICAEW Revision Resources: Some Important Points to Note

A5.1   Continuity from the BC Question Bank

As we have mentioned many times elsewhere in this book, the evolved ACA paper in Strategic Business Management is an evolution of the previous Technical Integration Stage **Business Change** paper. Several members of the ICAEW Business Change examiner team have moved across to the SBM examiner team so we would expect SBM to take largely the same direction as Business Change.

This is unfortunately evidenced by the fact that the majority of questions in the SBM Question Bank are **adapted versions of Business Change questions from the Business Change Question Bank**. Although the relevant Business Change questions have been updated with additional Exhibits and SBM-style Tasks, these questions have not been drafted from scratch with SBM in mind.

In our opinion, these "recycled" questions may not be quite as useful in preparing for SBM as questions written entirely from scratch with SBM in mind: SBM has been specifically designed to provide more of a "bridge" to the Case Study examination than the old Business Change paper and involves longer Exhibits and a different mark allocation across the different parts of the syllabus. Additionally, in our opinion, the "recycled" questions do not contain enough emphasis on Assurance and Ethics. The table below analyses the questions in the 2018 edition of the SBM Question Bank:

Analysis of SBM Question Bank – Continuity from BC Question Bank

Question	Marks (SBM)	In BC QB?	Marks (BC)	Change in marks
Hobart plc	**55**	**No**	-	-
Knowhow plc	55	Yes	40	15
Fowler Ltd	55	Yes	40	15
Homez	42	No*	42	0
Pickering Packaging Ltd	42	Yes	35	7
Zaltan plc	60	Yes	40	20
Hottentot Hotels Ltd	55	Yes	40	15
Zappo plc	60	Yes	30	30
Safetex plc	60	Yes	40	20
Coopers Coffee Company Ltd	45	Yes	30	15
Delta plc	55	Yes	40	15
Rafford plc	40	Yes	40	0
Connor Construction plc	40	Yes	30	10
Optica Scientific Instruments Ltd	40	Yes	40	0
Hyper-Thin Glass Ltd	60	Yes	40	20
Raul plc	55	Yes	30	25
Geo Carbon Engineering plc	40	Yes	27	13
Krown Jools plc	40	Yes	40	0
Coriander plc	45	Yes	40	5
Luminum plc	**62**	**No**	-	-
Horora plc	**40**	**No**	-	-
Puller plc	**55**	**No**	-	-
Quanta	**60**	**No**	-	-
Galaxy Travel plc	**60**	**No**	-	-
Latchkey Ltd	**60**	**No**	-	-
Plumbrite plc	**55**	**No**	-	-
Western Wheels Ltd	**40**	**No**	-	-
Stark plc (SBM Sample Paper)	**55**	**No**	-	-
Looster Lagoona plc (SBM Sample Paper)	**45**	**No**	-	-

* Homez was an ICAEW Mock question for the previous Business Change syllabus

Based on the above analysis, questions marked in bold appear to be new questions not contained in the 2015 Business Change Question Bank[101] nor in the Business Change Electronic Question Bank reviewed below. (The final 2 questions in the table above – Stark plc and Looster Lagoona plc – are contained in the single Sample Paper created specifically for SBM before the first July 2014 sitting.) We have also confirmed that the questions in bold have not been questions in real Business Change examinations since July 2011. We would therefore advise you to start with these questions first and come back later to the "adapted-Business Change" questions.

We have then calculated the change in marks for those questions which have been adapted from the Business Change Question Bank (or, in the case of Homez, a Business Change ICAEW Mock examination): **our concept here is that the more marks have been added, the more fundamentally the question has been changed and therefore the more value it should be for SBM-specific purposes**. Therefore, if you do not have time to do the whole question bank but have completed the new SBM-specific questions, start with the adapted questions with the highest number of marks in the "Change in marks" column first.

As we know that your time is limited, we hope that the above will help you to prioritise your time.

A5.2 The Electronic Question Bank: An Underutilised Resource

In addition to the more well-known standard ICAEW Question Bank (sold as a hardcopy book by ICAEW and used as standard by all tuition providers), ICAEW also produces an "Electronic Question Bank" which is available only to approved Partners in Learning.

The Electronic Question Bank contains further practice questions in Word document format, with the aim being that tuition providers use these questions on their courses. **From discussion with our taught course students, we know that many students are not provided with this resource.** Given the lack of new SBM questions in the standard hardcopy Question Bank (see above) and the relative lack of real past papers to practice, we believe that the Electronic Question Bank could be a useful resource and we recommend that you obtain it from your tuition provider.

At the same time, we have some caveats regarding this additional resource.

Firstly, as the following table shows, many of the questions in the SBM Electronic Question Bank are "recycled" Business Change questions but without the addition of marks or adjustments to the text that we see in the hardcopy SBM Question Bank i.e. there have been no real updates:

---

[101] These questions may, however, be contained in earlier editions of the BC Question Bank or other ICAEW materials. The table only compares the latest available Question Bank for SBM with the 2015 Business Change Question Bank (the final edition published as Business Change was not examined after July 2015).

**Analysis of SBM Electronic Question Bank – Continuity from
Business Analysis Questions in the BC Electronic Question Bank**[102]

Question	Marks (SBM)	In BC EQB?	Marks (BC)	Change in marks
Brady	**30**	**No**	**-**	**-**
Guestway Hotels	**23**	**No**	**-**	**-**
Qualserve	**28**	**No**	**-**	**-**
Maltis Supermarkets	**30**	**No**	**-**	**-**
Bryant & Watson Advertising	**30**	**No**	**-**	**-**
Tony Rossi	**28**	**No**	**-**	**-**
Taywell	**25**	**No**	**-**	**-**
Martigate	**20**	**No**	**-**	**-**
Fonezone	**20**	**No**	**-**	**-**
Stored for You plc	25	Yes	25	0
ACE Ltd	25	Yes	25	0
Try-it plc	25	Yes	25	0
PizzaClub plc	25	Yes	25	0
Rocky Road Institute	24	Yes	25	(1)
BST Motors Co	25	Yes	25	0
Holt plc	25	Yes	25	0
Nestlehoff Restaurants	**25**	**No**	**-**	**-**
Silver Spoon Serving plc	**35**	**No**	**-**	**-**
Mugswamp plc	40	*	-	-
Yolland plc	45	*	-	-
Kramp plc	40	*	-	-
Archen plc	45	Yes	30	15
Harper Ltd	45	*	-	-
British Flint plc	**45**	**No**	**-**	**-**

When the 2017 Electronic Question Bank was created, 8 further questions were added compared to the 2016 edition. However, several of the 8 additional questions were based on previous Business Change mock examinations rather than being original SBM questions: these have been marked with a *. Whilst these were not strictly in the final BC Electronic Question Bank, they are "recycled" BC questions.

The 2018 Electronic Question Bank is largely unchanged from the 2017 edition as only one change has been made: for 2018, Homez has been "promoted" out of the Electronic Question Bank into the standard (i.e. not the Electronic Question Bank) Question Bank whilst Archen has been "demoted" out of the standard Question Bank into the Electronic Question Bank. This represents a switching of places between 2 ex-Business Change questions so does not have a significant impact on the primary focus of this Appendix (the identification of questions which are definitely newly-drafted for SBM).

Secondly, of the remaining apparently new questions in the Electronic Question Bank, most have a **relatively low number of marks for an SBM question** (in the range of 20 to 30 marks whereas the real examination papers to date have had a marks split of 60:40 marks). You may therefore not find these questions as useful in terms of time management but the technical content is still worth looking at.

---

[102] We have also reviewed the questions in the TI Corporate Reporting and Audit Electronic Question Banks (2014-15 editions, the last editions published before the final sitting of the TI syllabus examinations in July 2015): none of the listed questions appeared in those elements of the Business Change materials.

A5.3 Use of ICAEW SBM Mock Examinations as Preparation

ICAEW provide all Partners in Learning with access to 2 mock examinations for use with students as preparation for the examinations. At the time of writing (March 2018), the following mock exams and questions were available:

July 2014 Mock Exam 1

Q1   Kesteven Plastics Ltd
Q2   Tigershark plc

July 2014 Mock Exam 2

Q1   Selworthy plc
Q2   Yolland plc

November 2014 Mock Exam 1

Q1   Davrina plc
Q2   Kramp plc

November 2014 Mock Exam 2

Q1   Power Products plc
Q2   Candide plc

July 2015 Mock Exam 1

Q1   Fashbook Ltd
Q2   Chocolait Cravings plc

July 2015 Mock Exam 2

Q1   Selworthy plc
Q2   Projecta Contractors plc

November 2015 Mock Exam 1

Q1   Davrina plc
Q2   Textiles with Care plc

November 2015 Mock Exam 2

Q1   Power Products plc
Q2   Western Wheels Ltd

July 2016 Mock Exam 1

Q1   Biaggi Ltd
Q2   Chocaulait Cravings plc

July 2016 Mock Exam 2

Q1   Selworthy plc
Q2   Projecta Contractors plc

November 2016 Mock Exam 1

Q1   Davrina plc
Q2   Textiles with Care plc

November 2016 Mock Exam 2

Q1   Power Products plc
Q2   Western Wheels Ltd

July 2017 Mock Exam 1

Q1   Biaggi Ltd
Q2   Sorrentine Advertising Company Ltd

July 2017 Mock Exam 2

Q1   Fashbook Ltd
Q2   Projecta Contractors plc

November 2017 Mock Exam 1

Q1   Davrina plc
Q2   Rammond Paints

November 2017 Mock Exam 2

Q1   Hapsburg Bottled Beers plc
Q2   Power Products plc

We would note that both questions in July 2014 Mock Exam 1 are questions contained in the Business Change Question Bank. Both questions in July 2014 Mock Exam 2 are questions from past Business Change examination papers (November 2011 and November 2008, respectively). Whilst both questions have been updated to some extent for SBM, we would note that **the questions have not been drafted specifically for SBM and this could lead to differences in emphasis and style of Tasks set**.

Both mock exams set ahead of the November 2014 exam, on the other hand, appear **to be new questions drafted specifically for SBM**: we could not find these question names in the Business Change Question Bank, past real Business Change exams nor in the Business Change Electronic Question Bank.

With the exception of Selworthy plc (Q1 in July 2015 Mock Exam 2), the mocks provided ahead of the July 2015 examination appear to contain original questions drafted for SBM: we could not find these question names in the Business Change Question Bank, past real Business Change exams nor in the Business Change Electronic Question Bank.

Q1 of November 2015 Mock Exam 1 repeats a question from the same Mock Exam one year earlier but other than this the questions provided ahead of the November 2015 examination appear to contain original questions drafted for SBM: we could not find these question names in the Business Change Question Bank, past real Business Change exams nor in the Business Change Electronic Question Bank.

The 2 mocks issued before the July 2016 examination are mainly repeats of earlier questions, with the exception of Q1 in Mock Exam 1 (Biaggi), which is newly written for SBM.

The 2 mocks issued before the November 2016 examination simply repeat the equivalent mocks issued before the November 2015 sitting.

The 2 mocks issued before the July 2017 examination are mainly repeats of earlier questions, with the exception of Q2 in Mock Exam 2 (Sorrentine Advertising Company), which is an amended version of a Business Change Question Bank question which used to be contained in the SBM Question Bank.

The 2 mocks issued before the November 2017 examination are mainly repeats of earlier questions, with the exception of Q1 in Mock Exam 2 (Hapsburg Bottled Beers) which used to be contained in the SBM Question Bank but was dropped for the 2017 edition of the Question Bank. This question is an updated version of a Business Change Question Bank question which was worth 40 marks as a Business Change question: as SBM November 2017 Mock 2 Q1, Hapsburg Bottled Beers is now worth 60 marks, representing a fairly substantial update (including the addition of marks relating to data analytics (not a subject which was part of the Business Change syllabus)).

Based on the above points, if given a choice, we would suggest **sitting the November 2014 or later mocks as a priority** and then perhaps also doing the July 2014 mocks but bearing in mind that the latter were not designed specifically for SBM. There has recently been a lot of repetition of questions in the ICAEW mocks so this unfortunately does not provide new questions to practise at each sitting ... so why not consider our own SBM Mock Exam Packs to obtain further exam-standard practice with the added advantage of detailed tutor tips and tricks? Please see page 4 for further details on our own original SBM Mocks.

Printed in Great Britain
by Amazon